EDDIE CONDON'S TREASURY OF JAZZ

EDDIE CONDON'S TREASURY OF JAZZ

Edited by
EDDIE CONDON AND
RICHARD GEHMAN

GREENWOOD PRESS, PUBLISHERS
WESTPORT, CONNECTICUT

Library of Congress Cataloging in Publication Data

Condon, Eddie, 1905-1973, ed.
  Eddie Condon's Treasury of jazz.

  Reprint of the ed. published by Dial Press, New York.
  1. Jazz music. I. Gehman, Richard, joint ed.
II. Title: Treasury of jazz.
[ML3561.J3C58 1975]   785.4'2   75-2693
ISBN 0-8371-8032-5

DESIGNED BY WILLIAM R. MEINHARDT

© 1956 by Eddie Condon and Richard Gehman

All rights reserved.

Originally published in 1956 by The Dial Press, New York

Reprinted with the permission of The Dial Press

Reprinted in 1975 by Greenwood Press, Inc., 51 Riverside Avenue, Westport, Conn. 06880

Library of Congress catalog card number 75-2693
ISBN 0-8371-8032-5

Printed in the United States of America

10 9 8 7 6 5 4 3 2

This book is for
EARNEST ANDERSON

ACKNOWLEDGMENTS

Balliett, Whitney, "Pandemonium Pays Off," copyright 1954 by *The Saturday Review;* "Kenton: Artistry in Limbo," copyright 1955 by *The Saturday Review.* Reprinted by permission of the author.

Beaumont, Charles, "Black Country," copyright 1954 by HMH Publishing Corp. Reprinted by permission of Harold Matson Company.

Borneman, Ernest, "The Jazz Cult," copyright 1947 by Harper & Brothers. Reprinted by permission of the author.

Boyer, Richard O. "Bop: A Profile of Dizzy." Copyright 1948 under the title "Bop" and reprinted by permission of the author.

Brown, Carlton, "Bill," copyright 1946 by Fawcett Publications. Reprinted by permission of the author.

Columbia Records, "Bix," the album notes from "The Bix Beiderbecke Story" by George Avakian, copyright by Columbia Records, Inc. and reprinted with their permission.

Condon, Eddie, "This Is Jazz" and "Turk," copyright 1955 by *Holiday.* "Bix" from *We Called It Music,* copyright 1947 by Eddie Condon. Reprinted by permission of the publishers, Henry Holt & Co.

Condon, Phyllis, "Eddie," excerpts from an article in *Good Housekeeping,* copyright 1956. Reprinted by permission of the author.

Crosby, John, "The Sun Never Sets," copyright 1954 by the *New York Herald Tribune,* Inc. Reprinted by permission of the author.

Duke, Osborn, "Oh Jazz, Oh Jazz," copyright 1956 by Osborn Duke. Used by permission of Harriet Wolf.

English, Richard, "The Battling Brothers Dorsey," copyright by Richard English. Reprinted by permission of Paul R. Reynolds & Son. This article first appeared in the *Saturday Evening Post.*

Feather, Leonard, "Dave," copyright 1954 by *Down Beat;* "Bird," copyright 1955 by Odhams Press Ltd., London: both reprinted by permission of the author.

Ferguson, Otis, "Bix," excerpts from "Young Man with a Horn," copyright by Otis Ferguson. This article first appeared in the *New Republic.*

Foote, Shelby, "Ride Out" from *Jordan County,* copyright 1954 by Shelby Foote and "Tell Them Good-Bye" from the *Saturday Evening Post.* Reprinted by permission of MCA Management.

Frazier, George, "Eddie" from an article in *True,* copyright 1946 by Fawcett Publications; "Lee" the album notes from "Lee Wiley Singing Rodgers and Hart," copyright by Storyville Records, Inc.; "Pee Wee" copyright by Hearst Publications; all reprinted by permission of the author.

Gehman, Richard, "Eddie Condon," from an article in Park East, copyright 1952 by Family Circle, Inc.; "Lionel Hampton," from an article in the Nation's Business, copyright 1954.

Gleason, Ralph J., "Duke Ellington," copyright 1953 by the San Francisco Chronicle and used with their permission.

Hammond, John, "Twenty Years of Count Basie," copyright 1954 by Down Beat.

Hentoff, Nat, "Jazz and the Intellectuals," copyright 1955 by the Chicago Review. Reprinted by permission of the author.

Holmes, Clellon, "The Horn," copyright by Direction. Reprinted by permission of MCA Management.

Jones, James, "The King," copyright 1955 by Playboy. Reprinted by permission of the author.

Kempton, Murray, "Duke Ellington," copyright 1954 by the New York Post Corp. Reprinted by permission of the author.

Kersh, Gerald, "The Musicians," copyright 1946 by Gerald Kersh and reprinted by permission of McIntosh & Otis. This story first appeared in Harper's Bazaar.

McMaster, Lawrence, W., Jr. Excerpts from a conversation with Dave Brubeck, a CBS television program by Ben Kagan.

Millstein, Gilbert, "Eddie," copyright 1955 by the New York Times Inc.; "The Commodore Shop and Milt Gabler," copyright 1946 by Gilbert Millstein under the title "For Kicks." Reprinted by permission of the author.

Reisner, Robert George, "Bird," copyright 1956 by Robert George Reisner and used with his permission.

Shaw, Artie, "The Rehearsal" from The Trouble with Cinderella, copyright 1952 by Artie Shaw. Reprinted by permission of the publishers, Farrar, Straus & Cudahy.

Silverman, Al, "Fats," copyright 1955 by Saga. Reprinted by permission of Sterling Lord Agency.

Simon, George T., "The Real Glenn Miller," copyright 1954 by Metronome. Reprinted by permission of the author.

Stearns, Marshall, "Rebop, Bebop and Bop," copyright by Marshall Stearns and used with his permission. This article first appeared in Harper's.

Sylvester, Robert, "The Lost Chords," copyright 1956 by Robert Sylvester. Used by permission of the William Morris Agency.

Weeks, Jack, "The Funeral of the King," copyright 1950 by Popular Publications, Inc. Reprinted by permission of Harold Matson Company.

Zolotow, Maurice, "One Night Tour," copyright 1941 by Maurice Zolotow. Reprinted by permission of Harold Ober Associates.

CONTENTS

                           Introduction   xv

ONE: EDDIE AND THE MUSIC

PHYLLIS CONDON, GEORGE FRAZIER, GILBERT MILLSTEIN, RICHARD GEHMAN:
                       EDDIE CONDON   3

EDDIE CONDON:
                          This is Jazz   21

ERNEST BORNEMAN:
                         The Jazz Cult   33

NAT HENTOFF
   Jazz and the Intellectuals: Somebody Goofed   68

GILBERT MILLSTEIN:
      The Commodore Shop and Milt Gabler   80

WHITNEY BALLIETT:
                    Pandemonium Pays Off   101

JOHN CROSBY:
                      The Sun Never Sets   108

TWO: SOME FRIENDS OF EDDIE'S

GEORGE AVAKIAN, OTIS FERGUSON, EDDIE CONDON:
                                  Bix   113

AL SILVERMAN:
                                    Fats   128
GEORGE FRAZIER:
                                    Lee   143
CARLTON BROWN:
                                    Bill   149
LEONARD FEATHER:
                                    Dave 162
GEORGE FRAZIER:
                                Pee Wee 170
EDDIE CONDON:
                                    Turk 176

THREE: THEY CALL IT MUSIC

MARSHALL STEARNS:
            Rebop, Bepop and Bop 187
RICHARD O. BOYER:
            Bop: A Profile of Dizzy 206
LAWRENCE W. MCMASTER, JR:
            A Conversation with Dave Brubeck 222
LEONARD FEATHER, ROBERT GEORGE REISNER:
                                    Bird 228

FOUR: THE SALES CONVENTIONS

RALPH J. GLEASON, MURRAY KEMPTON:
            Two Views of Duke Ellington 245
JOHN HAMMOND
            Twenty Years of Count Basie 250
BENNY GOODMAN:
            That Old Gang of Mine 258

CONTENTS xiii

GEORGE T. SIMON
      The Real Glenn Miller 275
RICHARD ENGLISH:
    The Battling Brothers Dorsey 286
RICHARD GEHMAN:
        Lionel Hampton 299
WHITNEY BALLIETT:
     Kenton: Artistry in Limbo 309
ARTIE SHAW:
         The Rehearsal 312
MAURICE ZOLOTOW:
        One Night Tour 323

FIVE: JAZZ STORIES

JAMES JONES:
           The King 337
SHELBY FOOTE:
          Ride Out 350
CHARLES BEAUMONT:
        Black Country 384
CLELLON HOLMES:
          The Horn 406
JACK WEEKS:
     The Funeral of the King 424
ROBERT SYLVESTER:
       The Lost Chords 435
GERALD KERSH:
        The Musicians 448
OSBORN DUKE:
       Oh, Jazz, Oh Jazz 461

INTRODUCTION

AMONG THE 25,000-odd people who turned up at the 1955 Newport Jazz Festival was Charles Andrews, the television writer-director-producer, a thinker part of the time and an agreeable fellow all of it. After registering a few bleats over the absence of such hot bands as those of Ace Brigode and Wayne King, he parted with an observation.

"People who like jazz," he said, "are like little children. They not only like to hear jazz all the time, they also like to hear about it. As kids like to hear about Little Bo-Peep and Goosey Goosey Gander all the time, so jazz fans want to hear the story of jazz over and over. 'Tell me a story,' they say, and then sit rapt while somebody tells them how jazz started down in New Orleans, moved up the river to Chicago, was influenced by men from Kansas City and Memphis, then moved on to New York, etc., etc."

This notion gave us pause; George Joel, a drummer who operates The Dial Press on the side, gave us impetus. He arrived at Condon's one night, booted the regular drummer off the stand, and got down to business. "If I can mess in your dodge," said he to Condon, between paradiddles, "you can get into mine. Write a book."

"I wrote a book," Condon said. "It enjoyed a wide sale among people trying to find themselves in the index."

"My books have no indexes," said Gehman.

"Come on," said Joel. "Get to work."

Someone then remembered Charlie Andrews' remark (it was the next morning, when the air was purer, if perhaps not necessarily clearer). We decided that maybe he had had an idea, and the next thing we knew we were working on this anthology.

The Condon-Gehman collaboration, which may possibly never take its place with Beaumont and Fletcher, Addison and Steele, Buck and Bubbles and Moscowitz and Lupowitz, was born after the death of Thomas Sugrue, who assisted Condon in untangling the punctuation for *We Called It Music* (Henry Holt, 1947). It began under the auspices of Fleur Cowles, who was then *Flair*-ing. We closed that enterprise; our piece on John Steinbeck, written under Eddie's name, appeared in the magazine's last spasm (we got in, Condon has noted, just before the sheriff). We were reunited by *The American Mercury*, when it was run by Lawrence Spivak, where we committed a few errors which aroused practically no interest in limited circles. Then, one night, Ted Patrick, who edits *Holiday* when he is not playing tennis or opening Hilton hotels, wandered into Condon's club and insisted that we attempt something for him. The result was *This is Jazz*, the second story in the book. That effort in turn attracted the attention of a fellow named Hearst, who owns some newspapers. Hearst, who evidently has great respect for his readers' patience, thought they might be willing to struggle through a record column. He sent Frank Coniff to give us a few ground rules. Coniff gave us one. "Write a weekly column," he said.

If we last until this book appears, the column will be two years old. Our mail response has been unprecedented: an insurance salesman solicited us, a lady wrote asking our advice on removing unsightly hair from her upper lip, and a gentleman in Queens begged our help in disposing of his collection of Helen Kane records.

That brings us up to George the Jewel. This book is a collection of stories and articles about jazz of all kinds. Some of the things we wrote, others were done by people who know more about the subject than we do. Most of them appear in their original form, as they were before those straight-haired, horn-rimmed girls on magazine copy desks managed to get hold of them. In some cases we have interrupted the text here and there to make some comment or rebuttal. In other cases we have made single pieces by patching together parts of the work of three or four writers. There is work here that has appeared on record album covers, on television, in the trade journals and the popular magazines and even the literary quarterlies. A little of the material has been cut slightly, but not enough to spoil the flavor.

In selecting these pieces we followed only two rules: they had to be fun to read and they had to contain at least some information. Also, we tried to find material that had not been reprinted previously. We make no apologies for omissions or inclusions, although we are fully aware that there are many important jazz events and performers which ought to be at least mentioned in the book. It is a bit unusual for an editor to print a piece about himself, but Gehman takes sole responsibility for the story about Condon, principally because the latter is, as Marshall Stearns kept saying at Newport in 1955, a legend. Certain people may be shocked by this candid exposure of the legend's capacity (Condon, for example, was shocked into a drought that lasted a full thirty minutes).

We are indebted to many people for suggestions and assistance, notably John Hammond, Leonard Feather, George Simon, James T. Maher, Robert George Reisner, Marshall Stearns, Bud Bohm, Donald Congdon, Don Allen and James Silberman. We also want to thank the Institute of Jazz Studies for making its files available to us. Complaints, naturally, should be addressed to Charles Andrews.

EDDIE CONDON
RICHARD GEHMAN

New York, January, 1956.

ONE:

EDDIE AND THE MUSIC

PHYLLIS CONDON, GEORGE FRAZIER, GILBERT MILLSTEIN, RICHARD GEHMAN

Eddie Condon

NATURALLY, EDDIE GETS the first piece—if only for the benefit of recluses and others who have never known him. I have used my own story as a framework, and patched into it parts of George Frazier's, some stuff from Phyllis, Eddie's wife, and parts of Gilbert Millstein's piece that appeared in the New York Times when Eddie's saloon was ten years old. Also, I've added some Condonisms which have not appeared in print before.
R. G.

It is impossible to separate the man from the music, of course, but an attempt can be made. The best way to do it, I feel, is to let the reader listen to him on the telephone. He called me up one day in the winter of 1952 and, as usual, wasted no time on introductory remarks.

"Say," he demanded, "you ever know a newspaperman named McLemore? Henry McLemore?"

"I've met him. What about him?"

The admiration in Condon's tone was tempered by regret. "What a real barrelhouse guy," he said. "He came down to the joint last night. With him, if the whisky isn't straight, you're a fag." He paused. "What you're speaking to now is the remnants."

"Tasted a few, did you?"

"Put it this way," said Condon solemnly. "Very few bottles won a reprieve. Listen. Let's go up and get a transfusion in the Numerical Place." He was referring to Twenty-One, a restaurant he holds in esteem.

Although I have known Condon a long time, I am always amazed at his capacity. "You mean," I asked, "you're going to go drinking again?"

"Naturally," he said. "I got to get myself half-soled."

And so he did. He always does. And yet, miraculously, he continues to function, and to cause his friends to speak of him as they would speak of some wonder of nature, such as a reliable geyser. Here is what one of them has said of him.

GILBERT MILLSTEIN: In December, 1945, having long since subdued his art or at least reduced it to manageable proportions, Mr. Albert Edwin Condon, the celebrated hot guitarist, who is also the La Rochefoucauld of Dixieland jazz music, put aside the things of his childhood and locked himself in the stifling embrace of commerce, thereby causing most of his acquaintances to shy in alarm or titter nervously, according to their dispositions. He opened a narrow freehold in Greenwich Village, peopling it with six of his instrumentalist friends in addition to himself, graciously lent the place his own name, made money and even appeared frequently on the bandstand, picking away fastidiously at the guitar, which he was supposed to do.

In December, 1955, on the eve of his tenth anniversary as a performer-proprietor, Condon was an unchanged man, still standing 5 feet, 7¾ inches high in his own vaulting imagination, although he is a shade more than somewhat smaller in fact. While he turned fifty in November, his appearance was one of extreme youth preserved with the dreadful perfection of a beetle in amber.

RICHARD GEHMAN: Or in Scotch. In my original piece on Condon, I calculated that in seven years Eddie had drunk approximately 5,102 bottles, or 425⅙ cases, or about half a carload of what he calls "imported Scotch-style whisky."

This figure actually was the barest minimum. It was based on the fact that Condon drinks anywhere from thirty to forty one-ounce shots of whisky per night, virtually every blessed night of the week, every single week of the year. Many nights he drinks more. Cumulatively, the total he consumes on heavier-drinking nights certainly balances those infrequent periods when he drinks nothing at all. He generally goes on the wagon for about two weeks out of each year, "just to see how it feels." When "on the wagon," he drinks beer.

It should now be made clear that Eddie Condon is not a drunk. A drunk is a man who slobbers, falls down, sings, leaves his overcoat in bars, calls up old girls, and fails to show up. Condon has lost a raincoat or two in the past couple of years, but he never slobbers, falls down only when pushed or struck by a moving object such as a Mack truck, always shows up when he has made an appointment, and does not call up girls for a very good reason: he is happily married. Here is what Phyllis, his wife, has to say about that.

PHYLLIS CONDON: To his many admirers Eddie is one of the fabled names of American jazz, but to our ten and twelve-year-old daughters, Maggie and Liza, and to me, Eddie is Uncle Da Da, a funny but appropriate name Maggie gave him when she was two. Uncle Da Da is the kingpin of a household whose family life is about as formal as Huckleberry Finn's. I've heard it called mad, wild, crazy. We think of it as free, easy, all our own—and perfectly suited to our individual schedules and tastes.

We make our headquarters in two homes at once—our nine-room town apartment on Washington Square, in New York City, and our house on the shore at Monmouth, New Jersey. In the winter we operate chiefly out of the Washington Square house, only three blocks from Eddie's club. Eddie works on the late-night to-early-morning club shift; I work the standard nine-to-five hours as a writer in an advertising agency; and the children live on still a different day span: They go to boarding school near the Jersey house and join us in town on weekends. That way Maggie and Liza can eat, relax, study, and play like other normal children, by the clock. In the summer we all spend at least half the week together at the shore, where the kids swim, ride horseback, roam around on bikes, wander with the dog over the bright sunlit beaches, and mother a menagerie of parakeets, turtles, goldfish, chameleons, tadpoles and cats. Wherever we are, friends and relatives come drifting into the house whenever the spirit moves them; they're always welcome to sit down and share our never-ending assembly-line buffet.

Occasionally we have a family dinner in New York at the Club, where the steaks are hot and the music delicious. I can't honestly call the Club quiet or intimate—not with jazz fans stopping by for autographs and Wild Bill Davison blasting away on his horn. Before the crowd comes on, Maggie and Liza usually ask Eddie to let them play "four hands" on the big piano. (This is a special treat, since there are few pianos that get more meticulous tunings than the Condon concert grand. It's groomed twice a week, by an expert tuner, for the hard eight-hour workout it gets each night.) These piano duets are sort of half-and-half— a mixture of the formal music the girls have both studied since they were six and the make-it-up-as-you-go-along ideas they get from Eddie.

I met Eddie—at a jam session. Some mutual friends, trying to "educate" me about jazz, introduced us. Eddie was thirty-six, single, and, then as now, exactly fitted the nickname "Slick" he acquired in Chicago. It was clear that steady girls didn't fit in with his budget, his offbeat attitude or his carefree bachelor ways. There seemed to be absolutely no way to "motivate" a date with Eddie. But shortly after we'd met, he asked me if I'd mind calling him on the telephone promptly at three o'clock the next day: He had an important appointment and couldn't rely on the telephone girls in his small musicians-and-actors hotel to wake him. That single telephone call became a perfect lead-in to a daily five o'clock date. In no time at all it took me everywhere. Backstage at the Paramount to meet Frank Sinatra. To cocktails at Sardi's with Burgess Meredith, Henry Fonda or Bing Crosby. And finally down to a little church on Washington Square to be married.

After Liza and Maggie were born, we found our present long, cool, old-fashioned apartment on Washington Square, occupied up to that time by Amy Vanderbilt. Now, through our front windows, in summer we look out on the leafy treetops of Washington Square, in winter on cheerful scenes of children, park sitters and brightly clad strollers in the snow.

RICHARD GEHMAN: This does not mean that Eddie permits his domestic life to intrude upon his music—or, for that matter, his drinking. He goes right on with both. Sometimes he has terrible hangovers—he calls them "holdovers"—but he seldom complains. When he does, his cries of agony take a comic turn. Robert Ruark told him one day that he recently had recovered from one of his recurrent attacks of gout.

"Is that so?" Condon said. "I had the gout when I woke up today—right between the ears."

GEORGE FRAZIER: Condon is, by his own unblushing admission, one of the world's most dependable authorities on the subject of hangovers. As such, he is inclined to turn up his pug nose at the innumerable remedies which other men have proposed from time to time for this self-inflicted form of torture. He is equally disdainful toward the defeatist school of thought, led by the late Robert Benchley, which maintained, "There is no cure for a hangover but death."

"For a bad hangover," prescribes Condon, "take the juice of two quarts of whisky."

RICHARD GEHMAN: Condon's hangovers are never the result of accidental drinking. He walks into all of them with his eyes open. His nightly consumption has a quality of cold, single-minded efficiency, like that of a python swallowing a suckling pig whole. He first pours an eight-ounce glass half-full of Scotch (his brand is Dewar's White Label, or if he can't get that, John Begg; when a friend asked him what he took when he couldn't get the latter, he replied simply, "Scotch"). Next he adds water almost to the brim of the glass and twists and drops in a lemon peel. After muddling it, he stares thoughtfully at the drink for several minutes and downs the first half. In another five-minute interval he destroys the remainder.

"I'm no sipper," he has said.

A companion who loves Scotch once asked Condon why he insisted upon disguising it with the lemon peel. Condon became confidential. "You know," he said, with utmost sincerity, "I can't stand the taste of hard booze of any kind."

The friend, who had just witnessed Condon putting away five Condon-sized drinks in less than thirty minutes, stared at him aghast. "Then why in God's name do you drink?"

"Why, to get loaded," said Condon.

Sam Boal, the writer, last year mentioned to Condon in a telephone conversation that he was sitting at home having, as he said, "a delicious drink of whisky."

"What did you put in it to make it taste that way?" Condon asked.

Boal is one of a small, rather select group of approved Condon drinking companions, an oddly-assorted circle linked mainly by admiration for his music and for him. In addition to such musicians as Bill Davison (Condon calls him "Wild Bull" or "Wild Pitch"), Ralph Sutton, Zutty Singleton, Pee Wee Russell and other musicians, the list of apostles includes Mischa Reznikoff, a naturalized Russian with a heavy accent and considerable talent as an abstract painter; Squirrel Ashcraft, a Chicago lawyer who enjoys playing barrelhouse piano; actors, such as Yul Brynner; newspapermen, such as Ruark, McLemore, and Bugs Baer; writers, such as George Frazier and John Steinbeck; a former suitcase thumper named Josh Billings, who now devotes his time to photoengraving and sports cars; Ernie Anderson, publicity man for Mike Todd, who was the promoter of Condon's series of Town Hall jazz concerts during the war; Lee Wiley, the singer, and Minerva Pious (once Mrs. Nussbaum on the old Fred Allen radio show); Jackie Gleason and his press agent, Lee Myers, and anybody who happens to be along with any of the foregoing. Condon also has a vast acquaintance among, and a mysterious affection for, all kinds of midwestern manufacturers of valves, sprockets, brakes and articles of apparel. The president of one of the nation's largest automobile companies is one of this group. He is a man who can't drink but has never learned it. Condon customarily introduces him by saying, "This is T———. When he's sober, he makes cars."

It is no coincidence that most of Condon's cronies are capable of assimilating Hogarthian quantities, but this is not his sole criterion for a friend. He seems to choose his companions for their deficiency in hypocrisy, their dependability in any crisis (such as the supply of booze running out), their good manners, their talent, and, above all, their talent for turning an original phrase. Whenever one friend says something worthy of repetition, Condon hastily calls and informs all the others he can locate.

GEORGE FRAZIER: Like Condon himself, his associates are, if not impressively rugged, nevertheless individualists. They also are all of a piece in their devotion to the brand of jazz which adolescents are prone to refer to as "out of this world." Condon would wince at that description of his kind of music, pointing out rather testily that it is jive talk, a form of self-expression repellent to his conservative tastes. For although he is in many respects the average musician, in others he is the direct antithesis of the characters who spout jive and bop talk as if it were a glittering testimonial to their musicianship . . . He is a precise elocutionist who writhes at the sound of such phrases as "Whatcha say, man? Man, whatcha really know? Man, where you been hidin', anyway? Hip me, man." A few nights before the fall of Germany he was presented with a golden opportunity to express his withering contempt for this sort of thing. A youngster who had presumably been reading too many issues of *Down Beat* (which Condon refers to as "Brow Beat" or "Dead Beat") approached him and said, "What's cookin', man?" Fixing him with an icy glare, Condon replied, "Hitler."

Condon abhors snobbery and pretension in any form. A few years ago, a *Time* researcher with a pseudo-Groton accent interviewed Condon and, in the course of his questioning, asked, "Now what about Pee Wee? (He pronounced it "Pay Way") Is he drahftable?"

Condon raised a shocked eyebrow. "Payway!" he said. "If the Japs happen to invade the ice skating rink at Rockefeller Plaza, Payway is a cinch to be called up for limited service."

RICHARD GEHMAN: Once Condon has made up his mind that an associate is a friend, his loyalty is unrelenting. When he writes a magazine piece and tells an anecdote about someone he knows, he goes through the writhings of the damned in trying to decide whether or not to use the person's name. Usually he winds up by calling him "a fellow I know." Once a well-known musician whom he had played with for years, bounced a check for $500 in the saloon. Pete Pesci was outraged. Condon told him to be calm. "He may show up," he said. The man has been working around New York for years, but he has never again put his head inside Condon's door. Still, Condon often says, "You can't tell—some day there may be a tremendous atonement. He might come walking in and give me a Cadillac or something." Another of Condon's pals of old had a habit of getting married in whatever town his orchestra was playing. He also liked to fly back and forth across the Mexican border in his own plane, carrying Mexicans purely for company. Unfortunately, many of the Mexicans neglected to gain permission for entry and, once here, failed to return. In telling this man's tale, Condon seldom mentions his name; he states only that the man was not a bad trumpet player. "Is he in jail now?" I once asked.

"Let's say this," Condon said. "He's now leading a band in a place where it's almost impossible for him to play one-nighters."

Condon is a sucker for touches from down-and-out musicians. I have seen him dole out anywhere from fifty to a hundred dollars in an evening to people who quite obviously may never repay. This is one of the few bones of contention in the Condon household, and as a gesture toward settling it once and for all, Phyllis now forbids him to operate his own checking account. She handles all finances and doles out cash to him as he needs it.

PHYLLIS CONDON: Since he never carries a billfold and is rarely caught with any currency larger than a five-dollar bill on his person, our country household is often awakened at dawn: Eddie missed the last common carrier to New Jersey and hired a chauffeured car for the trip from New York. When this happens, the $40 fare collected on delivery comes out of a special family sugar bowl, known to me privately as the "Who Does He Think He Is Anyhow, a Millionaire?" fund.

RICHARD GEHMAN: One night as Condon and I were going out, he approached Phyllis for his allowance. She handed him a hundred dollars. "Don't give this all to the same person," she said. Their casual, everyday conversation would qualify them for vaudeville. Once, when Phyllis had become more than usually concerned with Eddie's drinking, she typed up a ghoulish list of musician friends who had died of liver trouble and handed it to him without a word. He studied it. "There's a drummer missing," he announced, and handed it back.

Phyllis makes an excellent straight woman. One night the two of them were discussing a trip to the country. "Let's plan on leaving at ten," Condon said. "Oh, let's not make any plans," said Phyllis.

"We got to make plans," he said, "so we'll have something to cancel."

Another time they were having dinner at Luchow's, the famous old German restaurant. Condon ordered a ham-and-cheese sandwich on rye. A moment later the waiter returned and apologized. "There's no rye, sir—there's a breadtruck driver strike on."

Condon considered for a moment. "Tell 'em to put it on a couple of pieces of picket board," he said, agreeably.

Such lines are delivered in a dry monotone between teeth that appear to be nearly clenched and lips that barely open. Condon rarely laughs aloud. If there is one type that he does not resemble at all, it is the popular conception of the jazz musician.

PHYLLIS CONDON: Eddie still has the look of that sixteen-year-old beamish boy with the banjo—with his sporty bow ties, his dapper haberdashery, his electric way of skittering and darting around a room, and his baffling staccato talk, I think one reason why Eddie has no gray hair or ulcers is that he ignores clocks, time-tables, musical scores and all other man-made plans —including the arrival and departure time of boats, trains, and buses.

RICHARD GEHMAN: Condon's demeanor on the bandstand is akin to that of a hamlet undertaker trying to convince the bereaved that they owe it to their loved one to invest in the $750 casket. Some nights when he is in town, Jack Teagarden, naked trombone in hand, may wander into the joint, sit upon the stand, remove the bell of the instrument and play into a water glass and Billy Butterfield has been known to bring his volcanic trumpet into a Condon session for the sheer hell of it. Condon never fawns over these visiting stars, but he may lean down from the bandstand and say to a friend, "Lucky you came tonight." When he is speaking of someone he admires, such as Johnny Windhurst, a twenty-four-year-old trumpeter who plays a little like the great Bix, he couches his phrases cautiously. "I can't say he bothers me," he says. He brushes aside all praise of his own playing. If someone mentions that his guitar is not ably powerful in his rhythm section (he never takes a solo), he stares almost indignantly and says, "I knew the whisky was strong in here, but I didn't know it was that strong."

Much of his conversation is couched in this kind of understatement. One morning after the saloon closed I drove him to New Jersey. It began to rain as we started out. At Linden, New Jersey, we had to stop for a red light. The Esso refineries are located there, and the ugly silver tanks sit like enormous tombstones in the stinking marshes. The air is continually smoky and sooty, the gray sky seems to blend with the brown desolation of the landscape, and by the roadside are several old workmen's shacks plastered with windtorn circus and movie posters. As we were waiting for the light to change Condon surveyed this scene with interest.

"Phyllis and I have been thinking of buying out here," he said. . . .

Of Condon the New Jerseyite, Phyllis has this to say:

PHYLLIS CONDON: Eddie enjoys Jersey peaches, tomatoes, and the salt air, but he's not at all domestic or handy around the house. Behind the wheel of a car he's enough to give anyone a nervous breakdown—never knows which turn to take to the post office, church, or general store—so I do the chauffeuring and leave Eddie free for the children. He's old-fashioned in some ways; he'd much rather see them in starched, ruffly dresses than in blue jeans, for example, but he's given up on that fight. He and Maggie have a special understanding that goes back to those days, six years ago, when she left us to spend several months in the polio ward of a New York hospital. We could see her for only half an hour Sunday afternoons; then we'd have to wave to her in her small hospital wheel chair and say, "So long, Maggie. See you next week." Today the leg that was paralyzed is perfect, and Maggie and Eddie and our beagle, Punch, go off roaming for long walks to make up for lost time.

Of course Eddie can't stand spending more than a few days away from the magic isle of Manhattan. Its music, its chaos, its perpetual change and motion, its never-ending carnival of fun, are definitely his dish.

RICHARD GEHMAN: As Phyllis indicates, Condon literally never gets enough of jazz. Two or three nights a week, after closing his place at four A.M., he may get together a group of friends and go uptown to Joe Mah's Confucius, a late-hour chop-suey establishment on West 52nd Street which has become a musicians' hangout. Other players from other saloons wander in and join the party. The food in the Confucius is exceptional, but it is not exceptional enough to curb the restlessness that possesses them all. Before long, this ingrown desire for expression begins to boil over the table, and one or another may begin tapping his fingers rhythmically. At this point, Mischa Reznikoff, who is almost always in the party, may say in his rough, bearish voice, "Come on op to my place," and as one man the group gets up and piles into Josh Billings' Jaguar drop-head coupe or Johnny Windhurst's Rover (during the last year Condon's musicians have gone mad for foreign automobiles).

Reznikoff and his wife, the photographer Genevieve Naylor, live in a huge converted stable on East 69th Street. The ground floor is one vast room, in the front third of which Miss Naylor takes her studio shots. The rear two-thirds looks as though it was designed for sizable parties, which was indeed the case. It is decorated with Mischa's huge abstract paintings and some statues he has contructed from coat hangers and whisky-bottle tops, and with hundreds of Parliament cigarette boxes on which he has drawn curious angular faces. There is an upright piano in one corner, and near it the microphone for Mischa's tape recorder. Inspired by Mischa's booze, perhaps even stimulated by his wildly colored paintings, and unfettered by night-club audiences, the boys stand about, sit on the floor or on chairs or a large table, and improvise chorus after chorus of the old, nearly forgotten tunes, such as "Nobody Knows and Nobody Cares," "Peggy," and even, sometimes, "Wild Man Blues" or "Grandpa's Spells." Other musicians and singers or devotees may arrive, and the sessions have been known to go on for days. One Friday morning a friend of mine and I arrived at five A.M. At nine, I staggered out into the blazing sunlight. Next evening, the party was still going strong. My friend did not leave until the following Sunday afternoon at four.

GEORGE FRAZIER: Condon has been behaving this way all his life. He was born in Goodland, Indiana, where his father ran a saloon. Later the family moved to Chicago, where Eddie enrolled at Chicago Heights High School. He had been there only a short time when he decided to quit and go into the music business. Chicago in the nineteen-twenties was the hub of the jazz universe and everywhere that one went he tripped over untaught geniuses who were destined to emerge in later years as barrelhouse saints. The music they made along the South Side in those nights was heartfelt and prophetic. Louis Armstrong was there, showing the boys how the trumpet could be made to sound; and Jess Stacy, King Oliver, Beiderbecke, Benny Goodman, and Frank Teschemacher. And although all of them have long since become big, resonant names, at the time they were merely kids who, in the popular view, were wasting their youth and health in gin mills. Condon came of age in such surroundings.

His first instrument was, of all things, the banjo ukulele, a medium of expression that is happily out of style at the moment. In those giddy years, however, the banjo uke was as much a craze as John Held, Jr., autographed slickers, Clara Bow, and Keep Cool with Calvin Coolidge. Despite the fact that his occasional inarticulate singing these days would not seem to indicate as much, Condon began his musical career as a vocalist. In an indiscriminating era when Billy Murray, the Happiness Boys (Billy Jones and Ernie Hare, the Interwoven Pair), the Silver-Masked Tenor, and the Clicquot Club Eskimos were not without their devotees, Condon may have sounded passable. But by no merciful stretch of the imagination could he have sounded anything more than that. He apparently realized this, because before long he turned to the banjo.

Condon likes to talk about the hallowed jazz men who were kids with him in Chicago, but he prefers to discuss their lives rather than their music. "Listen to his records," he will often parry when asked for his opinion of a man's talent. "They'll tell you more than I can." As a prima facie authority on such idols as Beiderbecke and Teschemacher, his comments possess a validity notably absent from the small talk that has enshrouded both men since their untimely deaths. Toward such heroes as Benny Goodman and Tommy Dorsey, he has a calm objectivity which takes the form of such innocent nicknaming as "Benny Badman" and "Tommy Torso." As a matter of fact, his respect for both Goodman and Dorsey is abundant, because he knows the pitfalls of his profession well enough to appreciate the fullness of their accomplishments. But for a comparative johnny-come-lately like Artie Shaw, whom he regards as a poor-man's Goodman, he has unmingled contempt. "All he needs are the glasses," is Condon's succinct way of expressing his distaste for Shaw's blatant aping of Goodman's style.

Condon's iconoclasm toward the famous names of popular (as opposed to hot) music is invariably pronounced with a redeeming good humor. One evening, when he was at a party where some Eddy Duchin piano solos were being played on the phonograph, a gushing girl approached him and said, "Don't you simply adore Eddy Duchin, Mr. Condon? What I mean is, he really makes the piano talk, don't you think?" Condon raised an eyebrow, jerked his head back as if he were ducking away from an uppercut, and said, "He certainly does. The piano says, 'Please take your clumsy hands off me.'"

RICHARD GEHMAN: Condon moved east in the late twenties. Along with Red McKenzie, who played comb and sang, Josh Billings (suitcase), Gene Krupa and some others, he invaded New York and began working in whatever speakeasies offered employment. The best job he ever had was at John Perona's Bath Club, although he recalls that one with pain because the customers insisted upon playing comb, McKenzie-style, along with the band.

That job was exceptional. Most of the time, he has said, he was unemployed and living on "transparent hamburgers." The diet did not affect his sense of humor in the slightest. In fact, he appears to recall those days with a certain amount of enjoyment. In one of his Hearst columns last year, he wrote:

> Back in the mid-thirties jobs were scarce for jazz musicians and food was even scarcer.
> Marty Marsala, a trumpet player who sometimes engaged

drums in combat, found a Chinese restaurant where the asking price was not too unthinkable. You could get an entire dinner there for twenty-five cents, including dessert. One night the two of us managed to get the necessary trump together. We went up to this place for a meal. It was the first food we'd had in some time, and there was nothing wrong with it except that it was mildly inedible.

Marty found that the hot English mustard they put on the table improved the quality of the food enormously. Bud Freeman, who heard about it later, asked if we used so much of it because it improved hangovers.

"We used it so we could taste the food," I explained.

When we'd had all that was allowed, the waiter came and asked if we wanted dessert meaning almond cakes or vanilla ice cream.

"Bring us some vanilla ice cream," said Marty— "—and some more of that hot English mustard."

Condon's first impact on the national consciousness occurred when he and Ernie Anderson put on a series of concerts in Town Hall. The first one was sparsely attended, and Condon addressed the audience as follows: "Lady," he said, "and gentleman." But after that they began to catch on. There were air shots forthcoming. During the war, he and his boys made V-disks and broadcast on the Armed Forces network. The next thing he knew, he was a national figure and people began urging him to open a saloon. Before that happened, however, there was a long period of servitude in Nick's, the famous jazz tavern at Seventh Avenue and Tenth Street. When the comprehensive history of jazz is written,

GEORGE FRAZIER: Nick's will probably demand considerable space. It is a large room and over it hangs a pall of bluish smoke, a blurred hum of conversation, and the wonderful beat of a good little band. Along the paneled walls are stuffed heads of animals and, near the entrance, a framed set of the imposing ribbons won by Nick's Boxer bitch, Duchess, who used to put in an appearance several times in the course of an evening to lap up a saucer of beer and sniff the customers. The men's room attendant for years was a short, excitable man named Benny, who was referred to by Condon as either Benny McToilet, Benny McCann, or Flush

Gordon. As men's room attendants go, Benny was exceptional. He was especially dear to the hearts of those gentlemen who had the urgency to invade his sanctum more than once during an evening. When he was tipped for his ministrations, Benny presented his benefactor with a small coupon which, when shown on subsequent visitations, absolved the holder from the moral obligation of leaving another tip. Condon used to call this the "P Coupon." Once Condon was in the men's room when a novelist whose brilliant career had degenerated into chronic alcoholism, the loss of his teeth and a vicious disposition, stumbled in and proceeded to pick a fight with him. "Look," he said. "Let's not try to see who's king of the men's room, John. It wouldn't be a fair fight anyway. I stand to lose my own teeth."

GILBERT MILLSTEIN: Condon has said that the idea of opening his own club had been implanted in him first by the actor, Burgess Meredith, who telephoned him late one night from New York while Condon was playing in Chicago. "I turned him down," Condon disclosed. "He partially scared me to death. It seemed noisy on his end and it was certainly too noisy on mine. I figured he'd probably sober up or get sane or get hold of himself the next morning." Actually, it was a jarring accident of fate that put Condon in business. Nick Rongetti raised the band's drinks a nickel. "We began risking pneumonia and going across the street to Julius', the home of the fake cobwebs and the real sawdust," Condon continued, "where I got to know a guy named Pete Pesci. The drinks were a nickel cheaper and besides Pete'd buy one once in a while."

Pesci succeeded where Meredith had failed. "Pete's now my manager," Condon said recently with emotion. "The intricate business details will here be omitted. "When the news broke among the competition and the whisky dealers," Condon said, "the word was, 'Where's he going to get the whisky?' It was tough right after the war." He paused for what obviously was going to be an effect. "We opened with scotch," he finally said with quiet pride. "Not scotch-type or scotch tape. The turnout was fantastic. At ten o'clock the guys were still sticking the mirrors on the posts. We had to keep everyone in the bar. Tommy Dorsey came by and asked, 'How're things going?' I told him, 'We're doing the greatest vestibule business in town.'

"Following day, over at Julius', talking about the opening, somebody said, 'I went over and couldn't get in.' My brother Pat said, 'You couldn't get in? I'm his brother and I couldn't get out.' "

The great improviser said his most nervous days had been the five months he waited for a liquor license. "The only weight I gained," he observed, "was under each eye." The place almost failed the following summer, however, for lack of an air-conditioning system. Thereafter, everything was, as Condon put it, "rosy dosy." When asked what the most spectacular thing was that had ever happened at the club, Condon answered, "Staying open." He was then queried as to what he considered his major function to be and replied, "I show up. I can walk to work in three and a half minutes cutting through Washington Square on the bias and I can reel back home in 100-½ minutes on the same bias."

The club's policy, Condon said, has always been, "We don't throw anyone in and we don't throw anyone out. There was one instance when we almost had to throw a guy out because he insisted on playing the You-Hum-A-Song-Game. (Condon is severe about customer requests. If, for example, a man wants the band to play "Royal Garden Blues," it invariably responds with "The Man I Love.") This was some guy named Windsor. Ookey-Dookey Windsor. The only thing saved him was his wife. The joint was loaded with Windsors that night. They were sitting right in front of the band. I, of course, bending back for nobility, offered them a table, a little comfy table on the stand. All of a sudden, Dookey gave up humming for the nonce."

RICHARD GEHMAN: The opening of the saloon launched a new phase in Eddie's life. Although it is not as rough as it once was, his current schedule is no soft touch. Strangers often express incredulity at Condon's ability to lead the sort of life he does and still carry on a fairly normal family life. Actually, the drawn-out parties are the exception rather than the rule. Most nights he goes home immediately after he has had a bite to eat. He leaves the saloon as soon as it is locked up and walks the two blocks across the Square to his apartment where he undresses, puts on a pair of blinders, and falls into a rocklike slumber, from which he emerges at two or three the next day.

PHYLLIS CONDON: Luckily, Eddie's original idea for "decorating" his bedroom was turned down by the landlord. He wanted it painted jet black, ceiling and all, but had to compromise on dark green. Eddie started traveling with a little jazz band in Illinois when he was sixteen, and until we were married he had been suffering from light, noisy, hotel bedrooms, where traffic and sunshine plagued his sleeping hours. What could be finer than a jet-black bedroom of his own?

It is almost impossible to make the room neat or presentable. Half of one entire wall is a necktie rack strung with gay chintz, denim, calico and gingham bow ties. The rest of the room is a welter of business cards, phone numbers, appointment slips, news clippings, photographs, post cards from Johnny Mercer, dozens of pairs of shoes on shoe trees, and Eddie's souvenirs.

Important names don't impress Eddie, but any reminder he gets from an old friend is precious. He keeps every gift card, note and incidental message that Bing Crosby has sent with presents to our Liza, Bing's goddaughter, and he refuses to throw away his complete collection of last year's Christmas cards—at least until he gets a new collection come next December. About once every three months Eddie sorts over the litter and does what he calls "filing." This consists of throwing the obsolete memos into the wastebasket and putting the photos and post cards into neat piles. This goes on and on, but I must admit he never loses anything. His one warning to me and the cleaning woman is, "Don't move any memos." So we just dust around them.

RICHARD GEHMAN: Phyllis handles the matter of Condon's peculiar eating habits with the same dispatch: she leaves food where it can be seen, and keeps large jars of vitamin capsules in all rooms of the house. When Condon arises, he goes immediately to the kitchen and drinks a quart of milk—sometimes, in fact, two quarts. Then he is ready for his breakfast, which consists of several carrots, some celery, lettuce and other leafy vegetables hurled into a Waring blender with yogurt, wheat germ, and some unidentifiable health-store products. It looks fearful and tastes just as bad, but he drinks it down. Thus fortified, he faces the day. In the evening he has one large meal, usually a steak. As Phyllis pointed out, his diet is unusual, but it's very healthful. It also may be a kind of defense against the comments on his drinking he must listen to. He is a great worry to everyone who knows him well, and the concern of his friends is intensified by the fact that on two occasions in fifteen years he has had severe attacks of pancreatitis. He was given up for dead both times. After each one, doctors warned him that his next drink might be his last. Condon's reaction to these cautionary statements was typical. "I changed doctors," he said. There is another school of thought, to which I belong, which maintains that Condon might well outlive us all.

Nearly everyone has given up trying to persuade him to quit drinking. Pete Pesci, his manager (Condon calls him "my night damager"), is the lone exception. Pete keeps after him, and after his friends. When Condon turns up at the saloon with some pal, Pete gives the pal hell. One night after Condon and an old Chicago acquaintance, Bud Bohm, had had dinner uptown, Bohm refused to accompany him to the club. "Every time I go down there, Pete gives me hell," Bohm said.

Condon nodded. "You're bound to get in trouble," he said, "if you keep going to that place with me."

At no time in our acquaintance or in anybody else's memory has Condon ever given a hint as to the underlying causes of his toping. He undergoes no personality change as he drinks. Whatever there is that's worrying him is buried so deep it probably never will come out. He exhibits none of the feelings of persecution, outbursts of temper, excesses of hilarity that mark the common neurotic—but every once in a while he does give some thought to himself, and on such occasions he wonders what on earth could be the matter with him. One night at dinner he seemed especially introspective, and I asked him what was on his mind. "I'll be damned if I know," he said, softly. "Maybe I ought to go see a psychiatrist." Then he shook his head. "But," he continued, "can you imagine me goin' into a guy's office and saying, 'Look here, Moishe, I'm crazier'n you are, and . . .'" he slapped his wallet pocket smartly, "'. . . I got the money to prove it?'"

EDDIE CONDON

This Is Jazz

This is my piece. Dick gave me an assist after Holiday magazine had asked me to do it. It first appeared in May, 1953, and has been updated.

E. C.

We were unloading ourselves from the bandstand after playing a set, and there were some jazz scholars lurking in wait for us. It was easy to tell they were scholars, because they all had short haircuts and wore heavy-rimmed spectacles and used words like "polyphonic" and "antitonal" and others I wouldn't remember even if I could. One grabbed Wild Bill Davison's sleeve. Bill knew what was coming; he tightened his jaws on his gum.

"Mr. Davison," the scholar said, "when you start on a trumpet solo, what do you think about?"

"Man," said Mr. Davison, "I don't think about *nothin'*. I just blow."

I bring this up to show that the average talented, resourceful jazz musician is no mathematician. He doesn't plan out solos; he picks up his horn and away he goes, moving along from bar to bar. That's the essence of jazz music: improvisation. Even when a man has some sort of general framework in mind, he finds it hard to put in words. Well, one day the editor of this magazine asked me to put down a few words about my kind of music and musicians. I've been accused of playing guitar, and I can't deny that my dues are paid up in Local 802, but let this be a warning: what you hear next will be strictly improvisation.

Those scholars that bothered Wild Bill brought to mind Joe Rushton in a roundabout way. Joe and I were friends back in Chicago. He played good bass saxophone and rode a motorcycle. He used to strap the saxophone to his back and take off on the cycle to various engagements. After a while he joined Benny Goodman's band and had to travel in the bus. He reluctantly put his motorcycle on blocks in a garage. Another friend of Joe's and mine, Squirrel Ashcraft, saw Joe one day when Goodman's band came into Chicago. Squirrel asked him if he'd had a chance to ride his motorcycle lately. "No," said Joe, sorrowfully, "but last Saturday I went down and sat on it." Later Goodman was playing a hotel job in New York; I was there then, too, trying to play anywhere I could, and I bumped into Joe on the street. He told me he was staying in some ninth-rate menace over on the West Side. This seemed odd to me, since at that time Goodman's band was doubling and tripling and had about a thousand commercials, and his boys certainly weren't running out of trump. I saw Squirrel and happened to ask him, "How come Joe's living over there at that sewer?" Squirrel said, "Well, he's got a relative or two, and several other dependents, and of course," Squirrel added, "he's got to give that motorcycle seventy-five dollars a week." Then Squirrel reminded me of another Rushton story. This also happened in Chicago. I'd gone there on a job at the Brass Rail with Jimmy McPartland, George Brunis and some others; it was my first trip back after about a hundred years in New York. One night Squirrel committed a party for some of us who'd been around town in the old days, and we took our instruments along, figuring to make some records for Squirrel on his equipment. Joe came out on his motorcycle, the bass saxophone strapped to his back. He was very eager to use that recording apparatus. The rest of us were very eager to use Squirrel's booze. "Come on, fellows, let's make some records," Joe kept saying, and we kept ignoring him.

Finally, in desperation, he went outside, got the motorcycle, wheeled it in the house, set it up in front of the equipment, kicked it off and recorded it. I don't know where Joe Rushton is today, but I'll bet I know where the motorcycle is. He's got it under a bell jar.

(When last heard from Joe Rushton was working in Hollywood with Red Nichols.—R. G.)

The connection between Joe Rushton and those jazz scholars is probably just about as clear as any record Moondog ever made, so I'll try to explain. Joe and the scholars had this in common: they were cultists. Joe was a member of the motorcycle cult; the kids belonged to the jazz-music cult. Cults aren't exactly uncommon in this country. There are cults made up of guys who like to fly box kites, cults of guys who drink only cheap whisky even though they can afford better, cults of folks who like to go to Fire Island—everybody, it seems, cults it up to some degree. Sometimes people even get sort of reverse cults going, made up of those who particularly *don't* like something.

(Later in the book, Ernest Borneman has some more to say about cults.—E. C.)

I can't explain cults any more than you can. A guy I know suggests it might have something to do with the American people's habit of joining the Elks, the Woodmen of the World, the Mystic Knights of the Sea, and the crowd around the bar at Toots Shor's. He may be right. I wouldn't know; I'll leave the anthropology to Doctor Mead.

One thing I do know: there are many jazz cultists who can't leave jazz alone. Instead of sitting there listening to it and enjoying it, and maybe beating time with their hands or feet, they're always talking, talking, talking about it, hashing it over, chewing it up, and in general trying to make this music into something it isn't.

There are three or four different types of jazz cultists, all equally unbearable. First, there are those scholars who use the high-blown phraseology and are always talking about "fluidity of tone," "derivation," "tonal color," and other ridiculous phrases. Quite often these guys talk editors into paying them for using those words in public, and this is very good for those who like surrealism. Whenever I read Ulanov, Panassié and the rest of those archivists I always have to ask Phyllis to translate for me. They throw her too. About the only word I understand in their writing is "sound," and they sure make a lot of it.

The first cultist I ever knew was that well-known arranger and literary man, Milton "Mezz" Mezzrow. Back in Chicago during the late twenties, Mezz, who played a little clarinet (a very little) when he wasn't arranging, used to load up a bunch of jazz-crazy kids in a big green Willys-Knight and drive out in Grant Park. I remember that Frank Teschemacher, who played a lot more clarinet than almost anybody else did, used to go along, and Dave Tough, the drummer, and sometimes Frank Billings, known as Josh, who played an interesting suitcase with a pair of whisk brooms. Mezz always took along a nice supply of bottled goods, so it wasn't too hard for him to get an audience. He would sit there in the front seat, banging on the steering wheel with his hands to keep time, eulogizing on rhythm and syncopation and the purposes of them, talking in phrases that were over even *his* head, oralizing the poor music right into the ground. Dave Tough used to sit there nodding at everything Mezz said. Once I asked him why. "Well," Davey said, "he's got the ideas *and* the whisky."

Another kind of cult I've noticed around is the one made up of people who always insist on hearing "Wild Man Blues," "Grandpa's Spells" and other tunes that were written before Martin Van Buren. To these people, "Basin Street Blues" isn't acceptable because it's too new, and Sidney Bechet, the great old soprano saxophonist, who must be at least two hundred years old by now, is a youngster.

These cultists regard the Red Onion Jazz Babies as upstarts, and unless a record is a half-inch thick, has grooves only on one side, and a photograph of Thomas A. Edison on the label, they won't foul their hi-fi's with it. One night in my saloon I heard two of these bums discussing Louis Armstrong who is old enough to be grandfather of both of them. One suggested that Louis' trumpet sounded pretty good. "Yes," the other said judiciously, "Louis is coming along, coming along."

(*Of late this type has been getting numerous. See the Turk Murphy piece later on.*—E. C.)

A third kind of cultist is very embarrassing to me. These are the boys who insist on knowing every last fact about every record ever made—where the deed was done, who was guilty of it, the temperature of the studio, whether or not music was being read. These are the same boys who can tell you the exact personnel of every side ever waxed by Cook's Dreamland Orchestra, and they can recite all the aliases that Duke Ellington's band ever used on labels (Duke himself probably couldn't remember half of them). I have a fairly average memory, but I've never been able to help these guys much; I never seem to remember exactly who made what when, any more than an old plumber can remember the location of some pipes he fixed in your cellar eighteen years ago. These cultists often get into some pretty hot arguments over dates and personnels.

The fourth variety of cultist does absolutely nothing to ease my nerves. He is the worst of all. He's a pseudo-cultist, the man who comes up to me and behaves as though he's got every record I ever made and several I'm not sure I ever heard. To hear him tell it, this guy thinks the sun rises and sets on my head. One came into the saloon one night and, after filing several hundred thousand words about my saintliness, wound up by saying, "Now, Eddie, I want you to go up there and play me some real hot *trumpet!*" I restrained myself. "Please don't expect me to be at my peak," I said, "because I've been having a little trouble with my embouchure."

I don't want to rap the fans too much, because they're a necessary commodity. But I do object to people who regard this music as their very own as though they invented it. This music belongs to everybody; nobody's got a license on it that I've ever heard of. And I want to complain about people who keep insisting on referring to it as an Art Form, in capitals, as though they can't get used to the idea that it is one. Art Form, my foot. Canning vegetables is an art form, and so is driving an automobile and getting a sun tan. To a musician who plays jazz music for a living in a band like ours, the cultists are merely bewildering. No musician can explain jazz. A jazz musician is a jazz musician for the same reason that a man goes to the Luxor Baths because he likes the towels. He plays because it feels and sounds good to him or because he can't abide scored music. Jazz music is human music; when you're playing, nobody's going to write you a summons if you make a mistake or two. Once Peanuts Hucko, the clarinetist, was talking about a trombone player we know. He said, "He's the kind of a guy who goes for a wrong note and makes it." There was nothing malicious in that statement.

There are no hard-and-fast rules for jazz music, as a lot of the cultists would have you believe. The manager in our saloon, Pete Pesci, and his assistant, Bill Funaro, understand this simple truth very well, which is why we get along. They don't tell the musicians how to play "It's Tulip Time in Holland" (although they might request it occasionally, which is all right); and we don't tell them how to select beef. The musicians in our band have only two rules; shoes must be worn on the stand, and anybody who falls off must get back under his own power.

Back in the old days, God knows, some of us might have been glad for a cultist or two. At that time, there were few enough musicians *playing* the music, let alone people making a fetish of it. Whenever the opera lovers and longhairs heard it, they would shudder the way I do when a Lester Lanin Blatsch smites my ears. Those nose-in-the-air critics were very fond of saying that jazz would never last . . . that it was a fad and would die out like mahjong or spats. I don't have to say that the music fooled them. Jazz grew in popularity right from the beginning, and today it's more widely accepted than any of us ever thought possible. Almost every good-sized city in the country can boast two or three jazz bands that aren't bad. During the war, the Army transcriptions that my boys and I made were voted the most popular of all those sent overseas, in both the Atlantic and the Pacific theaters. I don't necessarily attribute that to our sterling performances; it just means that there is a large, eager, and devoted audience for this kind of music.

(And during the past year, *it's* exceeded everyone's expectations.—R. G.)

For the benefit of symphony lovers who may be reading this out of sheer desperation, this is probably as good a spot as any to break for a quick rundown on the development of jazz. In a way I hate to do this because it's infringing on the cultists, and I don't want to spoil their fun. But there are so many misapprehensions and fallacious conceptions floating around, it seems as though somebody ought to call the roll every once in a while. The impression still persists, although not as strongly as it once did, that jazz is low-brow music. I don't know who started this myth, but if I ever meet him I plan to ask him to make his next one strychnine on the rocks. Hearing jazz referred to as "low-brow" music is as distasteful to any musician as hearing people referred to as "little" people. (*Little* people, for God's sake! As Joe Mitchell once said, "They're as big as you are, whoever you are.") I once played a job with a band at the Otto Kahn estate at Cold Spring Harbor, and if that's playing for low-brows, then I'm planning to invite Meyer Davis to join my organization. I know of a professor up at Penn State who has a tremendous collection of jazz records; and I never heard anyone remark on his resemblance to Piltdown man. Low-brow music! As I said before, it's music for everybody.

Development. Well, it started out in the South. Most people blame New Orleans, mainly the Storyville section of the city. The music was played first by Negroes, but it was not, as so many people seem to think, music right out of the heart of Africa; anybody who has ever heard any records by African natives knows that while the beat in jazz may be derivative (just call me Culty), the two kinds of music are as far apart as the clarinets of Benny Goodman and Pee Wee Russell. In New Orleans, the Negroes had burial societies; you paid your money in every week, and when you finally turned your face to the wall you got a gangster's funeral. According to the stories I heard, the funeral processions were always followed by a band, generally one that was heavy on the brass. They played slow, mournful music all the way to the cemetery, and on the way back they started swinging it up, as though they were celebrating the fact that they hadn't been the one who stayed there. They called it "jass" in those days. I don't know why; ask some cultist. That was around 1870, maybe earlier.

This music came out of the Negroes' hearts. It was simple and direct and emotional; it told about how hard they had to work and how life was bleak, and it also told how on Saturday nights with a girl and a glass things weren't too unpleasant in the world. And because it was music that came right out of those human beings, uncluttered by phoniness and pretense, it began to catch on with other groups. As the late Thomas Sugrue once wrote:

"All kinds of music went into it—work songs, hymns, blues, marches, ballads, minstrel tunes, and folk songs brought by Italian, Irish, Spanish and French immigrants. It all came out jazz. The players originated basic melodies and performed them for their fellow musicians, who contributed their improvisations, different each time the tune was played. The melody was just an idea, a base on which to build variations."

That pretty well sums up why jazz is the only true American music—it's melting-pot music. A man doesn't have to belong to any particular nationality or have a certain shade of skin to be able to play jazz. And while we're on the subject, he doesn't have to belong to any specific church either. In our band at the saloon we've got two Negroes, a Jew, a Catholic and some Protestants, and I've never noticed any friction except over what key we ought to play in. And I never knew anyone who wanted to start a race riot because whites and Negroes were playing together. Jazz has done a great deal to break down the walls between the races—which was truly proven when Ernie Anderson, the publicist, and I took mixed groups into many concert halls, including some in Southern cities.

From New Orleans, the music went up the river on the old side-wheeler steamboats. It paused briefly at Memphis, took on some experience and local coloration, and went on north until it reached Chicago. (The riverboat days were long before my time; I mention this only because a lot of people persist in asking me how it was on those old packet boats.) From Chicago, the music spread out all over. Today you can even hear it in Southern California, over and above the moaning of the faith healers, the brain wavers and the undertakers.

(*To get an idea of how widespread it has become, see John Crosby's piece.—E.C.*)

In Chicago during the mid-twenties, the two great old men from New Orleans, King Oliver and Louis Armstrong, had bands that made you want to cry, they were so fine. A lot of us around town in those days, kids barely out of Buster Browns, listened to that music and got the itch to do it ourselves. Before long we'd got instruments and were trying to imitate them. At seventeen, I was already a veteran of Hollis Peavey's Jazz Bandits; we'd played one-nighters through Wisconsin, Minnesota and Iowa, making music for farmers for a whole summer. In Chicago I got myself a long-necked banjo and fell in with some other kids who were dying to see what they could do with this music: Gene Krupa, Benny Goodman, Dave Tough, Bix Beiderbecke, Bud Freeman, Wild Bill Davison, Frank Teschemacher, Joe Sullivan and many others. We used to take jobs when we could get them, which wasn't very often. Most of the time we had nothing to eat, but we had the music and that was enough.

The strict New Orleans style of music featured very few solos. When Louis and King Oliver got to Chicago they soloed all the time, and that, I suppose, was what led to "Chicago" jazz. (I say "I suppose" because that's a matter for the cultists to argue about.) The way the music went, the trumpet would take the melody and other instruments would play with it and around it. A band was most often composed of piano, drums, banjo, bass, trumpet, clarinet, trombone and sometimes a saxopone. The band would play one or two choruses together and then each man would have a solo; after everybody'd had a turn, there would be another all-out chorus, or sometimes sixteen or seventeen. Nothing was written down; nothing ever was played the same way twice. In our band at the saloon we still follow pretty much the same pattern. About the only difference is that the boys are older and more expert and, just possibly, a little louder. When I first started out I played banjo exclusively, and most bands featured banjos and a tuba, but those two instruments were gradually replaced by guitar and string bass. You seldom hear of a tuba in a band any more, and the banjo went out with silent movies.

(*Of course, that doesn't include either the Turk Murphy or Wilbur De Paris bands. —R. G.*)

All through here I've been speaking of our kind of music as jazz, and that isn't quite fair either to the word or the music.

Jazz as it's used today is too elastic a word. Jazz is sometimes played, for example, by a Hugo Winterhalter-type of band—scored jazz, that is. I suppose even Lombardo could be said to play jazz, in a sense. During the thirties, when Tommy and Jimmy Dorsey and Benny Goodman and Artie Shaw had those big bands of theirs, what they played was jazz—part of it was scored, and part of it, such as the solos of Bud Freeman and Jess Stacy and others, was improvised. They called it "swing." Then, just before and during and after the war, along came Stan Kenton and other big bands; they borrowed from Ellington and from composers like Bartok and Ravel and Debussy, and they played ambitious arrangements that they called "progressive." It was all out of the same grab bag. There are many, many kinds of jazz, but the main thing to bear in mind about it is that the best of it is improvised; it's the idea of the man who's playing it. We just call it music.

I can't leave this without mentioning bop.

I have never been found guilty of bop, and if I manage to retain a grip on my compass, I won't ever be. Bop, to me, is improvisation without sense. The first time I ever heard the word used was by Buck, of the old dance team of Buck and Bubbles; he would clap his hands and cry, "Bop!" when he took a time break. Later, when some of those bozos with the goatees and the red berets started playing that nervous noise, it sounded to me like nothing but time breaks . . . or maybe no breaks at all. My final statement on bop was made one night when Charles Ponzi, a waiter in our place, dropped a tray of dishes. I said, "Boys, none of that progressive stuff in here, please."

(For a less frivolous discussion of bop, see Marshall Stearns' piece. I wish I could get Eddie to see it.—R. G.)

The music that my boys and I like has been around now for so long that a few classics have established themselves. Nobody could ever explain how these classics came about; like any good, inspired, sense-making solo, they just happened. The standard way to organize a band in my set is to get out the telephone book and make a few calls to fellows you know to be sympathetic. Many, many record dates have been put together that way, and

THIS IS JAZZ   31

some of the best jazz of all time has resulted from such sessions. I am no expert, although I've been involved in a few record dates. And I'm hardly a collector, for the only records around our house are those hot Howdy Doody sides that Maggie and Liza, the kids, are wearing out the grooves on. But if I had to take a bunch of records off with me to a desert island, I suppose I'd pick: "Knockin' a Jug," by Louis Armstrong; "Minor Drag," by Fats Waller, "A Jam Session at Commodore" ("A Good Man is Hard to Find"), by a group of assorted fugitives, including Muggsy Spanier, Pee Wee Russell, Bobby Hackett, Joe Marsala, Miff Mole and others; "One Hour" by the Mound City Blue Blowers; "It's Right Here for You" by a fellow named Eddie Condon; "The Eel," by Bud Freeman's Summa Come Louders; any group of Bix Beiderbecke's sides, and—well, if I go on like this I'll improvise myself right out of space. It all depends on your own taste; those are a few sides I remember with favor. But I can't say I've ever been bored with any of my kind of music.

Whatever the forms jazz has taken, there's one thing sure: it's spread all over the world. In France it was "discovered" by a man named Panassié, who wrote "Le Jazz Hot." Panassié was a real culteriner, and he had very definite ideas which upset some of us. We couldn't understand why a Frenchman would write a critical book about music that wasn't native to his own country; after all, as I said, in a remark that's been repeated ad absurdum, we don't try to go over there and teach those Frenchmen how to jump on a grape. Panassié started the jazz craze in France, however, and it's now enjoying a big vogue everywhere in Europe. As this is being written, there are many Americans making killings in the European capitals. But the local bands over there, I hear, aren't first-rate. They're all inferior because they're imitative; most of the musicians have learned what they know from American records and American visitors. And because there are so few musicians, they get stale and fat from lack of competition. Something even seems to happen to Americans who go over there for extended visits. Ernie Anderson came back from Europe last year and told me about a band that Mezz Mezzrow and Zutty Singleton, the drummer, had in Paris. I asked him what kind of band it was. He said, "Well, it was a good enough little band—and then, *in walked Mezz*. I tell you the kind of band it was—they started out with "Wild Man Blues," and *then* went back."

Because much of the early jazz was produced in gin mills and speakeasies (and still is today, as far as that goes), many people have the mistaken impression that all jazz musicians are hopheads, weedsters, drunks and free-style hellers. It just isn't true. Many musicians I know have raised a bit of cain in their day; Wild Bill Davison didn't get his nickname because of his docility. But many of the best musicians are family men who live in suburban neighborhoods and keep hours as rigid as a railroad dispatcher's. They have outside interests and hobbies like anyone else; in fact, at a time when the boys in our band started building model trains and setting up a system in the basement of the saloon, we used to have a hard time getting them back on the stand. I've known a musician or two who smoked marijuana or peddled it, but high-school kids use up more of the stuff, and the customers drink more whiskey than the musicians (it's very hard for a man to play an intelligent chorus when he's plastered). As far as that old saw about dying off young is concerned, let me point out Louis Armstrong, the Dorseys, Duke Ellington, Sidney Bechet, Pee Wee Russell, George Wettling and Gene Krupa. They were all going strong thirty years ago, and I see no sign of their arteries hardening. As for me, I've made two guest shots at hospitals with pancreatitis. Each time the doctors said it was my farewell performance. I've never felt better.

This does not mean that the old-timers have a Japanese keylock on the music. Far from it; there are plenty of youngsters coming along, all of them as nuts about this music as some of us were back in Chicago during the twenties. To me, this proves that the people who are always talking about how jazz is dying out can only achieve, as Joe Frisco used to say, a severe state of hoarseness. The very fact that the lights have been burning in our club for ten years ought to prove that jazz is very far from dead; after all, Consolidated Edison has never been noted for a sloppy credit policy. Jazz will never die out as long as some guys get a bang out of the beat and others like to listen to it.

Even the cultists won't kill it.

ERNEST BORNEMAN

The Jazz Cult

ERNEST BORNEMAN IS an anthropologist, musicologist, novelist and film producer. *If you've got to have cultists let's have painless ones, like this one. Essentially, this is Borneman's story of his own interest and ultimate involvement in jazz, particularly interesting because it gives an excellent picture of the growth of the movement in Europe and the British Isles. But it is much more than that. It is also a history of The Great Revival of Bunk and The Battle of the Subsidized Critics.*

Once upon a time, long long ago, when I was still innocent in mind and a square was an equilateral rectangle to me and not a sad cat, my teacher at the Phonogram Archives of the University of Berlin held up a little ten-inch shellac disc and said, "Borneman, what do you think this is?"

"A phonograph record," I replied, smart as a whip.

"Ah," said the old man, who had been teaching comparative musicology for twenty years and was not easily fazed by youthful enthusiasm, "Ah, yes indeed. But what *kind* of a phonograph record?"

Temptingly, there presented itself to me the prospect of capping the question with a neat turn of phrase about a *round* record or a *black* record or a *shellac* one, but the old man was treacherous and I had an uneasy feeling that the whole thing might blow up right in my face like a trick cigar. After all, how could I be sure it wasn't a *rubber* disc or an *acetate*? The thing to do was to play safe.

"Let's hear what it sounds like," I said cautiously.

"Indeed," said the old man. "Let us by all means." He wound up the clockwork motor and turned the horn in my direction. Those were the days of hand-cranked phonographs and large metal horns, and there always was a good deal of bustle and commotion before the music could start going round and round.

Encouraged by the complex preparations, and prematurely emboldened by easy applause, I turned foolhardy and said, "It may be difficult to decide what sort of record it is until we have actually heard the music."

"Music?" the old man asked. For a moment he seemed taken aback, but he recovered quickly. "Indeed, indeed. An excellent suggestion: cautious, empirical, and fully endowed with the experimental spirit; a perfect demonstration of the scientific manner." He placed the record on the turntable, released the brake, and gently lowered the needle into the first groove.

The sound hit me like a dynamite blast. I clapped my hands over my ears and thought: Uh-huh, I should have known. It was a trick cigar.

"Excellent," said the old man. "Swift reaction to stimulus. Sensory perception: first rate. Highly developed motor behavior and good physical co-ordination. Thank you." He lifted the needle and stopped the record.

I took my hands from my ears and asked, "What in the world was that?"

"Ah!" The old man gave a long sigh of appreciation. "Music, of course. Was that not what you said we would find if we played the record?"

"You fooled me," I said reproachfully. "That was unfair."

"Not so." He raised his index finger like a monolith. "Not I. The *musicians* fooled you."

"Musicians?"

THE JAZZ CULT   35

"Indeed, sir. A *quod libet* of staggering ingenuity. A specimen of collective improvization that makes your *super librum cantare* sound like amateur stuff. Talk to me of Frescobaldi and Paganini and the rest of your great extemporizers! Why, here you have the transition of primitive heterophony into pure impromptu counterpoint. Here is an urban folk music that makes your flamenco guitarists and *cante hondo* singers sound like old-time country musicians! It's the real link between improvisation and composition, folk music and art music, the polyphonic age and the modern tradition. It's jazz music!"

He pronounced it *yutz mooseek*. It was the first piece of New Orleans jazz I ever heard and it was the first, I think, ever to be heard within the solemn premises of a higher institute of learning. The old man was Dr. Erich von Hornbostel, whose work in comparative musicology laid the foundation for much of the research now being done on Afro-American music in American universities, and the record was "Ory's Creole Trombone" by Spike's Seven Pods of Pepper, recorded in Los Angeles in 1921 by a group of New Orleans Negroes on the defunct Nordskog label. Ten years later a friend of mine picked up a copy of the same record with the Sunshine trade mark pasted over the old Nordskog label and the name of the band changed from Spike's Seven Pods of Pepper to Ory's Sunshine Orchestra. He paid a nickle for it in a Halsted Market junk shop and sold it three months later to a San Francisco collector for $125.

Three days after the ear-splitting operation at the Phonogram Archives, on a fine summer night in 1930, our Herr Professor—wearing the kind of collar which, on Dr. Schacht's neck, has attracted a considerable amount of ill-advised attention since then—and a group of six students, one of them in decorative short pants of yellow chamois leather, set out on an extracurricular mission to a great big barn of a night club called the Haus Vaterland.

This was quite a place. It was six stories high and each story was decorated in a different manner to represent a different part of the world. I remember vaguely that one whole floor represented a vineyard on the Rhine with little paddle-wheelers passing on a model river and that artificial thunderstorms shared the attraction with choirs of buxom Rhinemaidens. We, however, had come to admire neither the Rhinemaidens nor the thunderstorms but a soprano saxophonist named Sidney Bechet, who had reached Europe in 1925 with Will Marion Cook's Black Revue and after touring Russia and playing with Noble Sissle's Orchestra in Paris, had been stranded in Berlin.

After pointing out the Africanisms in Bechet's phrasing, Hornbostel told us that his father had heard Frank Johnson's Negro brass band playing a command performance for Queen Victoria in 1841 and the Fisk Jubilee Singers in Hamburg in 1878, and that he himself had heard Jim Europe's 369th Infantry Band representing the U.S.A. in 1918 during the victory celebrations at the Tuileries. Since then, he told us, he had gone to hear Eddie South in Budapest in 1920; Elgar's Creole Band with James P. Johnson, Buster Bailey, Darnell Howard, and Wellman Braud at the London Empire in 1922; Louis Douglas and Josephine Baker at the Champs-Elysees in 1924; the New York Singing Syncopators in Holland in 1925; Sam Wooding at the Ufa Palast in Berlin during the same year; Al Wynn at Levy Wines in Berlin in 1928 and Toby Hardwick in Paris in 1929. This, he said, was true devotion to the tough academic tradition of relentless intellectual pursuit. He reminded us, especially, of the great physical strain and the sacrifice of quiet study that was involved in these long and tiresome journeys. We sympathized and were sent by Sidney Bechet and the blues.

This, I suppose was my initiation into the secret cult of the faithful. My graduation, however, did not occur until three years later when I arrived, with my second pair of long pants securely held up by genuine silk-embroidered Tyrolean leather suspenders, among the discreetly amazed undergraduates of Cambridge. A helpful roommate, to save me from damnation, quickly introduced me to the three holy talismans of English undergraduate society—gray flannel bags, a checked brown tweed jacket, and a portable H.M.V. gramophone with a set of Parlophone New Rhythm Style records. Then we went out punting on the river.

As you made your laborious progress pushing your unstable flat craft past other unstable flat crafts on the crowded river, you passed, as in a stroll through a rehearsal studio, from one radius of music into another. Sometime during the nineteen-twenties the Parlophone Company in England had begun to reissue thousands of the rarest American jazz records under such fine Barnum and Bailey labels as the *First and Second New Rhythm Style Series*, the *Super Rhythm Style Series*, the *Super Swing Series* and the *Miscellany Rhythm Style Series*, and in the summer of 1933, when I first passed through that strange tunnel of sound which stretched along the river between the solemn walls of perpendicular stone, little else was to be heard than those tough, brassy Parlophone reissues of the twenties and thirties.

Among those I learned to like best were two records credited to "Louis Armstrong and his Washboard Beaters" although neither of them sounded much like Armstrong to me. One was a rough-and-tumble thing called "Cushion Foot Stomp" with a fine abandoned scat vocal; the other, a jazzed-up paraphrase of Stephen Adams's "Holy City," was called "Black and Tan Fantasy." One day during the long vacs I played them for a stern-faced young medical student whom I shall call Norman. He lived with his mother in a small musty house near Golders Green; his father had been a doctor, and in a huge attic which had been his father's study, among test tubes, small embryos in alcohol, and old medical drawings showing the insides of various animals in layers upon layers of fold-back cardboard flaps, Norman's collection of records was piled up from floor to ceiling in solid towers with the weight and thickness of a primeval forest. One wall, to the right as you entered this shellac jungle, was solidly upholstered with old record catalogues and back numbers of such musical trade journals as *Down Beat*, *Metronome*, and *Melody Maker*. On a desk, towards the left rear of the room, were the letters from record collectors the world over. All these letters ran approximately like this:

Dear Norm:
    Will trade Louis' Gennet 5627 "Of All the Wrongs" with Red Onion Jazz Babes in excellent condition (slight chip one side not touching first groove) for mint copy Clarence Williams' Blue 5 "Texas Moaner Blues." Also

have Sippie Wallace vocal "A Jealous Woman Like Me" with Armstrong cornet in fair condition. What offer? Will take any Bessie Smith with James P. Johnson on piano in good or excellent condition.

Yrs. Dr. L. Y. Yen
University of Canton, China

Norman, I think, was the first real jazz collector I had ever met. In more than one way he struck me as a completely new mutation of man. He was taciturn to the point of inarticulateness. If he spoke at all, he used words of one syllable and dropped them, through tightly closed teeth, from what seemed like a small cavity between his upper left molars. His mind had the scope and infallibility of one of those electronic brains that comes up with an answer to any kind of question you can think of. After I had played my two Armstrong Washboard Beaters for him, I could almost see this extraordinary machine clicking into action:

" 'Cushion Foot Stomp' . . . That's Parlophone R3383 . . . that's an Okeh original . . . that's not Armstrong at all . . . guess it must be Clarence Williams' Washboard Band . . . wrong label . . . will be a collectors' item soon . . . keep it.

"Now 'Black and Tan Fantasy' . . . that's Parlophone R3492 . . . master number 81778C . . . that's Okeh 40955 in the original . . . an Ellington tune . . . Ellington and Bubber Miley . . . that's not Miley on trumpet though . . . Miley was sick the day they recorded . . . probably Jabbo Smith . . . good man too . . . wrong label again . . . keep that too."

"How in the world do you know about these things?" I asked. "How do you learn? Where do you get the facts? Where do you get the records?"

"Meet you six o'clock Caledonian Market tomorrow."

"Why? What's the idea?"

"Show you."

"That's a bad time to show me anything. I've got a date with a girl from L.S.E. at 6:30."

"Not six at night. Six in the morning."

"What?" I was outraged. I hadn't been up at six o'clock since the last boat race. But at six sharp the next morning, on a miserable gray day, I found myself getting off a tram at Caledonian Road, and there was Norman with the rubber cushion and the little black book under his arm.

Now many stories could be told about the rubber cushion, but in fairness to surviving victims we shall here merely concentrate on the little black book and say that it is the first piece of field equipment required by the trained record hunter. No expedition to the junk markets or the secondhand shops should ever be undertaken without it. Other equipment such as soft rubber knee-caps for low-level work on cellar shelves, or collapsible stepladders for high-level work on cupboards and attics can safely be left to a later stage of development. The little black book, however, is basic and indispensable, and this lesson was brought home to me with a vengeance almost at once.

The old Caledonian Market at that time was a huge empty expanse of cobblestones and metal tubing in the dreariest part of North London. On certain fixed days of the week, however, this sad no man's land took on the miraculous color and gaiety of an oriental caravanserai. The junk traders moved in, and there was nothing in this whole wide world that did not suddenly become available for sale or trade within a mile of the market center. More amazing still than the precious things spread out on the cobblestones were the utterly useless ones. You could sink into endless reveries at the secret line of reasoning that must have moved the old woman in the Spanish shawl to offer the broken handle of a Queen Anne water jug for sale; or you might spend hours trying to imagine what lay behind the stern-faced man with the steel-rimmed glasses who had nothing for sale except bowls upon bowls of rusty paper clips.

Norman, however, with the no-nonsense manner of the professional collector, had no time to spend on idle speculation and made straight for the first stand that offered an old washbasin piled high with dirty phonograph records for sale. In my childish ignorance of the profound fact that each collector has his own secret method of washing, grooming, and straightening old records, I would have passed the miserable pile of worn-out discs without a thought of possible salvation. But Norman stopped me curtly, spread out the rubber cushion on the cobble-stones, kneeled down as if in prayer, and began to sift the old discs with the agility of a trained cardsharp shuffling a marked deck of cards.

I thought I had gained sight of an old Romeo record by the Broadway Broadcasters, and I fished it out just as Norman was about to discard it. In Cambridge I had picked up a record by the same band which had Benny Goodman and Jack Teagarden on clarinet and trombone, but when I told Norman that I'd like to have another one by the same group he merely looked at me sternly and shook his head.

"But I like Goodman and Teagarden," I said petulantly.

Out came the little black book. Up to "B" went the index finger, and there it was—Broadway Broadcasters. In Norman's neat collector's calligraphy, the entry read: "This is a highly misleading studio group. The name was used by the Lincoln, Romeo, and Perfect labels for various odd combinations. The few records that actually have Goodman, Teagarden, and MacPartland should be carefully remembered. Their master and release numbers are as follows." There followed a list of cryptic figures.

Norman pointed at the disc I had selected and said: "You see the number in the book?"

Shamefacedly, I shook my head.

He closed the book smartly and with finality. I returned the record to the discards and we marched on.

Many years later I learned that Norman's father had left him a total legacy of ten shillings. This minor fortune Norman had invested in records bought at a penny each in Caledonian Market, and out of the proceeds of an ensuing trade which literally spanned the whole globe, he had financed his entire medical studies. He is a doctor now with a good practice, and I understand he no longer trades in records.

In 1936 I went back to London to work with Criterion Films, Douglas Fairbanks, Jr.'s production unit for United Artists, and since apartments were almost impossible to find, I moved in with two prominent collectors whom I shall call Chick and Chuck. A weird and wonderful life thus opened up before me. We got up in the morning to the haunting sounds not of the alarm but of

THE JAZZ CULT

Billy Banks's "Bugle Call Rag" which had Red Allen on trumpet, Pee Wee Russel on clarinet, and Zutty Singleton on drums; an ingenious mechanism rigged up by Chuck linked the phonograph to the clock. For our toilet, we had a blues called "Shave 'em Dry." We dressed in time to Goodman's "Shirt Tail Stomp" and had breakfast with the Boswell Sisters' "When I Take My Sugar to Tea." All through the day, the telephone would ring and strange characters whose names and voices were utterly unfamiliar to us would try to sell, buy, or trade records. Others would phone in news of bands in London, Paris, or Chicago. Pretty little girls would drop in at all hours of the day or night, turn on the phonograph, and walk out again with a vague look of sorrow on their pretty faces. The BBC or the H.M.V. Company would call up from Regent Street or Hayes, Middlesex, to ask us for the recording date on an old Victor record or the address of a long defunct recording company.

Chick, who had given up listening to records long ago so that he could more wholeheartedly devote himself to the serious business of cataloguing all the records he could have heard if the cataloguing had left him any time for such idle fripperies, had entered into negotiations with two obsessed Frenchmen named Hugues Panassié and Charles Delaunay, who were editing a magazine named *Le Jazz Hot* in Paris; while Chuck was trying to work out a foolproof index to his records which would permit him to lay his hands on any sample of any musician's work within ten seconds. As time went on, the index grew considerably more bulky than the records themselves, and although Chuck finally reached his goal of finding any given disc within ten seconds, he must have spent at least ten years of his life trying to perfect the system.

(*This is a common habit of many cultist-collectors. A friend of mine has five thousand wonderful records, but he never plays them unless I visit him and insist on it.*—R. G.)

Conversations between Chick and Chuck had a certain dreamlike quality which is hard to reproduce in the cold light of history. One of Chick's particular obsessions was the organization of an International Federation of Rhythm Clubs which would hold sufficient power to persuade all radio stations and phonograph record manufacturers to turn away from their misguided ways and concentrate henceforth on the straight and narrow path of righteous jazz music. He based his pattern of argument upon an extraordinary phenomenon called the British Rhythm Club Federation, which was the brain child of a genial, chubby little Cockney named Bill Elliott. Every week, on a certain selected night which was to be kept free from all other engagements, Chick, Chuck, and I set out on a lengthy safari to the basement of the Mecca Café in Chancery Lane, where Bill Elliott held court among the devotees of the Number One Rhythm Club.

To understand the function of this sort of organization in the life of the European jazz fan, his utter dependence upon phonograph records will have to be remembered. Cut off from the living music by time as well as space, he submits to a peculiar shift of values. The record becomes more important than the music; minor musicians who have left recorded examples of their work behind them become more important than those major musicians who for one reason or another have never got around to a recording studio; and the man who has met the musicians and knows his way through the maze of records becomes more important than the musician himself. Thus the peculiar and altogether top-heavy standing of the so-called jazz "critic."

At the weekly meetings of the Number One Rhythm Club, one such "critic" after another would make his stand before the public by putting his favorite records on a big phonograph and expecting the entranced members to nod their heads in unison to the succession of adverbs and adjectives that formed the basis of the running commentary. Every once in a while a "critic" who had once had his shoes shined by Bix Beiderbecke's favorite bootblack would give a guest recital, and those evenings were the highspots of the season.

Sometime in 1935, on a pleasant April Sunday, Bill Elliott of the Number One Rhythm Club, the late P. M. Brooks of the *Melody Maker*, Edgar Jackson of the *Gramophone*, Eric Ballard of *Hot News*, Leonard Hibbs of *Swing Music* and an enthusiastic multitude representing Rhythm Clubs from as far north as Glasgow and as far south as Torquay crowded into the neo-lavatorial splendor of the Royal Hotel in Bloomsbury and voted the British Rhythm Club Federation into existence. Bill Elliott wanted to call the thing British Federation of Rhythm Clubs, but Percy Brooks, with the nostalgic wisdom of the old newspaperman, warned sternly against the initials B. F. Thus strengthened in our knowledge, we proceeded with the formation of "area committees" covering the whole of the United Kingdom like a well-organized Gestapo network.

We were supposed to represent four thousand determined members, but somehow no more than one member could ever be found who was wholly in agreement with himself, and thus the jazz movement continued living up to its highest tradition. Chick continued to catalogue the records he would never hear, Chuck clocked the efficiency of his index with a stop watch, and the Rhythm Club members nodded sagely in unison.

In 1939 the war put an end to these pleasant pastimes and I went to work for the Films Division of the Ministry of Information. In the old days, at the Psychological Laboratory and later at the Phonogram Archives of Berlin University, we had spent a good deal of time and effort upon the job of finding a method to record, in visual patterns, such musical intangibles as width and frequency of vibrato, inflections of timbre, and microtonal variations of pitch. Hornbostel's pet idea at that time was that the conflict and resolution of two patterns of culture was most clearly revealed in the folk music of mixed populations and that American Negro music was one of the most fruitful fields for the study of this process of acculturation.

When the war broke out, we used a similar line of reasoning and a similar apparatus to trace the social and regional background of enemy radio speakers. Most of the work was done with photo-electric cells and 35mm motion picture film, and very similar machinery was later used in the United States by the Bureau of Standards to study the amounts of ozone in the various strata of the upper air, and by Dr. Waterman at Northwestern University to chart the regularity of pitch variations in the five-tone Ibo language of West Africa.

Two years later, in the second year of the war, I found myself assigned to do some motion picture work of a different sort for the Canadian Government, and for the first time in eight years a new opportunity offered itself to continue some of Hornbostel's work on American Negro music. We went out into the field with two anthropologists, Marius Barbeau and Laura Boulton, to record examples of Indian and Eskimo music, and in the process of recording them on film, some of Hornbostel's earlier suggestions were amazingly well confirmed.

This offered the temptation to continue the work with samples of African and American Negro music. As a trial venture, I wrote to a number of American collectors whose names I found in the small jazz magazines and asked them whether they had any Negro records other than jazz—worksongs, spirituals, streetcries, field hollers, nursery rhymes, and similar things. One of these letters came to the attention of the editor of one of these little magazines, and after some cautious enquiries about my general views on music, he asked me whether I might be able to do an article for him on the history of Negro folk music and its possible relationship to early jazz.

The idea seemed acceptable, especially in view of the fact that it proved just about the only method of shaking the editor loose from some of his precious records, and as my need for additional recordings proved continuous, the first article grew into a regular series under the title "The Anthropologist Looks at Jazz."

I had agreed to conduct a Question-and-Answer column in which readers could air all queries and grievances to which the article might give rise, but I had not expected to find myself in the midst of an intramural battle which made the Wars of the Roses look like a custard throwing contest on a Hollywood lot.

In April 1944, within two weeks after the appearance of my first innocent contribution to the *Record Changer*, I received eighty-six letters from angry readers telling me that I was strictly from nowhere with my quaint ideas of what made jazz tick. All I had been asked to do by the editor, and all I had tried to do in good faith, was to write a short piece on the African roots of American Negro music in general and of jazz in particular. What my readers read into it was something like an attempt to set off a small atomic bomb at 52nd and Broadway.

In a humble way I had said that I liked the early kind of jazz much better than some of the later kinds, because it seemed to have preserved a good deal of the dignity of rural folk music, but that the attempt to revive it now seemed to me as funny as the organized revival of folk dancing among the rural citizens of Greenwich Village. This innocuous piece of logic was my downfall; it landed me flat on my rear in the most exposed position between the contending forces of jazz—the Fundamentalists and the Modernists.

Jazz, according to the Fundamentalists, began in the eighteen-eighties with the playing of blues and ragtime by the Negro brass bands of New Orleans. The first of the jazz cornetists was a barber named Bolden, born in 1863, whose band, according to Bunk Johnson, his second cornet player, was the best jazz band there ever was "because it did not read at all." The music, say the Fundamentalists, began to decline when the musicians learned to read and gave up collective improvisation on blues and ragtime themes for written arrangements of Tin Pan Alley tunes. The fact that solo improvisation continues in modern swing music is of small importance to the Fundamentalists because, in their interpretation, the accent of importance rests upon the collective nature of improvisation; the solo, they say, is a form of vanity in which all the indulgence of jazz survives without any of the discipline which is its organic counterpart. This discipline, in the best of jazz, is derived from the individual performer's need to build his melodic line in such a manner that each note he plays will be in harmony with each note that the next man will simultaneously improvise.

Since the elementary laws of harmony require a minimum of three notes to form a chord, the essential jazz orchestra should have three wind instruments—no less and no more; and since jazz is essentially rhythmic music, a rhythm section made up of drums, bass, and guitar or banjo should be added. The piano is optional, and the sole function of the rhythm section should be to mark the beat and the basic chords. The modern tendency of the piano, the bass, the guitar, and the tuned drums to act as solo instruments and play whole melodies on their own is abhorred by the Fundamentalists as an essentially unorganic use of jazz instrumentation. The organic use of the basic instruments calls for the cornet or trumpet to play the melodic lead, the clarinet to play a syncopated obbligato, and the trombone to fill in the harmony with propulsive glissandi. This, the Fundamentalists say, with profound faith in the vanished perfection of man before the Fall, was exactly the shape of the band and the style of performance in the good old days before commercialization killed the cat.

It is a neat, persuasive, and musicianly argument with all the loose ends prettily tucked in. Alas, the counter-argument of the Modernists is equally neat, persuasive, and musicianly; it grants the historic part of the argument and says *so what*: New Orleans jazz may or may not have been as good as you say, but it is a dead music now; the founding fathers of the music have grown old and can't play any more; the youngsters are trying to do something new. Encourage them instead of telling them to play like their granddaddies; let them learn to read and write music; teach them all about harmony and counterpoint and give them proper instructors so that their instrumental technique may become as accurate and reliable as that of academically trained musicians.

(*At the time Borneman wrote this, Turk Murphy and the West Coast revivalists had not yet begun to blare.—E. C.*)

Ah, says the Fundamentalist in reply, that sounds pretty as an argument but it sounds awful as music. Just listen to those youngsters who have learned all about harmony, notation, and instrumental technique. All they do with their fine academic equipment is imitate the worst mannerisms of the European romantics—chromatic runs, whole tone scales, triplets, successions of eighth notes, and the facile exoticism of impressionist timbres and tone colors. At best they are *almost* as good as the Europeans whose work they ape. The New Orleans jazzmen, by distinction, were good precisely because they neither knew nor cared for the European tradition. Since they didn't know the rules, they triumphantly accomplished the impossible, laying the foundations of what might well have become the only native school that American music has ever been likely to produce. Instead of this, your modern bop musicians have sold their birthright for a stale mess of European pottage.

That is where the battle stands, and it is a stand as hopelessly stalemated as any controversy between adversaries who know more about their opponent's motives than about their own. Each camp has gone a long way toward breaking down the logic of the other camp into its component elements, and often enough the devil of calumny has raised his ugly head among the philosophers. Advocates of the New Orleans school have charged for some time that the most literate advocates of the modern school, while posing as objective critics, have in fact been paid all along by certain musicians of the modern school as their personal agents, and that the whole argument of the novelty-for-novelty's-sake school therefore has no more critical significance than a publicity blurb. They have charged, in detail, that the music critic and jazz yearbook editor of a certain pin-up magazine has been and still is on the payroll not only of a famous New York night club owner and jazz promoter but also of one of the large music publishing houses; that a new song, specially commissioned and plugged by his magazine, has been composed by one of the "critic's" favorite pianists, published by the brother of the pianist's employer, and recorded by his client; and finally that one of the oldest and most respectable magazines in the dance music field has recently become a thinly veiled puff-sheet in the hands of one or two slick operators whose strong line in defense of the "modern" school has at times been motivated less by aesthetic than by financial considerations.

All this may be a somewhat unkind view of what is in reality a happy coincidence of certain critical and economic factors. There is really no reason why one of the editors, who also acts as tunesmith, verse doctor, and recording supervisor for a number of phonograph companies, should not be genuinely enough enamored with his own work to give specially favorable marks to it whenever he acts as co-editor of the magazine's monthly record review section.

And it is, of course, quite possible that an artist who is reviewed in one issue of the magazine as "an agonized and agonizing girl singer" might have improved so much while singing one of the editor's tunes that he may justly review her three months later as "a hefty sounding, earthy blues singer;" but this sort of thing is always likely to give rise to false impressions among the cynics.

At one time, one of the editors said: "You can listen to each of the five trumpet players in Lionel Hampton's band, and every one of them will take a chorus which, had it been discovered on some obscure old record, would be hailed as a genius by the Jelly Roll Network." This caused a great deal of bewilderment among the Fundamentalists, not only because of the odd grammatical structure of the sentence but also because of the fact that the editor had just become Lionel Hampton's press agent and the happy coincidence of economic and aesthetic considerations placed a gentle strain on the credulity of the faithful.

These hard thoughts, however, should not be taken too seriously. The more adult minds in the Fundamentalist camp have long discovered that the real link between the economics and the aesthetics of the dance band business is far stronger than the odd sample of the itchy palm or the straight payoff might lead you to believe. What really matters is the old jazzbander's profound shame for the years of poverty, illiteracy, bad hooch, and bad company from which he has happily emerged at long last. Certain rackets—boot-legging, illegal narcotics, gambling, and prostitution—have always been associated with the early history of jazz. Add to this, in the case of the Negro musician, the whole aura of shame, misery and subjugation that surrounds the history of jazz in the South, and you get a profound complex of early humiliation that can be most skillfully exploited by any white man who offers a neat scheme of moral rehabilitation based upon a disparagement of the old jazz and a glorification of the new school which, at the small expense of a good press agent's salary, will guarantee admission to the ranks of musical respectability.

The question of purpose and content has been completely eliminated from the critical standards of the modern school. The only criteria of value are novelty, accuracy of technique and complexity of harmonic structure. To this has been added, with a shamelessness unprecedented in musical history, the criterion of financial success. "Take a good look at Louis Prima," says *Metronome*, "at Lionel Hampton. At Benny Goodman. And, of course, at Duke Ellington. Who has more money?" Then compare these local-boys-who-made-good with those failures, those old timers who are frustrated by the fact that Art Tatum "is gaining yearly in prestige, earnings, and success; and is playing concert dates, while their own favorite pianist is still working in a Greenwich Village cellar."

"At last we know," said the Fundamentalists when this dramatic new criterion of value was revealed. "Walt Whitman was a bum in the poetry racket; his *Leaves of Grass*, which he spent his whole life writing, didn't net him what a radio jingle writer pulls down for one job. Now take the author of Super Suds ditties—there's a poet! He *sells*!" Or take the defenders of the modern school themselves, adds the Fundamentalist, getting hot under the collar. Look at what musical giants they proved themselves when they hit upon the guaranteed-success idea of the national jazz music poll. "Look at Mr. F.," says Art Hodes, editor of the *Jazz Record*, whose feud with Mr. F. is one of the noble myths of the modern era. "Mr. F., an influential writer on 'le Hot' (meaning the mags that employ him reach many souls) also considers himself quite a pianist. He becomes a member of the musicians' union, which gives him the right to mix and mingle with all and sundry. This turns out to be a good investment. Mr. F. looks up Mr. S., who is in the recording business, and lets him in on a secret. 'How would you like to record the winners of the nation-wide poll that the Looking-Forward-to-the-Future Mag is conducting?' Mr. S., being in the business for other reasons than health, answers 'who wouldn't.' Mr. F. now approaches each musician who is soon to be declared a winner on his respective instrument, and offers him a record date. They accept. Why not? They're immediately glorified, their incomes increase, and they're sure to get good reviews."

Shifting his weight from the economic to the aesthetic scale, Mr. Feather replied in *Esquire* with one of his famous blindfold tests. What's all this nonsense about Art, he said sternly. "Jazz, seen from the inside looking out, is a matter of notes, chords, and facts . . . expert analysis in place of emotional ecstasies." And what is "overwhelming" about Edmund Hall playing "a B Natural against an F Seventh chord?"

"Ah," said the *Jazz Record* sadly, "you might equally ask, Mr. Feather, what is so particularly caloric about 'Full fathom five thy father lies' since it is made up of but six common words, four of them in simple alliteration . . . You have cast your lot with those who insist that a sunset is nothing more than the diffusion of light by suspended dust particles—and I'm sure you want to know what's so 'overwhelming' about that."

"Really, Mr. Feather," said the *Record Changer*, "you're much too bright to plead this sort of thing with your tongue all the way out of your cheek. Could it be that your whole argument in praise of the 'modern' manner is motivated less by your honest musical conviction than by the fact that you were still in your short pants when the real thing was going strong? If I told you that you and I could build a pretty little million-dollar business out of selling ye olde jazze musick to the suckers, would you come over and join me in my streamlined new antique shop?"

The Modernists, always fast on the uptake, were quick to see the double-edged nature of this most unkind cut. Turning around at the aggressor they asked severely: "And where was you, daddy, when Buddy Bolden stomped 'em down? Could it be, Jack, that your strange passion for the olden times is just a veiled attempt to recreate the things you missed when you were in your cradle?"

Couldn't it be, the Modernist asks, pressing on, that your whole argument is motivated not by true musical conviction but by an endeavor to derive vicarious satisfaction from an association with the tough, nostalgic, fabulous characters of the red light district days? You, whose own experience of life's purple patches has always been limited by moral education and natural timidity, couldn't it be that what you're really after isn't music at all but the spurious sense of action you get by identifying yourself with men whose music has become a symbol of the sinful life to you?

And they quote the case histories that tend to substantiate their theory: John Hammond, Jr., one of the earliest and most influential jazz "critics," came from an extremely wealthy family and after years of slumming among Harlem musicians found himself in the almost insoluble dilemma between an increasingly strong identification with the left wing of the labor movement and a tempting offer from a major recording company to act as their professional talent scout and recording supervisor. The company knew that more than a small share in the modern vogue of swing music was due to Hammond, who sponsored the first of the modern swing bands, Benny Goodman's, in 1934, and whose sister later became Goodman's wife. They knew that Hammond had brought Count Basie's Orchestra from Kansas City to New York and had thus started the first of the modern Negro jump bands on its way. They remembered, with particularly mixed emotions, the most instructive story of the lot—the story of John Hammond and the boogie.

Hammond, so the story goes, had found an old beat-up Paramount record named "Honky Tonk Train Blues" in a junk shop and had vainly advertised for two years in all Negro newspapers for any information leading to the discovery of its composer and performer, Meade Lux Lewis. One night in 1936, on a talent scouting tour in Chicago, he heard a pianist named Albert Ammons, whose style reminded him vaguely of Lewis. He asked Albert whether he could play a tune named "Honky Tonk Train Blues," and whether he'd ever heard of a pianist named Lewis. "Why, man," said Albert, "Lux's my very best friend."

Lewis, it appeared, had left the music business years ago to work with Ammons as taxi driver for a company that had installed an old upright piano in its office to keep its drivers away from the ginmill across the street. Hammond found him working in a south side garage and whisked him off to New York to play a concert at the Imperial Theater. When Café Society opened in 1938, Hammond got him to play the opening together with Ammons and a third pianist from Kansas City, Pete Johnson, whose praises Basie and Ellington had sung for many years. This was the famous boogie woogie trio which started the whole modern rumpus.

Small wonder that this sort of *deus ex machina* existence, which may change the musical taste of a whole nation, has a way of giving the critic a feeling both of omnipotence and of an almost overwhelming identification with the musician upon whom the

Pygmalion act has been performed. Hammond's recent breach with Goodman has therefore been interpreted as something more than a symbolic attempt to break away from the statue to which he thinks he has given life and which, with apparent ingratitude, has deserted the counsel of its mentor.

Three of the founding fathers of the Fundamentalist cult have recently gone through the first stage of this experience: William Russell, the dean of New Orleans jazz collectors, a skilled performer on many rare oriental instruments and a composer of percussion music within his own right; Eugene Williams, the editor of the first American jazz magazine, *Jazz Information*, and until recently a recording supervisor for the Decca Company; and Rudi Blesh, a San Francisco architect, who after a series of jazz lectures at the San Francisco Museum of Art was persuaded to give up his practice so as to devote all of his time to jazz. These three men, and a few others whose names have appeared among the contributors to the *Record Changer* and the *Jazz Record*, have been closely associated with the recent "rediscovery" of such old-timers as Bunk Johnson, Kid Ory, Mutt Carey, Bertha Chippie Hill, Montana Taylor, and Mr. Freddie Shayne. Of these case histories, the Bunk Johnson story is by far the most instructive.

Such graduates of the New Orleans school as Louis Armstrong, Sidney Bechet, Clarence Williams and Richard M. Jones had mentioned for many years that one survivor of the original Buddy Bolden band, the primal horde of jazz, might still be around somewhere in the deep Southwest. No one remembered his name for sure. All they had to go by was a nickname, "Bunk." Some thought he was in Electra, Texas; others were sure he had moved to the West Coast. Louis Armstrong suggested New Iberia, Louisiana, and the boys decided to play a long chance and send a letter to the postmaster of New Iberia, requesting that he "deliver the enclosed letter to a Negro cornetist known to all musicians in New Orleans, whence he came, as 'Bunk.'" A month later, the first of the fabulous Bunk Johnson letters hit New York. It was one of the most moving things that had ever happened in the rich cavalcade of the music. There was in it the dignity of an Old-Testamentarian lament and the fierce authenticity of the Scottsboro story. It was the real thing.

> Dear Friend, your letter was received and was more than glad. . . . Now a picture of mine is what you want and that is something I haven't got. . . . I am here only making out now. For we have work only when Rice Harvest is in, and that over, things goes Real ded until Cane Harvest. I drive a truck and trailer and that only Pays me a $1.75 a day and that do not last Very Long. So you all know for sure just about how mutch money that I makes now. I made up my mind to work Hard until I die as I have no one to tell my troubles to and my children they can not Help me out in this case. I have been Real Down for about Five years. My teeth went bad in 1934 so that was my finish playing music. I am just about to give it up. Now I haven't got no other way to go, but put my Sholder to the wheel and my nose to the grinding Stone and put my music down. . . .
> Now for the taking of the picture of mine you can have one or six now six will cost $5.00 and if you care to pay for six I will be glad because Armstrong wants one. I would like to give Williams one, Foster one, Bechet one, and I would like to keep one which would be the six. Now if you only want me to take one I will do so. So you can send me what you think about it for one or six. Now if there is some things that you would want to know about music please let me know when you answer.

There were a great many things the boys wanted to know about music, but they had to wait a long time for the answer:

> My dear kind Friend only a few words I want to say to you about my delay in sending you these pictures and these letters. Now I'm pretty sure that you all know just how everything is down south with the poor colored men. The service here is really poor for Colored people we have no colored studios. This a cajun town and in these little country towns you don't have a chance like the white man so you just have to stand back and wait until your turn come. That is just the way here so please do not think hard of me, you think hard of the other fellow. You all do your Very Best for me

and try and get me on my feet once more in life. Now here is just what I mean when I say the word on my feet I mean this, I wants to become able to play trumpet once more as I know I can really stomp trumpet yet. Now here is what it takes to stomp trumpet, that is a real good set of teeth and that is just what I am deep in need for. Teeth and a good trumpet and then old Bunk can really go.... Now I truely thank you for the treet of the money. They come in need time. I did not have a penny in my house or no place else. Do tell my dear old pal Clarence Williams to write me and to send a few late numbers of his. Now I can not play them but I can think them. Oh Boy that will make me feel good anyway if I have not got no teeth I can have some thing to look at when I get to thinking about the shape I am in and have no good way to go but work just as I could get it, some weeks nothing at all. Now you tell Louis to please send me a trumpet as he told me that he would and you all do your best for me. From a old good kind Friend as ever and will all ways be so answer me at once.

The boys raised money for a trumpet and a set of teeth. Sidney Bechet, the New Orleans clarinet player, wrote to his brother who was a dentist in New Orleans and asked him to fix Bunk with the best denture money could buy. Bunk went to New Orleans and wrote:

Just a few lines to let you here From me and also to let you know that I did Received the money order. . . . Here was the thing that I had to do to get something to play on. Now I had to start out hussling my Fare to New Orleans and I did Real good and made a good Bargain with the money that was sent to me. Now I got two instruments. I got a cornet and a trumpet. Now they are cheap made instruments I bought them at Fink's Pond Shop on South Rampart near Perdido St. second handed. Now I am able to make my Start. Now I'm able to play at home Everyday until my lip gets in Shape. So do write me at once and let me here from you and I thank you all ever so much for the fixing of my mouth and for all you have done for me. Your Kindness will never be forgoten By Me and my Family.

Here is our Very Best Regardes to you and all of my dear Friends. I will close all from your true friend
                                                    Bunk Johnson

Rudi Blesh, who was lecturing on design at the San Francisco Museum of Art, was asked by the curator, who had played drums in an amateur jazz band during his university days, to give a series of lectures on jazz, featuring Bunk Johnson on trumpet. On the day before the scheduled concert, Blesh still didn't know whether Bunk was going to make it. There was a sharp fifteen-minute train connection in Los Angeles, and Blesh was worried that the old man would miss it. But Blesh didn't know about the jazzmen's underground organization.

Coming through Texas, Bunk couldn't get a seat on the train, and he had to sit in the aisle. He sat on his trumpet case so it wouldn't be stolen, but he went to sleep and someone stole his new shoes and hat. Then, along somewhere in New Mexico, one of the porters from the Pullman cars came through and said, "What are you doing here, man?" Bunk looked up and saw Papa Mutt Carey, the only other surviving New Orleans trumpet player of his age. They had not seen each other in twenty years and each of them thought the other was dead.

Then and there, Papa Mutt took Bunk under his wing, found him a seat, and saw to it that he made his train in Los Angeles. Bunk arrived only four hours before curtain time. He was then sixty-four years old. He had never spoken through a public address system, but he stepped up to the microphone and gave the capacity audience a flawless history of New Orleans jazz. "He had all the poise in the world," Blesh says.

They put on another concert and had over a thousand standing in the halls and in an overflow room. They hired the Geary Theater and brought in Mutt Carey from the Pullman Company and Kid Ory from Los Angeles. NBC put out the last half hour on their Pacific Coast network. The OWI transcribed and broadcast it overseas. *Esquire* magazine put on a concert and the New Orleans Jazz Foundation put on another. Blesh tried to keep Bunk in San Francisco to form a permanent band, but the AFL local didn't like the idea of a mixed band, and so the CIO offered them their union social hall. White and Negro musicians from all over America dropped in to play with the band, but in the end the AFL found a way to break this up on the color line issue.

Gene Williams found a hall in New York, the old Stuyvesant Casino, built a band of New Orleans old-timers around Bunk's trumpet, lodged the band in his old brownstone apartment where they cooked red beans and rice in a bucket every night, and stood back waiting for the big things to happen. They happened simultaneously in *Time*, the *New Yorker*, and the *Herald Tribune*. After that there was no stopping it. Decca, Victor, and Blue Note picked up the band for recording sessions. Gene Williams wrote a review of the band which was so studded with superlatives that it was embarrassing to behold. The Fundamentalists gathered in a solid phalanx and said: *This is it. We have arrived.*

James Jones' short story in the fiction section also deals with the events Borneman describes here. And I have a footnote to prove that some of the fans were, as Condon has said, really full of Bunk. Just after the war, a friend of mine bummed a ride to the west coast with a young man I'll call The Critic, a Bunkster of the most rabid kind. The Critic's father also rode along in the car. All the way across the country, The Critic brought Bunk into the conversation whenever possible. If politics came up, The Critic would say, "You know what Bunk says about that?"—and then quote one of the old man's dubious pontifications. If the party stopped for a bowl of chili, The Critic inevitably remarked that it was not as good as Bunk's recipe for red beans and rice. Bunk's views on theology, philosophy, mathematics, physics and whorehouses were exhaustively and exhaustingly aired. Meanwhile my friend and The Critic's father, an old gentleman of about seventy, endured all the Bunk in the back seat, the old man fortifying himself with occasional nips at a pint and reminiscences of the days when there was a racetrack at Sheepshead Bay in Brooklyn. By the time the party reached the west coast my friend was thoroughly sick and tired of The Critic, not to say of Bunk, but common courtesy demanded that he express his appreciation for the ride. He did. The Critic accepted the thanks rather abstractedly, and my friend felt called upon to add something. He said, "Also, R——, I want to tell you that I enjoyed making the trip with your father. He's a very nice old guy, and it was a pleasure knowing him." The Critic nodded. "Yes," he said, "Dad is a nice guy. I never realized it for a long time. And you know how I know what a nice guy he is? Bunk liked him."—R.G.)

But watch what happened among the Modernists. Metronome said, "These records are laughably out of tune, unmusical and antimusical. Anybody who tells you otherwise, be he William Russell or Charles Edward Smith or Buddy Bolden himself, is guilty of gross deception, net deception, and self-deception. Metronome says, 'Bunk is the bunk.' You can quote us."

When the Fundamentalists read this review, they were delighted. "Look," they said, "you see what happened? At long last the slick boys have lost their smugness. Now they've got nothing to say but a few epithets. And you know why? We've touched the one point they respect. We've made a financial success of the band!"

"Yes," said the Modernists in reply. "You've made a small sort of success out of the band, but you didn't make it out of the music. You dramatized a personality, as you always do, and this time you got the public to identify itself with Bunk Johnson and his riches-to-rags-to-riches story. As far as you are concerned, he might just as well have been the overlord of the New Orleans tenderloin and not the King of the New Orleans trumpeters." And to prove their point, they quote the story of the boys at Wethersfield:

Four or five years ago, a Chicago collector named Preston Flower received a letter from Connecticut State Prison asking him where second-hand records might be bought most cheaply. Flower quoted typical collectors' prices ranging from an average of two dollars to a maximum of two hundred dollars and sent eighteen records of his own—with his compliments.

Two years later, a new American discography was published— in Connecticut State Prison. Hundreds of collectors had contributed records from their own stock-piles to help the boys at Wethersfield in their labors. A young white trumpeter tipped off a pianist friend of his to a bargain in a second-hand horn. A famous Negro trumpeter tried it out, and the editor of a small jazz magazine shipped it off to Wethersfield. A letter came back that had the same feel to it as the first Bunk Johnson letters:

> Yesterday afternoon I took the horn out in the yard where I could play it and though my lip is far from being in shape, I found that the horn has a wonderful tone, it is easy to blow, slurs easy, and high C and D are easy to get. Am I happy? To tell you the real honest truth, I don't believe a pardon could have made me any happier. I really mean that. Here I have a horn that is a beauty and everything a guy could ask for . . . You might make arrangements for me to get some kind of work to do, so I could pay you back. Well, I say, send the work on to me; this horn is worth anything I can do for you.

This story had a great many repercussions. Some of the Modernists said that the collectors would never have bought the trumpet if the man at Wethersfield had not purchased their favor first by currying to their collectors' fancies, and that the collectors' whole interest in him was probably motivated less by genuine charity than by a spurious quest for the great spiritual father whose sinful world of tough masculine action was forever barred to them by the poverty of their own timid and academic minds.

This made the Fundamentalists extremely angry. It seemed in bad taste and it smacked of something which everyone thought had happily been buried at Nuremberg. Art Hodes, in the *Jazz Record*, said wearily, "And so the New Order boys go merrily on their way, increasing the sale of the mags they write for. They're happy—they've found a minority to pick on, just as Hitler made use of a minority in his country . . . They haven't wasted their time fighting for beliefs that didn't pay off in cash. That register rang loud and lustily for them. . . ."

The Modernists, not to be outsmarted, turned the lance right back at the Fundamentalists. They found a good publicity slogan for the enemy—the "Moldy Figs"—and off they went. "The Moldy Figs," said Leonard Feather in *Metronome*, "are to music what Rankin and Bilbo are to politics and Pegler to the press. They are the extreme right-wingers of jazz, the voice of reaction in music. Just as the fascists tend to divide group against group and distinguish between Negroes, Jews, Italians, and 'Real Americans,' so do the Moldy Figs try to categorize New Orleans, Chicago, swing music, and 'the real jazz.' Just as the fascists have tried to foist their views on the public through the vermin press of *Social Justice, The Broom,* and *X-Ray,* so have the Figs yapped their heads off in the *Jazz Record, Jazz Session,* and *Record Changer.* Just as the Gerald L. K. Smiths regard America as a private club to which refugees and members of various races cannot be admitted, so does the right-wing jazz group limit itself to a clique in which a nineteenth century birth certificate from New Orleans is almost the only admission ticket, while all young, aspiring musicians of today are barred and branded as 'riff musicians' or jump and jive men."

There is a certain truth to this. Such high priests of "Dixieland" and "Chicago" jazz as Eddie Condon have often allowed their wit to run away with their discretion. When Hugues Panassié, the French apostle of New Orleans jazz, failed dismally to rank Eddie among the dozen top guitar players, Eddie smartly rapped Panassié across the knuckles with a quip that has become history: "How come the French cats are telling us how to play jazz? Do I tell Panassié how to jump on a grape?"

When Eddie, in *PM,* of all places, used terms like "Gellis dialect" and "watermelon accent," the Jewish and Negro musicians became a little restive. But, significantly enough, the worst offenders in this pretty little game of patriotic name-calling have been the Modernists themselves.

(*To begin with, I've never used the word "cat" in that sense in my life. Second, Borneman obviously did not understand the manner in which those other two phrases were used. PM did, though.* —E. C.)

"For a critic who has hardly ever heard the real jazz, read Panassié's "The Real Jazz,'" says Leonard Feather in a lopsided recommendation in *Metronome.* Next someone named "Hope" picks up the *Metronome* cudgels for America First by aiming another good blow at the furriners: "With Europe in the toils of reconstruction, the jazz cult is again beginning to rear its curiously deformed head in numerous centers, notably the French capital. The *Hot Club de France*, whose purpose before the war seemed to be nothing more than to make confusion more confounded, is appearing once more in Paris in . . . the kind of muddy, ill-formed thinking that is going to befuddle the French public as to what is and is not the real jazz. Barney Bigard's description of Panassie's first book on jazz as 'without doubt the worst book I ever read in my life' might go double for . . . the appallingly misguided French pseudo-critic. . . . It is difficult to regard Panassié's view with anything but mild amusement."

And then, without a visible trace of amusement, Mr. Hope proceeds to beat the life out of poor Panassié. "Caldonia, Caldonia, what makes your big head so hard?" asks the balladist, and the answer, of course, is the little round shellac disc with the hole in the center.

Since the European jazz lover is almost entirely dependent on phonograph records, he finds himself automatically in sympathy with collectors in other countries, including the U. S. A. All collectors are Fundamentalists. The disciples of the modern school may pile up a small collection of their favorite records, but since their standard of value is largely based on novelty, they rapidly get tired of yesterday's records and as a result they generally give up collecting before they have really begun. The Europeans, on the other hand, or the non-American jazz lovers in general, are the collectors *par excellence*. Nowhere, except among the European collectors, will you find tidbits like these:

> There are several distinct kinds of Gennett records, including a green labeled semi-classical series (10,000 up), the dark blue 4,500 popular series, which ended about 5,700 in 1925, the red 3,000 series, similar to the blue, which followed the latter through to 1927, and the black electrically recorded type (6,000) known as Electrobeam Gennett which was mostly a "popular-only" series from 1927 to 1930. Interesting jazz is to be found on all but the first-named, of course, and, as everybody knows, it was for Gennett that three great pioneer jazz bands first recorded—King Oliver the New Orleans Rhythm Kings, and the Wolverines.

While dealing with Armstrong, those resolute souls like myself who dream of a complete Armstrong collection, can start searching again. Two sides, made immediately after the *Knee Drops* session under the name of Carrol Dickerson & his Band have Armstrong solos. Titles are "Symphonic Rapps" (400992) and "Savoyager's Stomp" (400993). They were only issued on Argentine Odeon. Another new item is the German Brunswick "Tiger Rag" and "St. Louis Blues." I recently obtained this and find that the former is a different master to the French Brunswick versions, while the latter, bearing masternumber 1478, is a new version. While on the subject of second masters, the English Brunswick "Down in Honky Tonk Town" is from a different master to the American release, while Swiss Decca F8055 of Louis' "Swing That Music" is a different master to both the U.S. and English release.

And here is a major tragedy from an English jazz magazine named *Record Information*:

> Peter Tanner's inclusion of Bessie Smith's "Young Woman's Blues" as an example of the late Jimmy Harrisson must have come as a shock to those who knew that glorious record. It certainly did to me! It so happens that there is not the slightest trace of trombone on the record, though it does contain some of Joe Smith's finest, broad-toned, low register cornet. *The label of the U.H.C.A. reissue wrongly lists Harrisson.* I have never heard a Bessie Smith which features Jimmy; when she used a trombone, it was almost always the late Charlie Green. At any rate, Green is responsible for most of the accompaniments which were at one time credited to Harrisson. But that hardly excuses Peter, who has chosen as an example a record which contains no trombone at all!

This has an old, familiar sound to me. The first piece of solemn prose of this sort that I ever saw was the dance music section of a German phonograph record catalogue of 1931 or 1932 which was signed by someone named Dietrich Schultz-Koehn, Konigsberg, East Prussia. It struck me at the time as a most characteristic sample of the German professorial mind in action, but it never occurred to me to associate it with the jazz cult until fifteen years later, when Allan Morrison, in *Stars and Stripes*, described his meeting, in the no-man's-land between the lines at St. Nazaire, with a German officer named Dr. Dietrich Schultz-Koehn. Morrison was almost overwhelmed by the absurdity of the situation, that a commissioned soldier of the master race should have no greater demands upon his enemy than the most agonized desire for news from 52nd Street. A year later, when Charles Delaunay, the son of the cubist painter, came to New York to record some American jazz musicians for the French *Swing* label, he told the rest of the story.

The French jazz collectors, he said, had converted their whole organization into an underground network with American jive talk as code for underground messages; some operations were carried out with the knowledge and co-operation of a few German officers including one Dietrich Schultz-Koehn, whose whole political thought had been influenced by his study of American Negro music.

The Paris Hot Club, the federal headquarters of the Hot Club of France, at that time owned a three-story building in the Rue Chaptal where American and British agents, under the guise of record collectors and jazz fans, could easily mingle with the underground members of the Hot Club. This setup worked well as a message center until October, 1943, when the Gestapo raided the building and took all persons found on the premises to the Fresnes Prison. Two of them, including the president of the Marseilles Hot Club and a secretary of the Paris club, were killed off in the gas chambers. Delaunay was held for four weeks and then released for lack of evidence. When he came out of jail, he finished editing the fifth edition of his encyclopedia of jazz, *Hot Discography*. The German authorities had forbidden publication of more than 500 copies, but a group of Belgian jazz collectors had provided Delaunay with sufficient blackmarket paper to print 2,500 copies, and as a result he decided to publish five separate editions, all of them numbered from 1 to 500 but each of them distinguished from all others by a diminutive printer's mark. These five underground editions have since become collectors' items of more than sentimental value, not only among the jazz collectors but among bibliophiles of all nations.

The Modernists were not pleased with this at all. They decided to query the whole show:

"Before one can place much faith in the claims of Panassié and his cohorts, it might be desirable for someone to clear up the mystery of the critic's activities during the occupation. A couple of stories have reached the United States that do not reflect well on Panassié, but they are unconfirmed."

When Panassié, in a letter to the editor of the magazine that carried the article, asked gently for an apology or a verification of the charge, the editor gallantly printed this elegant specimen of double-talk:

"To be entirely blunt about it, jazz circles in the United States were alive with rumors that M. Panassié was a Vichyite during the years following Marshal Petain's capitulation to the Germans. We are glad to print here the fact that Hugues Panassié was in no way a collaborationist. But as for rumors—M. Panassié's *Bulletin du Hot Club de France* has printed some honeys—such as the report that Harry Carney (Duke Ellington's baritone sax player) had been discovered in Marseilles!"

This pretty exchange of courtesies is offered here not as an example of virtue on one side and vice on the other but merely as a mild sample of the bitterness and confusion to which the jazz cult has given rise. As if to stress the irreparably schizoid nature of its argument, the magazine that had printed the attack upon Panassié found it incumbent to print on the next page a glowing report on the heroic stand of the Belgian jazz fans who had supplied Delaunay with paper for the *Hot Discography*.

To get around the German ban on dancing, the Belgians had organized some forty Swing Clubs and Hot Clubs which covered the whole country with a network of musical relay stations. Their total membership reached 10,000; they organized concerts, gave record recitals, and formed music appreciation groups. Since American songs were *verboten*, such titles as "Tiger Rag" and "Honeysuckle Rose" became *La rage du tigre* and *Rose de miel*; "Exactly Like You" became *Exactement comme vous*; "Tea for Two," *L'heure du the*, and so on. In 1941 the *Propaganda Abteilung Belgien* became suspicious and began to monitor the meetings of the Hot Clubs. A tea dance of the Hot Club de Belgique held at the Palais des Beaux Arts in Brussels on April 13, 1941, elicited such program annotations as "Swing-Jew" and "Anglo-American Music without control" left behind by an incautious Gestapo officer.

He had good reasons to be suspicious: the general manager of the Decca Company of Belgium had equipped his car, a new Packard Super Eight, as a traveling recording studio for the leaders of the Belgian resistance movement. When the Gestapo queried him about the car, which would have come in handily for their own purposes, he produced a certificate of sale to a man who had died one month after the purchase and claimed that he had no idea what had become of the car since.

Meanwhile, at night, the studio went on recording American jazz (sung in English) and employing Jewish musicians on the Gestapo black list. One night, when the Gestapo raided and sealed the building for a thorough search, they forgot one special elevator leading from the basement into the factory; with this elevator, the Belgians removed all matrices and other incriminating evidence. Three days after the retreating Germans had smashed up what they thought was all available recording equipment, the Decca people had the studio sufficiently well in shape again to record Pierlot, Gutt, Spaack, Van Zeeland, and other leaders of the Free Belgian Government.

The accent of importance here is not the fact of heroism which, during the war, became so universal as to be taken for granted, but the transformation of something as bland and apparently asocial as jazz into a powerful spring of action. Jazz, which began as the American Negro's music of protest and assertion, and which, in the hands of white tunesmiths and arrangers, had long been debased from a powerful stimulant to a poor soporific, thus proved that in times of action it still held the power to sway man's will against his overlord.

That the Teutonic conquerors were by no means unaware of the latently rebellious nature of jazz became particularly evident in the Netherlands where the *Propaganda Abteilung Holland* issued an amazing document to all members of the Dutch musicians' union. In its knowledge of technical terms and its awareness of their musical significance, this manifesto is not likely ever to be equaled by any other government department; in its

THE JAZZ CULT 65

racial, social, and religious overtones it will, we hope, never be attempted again by any government in mankind's future history. It is hard to imagine the mechanics of a human brain which in the midst of a life and death struggle can find the perverse thoroughness of mind to say "licks and riffs repeated more than three times in succession by a soloist or more than sixteen times for one section or for two or more sections" are forbidden, but a special permit may be granted "where such music is interpreted by persons having two or more Negroid to Negritic grandparents."

Yet some of this utter solemnity and single-mindedness of purpose emerges from the work of the European jazz fans themselves, and if any human explanation can be found to make the Nazi jazz manifesto intelligible, such explanation will probably have to be derived from the give-and-take relationship between the maniacal lack of humor of the European jazz lovers and the corresponding lack of humor among their wartime overlords. A few brief passages quoted verbatim from European jazz magazines may serve to illustrate this point:

From England, where there are more than fifteen periodicals exclusively devoted to jazz:

> Members of the Jazz Sociological Society which leans towards the anarchist party in politics, and members of the Jazz Appreciation Society, which is affiliated to the Communist party, have recently fallen out over the social interpretation of certain jazz, blues, and boogie records. . . .

From Spain:

> Little news of jazz activities have reached us from this country since the end of the civil war. It is now known that one of the prominent Spanish collectors, Pedro Casadeval, will shortly edit a jazz review and issue records by Spanish musicians. . . . It is hoped that the once flourishing hot clubs will soon be able to reform under less unhappy conditions.

From Holland:

> The well-known Dutch orchestra, The Ramblers, was recently banned from radio broadcasting and other en-

gagements for collaborating . . . It is feared that the most prominent European critic after Panassie, Joost van Praag, was murdered by the Germans. . . .

From France:

Nancy Cunard, who is now in Paris, reports that there is a great interest in jazz amongst the French intelligentsia. Picaso has a considerable collection of blues records, including many extremely rare items which a number of collectors would very much like to own.

From Turkey comes the following letter to the editor of an American magazine:

First of all we would like to introduce ourselves. We are jazz-fans, in fact, if you wish, jazz-maniacs, to perfection . . . By no means think that we are unrighteously praising you . . . We cannot help admiring the great frankness and excessive knowledge in your band reviews. . . . For heaven's sake carry on with your so-called 'disfavorable comments' on people like the Andrews Sisters, Bing Crosby, and especially what you classify as 'Mickey Mouse' bands, or else we are sure to perish! We simply cannot imagine why you Americans still listen to the sickening music of Guy Lombardo, Sammy Kaye, Freddie Martin, Ted Lewis, Wayne King, Blue Barron and Lawrence Welk. Whenever we have the misfortune of coming across the discordant music of these mediocre gentlemen, we find no alternative but to commit suicide. . . .

It is significant to notice that among the front rank "American" jazz critics there are the two sons of the late Turkish Ambassador to the U. S.; the five-feet-tall son of a wealthy Javanese planter, whose pretty girl friend, towering a couple of inches over him, used to refer to him as "my son"; a Danish baron; an English journalist and half a dozen others whose birthplace is far beyond the radius of Buddy Bolden's cornet.

A few days ago, I received a letter which began, "Dear Mr. Borneman: You, as a leading American jazz critic, might be able to . . ." This was the end. I knew I had gone too far. The ranks of the collectors had closed in around me. Only two courses remained open—desertion or lifelong servitude. The next day, a single mail delivery brought four letters: one from an irate Fundamentalist, attacking me savagely for showing insufficient sympathy with Bunk Johnson's clarinet player; one from a bitter Modernist, addressed to Old Moldy Fig Borneman, expressing scathing surprise at my attempt to consider Bunk Johnson's clarinet player as a *musician*; one from a happy Modernist congratulating me for putting the Moldy Figs in their place with my strong criticism of Bunk Johnson's clarinet player; and one from an enthusiastic Fundamentalist praising me for my strong stand in favor of New Orleans clarinetists in general and Bunk Johnson's clarinet player in particular.

This co-ordinated display of strong-arm stuff gave me the blue shakes. But in the same mail I also received a reassuring post card that calmed my rising fears for the future of mankind. It reads as follows:

Dear Mr. Borneman,
    For only 1 United States dollar bill and a self-addressed stamped Envelope I will send you the following information:
    (1) Where to get records of Boogie piano, Blues, spirituals, etc., etc., for only 20 cents a piece. Old records but in good playing condition.
    (2) Where to buy nationally advertised cigarettes at only #1.13 a carton. These are freshly packed cigarettes.
    (3) Where to get razor blades, 100 to a carton, at only 80 cents a carton.
    Hoping you appreciate our service and that we will hear from you soon.
                      Yours truly,
                      James Fitzpatrick
                      21 Barnes Street,
                      Waterbury 62, Conn.

This did the trick. I am not deserting. I have taken up smoking. I have begun to shave twice a day. I have become a collector. I even play boogie woogie. God help my poor wife.

NAT HENTOFF

Jazz and the Intellectuals: Somebody Goofed

> NAT HENTOFF *is an editor of* Down Beat. *This piece, reprinted from the* Chicago Review, *is going to make some people indignant, possibly because Nat seems to feel that only a few intellectuals have taken time to listen to the music. The very fact that the* Chicago Review *published the piece might seem to refute Nat's premise.*
>
> E. C.

"If America has a native musical voice," proclaimed a startlingly benign editorial writer of the *Boston Globe* recently, "it speaks through jazz."

If this suddenly respectable thesis is sound—and there has long been an excellent case for it—America's "native musical voice" is an alien tongue to most of the country's intellectuals. In accusatory fact, it always has been.

During the past half-century (while jazz has evolved from New Orleans brass bands to Brubeck polytonality), the American intellectual-artist has continued to search restlessly and often profoundly for the roots of his culture (along with his own). He has examined acres of its interlocking parts, from *The Day of the Locust* to *The Man with the Golden Arm*; *Winesburg, Ohio*; *Faithful Are the Wounds*; *Invisible Man*; and *Light in August*. There have been complementary socioeconomic-political studies and large numbers of essays, monographs, and even manifestoes on scores of aspects of "our American heritage."

But in all this searching one of the most unmistakable strains of American culture—both as a musical language and as a way of life—has been almost entirely overlooked. Jazz, it is true, has figured peripherally in the work of a few "serious" short-story writers, but almost invariably it has been handled in an ingenuously distorted manner, with the Negro jazzman in particular frequently masked in a "primitivism" more revealing of the writers' ambivalency toward Negroes than of jazz fact. Even Eudora Welty's passionate "Powerhouse" with its attempt at empathy is not without its Uncle Tom trappings. And the best-known stories in the field, Elliott Grennard's "Sparrow's Last Jump" (Harper's Magazine, May, 1947) and Clellon Holmes' "The Horn" (Discovery #2), though they are more knowledgeable than most and are free of "primitivism," none the less describe more than they comprehend.

There have been no novels even of jagged merit based on jazz. The widely publicized *Young Man with a Horn* was just this side of a *Ladies' Home Journal* serial, and the few subsequent jazz novels like Edwin Gilbert's *The Hot and the Cool* and Stanford Whitmore's *Solo* have been embarrassing. Osborn Duke's *Sideman* is more knowledgeable but hardly a *Red Badge of Courage*. None of our "major" novelists of the past few decades seems to have been more than remotely aware that jazz and jazzmen exist. It is as if Jelly Roll Morton, Bix Beiderbecke, and Charlie Parker were American Indians.

One might have thought that some of the poets would have found instant empathy with the lyricism and hotly dramatic self-expressiveness of jazz. But there have been no memorable poems marked by jazz. There have, of course, been fairly frequent echo-like rhapsodies on the theme of African drums, as well as a few homilies by Langston Hughes, but no wholly realized, deeply experienced poems. In fairness, I should note that American poet

Cid Corman, who edits *Origin*, claims that such of our newer poets as Creeley, Olson, Blackburn and Duncan (plus William Carlos Williams in several of his later poems) do reflect some of the pulsation of jazz. "They don't," Corman points out, "obviously have to be dealing with jazz as such, but their verse rises out of just such an impulse as jazz, their rhythms often suggest jazz, their language is usually firmly rooted in its world, they are sentimental, egoistic, terrified and terrifying, sometimes loud and noisy, sometimes fiercely sweet or strident, sometimes soft and low, so much blues." Nor have the dramatists taken any advantage of the explosive potential of a play about the jazzman, his relationships with his colleagues, and his often strangled relationship with the larger society.

The sociologists, writing psychologists, and cultural historians also have almost entirely ignored the existence, let alone the pulsating ramifications of jazz and the jazz life. An exception is the often too glib Anatole Broyard who has written a few essays on the subject for publications like *Partisan Review* and *Commentary*. A more valuable exception is a young psychiatrist, Norman Margolis, who has begun to write on jazz with some perception. There is also Howard S. Becker's unique study, "The Professional Dance Musician and his Audience" (The *American Journal of Sociology*, September, 1951).* Another valuable exception among social scientists is William Bruce Cameron, who has contributed "Sociological Notes on the Jam Session" (*Social Forces*, December, 1954). And Charles N. Fair is an essayist with a considerable degree of jazz understanding, judging by his articles in the *Avon Book of Modern Writing* and *Arts Digest*. But these and a handful more are very few when the field has been fertile for exploration so long.

Even in the specialized area of jazz historiography itself, there has as yet been no first-rate history of jazz. Barry Ulanov's *A History of Jazz in America* (Viking Press) is the best available but it seems hastily assembled in parts and is often overgeneralized

---

* Also by Becker are: "Some Contingencies of the Professional Dance Musician's Career" (*Human Organization*, Vol 12, No. 1); "Becoming a Marihuana User" (The *American Journal of Sociology*, November, 1953); and "Marihuana Use and Social Control" (*Social Problems*, July, 1955).

and generally disproportioned. Marshall Stearns of Hunter College, executive secretary of the Institute of Jazz Studies (the only organization devoted to correlating studies on jazz from all perspectives), has had a history in preparation for several years, and his could be the first comprehensive and accurate volume on the subject. Recently published and of value particularly for its early chapters is A *Pictorial History of Jazz* by Keepnews and Grauer (Crown).

There was, it should be noted, a valuable anecdotal volume (concerned largely with the early history of jazz) published a few years ago—*Jazzmen* by Frederic Ramsey and Charles Edward Smith (Harcourt Brace, 1939). Also of rare excellence is Alan Lomax's *Mister Jelly Roll* (Duell, Sloan and Pearce, 1950), a picaresque odyssey of an early jazz creator that is based largely on Jelly Roll's autobiographical reminiscences, recorded in his own words for the Library of Congress. Nearly as vital within its more limited milieu is *Big Bill Blues: William Broonzy's story as told to Yannick Bruynoghe*. This autobiography is thus far available only in the English edition, published by Cassell.

In contrast to the jazz understanding of Lomax was the manner in which the first volume of Louis Armstrong's autobiography, *Satchmo: My Life in New Orleans*, was edited. The book itself has a number of inadvertently controversial and provocative revelations about one jazzman's attitude to society (as best discussed in Orrin Keepnews' review in *The Record Changer*, Vol. 14, No. 2). But much of the volume's impact and idiomatic strength was diluted by an attempt to "fix up" Louis' prose style. The result reads too often like a finishing-school parody of what could have been a lasting record of a vitally individual American's idiom in music and speech.

An important reference volume, issued within the year, is Leonard Feather's *Encyclopedia of Jazz* (Horizon Press). The first book of creatively penetrating jazz criticism (as contrasted with previously emotional tracts) is also recent—André Hodeir's *Jazz: Its Evolution and Essence* (Grove Press, translated from the French.)

In any case, even within the limited field of jazz specialists, the contentious critics and quasi-historians have, except for a few books, also done surprisingly little to document well, explore deeply, or otherwise illuminate the rich, swift evolution of jazz. Only rarely have the musicians themselves been asked to talk or write, and usually the result has been mutilation, all-too-visible ghosting (the late Thomas Sugrue's unobtrusive handling of Eddie Condon's *We Called It Music*, was a partial exception); or, in one notorious case (Mezz Mezzrow's *Really the Blues*), a Munchausen-like self-canonization.

(*I feel bound to mention that Nat's last book, put together with Nat Shapiro, was called "Heah Me Talkin' To Ya." E.C.*)

As for regular journals within the field, there are only three in America—*Down Beat, Metronome,* and *The Record Changer.* While occasional articles of more than surface perception appear in the three, none of them regularly covers jazz with, let's say, the depth of perception *The Musical Quarterly* applies to classical music or *The Kenyon Review* to literary criticism. The reason is that there is no audience in this country as yet for writing of this degree of seriousness (and appreciation) concerning jazz. Nor are there more than a half-dozen writers who would be able to handle the subject with wide-ranged expertness if the audience were present.

The large-circulation newspapers and magazines give jazz as much attention as does radio—practically none. Recent exceptions are the *New York Times* (John S. Wilson), the *San Francisco Chronicle* (Ralph Gleason) and the *Washington Post* (Paul Sampson). The newspapers and wire services are indeed quick to use the handy caricatures of the jazz musician in their leads if a jazzman ever does get into trouble, but very, very few of their writers have either knowledge of or respect for jazz. When the leading jazz creator of this generation, Charlie Parker, died recently, he received front-page attention in the *New York Daily Mirror* only because he died in the apartment of a friend who was a titled European.

Parker, the most important modern jazz influence in many years, was ignored when *Time* finally decided to "recognize" jazz. *Time*, instead, gave its cover story to Dave Brubeck, a highly individualized modern jazz pianist of considerable resources but at some distance from Parker's jazz attainments. Brubeck, however, was "respectable" enough for *Time* because he had studied with Milhaud, was a favorite among collegians—and was white.

Not that *Time* is Jim Crow. Quite the contrary. But the concept of an American Negro musical innovator of Parker's freshness, originality, and complex power was quite beyond the knowledge or imagination of *Time*'s music editor—as it is beyond the ken of most American intellectuals, whether they work for Luce or write for the *Partisan Review*.

Our intellectuals are still largely ambivalent toward the Negro creator in our society. Whatever guilts and loose ends of fear make up this seldom wholly realized difficulty, it frequently exists not only in the intellectuals' relationship to jazz, but also in their daily relationship with Negroes—except those Negroes who are respectably degreed or otherwise well within the familiar western tradition of the arts.

As for radio, thanks largely to FM, classical music now gets some measure of air time in at least the larger cities throughout the country. Jazz, by contrast, is heard on very few stations and then usually on terms of constant probation. The same is true of all the other media—films, TV, etc. Only in recordings has there been a boom in the last two years and, ironically, it is now easier for most jazzmen to get record dates than steady work in a club for any length of time.

The jazz clubs are few, the hours exhausting, and the pay— except for a few "stars"—not enough to average up the many lean weeks in each year. There is hope of wider work opportunities in the concert field—both in the larger cities as managed through tours like Norman Granz's "Jazz at the Philharmonic" circuit, and in the colleges, as Dave Brubeck has been demonstrating. But the average jazzman still works under economic and psychological conditions that make it difficult for him to study, compose, or reflect.

So after fifty years as America's "native musical voice" jazz is still a widely unknown, largely untested experience for most Americans—intellectuals included. And the jazzman continues to suffer thereby. This often comes as a shock to European intellectual-artists who are generally more informed on the nature and range of jazz than their American counterparts. In fairness it should be added that the difference in understanding is often not great. The European intellectual only infrequently possesses a comprehensive knowledge of the idiom, but at least more European intellectuals are emotionally aware of jazz than their American counterparts.

More European visitors, for example, know that jazz is not the same as the "pop" music of the disc jockey and the juke box than do American intellectuals. Moreover, few European intellectuals—except the French—restrict their jazz listening only to Dixieland or New Orleans-styled music, as do most of those few intellectuals in America who profess to "appreciate" jazz.

This frequent preference, by the small number of American intellectuals who care about jazz at all, for early blues, New Orleans, later Dixieland, and "revivalist" jazz is yet another example of that odd ambivalency toward jazz (and particularly the Negro jazzman) that is shown by many intellectuals. The evolution of jazz through the swing era into the modern jazz of Parker, Gillespie, Tristano, John Lewis, Bud Powell, and Brubeck is denigrated by the intellectual Dixielander as "unpure," and as too infused with European influences. Actually Charlie Parker was fully as original at his stage in jazz history as Louis Armstrong was in his, but somehow the Dixieland intellectuals are more comfortable with the simple, "pure" jazz and blues that they can follow without the kind of intellectual and emotional effort they apply to Bartok quartets or Wozzeck. Could it be that these intellectuals are not yet willing to credit the Negro musician with the mental and emotional equipment to be complexly creative in a new Afro-American musical language?

Artists like William Grant Still or Marian Anderson can be readily accepted because they are a part "of us" in the language of their art and in their formal use of that language within the tradition of European-American "serious" music. And Huddie Ledbetter was O.K. because he was a "folk artist" and thus sufficiently removed from "us" in background and in the nature of his creative product to be "understood" as one would understand another, less intellectually "advanced" society.

But when artists like Lester Young, Thelonious Monk, Billie Holiday, and Bud Powell explode from within a largely ignored and thereby rejected part of our culture, then the intellectual's ambivalence toward the Negro as this kind of individualized creator is heightened. It's all very well for Negro intellectuals to move within our regular traditions (however avant-garde) of writing, painting, or composing or for them to be folk artists. But for the Negro to have created an increasingly complex musical language on an Afro-American base, a language that has become as original, as challenging, and as internationally stimulating as jazz, is quite another thing. Few intellectuals have allowed themselves to become aware of this predominantly Negro contribution to American culture, apparently because of their inability to acknowledge this kind and range of American Negro creation in the arts. (White jazzmen, of course, have been valuable contributors to the jazz language from New Orleans on; but during at least its first fifty years most of the basic advances in jazz have been made by Negroes, and the beginnings of jazz in the south and southwest in the early 1900's were based on three previous centuries of Negro work songs, play songs, spirituals, ring games, field hollers, blues, etc.)

What happens, then, is that rather than expose themselves to the full impact and complexity of jazz, most American intellectuals have either ignored it entirely or allowed themselves to dig only New Orleans-Dixieland and the blues; or, in a few cases, they have yielded to the extent of appreciating white modernists like Brubeck and Gerry Mulligan without being able often to "take" Parker, Monk, Gillespie, and the other innovators of modern jazz. There are also those like Harvey Breit of the *New York Times* who, in a review of *A Pictorial History of Jazz*, wrote: "The modern jazzmen seem to these ears noisy, unruly and sour. They look bland. And they are unproven. I would have voted an arbitrary halt (to this book) with the Benny Goodman quartet and the various comeback combos playing around town." Where would Mr. Breit propose to cut off a history of painting —with Seurat?

As a result of this mass goofing by the intellectuals with relation to jazz in the past several decades, jazz has lost a chance to have at least the core of an audience that has a sense of tradition —as well as an audience that could have supported and encouraged the jazz musician as it has, at least to some extent, the experimental writer, painter, sculptor, or composer.

The jazz audience, as it exists at present, is by and large a young audience. It is, says one psychologist, an audience whose revolt against its elders takes the form, among others, of appreciating the sometimes rebellious music of jazz. Because of the youth of the jazz audience and its predominantly nonintellectual habit of mind, the jazz audience is an inordinately cruel one, more cruel than the public for any other art form.

To a large extent the audience for jazz in this country is created anew each generation and its criteria of jazz excellence are almost uniformly the most "modern" and the most "progressive" developments of whatever year it happens to be. The generations before have usually lost interest in jazz in large numbers because most of their members have not had the intellectuals' discipline of mind and imagination and have not been able to absorb the rapid changes that have taken place in jazz in each generation.

As I pointed out in a recent article in *Down Beat* on the subject of the jazz audience:

"The practice of listening to jazz as a serious avocation is only 25 or 30 years old. There were only a few jazz 'fans' at the beginning of the 30's and many of that original band were unable to keep up with the swiftly changing patterns of jazz expression. These either dropped their interest in the art or continued to replay their Louis Hot Fives and Bix records while lamenting what they termed jazz's loss of 'purity.'

"The swing era generation also, in large part, found it difficult to pass from Benny Goodman to Charlie Parker. No other art form, in fact, has ever grown so quickly and dizzyingly as jazz, and not many people in this other-directed society have the strength as individuals to adjust their hard-won tastes to so roller-coasterish a pace. So the major percentage of the contemporary jazz audience is now formed of yet another new generation."

The result of this succession of audiences—with a very small band of exceptions who do encompass the range of jazz from Johnny Dodds to John Lewis—is that the jazz musician feels himself doubly isolated. He is not only ignored by the general public that opulently supports the "pop" singers and the Lombardos of the dance-band field, but his own small audience is a changeable and unstable support. In this decade, for example, such major figures of the swing era as Coleman Hawkins, Ben Webster, and Johnny Hodges have a rapidly diminishing audience. They are too "old" for the newest generation of jazz listeners.

The current jazz audience is largely composed of youngsters who believe that jazz began with Stan Kenton. The older jazz generation may occasionally play their fifteen-year-old records of Hawkins, Webster, and Hodges at home; but having lost touch with so much of modern jazz, they are no longer in the habit of actively supporting even that part of jazz that they continue to like.

So the older jazzmen face an increasingly bleak prospect and often their bitterness grows and grows. Not only is this changeability of the jazz audience a tragedy for individual jazzmen, but it takes away from "modern" jazz the kind of historically astute audience that could give more balanced encouragement and more knowledgeable support to the young jazz experimenters than is presently available. As it is, jazz continues to evolve, but the jazzman almost never thinks of looking to members of his audience for sound criticism or advice. In fact he has a certain contempt for that audience and will adhere seriously only to the judgments of his fellow musicians. This is not entirely bad, but certainly a relatively "enlightened" audience is more a source of spiritual strength to an artist than a collection of shrill "fans."

(A "relatively enlightened audience" is a source of strength mainly when it is relatively enlightened enough to shut up.—E.C.)

Jazzmen especially would welcome the warmth of even a small audience that had some real comprehension of jazz music and the jazzmen's problems as individuals. This quality of audience, of course, is rare in any field, but in jazz it is almost non-existent. The jazzman is, in terms of decades, newly self-aware of himself as an artist. The early New Orleans musicians were, in large part, urban "folk" artists and played mainly for their own pleasure and for the functional pleasure of their neighbors at dances, parades, weddings, and so forth, as well as for the more somber communal occasions like funerals.

Even through the twenties most jazz musicians were unaware that their language was an evolving "art." Jazz, for one thing, was too young; there were no "critics" (the first "serious" books on jazz appeared in the early thirties and were written by Europeans); and playing jazz was regarded by the musicians only as a way of making a living and as a necessary means of self-expression. As the language changed and grew richer in achievements and possibilities, jazz musicians gradually became aware of the value of their work as part of a permanently growing art form.

But this awareness and its accompanying pride were severely injured by the continued apathy of most of the public toward jazz and the relative shallowness of the swiftly succeeding generations of jazz listeners. In turn, jazz musicians became more and more of an in-group (cf. the previously cited study by Howard Becker, "The Professional Dance Musician and His Audience"), and the alienation of several of them from almost all reality but that of their music has often been frighteningly complete.

Contrary, however, to the frequent identification of almost all jazzmen with narcotics (it used to be liquor) by an otherwise uninterested public, the larger number of jazz musicians has been as responsible a section of the citizenry as any other vocational group. It is true, however, that the uncertain economic conditions of playing jazz and the general feeling on the part of jazz musicians that there are few sources beyond their fellow musicians from which they can gain any real measure of recognition has resulted in greater rootlessness among jazz musicians than among most other groups of artists. It is oversimplification to say that this rootlessness is the chief cause of the narcotics addiction that has indeed existed and still does exist to some extent among jazz musicians, but it is certainly an important cause.

The reasons for the narrowing of the jazz musician's personality and perspectives are too many and complex to be covered in a few general sentences here. There are indications that many of the younger jazzmen are breaking away from these circles of self-constriction, but a general feeling of alienation from the rest of society will persist among jazzmen for some time to come, because the feeling derives from the facts. Jazz, despite the adjectival honors it has received from abroad and the current focusing of interest on it here in the form of festivals like that at Newport, is still an unwelcome musical voice to most Americans, however unmistakably native.

(*This simply isn't so any more. Eddie Condon and his boys have appeared with three or four symphonies. So have many other musicians. The crowds everywhere attest to the music's ever-widening audience—a mass audience. It's true that last year Norman Granz' Jazz at the Philharmonic was barred from Kleinhans Hall in Buffalo, but that was because the audience that showed up for preceding concerts had been a little unruly. I wonder if Hentoff isn't wringing his hands because his intellectual friends listen to Bartok "seriously" and John Lewis for fun. Maybe he knows the wrong intellectuals.—R.G.*)

Had more intellectuals been free enough to comprehend the language of jazz in the past two decades, the position of this kind of music and of its creators might have been more secure psychically, if not financially. The intellectuals could have helped provide jazz with the nucleus of a historically oriented, sustainedly responsive, and challenging audience it has needed so greatly. And in turn, jazz had much to teach the intellectuals about free and complex expression of feeling in artistic idioms more deeply rooted in America than any other single manifestation of our musical culture.

Throughout these reflections I have, in a sense, taken it as "given" that jazz merits a devoted degree of attention as a music with unique depth, power, and limitless potential. For those who are skeptical words are by no means adequate to present the case for jazz as music. I would suggest you listen. Listen to jazz in the clubs as well as on records. And listen, if you can, to the musicians off as well as on the stand.

In the academies, the "little" magazines, and other centers of American intellectual activity, jazz is still America's unknown untranslated language. Yet all the intellectual need do is listen —to jazz and then to himself—to understand this language that has always been part of his heritage even when he refused to hear.

GILBERT MILLSTEIN

The Commodore Shop and Milt Gabler

THE COMMODORE MUSIC SHOP used to be a nice place to hang out in, as Gil Millstein indicates here in his story written when the shop was in its finest flower. As a matter of fact, that was where I first met Gil, one of the better writers who never graduated from the New York Times. I had the pleasure of making Milt Gabler's first record for the Commodore label, and unless I'm mistaken Gil Millstein had the pleasure of making Milt his first piece for The New Yorker. I want to say one thing about Milt. For a non-musician, he had better musical taste—and less hair— than anyone I've ever known in my life.

E. C.

In Murder on the Downbeat, a two-dollar dreadful in which everyone who is not killed feels called upon to talk learnedly about hot music, the Commodore Music Shop is mentioned by the hero, a rather offensive jazz critic on a New York newspaper. "A guy walked into the Commodore Music Shop the other day," he says at one point before the blood runs, "and offered them fifteen dollars apiece for every Gold Coast recording they could sell him, and they couldn't locate one for him for three times the price." The author's intention is clear. His hero is simply trying to impress the pretty heroine by a knowing reference to the theory that if a jazz record cannot be found by the Commodore it is not to be had. This theory is held by, among many others, Milton Gabler, the stocky, bald, bland owner of the shop, a small, tumble-down establishment at 136 East 42nd Street. Gabler enjoys telling people that in the unlikely event that his store can't find a specific classic hot record, it will manufacture its own version, equally fervid and possibly with the same musicians who made the original fifteen or twenty years before. That the Commodore should turn up in a murder story entertains but does not surprise him. The store's place in the up-and-down history of jazz has long been taken for granted by musicians, critics, and that special, intense public which collects hot records just a little more passionately than anyone else thinks is necessary. "We were," says Gabler, "the iron lung of jazz. Just like New Orleans was the cradle, we were the iron lung."

The iron lung was in bad shape itself early in 1937, having piled up, for art's sake, debts to the amount of twenty thousand dollars, when the editors of "March of Time" decided that jazz needed documentation and produced a film called "The Birth of Swing." The picture opened with a shot of a man walking into the Commodore. The camera moved on to the record racks and a sign advertising such revered exponents of the idiom as Bix Beiderbecke, Red Nichols, Muggsy Spanier, Frank Trumbauer, Kid Ory, King Oliver, Louis Armstrong, and Jimmie Noone —names that were known to fewer people in 1937 than they are today. Gabler was shown handing a presumably irreplaceable hot record to a customer. Then the film took up other aspects of hot music's nativity. The script for the picture was prepared by James H. S. Moynahan, an unreconstructed Dixieland-style clarinet player and chief publicity writer for "March of Time." "We wanted to show a place that typified jazz for the public," he explains, "one that was authoritative in the field. The Commodore is the biggest thing of its kind in the world. There is no jazz fan who doesn't know that. If the Commodore had been in Chicago or Persia, we'd have sent a camera crew there." The boost in "March of Time" helped, but not even that was enough to put the Commodore on a paying basis. The shop continued to operate well in the red.

The philosophy in back of the Commodore is based on an uncomplicated premise: that there are a lot of people whose idea of music is, as one critic has put it, "an informal gathering of temperamentally congenial jazz musicians who play unrehearsed and unscored music for their own enjoyment." Gabler has held firmly to this premise, and he has probably done as much as anyone to restore jazz to an eminence, not to say affluence, unknown since its severe decline in the early days of repeal. He has sold more hot records than any other music-shop proprietor anywhere. He has manufactured, under the Commodore label, some of the world's best hot recordings, and he has made them fashionable at the not inconsiderable price of a dollar and a half a copy. He provided meat and drink for a generation of hot musicians at a time when they were having trouble earning cakes and coffee and were not getting much fun out of their congenial temperaments. The fact that he does not know a grace note from a diminished fifth lessens neither his absorption in music nor the esteem in which he is held by musicians. "He has an ear like an elephant," one musician remarked not long ago. Evidently fearing that this description was inadequate, he added, "And he's the nicest bastard I know."

Throughout the jazz world, a turbulent and often bitter little planet housing as many cults as there are hot musicians, Gabler is given the credit for forcing the big "commercial" record companies, after years of neglect and Guy Lombardo, to devote a part of their output to what is perhaps arbitrarily known among its devotees as "righteous" music. "He started alone searching for good jazz," one writer reported a few years ago. "Now the record companies are almost bumping heads digging for unused masters, rare collectors' items, and unheard-of or long-forgotten jazzmen." The companies recognized Gabler's forthright pioneering in another way, too. They paid him the doubtful honor of taking back the master records of old and presumably worthless recordings they had rented to him so that he could reissue them under the Commodore label, and putting out the records themselves in fancy albums. Gabler was not disturbed by this. "The way I figure it," he says, "as long as it's a jazz record and somebody wants it and it's got someone on it, I'll sell it. What's the difference whether they make it or I do? It's jazz, isn't it?" Gabler is also acknowledged to be the man who first hit upon the idea of listing the names of all the members of the band on a record, an innovation so simple that nobody had any trouble copying it. Jazz collectors rank it somewhere between the invention of the wheel and the releasing of nuclear energy.

At one time, Gabler had almost a monopoly on the best hot records of the old days. That was after the Okeh Company, which had issued the majority of these records, had collapsed and been taken over by Columbia. It had folded in the early thirties, when the recording industry hit a long-time low and hot records were lying on bargain counters. Gabler went up to Okeh's warehouse, in Bridgeport, one weekend, dug through a hundred thousand records or so, tore off a fingernail opening crates, and bought enough of the hottest discs to just about corner the market. It was hardly the sort of monopoly to arouse the Department of Justice, because at the moment nobody else wanted the records, and, as a matter of fact, it took Gabler several years to dispose of them. The deal was profitable, however; he paid a dime apiece for some twenty thousand records that he later sold for from thirty-five cents to a dollar. A number of them, changing hands among collectors, have since sold for as much as thirty-five dollars. Another source of supply was the Salvation Army. The Army inevitably came into the possession of a great many records, hot and otherwise, in the course of collecting donations and was only too pleased to sell them for a cent or two apiece. This fountainhead has since dried up; too many collectors found out about it.

Gabler's prescience not only enhanced his already established reputation with jazz enthusiasts but presently brought him to the attention of Jack Kapp, then president of Decca Records. Kapp was a former boy wonder himself, having made Decca one of the big three in the recording business, and he likes to surround himself with Bright Young Men Who Can See a Future in the Organization. In 1941, Decca bought Brunswick from Warner Brothers and thus acquired some six thousand recordings in the Brunswick, Vocalion, and Melotone catalogues, but it didn't do much about them right away. (How a motion picture company happened to own Brunswick in the first place is one of those intricate sagas of big business that will not be dealt with here.) Gabler was already president of two tightly held family corporations, the Commodore Music Shop (founded by his father in 1926) and the Commodore Record Company (founded by himself in 1938), when Kapp discovered him. Gabler was rummaging in the basement of the shop one day when Kapp called up and offered him the job of bringing order out of his chaotic buy. Gabler asked him to hold the wire and explained, when he finally got back to the phone, that he had been looking for a record—a thirty-five-cent record—for a customer. Gabler spent a year classifying Kapp's acquisition, and apparently to everyone's satisfaction, for he is still with Decca, in a Monday-through-Friday job, as supervisor of the recording of all Decca's hot music and some of its sweet stuff. He has not given up the Commodore, however. Until recently he would work in the store evenings and all day Saturday. As a result, he has become something of a split personality, the Commodore side of which used to make Kapp nervous. "I don't want to know anything about Commodore," he told a friend of Gabler's. "Milt's future is with Decca. We modulated him into the general picture. The scope of the world passes in review before anyone's eyes who comes into this office. I've taken Milt out of the local neighborhoods and put him in touch with the world. Why, I've sent him to Chicago and California." The friend remarked that he had watched Gabler make a Commodore recording a few weeks before. "What?" said Kapp. "What's that? What day of the week did that happen?" He seemed only moderately relieved to learn that it had been a Saturday.

In his store, Gabler is noticeably informal, sometimes sweeping the floor while a small but earnest salon of regular customers follows him around. Now and then one of them takes over the broom, and usually a couple more can be found behind the counters, where they appear to be as much at home with the stock as the clerks. The clerks, often as not, are on the wrong side of the counters, talking to some of the musicians who for

THE COMMODORE SHOP AND MILT GABLER 85

more than a decade have regarded the Commodore as a year-round resort. Strangers are apt to become confused by these irregularities and every once in a while one of them asks a visiting pianist or trumpet player to wait on him, which the musician unhesitatingly does. In addition to Gabler and his father, the shop officially has five clerks, one of them a brother, two of them brothers-in-law, and the remaining two not even distantly related to him.

For five years, up through 1945, Gabler devoted his Sunday afternoons to a series of jam sessions he ran, from October to June, in Jimmy Ryan's night club, a narrow, low-ceilinged room on Fifty-second Street which Gabler picked out because of its moral tone. There didn't seem to be any goons hanging around, and Ryan, an ex-hoofer, is an earnest host who sees to it that when patrons ask for rye and water they don't just get watered rye. These jam sessions gave Gabler's customers a place to go when the store was closed—at any rate, from October to June. They showed up at the Ryan sessions season after season, looking as palely intellectual as ever, and sat in rows of chairs on the dance floor or at napkin-sized tables along the walls. The sessions were admired by both the hot men who played in them and the men of the big "commercial" name bands who came to listen to the kind of music their clientele wouldn't put up with. The jazzmen insist that there was a casual quality about the Gabler sessions that is not often achieved by other impresarios. At times it appeared to derive from the bottles he laid out for them behind the drums and to which they addressed themselves between sets. These bottles were judiciously supervised by Dr. Henry Sklow, one of Gabler's closest friends. Dr. Sklow is a small, neat, energetic dentist who finished Tufts Dental School, became a Commodore customer, and established a practice, in that order. He missed only two of the one hundred and fourteen Fifty-second Street routs, once when he was in bed with a temperature of 104 degrees and once when he hit 105.

It was in Ryan's that, in a sense, Gabler achieved fame, an honor which is not generally accorded owners of music stores and which he has worn lightly. The time had come, *Down Beat*, a widely circulated jazz-fan magazine reported, "to thank him publicly for all he had done for jazz and jazz musicians." The occasion was his thirty-second birthday. He was given a cake and a cigarette case, and every hot musician on the street who could get leave for the evening, along with some of their confreres from Greenwich Village, crowded into Ryan's to play ad-lib versions of "Happy Birthday" until 4 A.M. Gabler's wife, Estelle, who used to be a dress model and thus learned patience, had always regarded her husband as an eccentric who, when he didn't stay out most of the night, came home late to play loud jazz records for a few unwholesome-looking companions, and who was profoundly uninterested in her friends, substantial citizens but not jazz lovers. Gabler persuaded her to go to the party. "A few hours after I'd gone to sleep that morning," she recalls, "I woke up and looked at him and I realized he'd done it." She wasn't, when she stopped to think about it, sure just what it was he had done, but she could see why it might keep him out late.

Gabler's wife has become accustomed, if not resigned, to his erratic life. The Gablers and their two children, a six-year-old boy and a one-year-old girl, live in the top half of a two-family house in the Pelham Bay section of the Bronx. Gabler gets home for a late dinner perhaps two nights a week. Other nights, he arrives sometime between 2 and 5 A.M., depending in part on whether he has some important piece of business to transact at a nightclub bar and in part on whether he falls asleep on the subway and rides back to the other end of the line, which he does frequently enough. His nights are spent shuttling between Fifty-second Street and Greenwich Village to hear hot music. He has never been to either the Stork Club or El Morocco, where all the music is either sweet or Latin-American.

To this day, Gabler still presents an unconvincing portrait of a success, being partial to plaid shirts, battered moccasins, and jackets and trousers that not only don't match but don't even not match correctly. The oldest settlers at the Commodore cannot recall seeing him in a conventional suit. In appearance, he combines the more sinister features of Charles Laughton, Sydney Greenstreet and Peter Lorre. Actually, he is a mild individual made slightly mournful by a milieu of which he is a part but which he cannot fully fathom. "He walks like an innocent among the insane," a friend of his has observed. "He must be at least a quiet screwball himself. Otherwise he couldn't stay in the business. Jazz musicians and jazz collectors are frantic characters."

The Commodore's customers are not necessarily insane, but they are often uninhibited, and some of them are certainly off the beaten track. Two of them are inmates of a Connecticut jail who not only buy records by mail but have been cooped up long enough to have written and had published a hot "discography," which is what the trade calls a record directory. Neither one has ever seen the store. Then there is an Astoria undertaker who frequently drives to the Commodore in a hearse, sometimes stopping to pick up a client on his way over. He used to park in front of the place and stroll in in the grim garments of his trade. Gabler, a trifle worn from receiving condolences, finally persuaded the hot mortician to park his hearse down the block and leave his black gloves and hat in it when he comes to call. It is stashed in front of a saloon these days. Some customers, including one maharajah, have travelled literally halfway around the world to see the store and then have got lost in the lobby of the Hotel Commodore across the street. When they have at last found the right place, they may, as did an emotional Puerto Rican who had never before been in the United States, burst into happy tears upon being introduced to the proprietor. Gabler always rises handsomely to these occasions. He took the Puerto Rican into a booth, accepted an expensive cigar, and played a number of recent test pressings of Commodore records for him. The visitor was overwhelmed by Gabler's attention and Gabler was overwhelmed by the visitor's cigar. The booths at the Commodore are just large enough to accommodate one man and one small boy. Gabler used to decorate them with signs which read, "Certainly we allow smoking in the booths, but they're your lungs." It is protocol at the Commodore for a customer, as he leaves a booth, to fan the smoke out of it by swinging the door.

Gabler now and then thinks of installing soundproof booths, a project from which he has to be dissuaded by his customers, who like to hear what is going on in adjacent cubicles and are as likely to buy what someone else is playing as what they are playing themselves. The composition-board walls lend themselves nicely to art and legend, like the caves in the Pyrenees. Among the impromptu embellishments are the signatures of The Independent Dukes; Jimmy, Moose, Moe, and Mike; Sappy Sy, Oak Irish, Kind Face, and Hairy Harry; the Hot Club of Flatbush; the Deacon of Dodge City; the Olinville Avenue Ostentations, and Rim Shot Bill. Practically every Greek-letter fraternity in the land has registered in one booth or another. One draftsman with a surrealist turn of mind did the late Fats Waller as an overstuffed sofa and Eddie Condon, the hot guitarist, as a guitar in the Braque manner. In the Madison Avenue music shops, such things are considered bad form. These shops concede the Commodore's preeminence in a highly specialized field and steer any number of customers Gabler's way. The Commodore's hold over the international jazz set was demonstrated a couple of years ago by a correspondent who described himself as the "part co-organizer and recitalist of the Portsmouth Jazz Club and Ryde, Isle of Wight, and Fareham Portchester Jazz Conversion Society." He wrote Gabler that England's determination to get on with the war was all that prevented him from hastening to his side. "You are the King Pin of it all," he wrote, while robot bombs were falling within a few yards of him, smashing the society's Commodore imports and British national monuments. "You alone are responsible for the great output of jazz that we, the fans, enjoy." The part co-organizer added that a fellow of the society had reduced the membership to a state of mute admiration one evening when he remarked that he had a Commodore record of his own. The letter ended with a plan for the improvement of Anglo-American relations. "I'm hoping," it said, "to see an Allied jam session after this war, recorded at Commodore by British and American musicians."

A more fortunate Briton was one of the sub-editors of the *London Times*, also a hot fan, who was sent to this country on a journalistic errand at the height of the German submarine warfare in the Atlantic. He checked in at the store and bought two copies of "Strange Fruit," a chilling ballad about lynching that Billie Holiday, the celebrated torch singer of Fifty-second Street, had recorded for Commodore. The *Times* man took one with him and asked that the other be shipped to England. "One of us," he said to Gabler, "will get through." Because of its subject matter, which would not be likely to interest the average record company, "Strange Fruit" is often cited by Gabler's admirers as an outstanding example of his "sincerity," a term loosely construed in the hot trade to mean rectitude of a high order, or a disregard for money. This particular example of "sincerity," however, has furnished Gabler with his biggest commercial success. He has sold fifty thousand copies of "Strange Fruit" since the master record was cut in 1939, which is considerably more copies than he has sold of any other Commodore record. If a hot record he gets out goes over five or six thousand, it is considered a sensation. As a best seller, though, "Strange Fruit" scarcely ranks with Victor's "Chattanooga Choo-Choo," which sold over a million copies in one year. "Chattanooga Choo-Choo" is neither blue, hot, nor grim; its subject is Southern but noncontroversial. The Commodore recording of "Strange Fruit" was, until quite recently, the only one on the market. Keynote, another small recording company, recently had Josh White, the Negro folk singer, do it. The major companies have avoided it. Gabler was able to get Miss Holiday to make it for him only because Miss Holiday's employer, then Columbia, was afraid of it and was happy to let Commodore do it instead. Miss Holiday has since become a Decca performer, principally because of Gabler. He disclaims any social motive for making the record. "I did it for kicks," he says. "It was exciting." "Kicks" and "exciting" are important words in his vocabulary. He uses them as convenient, if inadequate, capsule descriptions of his reaction to the things that please him. He feels exactly the same way about Commodore's Eddie Condon record of "A Good Man Is Hard to Find," whose message is only vaguely sociological, as he does about "Strange Fruit."

Until 1940, the Commodore did business—or didn't do business—in a gloomy little establishment only nine feet wide, which was at No. 144 East Forty-second Street, several doors east of its second location, No. 136. The store somehow got through the early thirties, when, because of the wonders of radio, it was considered eccentric to own a phonograph. The shop at that time concentrated on other things—exploding cigars, dribble glasses, sneeze powder, rubber frankfurters, cameras, golf clubs, and Christmas cards, as well as such prize collectors' items as Louis Armstrong's playing of "On the Sunny Side of the Street" for the French Brunswick company. "It was a dingy, badly arranged, and hideous little firetrap," one of Gabler's old customers affectionately recalls. "A visit to the basement was really slumming. And when I think of some of the weirdies and weevils who used to infest that store! There was Milt, a very solid character, getting bald and developing a wonderful taste, sitting right in the middle of the damnedest collection of people and being responsible for the fact that you could buy absolutely first-rate jazz unloused up by commercialism." The Gabler taste became more and more wonderful as the years passed, and he plainly kept on avoiding commercialism, since in his best year he managed to be twelve thousand dollars behind in the rent and to owe other record companies more than eight thousand dollars. The Commodore's entire stock and fixtures were worth only about ten thousand dollars. Meanwhile the store was going broke trying to buy every hot record in existence. It almost succeeded in doing both. "Our credit was good," Gabler says today. "We owed everybody." The landlord, a somehow complaisant estate, murmured now and then but stayed its hand. Possibly there was no alternative. "I guess," says Gabler, who now pays his rent every month, "those estate people financed almost everyone on the block in those days except the theatre and the shoe-repair joint." For the Commodore, it was a nervous era of postdated checks. There was rarely anything in the cash register besides paper clips and night-club due bills.

In 1939, Gabler's father, who had started the Commodore as a radio shop and had finally turned its management over to his son, who converted it into a hot-music center, sank his last fifteen hundred dollars in his son's baffling new business. The store's books consisted for the most part of old envelopes, bits of brown wrapping paper, hat-check stubs, menus, and pages torn from record catalogues. The elder Gabler was astounded whenever an inventory revealed that the Commodore actually had on hand as many records as the books said were there. Why anyone should buy them, however, was beyond him. Gratified collectors told him Milton was a great man. This only increased his sorrowful puzzlement. How many collectors were there in the world, he wondered. He survived the years of doubt, and today he has a large financial interest in the business. He is now treasurer of both the store and the record company and is downcast only when a new competitor appears in the recording field. He is convinced that there will never be another store like his son's. When deliveries arrive, he supervises the opening of the boxes and albums, examines the records for flaws, playing them on a phonograph near the front of the store with a great show of technical knowledge. Jazz, like his son, bewilders him, but he is reconciled to it, now that he realizes it is a business.

When the old days became perilously difficult, record salesmen demanded cash on delivery, plus ten per cent of the back bill, with interest. They were still snapping at his heels when Gabler really gave them something to complain about by quietly starting to make his own recordings. The salesmen, when they discovered this, accused him of putting all his money into Commodore "dates," as recording sessions are called, instead of paying up. They even dug up evidence and began waving it in his face. The August 8, 1938, issue of Life contained photographs of a Commodore recording session. "Eddie Condon, guitar," read one of the captions, "worries over a point with Milton Gabler, who produced the records." (*It wasn't a point, it was a pint.—E.C.*) The salesmen demanded that Gabler do some worrying about the bills, too. "Doesn't it say here," one of them asked, " 'Gabler runs the Commodore Music Shop in Manhattan, mecca for hot-record collectors'?" Unable to deny such loud impeachments, Gabler would go through his pockets and collect enough money to appease his creditors for a day or so. Then he would retreat down the block to an inconspicuous bar known as the White Rose. There, over a glass of Irish whiskey and a beer chaser, he would plan another record date. Quite often he would be roused from his reverie by some jobless jazz musician plucking at his sleeve. Such men always knew where to find him. If he was not in the store, he was almost certain to be in the White Rose, elbows on the bar, underlip thrust out, in the midst of a vision of millions of people buying hot records and jazz musicians earning two hundred dollars a week. Then a ten-dollar bill secreted from the record salesmen might be split with a hungry clarinetist possessing a hallowed reputation and one shirt. Gabler optimistically called these touches "advances" for the man's next date, and occasionally they were. Sometimes the boys got four or five dates ahead; no one was ever quite sure which. Gabler's business arrangements with musicians have always been offhand; he has never signed a contract with the men who record for him.

Gabler has, among his mementos of this period, a broken drumhead from Zutty Singleton, an outstanding Negro drummer, on which is inscribed, "Milt, I've got to call you Mr. W.P.A. because you have been very good to poor band boys. I know, because I am one of them." Jazz musicians, recalling the bad years, are apt to be enthusiastic about Gabler. The tendency is especially strong in the men who play at Eddie Condon's and Nick's, two citadels of hot music in Greenwich Village. These men, an ordinarily diffident and suspicious crew, sentimentally call Gabler "the musician's friend." Condon says aggressively, "Milt picked me up off the floor." Having been assisted to his feet, he did not forget. He signed a contract with Decca some time ago only on condition that he be permitted to keep on making Commodore records too. Condon had received so much publicity because of his Town Hall and Carnegie Hall jazz concerts that he was in a position to say, when he was negotiating with the officials of one company that wanted him without any Commodore strings, "Where were you when all I was doing was making records for Milt Gabler? I make records for you, I make records for Milt. That's one thing you've got to put down."

Gabler was born on May 20, 1911, in an apartment house at 116th Street and St. Nicholas Avenue, a building he says his mother thought must be famous because it had an elevator. He was the first of Susie and Julius Gabler's six children. Mrs. Gabler, who was born in New York, had a great-great-grandfather who was chief rabbi of Vilna when that city was an imperial Russian possession. Her husband, to whom she was married in this country in 1909, came over here from a small Austrian village when he was thirteen. The village bullies beat him severely one day in the schoolyard for being a Jew and he went home in tears. His father gave him a large part of the family savings and sent him off to America. Julius worked briefly for an uncle who had a hardware store on Vesey Street, and then he became a streetcar conductor.

Milton's childhood was so unexceptional that it is little more than a pleasant blur in his mind. The family had a summer cottage at Silver Beach, in Throg's Neck. Gabler thinks that it was at Silver Beach that he fell in love with jazz. There was a wooden dance pavilion at the beach to which came a number of jazz bands, all of them undistinguished. Milton, in the terminal period of a singularly placid adolescence, learned to dance, but he preferred just standing near the bandstand and listening. He felt, however, that there was a certain monotony in the music, for each band played its tunes the same way every time. The reason, which he came to realize later on, was that the musicians played the songs the way they were written. He wanted something more, and he knows now that unscored music, in the form of hot and, as the phrase goes, inspired solos, was what he was yearning for.

Gabler's public-school career was hardly promising musically. At Stuyvesant High, from which he graduated in 1928, music was optional, and he didn't take it. Nevertheless, while he was still in high school he got himself into the record business by sheer persistence. His father then owned a small hardware store, on Third Avenue near Forty-second Street, as well as the Commodore, at 144 East Forty-second Street, which was several doors east of the present store. Milton was put to work in the hardware store after school. He professed an intense interest in nails, screw drivers, locks, wire, and hammers, but he cast an impatient eye at the Commodore. He asked one day whether it would be all right if he transferred to the radio shop. No one objected, whereupon Milton added casually that it wouldn't be a bad idea for the store to stock a few phonographs and records. After making the unnecessary proviso that Milton would have to handle all that himself, his father, who hadn't the slightest intimation of what lay ahead, said yes. The first order Gabler put in was for a hundred and fifty records, all current hit tunes made by popular bands, but nothing to get excited about, Gabler says today. Milton finished high school and started to take a business course at City College, whose commercial branch was then in Grand Central Palace, conveniently near the store.

It remained for an amorous radio salesman and repair man employed by his father to remove the last barrier between Milton and his destiny. This salesman had reason to believe that he had as much of a way with women as he did with aerials, a conviction in which he was confirmed by quite a few girls kept in East Side apartments by Wall Street brokers who had survived the grisly incidents of October, 1929. A large number of radios broke down in the neighborhood, and the salesman devoted so much time to fixing them that Milton missed a lot of classes at City College because he had to fill in for him. Finally the man was fired. Milton was put in charge of the radio-and-phonograph department, gave up the business course, and began to run up big bills for records. Before long, the records pushed the radios right out of the place, or at least into the basement. He still hadn't found himself, however, for most of his early purchases left him emotionally cold. Every once in a while, though, he would be stirred when a trumpet departed on a garish, apparently uncharted course or a clarinet made wholly unexpected sounds. Thus he listened to the music of Duke Ellington's orchestra and was tremendously moved by the trumpet solos of Bubber Miley and the clarinet of Barney Bigard, and Louis Armstrong's trumpeting had a similar appeal for him. Gabler began to concentrate on the kind of music that excited him. Happily for his career, it was around this time that his father gave him a financial interest in the store and turned over the management to him.

Like many other radio stores of the period, the Commodore had a loudspeaker above the door. Gabler played his favorite hot records over it so persistently that he attracted the nucleus of his present clientele rather quickly. He also attracted the police, who were in the midst of an anti-noise campaign. The loudspeaker was removed in the early thirties at their request, but by then the jazz set, instead of just listening on the sidewalk, had come inside. This group included not only young gentlemen from Yale, Harvard, and Princeton but somewhat older jazz lovers, mostly in publishing and advertising, who worked in the neighborhood. Both varieties provided Gabler with spiritual direction. They began by being kindly disposed toward a man who would play music all day that most people could not endure for an hour. From this they passed to the matter of further improving his taste. Gabler took eagerly to instruction and ended up by teaching his masters. The Ivy League boys dutifully came to class weekends and returned Sunday night to school to fill columns in their undergraduate publications with news about the Commodore Music Shop. Some of them were even permitted to work there during vacations. The advertising and magazine men spent their lunch hours, evenings, and all day Saturday at the Commodore. Eventually the shop became so popular that Gabler opened a branch on West Fifty-second Street, in the middle of the hot-music belt. The branch store did well, but after three giddy years Gabler decided to close it down because of the wartime shortage of both manpower and records. Before he did, however, Howard Bay, the theatrical designer, got so fond of the place that he worked up a window display that would have done for Saks-Fifth Avenue. "Just a little diorama gadget," Bay now says deprecatingly. "Just a little New Orleans sort of gadget." The gadget, which was never installed, was to have had a street scene and an interior of Mahogany Hall, a famous, long since departed New Orleans bagnio. It was in Mahogany Hall and lesser bordellos, during the early nineteen-hundreds, that, according to one determined school of thought, jazz was born. Bay planned to set up figurines of a number of the old-time musicians and a couple of the well-known girls of the era. Gabler liked the idea, but the Fifty-second Street store closed before Bay got the diorama finished. Gabler has lately thought that it would dress up the Forty-second Street store and he plans to call Bay in on the project soon.

Almost anything would dress up the Forty-second Street store. It has an anonymous exterior which gives it, in a dingy block of saloons, fruit stores, and shoe-shine parlors, a sort of protective coloration. A red-and-white electric sign, bearing the name Commodore, hangs at the entrance. There are records in the windows, and a number of the fancy albums the big companies now put their products in, but even these contrive to look tired and cheerless. Gabler trims the windows himself when he finds time, which he almost never does. One of his most recent innovations was strewing a few imitation flowers over the records. The neighboring shoe-shine parlor, with its gaudy neon tubing and its clock in the window, makes a much bigger splash. It is three times the size of the present Commodore and at least six times as big as the old place, which had a frontage of only nine feet. When the store moved, in 1940, Gabler, his father, his brothers, four other clerks, and whatever customers were around simply packed up everything and staggered westward from No. 144 to No. 136. The job took five hours. The new place is very much like the old one, only bigger. It has seven record booths; the other had two. No carpeting, no indirect lighting, no chromium—just a dump. Or, as Eddie Condon once said, "It's a shrine—the crummiest shrine in the world."

Gabler never feels that he has to get away from his customers. A couple of them usually wander around at night with him as he shambles from one hot-music establishment to another on Fifty-second Street or in the Village. Or, at the end of the business day, a few of them may help him close up shop, draw the shade over the door, and settle down with him to what one of them calls his "at homes." A considerable amount of liquor, provided mostly by Gabler, occasionally by the customers, has been consumed at these gatherings. It is seemingly an indispensable aid to the critical examination of new records and the hatching of plans for the future of hot music. One warm summer night in 1935, out of a haze of Tom Collinses, there emerged a remarkable, if evanescent, project. While Gabler, perspiring in his undershirt, was looking for a fresh glass, one of his customers, Marshall Stearns, then a Yale jazz enthusiast, turned off the phonograph they had been listening to and said, apropos of nothing that had gone before, "Milt, we ought to organize them."

"Organize what?" Gabler asked.

"Hot clubs, Milt," Stearns said. "The way they do in Europe. A national organization, thousands of clubs, headquarters right here in the Commodore." He paused for a moment, then said, "We could call it the United Hot Clubs of America."

Gabler, who is accustomed to the hatching of large ideas by

his patrons, said indulgently, "All right. I'll reissue a lot of good records under that label. We can print a magazine and hold jam sessions."

Stearns said, "I'll write to Hammond and Panassié right away."

"That's it," Gabler said amiably. "You go right ahead and tell them all about it."

John Hammond, an affectionate partisan of the Commodore, was in Europe on that particular night, but that did not prevent his being elected honorary president of the U.H.C.A. by Gabler and Stearns. Hammond also wrote Hugues Panassié, the French jazz expert, about the new organization, and he sent it his blessings. Stearns became secretary and Gabler treasurer and a number of membership cards were printed for the Commodore clientele. A board of directors, made up of a dozen New York Jazz authorities, held two or three very casual meetings, published a couple of high-toned pronunciamentos on pink paper, and then disbanded, satisfied that the U.H.C.A. would flourish because of its virtuous intent. It quickly sickened and died, leaving behind it only the name, which Gabler used as a label on fifty-seven records he put out within the next five years—reissues of old Brunswick, Vocalion, Okeh, and other companies' hot records to which he had leased the rights. The U.H.C.A. reissues not only brought back into currency such classics as Frank Teschemacher's "Prince of Wails" and Louis Armstrong's "Potato Head Blues" but, for the first time in record history, listed the personnel of the bands and the instrument each man played. Also for the first time, the labels were designed so that they would look good while revolving, an innovation perhaps not quite as overwhelming. This second idea was contributed by Richard Edes Harrison, the *Time* cartographer, who had been a member of the U.H.C.A.'s board of directors. For years, Harrison had been annoyed by the way records looked in motion.

Late in 1937, Gabler decided to make his own recordings. This decision was arrived at in the same informal, rather tangential manner in which he makes all decisions. It had occurred to him that simply reissuing jazz classics was not really reviving the idiom or giving it all the nourishment it so obviously needed. Also, the companies whose records he had reissued had refused to sell him the master records outright, and he suspected that if the U.H.C.A. discs became at all popular, the companies would take back their masters and start doing what he had done. That, as a matter of fact, is just what happened. For reasons no one can explain, no new hot music—as distinguished from popular dance music—had been recorded for some four years when Gabler made his decision to put out new records of authentic unscored, "uncommercial" hot music. The hot musicians themselves, he reasoned, had undoubtedly dug up a few new ideas since the old days and might like to record them. He expressed some of these thoughts to Eddie Condon, whom he found wildly receptive. He and Condon rounded up Pee Wee Russell, clarinetist, George Brunis, trombonist, and Bobby Hackett, cornetist, all three of whom were then playing at Nick's, a celebrated Greenwich Village bar-and-grill; George Wettling, drummer, who was in Red Norvo's orchestra; Artie Shapiro, bass player, of Joe Marsala's orchestra; Bud Freeman, tenor saxophonist, of Tommy Dorsey's orchestra; and Jess Stacy, pianist, of Benny Goodman's orchestra. The first Commodore "date," as a recording session is called in the trade, was held on January 18, 1938. This is considered by many specialists the most significant event in hot music since the birth of Louis Armstrong. The scene was a bleak but technically excellent midtown studio owned by one of the big recording companies. Gabler gave the musicians a brief, prayerful talk, Condon (who acted as conductor as well as instrumentalist) tapped his foot twice to set the tempo, and the eight performers, who had never before played together as a unit and were working without any written-down music, made eight recordings, improvising from beginning to end. Since then, Gabler has made something like a hundred hot jazz records. He has hired the finest white and Negro musicians he could and he has got results from them that are usually conceded to be better than those achieved by his competitors.

Hot musicians have given a number of explanations of why they do neater work for Gabler than for other recording men. "There's a ray comes out of him," one of them has said. "You can't help doing something the way he wants. Here is this guy can't read a note of music and he practically tells you what register you're going to play in just by the position of your head." Gabler himself thinks that perhaps he has a mesmeric appeal. "Maybe I'm a Svengali," he says. "Maybe they're more relaxed and they'll do things for me that might give me a kick where they wouldn't for anyone else."

As a rule, Gabler is perspiring, but still tender with admiration, at the end of a recording session. "They've got such big souls," he said to one of his friends not long ago, after a nervous date during which an accomplished but intemperate pianist had passed out. "One guy hits on something and the others pick it right up and there they are, composing while they play. The thrill I get is not knowing what's going to happen. I never can tell when I'm going to be lifted right out of my seat. That doesn't come with arranged music. You don't get knocked out. You don't get the bottom, the drive, the punch, the big, fat, hot note. A musician's got to have a heart and be able to play pretty things, too, things that say something different, when he takes a solo, and not just what he's heard somewhere else. He's got to know where the time is and be able to push and drive and not just be in there for the ride. He's got to know his instrument. Guys that know their instruments don't get lost. They know how to play the song and improvise on it and then come back and play what it is. Of course, when you get one of those frantic characters sitting in, he'll mess up everything and throw everybody off. I don't like those screamadeemas on the horn who have to make faces and blow high. That isn't jazz. A lot of people don't know that. Those guys get out on a limb and then they can't come back. They get themselves a one-way ticket to nowhere. Then they miss, and it's the worst thing in the world. You're following a thing and building it with one of these characters and suddenly he misses a note. He leaves you on the top floor and the whole works collapses. You don't have to raise the roof to create something."

In the process of delivering such oral essays, which he does only rarely, Gabler may bring up a plan to which he has given a great deal of thought. "I'd like to set up a foundation someday," he said on this occasion, "so that these hot men can get something in their old age out of the records they made in their prime—something like an A.S.C.A.P., with a special point system. Say you'd have a board and they would decide whether it was the trumpet or the clarinet or the trombone that made the record go, and the guy who did would get a certain number of points. Only thing bothers me is how you'd go about getting an agreement on the musicians who should get the dough. And there ought to be a foundation for the encouragement of new talent, too. The new crop'll be coming along now that the war is over. I don't know how it'll all happen, but it will.

"You know," he went on, with the air of a man confiding a secret, "it's not a nice thing to say, but some of the hot boys today came up from places of ill repute. Especially in Chicago. A musician would come out of high school and right away he'd get a hundred or a hundred and fifty bucks a week and what did he run into? Racketeers, loose women, pimps, and whatever else they ran into during prohibition. People with dough would take them home for a laugh or maybe a gal would get her hooks into them. Maybe the grind they went through in those years improved their music. Maybe we'll even go through some sort of cycle like that again and the clubs will start to jump. But maybe the music will develop without the terrible things you used to run into. Maybe a foundation would do as much good as a gin mill."

WHITNEY BALLIETT

Pandemonium Pays Off

THERE ARE TWO schools of thought on Norman Granz. One says that he has done more for jazz than anybody else in the country, and the other says he has done more for Norman Granz than he has for jazz. Both schools are partly true. Norman is the most active promoter anywhere around, and he is also one of the few strictly honest guys in the promoting end. Whitney Balliett here presents a high objective picture of "Mr. Jazz." Whitney is on the staff of the New Yorker and also writes for the Saturday Review, in which this story appeared in 1954.
E. C.

Some years ago, when jazz became portly enough to warrant its own cortege of critics, one began hearing, among other things, that this new music was an art of revolt. Nevertheless, just as this land was once a wind-rolled wilderness that has since been urbanely corseted by conveyor belts, advertising agencies, and respectability, so jazz has finally run head on into its potential master. He is Norman Granz, a lean, fast-talking, sandy-haired man of thirty-seven, who sends out single-handedly over a good part of the Western world a yearly series of jazz concert tours known as "Jazz at the Philharmonic" (JATP to the intimate), owns and operates a record company that has mushroomed so violently in the past few years that it has had to be split into three companies to accommodate overworked distribution facilities, and, as a canny, granitic businessman and the hope and fear of the rest of the jazz promotion world, is generally regarded as the first person who has ever been able to successfully mass-produce jazz.

The total worth of these enterprises is currently estimated by Granz at five million dollars. Of this, a million accrues from JATP, and the rest from his record firm. These staggering sums—staggering, at least, for jazz, since it was not long ago that jazz-men were frequently reported dying of malnutrition and exposure—are easily accounted for, if not easily explained. In 1955, JATP included eleven jazz musicians and a singer, who played in fifty-four American and Canadian cities where seventy-two concerts were held, as well as in twenty-five cities in Europe, where some fifty concerts occurred. The group appeared before approximately 400,000 persons, who paid from $2 to $4.80 for their seats.

Granz's recording activities, which are hastily sandwiched in between tours and business trips abroad, were equally cornucopic. Almost one hundred ten- and twelve-inch jazz LP albums were released on the Clef and Norgran labels, with a recent month finding a dozen new Granz albums flowing into record stores across the country. Columbia and Victor, who have again returned to the marketing of jazz in a big way, managed to release about forty albums apiece. In fact, perhaps fifty per cent of all the jazz records released last year came from Granz factories, a development that has become somewhat of an uneasy joke in the industry. Granz's recording efforts, in addition to being abundant, are encyclopedic. At present his catalogue lists seven LPs devoted to the work of Lester Young. Art Tatum is represented by twelve twelve-inch LPs, with more promised. Charlie Parker has eight, in addition to a three-record, $15 memorial album. Johnny Hodges has six. And Oscar Peterson, the thirty-year-old Canadian pianist, who has virtually been handmaidened into fame by Granz and has since become the Granz house pianist, now has twenty albums to his credit.

Granz, or "Mr. Jazz," as he is often affectionately referred to by his admirers, was born in Los Angeles, and attended UCLA, where, as a part-time quotation clerk with the Los Angeles Stock Exchange, he picked up some useful rudiments about money. After college and a stint in the Army, which was followed by a film editor's job at M-G-M, Granz, who was a jazz fan and a strong liberal, decided that jazz should be listened to in the pleasantest possible surroundings by the largest possible number of people of all races, creeds, and colors. The non-segregational concert hall was the answer. After running a series of successful informal concerts at the Los Angeles Philharmonic Auditorium he took, in the fall of 1945, a hand-picked group of musicians on a limited tour of the Western United States and Canada.

Unfortunately, the public, unlike Barkis, was not willing, and the tour collapsed in Canada after working its way up the West Coast. A few years later, with the assistance of names on the Granz payroll like Gene Krupa, Coleman Hawkins, Bill Harris, Flip Phillips, and Buddy Rich, and with the release of the first of eighteen on-the-spot recordings of JATP concerts, the public changed its mind. In the meantime, Granz had not forgotten his liberal instincts. He succeeded in taking his groups, which have been a consistent mixture of Negro and white, into those parts of the country where racial bias still persists, and three years ago had a rider put in certain of his contracts with theatre owners to the effect that if he, Granz, finds that any discrimination is practised against his audiences, the concert may be immediately cancelled.

Since the shaky days of 1945 Granz's acquaintances have been continually astonished by his drive and durability in a notoriously unsympathetic business. He works without any regular assistants, outside of a few harassed secretaries and a publicity agent—an office-in-the-hat type of operation that prompted an associate to refer to Granz the other day as a "walking corporation." Granz books almost all of his own concerts, an accomplishment that was of some proportions in the pioneering days, and that has since been partially alleviated by his practise of booking future concerts in a city while his men are playing it. In line with his recent efforts to give his enterprises a single, well-honed edge, Granz sometimes schedules concerts in new cities on the strength of his record sales in that city, for the roster of his recording artists, which numbers well over a hundred, is a fairly accurate mirror, past and present, of the personnel he has had in his various JATP groups.

Granz attends every concert JATP gives, acting as both M.C. and stage manager. Out front, he seems an almost timid figure, for he is distinguished in neither voice nor presence. Backstage, however, Granz is like a hurricane on the wax. "I go crazy at concerts," he said recently. "I lose my temper every five minutes. I yell at everybody. I'm rude. Every concert has got to go perfectly. If somebody goofs he pays for it." But if Granz is inflammable under pressure he is generally of temperate mien. Most of his musicians like working for him, and return to JATP year in and year out. There are, from time to time familial eruptions, of course, such as a falling out (which was recently repeated) a few years ago between Granz and Buddy Rich, the drummer. Rich blatantly announced through the pages of *Down Beat* magazine that he was through with JATP because Granz made his musicians play nothing but "junk." Granz answered by saying hotly that he never told his musicians what to play, and that Rich was a "liar" and an "adolescent." A short time later Rich was contentedly thumping away on a new Granz recording date, and appeared, as usual, in last year's JATP lineup.

Granz the businessman has occasionally made profitable room for Granz the jazz lover. In 1944, for instance, he supervised the only honest motion picture ever made about jazz. A short, photographed in color by Gjon Mili, and called "Jammin' the Blues," it won an Academy Award nomination for the best short feature of the year. (Many of the musicians involved, naturally, were drawn from the Granz-sponsored concert group then appearing in Los Angeles.) In 1949, when he was using the facilities of the Mercury record company, he issued a deluxe twelve-inch 78-rpm album which featured such oddities as Harry Carney, the baritone saxophone player, pitted against strings; the unorthodox arrangements of George Handy and Ralph Burns; an extraordinary unaccompanied saxophone solo by Coleman Hawkins, and generous quantities of the progressive music of Bud Powell and Charlie Parker. The album had, in addition, a folio of gorgeous jazz photographs, and the whole package, five thousand of which were printed, was priced at a cool twenty-five dollars. It was sold out in a year.

Granz was the first person to experiment widely with on-the-spot recordings, and with studio recordings that took advantage of the longer playing time per side of the LP. Record stores have been reordering them ever since. Three years ago he released a set of four twelve-inch LPs titled "The Astaire Story," which showed off Fred Astaire's singing and the sound of his dancing before a small Granz-picked jazz unit. It was widely panned by the critics, but has been just as widely accepted by the record-buying public, which tends to ignore critics, a fact that Granz is well aware of.

The products which Granz offers his public are accurate reflections of the bipartite Granz personality. Granz the businessman, who has, however, become increasingly dominant in recent years, is most aggressive when he is near the concert stage. Here he believes that a small-group, working within a loose musical framework, is the surest means of producing satisfying, freewheeling jazz. He chooses musicians who are the best or the near-best on their instruments regardless of school or style. This does not mean that Granz would be apt to hire an excellent, but largely unknown musician, for he is never unconscious of the drawing power of a name. (If Granz decides, though, that a certain musician, who is not well known, should become a member of a future JATP tour, he carefully builds his name during the preceding year by releasing several LPs featuring that musician's work.)

The result of these policies is a kind of nervous jazz that is somewhere between small-band swing and bebop. It is also a purely solo jazz, where collective improvisation or teamwork are left to other, more pedestrian jazzmen. This concentration on jazz as a solo art has brought off some weird musical achievements. One is a regularly featured trumpet battle—Roy Eldridge and his old pupil Dizzy Gillespie were the participants last year—

in which two trumpeters squeal at each other for chorus after chorus like a brace of stuck pigs. Another is a blinding, deafening drum battle, that invariably jellies the stoutest audience. Most of the musical materials employed are banal, being restricted to the blues at a variety of tempos, and to such weary evergreens as "How High the Moon" and a handful of Gershwin tunes.

From close observation Granz feels that the average age level of his audiences has increased in the past nine years, and that it is now somewhere between twenty-one and twenty-eight, which is probably a rather casual statistic, judging by the oceans of heated teenage faces one can find at any Granz concert. One might at first describe these audiences as the spiritual offspring of the sprites who jitter-bugged in the aisles and on the stage of the Paramount Theatre in New York in the late thirties when Benny Goodman first came to town. But at second glance, these present-day audiences are of a different, and more war-like tribe. They rarely move from their seats, yet they manage to give off through a series of screams—(the word "go" repeated like the successive slams of the cars on a fast freight), blood-stopping whistles, and stamping feet a mass intensity that would have soothed Hitler, and frightened the pants off Benny Goodman.

Granz the jazz lover is predominantly visible through his studio recording sessions. In these he has been responsible for a certain amount of excellent jazz, as well as a great deal of musical mediocrity. Granz officiates at every recording date, and ominously announces this fact on every record label and record sleeve with, respectively, the words "Recorded Under the Personal Supervision of Norman Granz" and "Supervised by Norman Granz." He also composes many of the liner notes for his albums, which have become noted for barrages of adjectives and their lack of information. Although Granz, as has been mentioned above, claims that he never dictates to his musicians, much of what emanates from his recording studios has come to have a distinct flavor. This flavor, as an observer recently pointed out, is reminiscent of good roast beef that has been left in the icebox too long. For, in spite of the fact that their personnels are often laundry lists of jazz royalty, many Granz records are, peculiarly, boring and cold. One reason for this may be that a good number of the musicians who appear on Granz recordings are also members of JATP, and, because of the nature of the music they must play seven months out of the year on the concert stage, their musical batteries, as it were, have gone dead. And if the requirements of a touring job with Granz often make his musicians artistically laconic, these requirements have also seriously stunted the musical growth of such talented men as Flip Phillips, Charlie Shavers and Buddy Rich.

When Granz inaugurated last year's JATP tour in Hartford, he had on his payroll eleven of the best jazz musicians money can buy. He paid them salaries that started at several hundred dollars a week, and ranged up to $6,000 a week for Ella Fitzgerald and $5,000 a week for Oscar Peterson. In addition to the European tour, which took place in the spring, and the fall tour of the United States and Canada, Granz released $400 worth of LP albums in those twelve months. To at least half a million potential customers around the world, Granz was doing for jazz what another prestidigitator, P. T. Barnum, did for midgets.

JOHN CROSBY

The Sun Never Sets

ANYBODY WHO DOUBTED that American music is spreading far and wide had only to read the newspaper accounts of the reception that European jazz fans accorded Louis Armstrong when he went on his triumphal tour in the fall and early winter of 1955. Hopelessly addicted doubters are also invited to look at Ernest Borneman's piece elsewhere in this book. Here is John Crosby, the distinguished radio and television columnist of the New York Herald Tribune and other newspapers, writing from, of all places, Zanzibar. Has Outer Mongolia reported in yet? I'm sure they must have a fan or two up there.

E. C.

Zanzibar

The sun, I keep telling the British colonials who surround the very pleasant bar of the Sailing Club here, never sets on Irving Berlin. Nor, for that matter on Cole Porter or George Gershwin or many another American popular composer. American popular music has swept around the world and has crossed borders that nothing else can get across in a way that, I think, has never been properly appreciated in the country of its origin.

You can hear American music in the oddest places and in the oddest forms. In the Tivoli Gardens in Copenhagen, a city whose charms have not been exaggerated by the S.A.S. which flew me there, I heard a symphony orchestra—about 150 pieces, I'd guess —do a symphonic rendition of "Way Down Upon The Swanee River," a body of water which is an awful long way from the Baltic.

Just the other night, a couple of us rented a rickshaw and attended a native dance out in the back woods here. There was a trumpet and drums and some stringed instruments and the music the boys were playing sounded as if it came straight out of Harlem. Well, I realize that Harlem and New Orleans are indebted to Africa for their rhythms and for many basic melodies. But melodies had certainly never been played in this way in native villages until they had been considerably retouched by Harlem, New Orleans and just possibly Chicago—and then returned to the land from which they sprang.

I have long since become accustomed to hearing American music in the bars and nightclubs all over Europe, but it gets into many other less obvious crannies. Listening to the radio station in Nairobi night after night in the wilds, we heard Dinah Shore, Frank Sinatra and the ubiquitous Bing Crosby singing songs they had recorded years ago.

American jazz in its purer forms had actually been kept alive in Europe, especially in France, while for a period of six to ten years it was under eclipse in America. It is still going strong in Europe, and since the war its influence has crept past some mighty unfriendly border guards. In the Iron Curtain countries American jazz has been repeatedly denounced as a nefarious form of American hooliganism, but it's a form of hooliganism that the authorities have had great difficulty in suppressing.

Addiction to jazz is a very virulent mania indeed. By making it illicit, the authorities have just made jazz that much more enticing. Teen-age addicts in Czechoslovakia and Hungary gather furtively around their radios and listen to new American jazz records, many of them played on our Armed Forces network. The moment the record is over, the addict sets himself down to record

—by what method I have no idea—not only the melody but also the arrangement. And then he and his pals have a jam session, reproducing a recording that was pressed in Chicago. That last scene from the Broadway hit "Silk Stockings" where the Muscovites play bootlegged American jazz in the Russian capital is not so far from reality.

I have always been intrigued by what the Europeans do to our dances. You can still see the Big Apple, a dance that hasn't been around back home for quite awhile, danced in France with a classical precision that it never had in the states. I keep thinking Sol Hurok is missing a bet in not getting a troupe of these French kids together to reintroduce into this country that wildly exuberant dance.

In a Roman nightclub, I was watching a couple of good looking young Italian kids doing a dance that seemed vaguely familiar. It was a couple of minutes before I realized they were doing the Charleston. Like the Big Apple, it had undergone some extensive alterations. Under the soft Italian skies, the Charleston becomes a very sexy dance, something it never was before. Where we used to kick and jump, the Italians—at least, these Italians—slither and roll. It was quite an experience.

While the Americans have had the field in popular music all to themselves for many years, it may not always be that way. The South Americans are coming up mighty fast. The sun, as I said, may never set on Irving Berlin, but it is becoming increasingly apparent that it doesn't set on the mambo, either. Even in Vienna, alas, you may have to sit through an awful lot of mambo before the wild gypsy violins take over again.

(*Any mambo is an awful lot of mambo, John.*—E. C.)

TWO:

SOME FRIENDS OF EDDIE'S

Note: This section is much shorter than it should be. It ought to include stories about Bud Freeman, George Wettling, Teschemacher, Red McKenzie, George Brunis and many others who have been associated with Eddie over the years. The fact is, we simply couldn't find good pieces about many of the friends, even on album liners. As Eddie has said, the historians at the Institute of Jazz Studies have their work waiting for them.

R. G.

GEORGE AVAKIAN, OTIS FERGUSON, EDDIE CONDON

Bix

ANOTHER PATCH-UP JOB. *We've used the Ferguson story, which originally appeared in the New Republic, as a scaffolding, and have added some stuff from* We Called It Music *and from Avakian's album notes on the three-volume Columbia "Bix Beiderbecke Story." The late Otis Ferguson was one of the first of the literate, readable jazz critics. George Avakian was too, and today is director of popular albums for Columbia.*

R. G.

OTIS FERGUSON: Bix Beiderbecke died shortly after his twenty-eighth birthday; the bulk of his music was played before 1929. But you can still buy his records, or some of them, and they make him seem as new and wonderful now as he was in those fast days on the big time, the highest expression of jazz when jazz was still young, the golden boy with the cornet he would sometimes carry around under his arm in a paper bag.
EDDIE CONDON: An interruption.
Frankly, I can't remember that Bix ever carried the horn in a paper bag, although I've read that report many times. I recall it as a cloth bag, the kind some musicians still use today. But

maybe I didn't have my eyes open too much of the time. There were days when I did, though, such as the day I met Bix for the first time. Tom Sugrue and I put it down in *We Called It Music;* it happened nearly thirty-five years ago. We said,

". . . I stood in the station and watched Pee Wee come at me with three other guys. One was a dude, the other was an ordinary human being. The third was a kid in a cap with the peak broken. He had on a green overcoat from the walk-up-one-and-save-ten district; the collar was off his neck. He had a round face and eyes that had no desire to focus on what was in front of him. Pee Wee introduced us. The guy in the cap was first.

" 'This is Bix Beiderbecke.'

". . . I'm stuck wtih this clam digger for two months," I thought.

" 'Hello,' Beiderbecke said. Great talker, I thought.

"The dude was next; his name was Wayne Hostetter. The ordinary human being was Johnny Eberhardt. Eberhardt was the saxophone player; Hostetter played clarinet and violin. Nobody said anything about Beiderbecke's instrument.

". . . Pee Wee said, 'Bix wants to go over to the College Inn and see Louis Panico. Let's walk over.'

"The College Inn was in the Sherman House, a loop hotel. Louis Panico was playing trumpet in Isham Jones' band. He was only eighteen, and had written 'Wabash Blues,' and was getting $350 a week. They'll never let us in, I thought. This corncobber probably has heard Louis on a record and hasn't any better sense than to think he can march in wearing that cap and hear him play. I fell back and walked with Hostetter, the dude.

" 'Is Beiderbecke our cornet player?' I asked.

" 'By way of understatement, yes,' Hostetter said. 'Wait until you hear him play. You'll go nuts.'

"I can believe it, I thought. What kind of music have these guys heard? What is their standard? How can a guy in a cap and a green overcoat play anything civilized?

"We walked right into the College Inn without being stopped. Pee Wee and Beiderbecke pushed their way up to the band stand. I spotted Panico about the time he saw Beiderbecke. His face lighted up like a drunk on Christmas Eve.

" 'Bix!' he yelled. He leaned over to shake hands and the boys in the band looked around as if free drinks had been announced. Beiderbecke must be something, I thought, but what?

"... My eyes were just getting used to the glare in there when Pee Wee said, 'Bix wants to go to the Friars' Inn.'

"Well, I thought, they let us in here, why not the Friars' Inn? The Friars' Inn was a flashy cabaret for big spenders. For music it had the New Orleans Rhythm Kings, the famous white jazz band. I had heard their records on Gennett. If any of the Rhythm Kings spoke to Beiderbecke he was somebody, cap and all.

"We walked in . . . right up the band stand. The players fell over themselves greeting Beiderbecke. Have I got to buy a cap to make good, I thought?

"Beiderbecke smiled like an embarrassed kid and muttered something. Then he got up on the stand and walked over and sat down—at the piano. 'Clarinet Marmalade,' somebody said. Bix nodded and hit the keys.

"Then it happened. All my life I had been listening to music, particularly on the piano. But I had never heard anything remotely resembling what Beiderbecke played. For the first time I realized that music isn't all the same, that some people play so differently from others that it becomes an entirely new set of sounds . . .

"The next day we got up as the train came into Cleveland. With nothing to do but sit and stare at the scenery from there to Buffalo I began to wonder again about the cornet. I got out my banjo. Eberhardt dug up his saxophone and doodled along with me. Finally Beiderbecke took out a silver cornet. He put it to his lips and blew a phrase. The sound came out like a girl saying yes. Eberhardt smiled at me. 'How about Panama?' he said. I was still shivering and licking my insides, tasting the last of the phrase. 'All right,' Beiderbecke said, 'Panama.' By itself, so it seemed, my banjo took up the rhythm. At last I was playing music; so far as I was concerned it could go on forever."

OTIS FERGUSON: I suppose the kids who grew up in the belief that Glen Miller is what it really takes to blow the roof off would wonder, in the midst of this rather dated small-band clamor, what they were listening to and why. Well, it's just jazz, kids, and as far as the groups in general go, not the best of its period. But

Bix, the fellow riding above and ahead and all around with that clear-bell horn, Bix had swing before the phonies knew the word. He had it at its best and purest, for he had not only the compelling lift of syncopation, the ease within an intense and relentless rhythm; he had music in a way of invention that is only found when you find a good song, inevitable, sweet, and perfect. He could take off out of any chord sequence, any good or silly tune, and wheel and lift with his gay new melodic figures as free of strain in the air as pigeons. He had a sense of harmonic structure that none can learn and few are born with; he had absolute pitch and absolute control of his instrument—in fact, no trumpet player I've ever heard could be so reckless and yet so right, so assured in all the range from tender to brash, from sorrow to a shout; his tone was as perfect without artifice as water in the brooks, and his lip and tongue and valve work so exact in all registers that he could jump into a line of notes and make it sound like he'd slapped every one of them square in the face. With this technical assurance, he never had to cramp and plan and fuss himself; he could start at any point and land on a dime.

This makes it sound too tossed off. He worked on his music, and worried always. Any jealous little stink-finger (and there were plenty around to envy and fear his talent) could always bring him down by low-rating the thing he'd just played; any musician who had something was the object of his admiration. He never got over feeling uneasy about his lack of facility in sight reading—but it was too natural and easy to play it by ear. He had a memory in music like nobody's business, and and could and at certain hilarious times did imitate a corny solo just preceding his, so closely note for note that the only one who wasn't holding his sides was the soloist himself, who figgered that young feller was rarin' to go.

I don't know anybody who did more in the way of opening up the set rhythm of jazz. Everything is written in four-four time, and the pace can be said to vary through twelve or fifteen standard tempos, from slow-drag to fast-jump. But Bix as he went along actually wrote his own time signature over the implied beat for dancing, by subtleties of phrasing, by delayed attack or a quick rush on ahead, and by the varying duration of a note.

It was no mere gut-bucket, emotion without control, virtuosity without pattern, louder and faster and higher. He sweat, and for all the ease of his solo in flight, the men around him would see the lines tighten in his face every time he stood up. One of the easy remarks in jazz is: He played it fifteen times, every one different. Bix played it different, all right. But when he got just the note of the chord, just the intervals, just the main line the way he wanted—that was his structure and there couldn't be a better, so why go off into new scales and razz-mah-tazz? At times—and you can hear it proved on half a dozen records—he would get a way of playing for the brass section and have the arranger leave that chorus blank; then he would get the boys together outside and play a phrase and then another, and then go back and play it in chords, patiently, carefully, just as he used to do with the glee club back in grade school in Davenport, note for note and chord for chord, until that part of the arrangement was a section in solo, established in the book and no need for writing. It couldn't be written anyway.

An analysis of his music as a whole would amount to a statement of most of the best elements in jazz—which is a little too much for this spot. Briefly, he played a full easy tone, no forcing, faking, or mute tricks, no glissando to cover unsure attack or vibrato to fuzz over imprecisions of pitch—it all had to be in the music. And the clear line of that music is something to wonder at. You see, this is the sort of thing that is almost wholly improvised, starting from a simple theme, taking off from that into a different and unpredictable melodic line, spontaneous, personal —almost a new tune but still shadowing the old one, anchored in its chord sequence. Obviously, without lyric invention and a perfect instinct for harmony, this is no go for a minute, let alone chorus after chorus, night after night. And yet here is this fantastic chap, skipping out from behind a bank of saxophones for eight measures in the clear and back again, driving up the tension with a three-note phrase as brash and gleeful as a kid with a prank, riding down the whole length of a chorus like a herd of mustangs—everywhere you find him there is always this miracle of constant on-the-spot invention, never faltering or repeating, every phrase as fresh and glistening as creation itself.

Just as characteristic was the driving rhythm against which he played, the subtle and incisive timing that could make even a low and lazy figure of syncopation explode like blows in the prize ring. Bix had a rhythmic invention that seemed inexhaustible, variety without straining; and in all his cross-rhythms and flights of phrasing, could mutter and whistle the general idea of the big full solo in "Riverboat Shuffle," which was on the back of "Ostrich Walk," which coupling just about represents the peak of a high and wonderful career—but why waste time with words and poor copies? One hears it, and is moved and made strangely proud; or one does not, and misses one of the fine natural resources of this American country.

EDDIE CONDON: Bix was always handicapped, it seems to me, by the blood relative-sounding musicians he played with. It was his bad luck to be forced to comport with some real hobos, musically speaking. Why, I remember one day when *Lennie Hayton* played drums on a record.

For that reason, every time Beiderbecke took a lunge, he'd bump into one of those Iron Chancellors. As soon as he came in for a chorus it sounded like somebody was in town, but when the others came in, it sounded as though they were all trying to leave town. It was too bad, too, for he was a very gentle guy.

OTIS FERGUSON: All of this makes him sound too perfect, like a church-going cousin always being thrown in your face. He was perfect only in music, and in the simple goodness and loyalty that was always there under the rusty tux with the soup stains, the underwear and socks you never could get off him for sending to the laundry until they fell off, and he'd borrowed them from you in the first place, like as not. As a kid he had wanted to be Douglas Fairbanks; he kept himself in trim and was great at skating, swimming, jumping over walls and the like, an all-around first in his neighborhood, and so generally hardy that an old sweater was all he found necessary for an Iowa winter. But music as it became a profession and almost a religion shut out his concern for just about everything else. Things were always happening to him, partly because he couldn't spare the time to study about them—missing the train, losing his tie, falling off the stand in a whirlwind of music racks, getting thrown out of the hotel.

Of his considerable achievements as a rumpot, people still speak with wonder and endlessly, and there were indeed some funny times, before the dark days. But one of his troubles was a capacity rare in brass men: he could tie quite a handsome one on without going technically fuzzy and lipnumb, so that he could stand up and get off those clear round notes as innocent as pie, and then solemnly take his seat in the middle of the whole boilerworks of a drummer's outfit. He lacked a natural brake in that; and his constitution was so good to start with that he wasn't retarded physically until he'd blown the fuse on the whole works. Also, he could make as big money as you want without having a dime, a very rough man on a dollar bill. Also, while no one ever suffered musical fools more gladly, stood by for and worked over them, he had no use for any stuffed shirt in music or anything else, except as a target for a slingshot. He'd run into any such rich spreading trees as quick and head-on as the horse in the fable; he wasn't blind, he just didn't give a damn.

The story of his musical career is outlined in the book *Jazz Men* about as well as it can be. The dates, the cities, the things done, the people met are established enough by now for a pattern, if only in fragments. But he had started in music early, and there is not so much known about that. His family was well off; his father was a good solid lumber merchant in Davenport, Iowa; his mother an amateur musician. There was always a piano in the house and there was a phonograph when few people had them. Bix (his real name was Leon Bismarck, for it was a family of German-American extraction) was a perfectly normal boy, except that he was always fussing around with music. He had a sister and an older brother, who was enough a hero to him so that he swiped the nickname Bix from him, and would not part with it. He lived in a big house across a sloping playground from the school, and the school was more a center of life than schools usually get to be.

There was the playground, the sliding and skating and wrassling, but there was also a lot of singing: the kind of spontaneous thing where a whole grade of kids will enjoy their cantatas and what-not so much that they not only start a ball rolling through the classes in general but work at it and get pretty good.

They used to have the run of the school at night for rehearsal; they used to have a barbershop quartet out on the fire escape. In one grade they wanted a piano for their own room, so they arranged a local concert, which was so successful they gave another, and before the year was out they had the piano, bought and paid for. One of those happy things that cannot be incubated, taught, or fostered.

Anyhow, Bix went through all the grades without being kept back, and in this social-musical atmosphere he was the number-one boy. Anything he heard he could play on the piano; anything he could play he could figure out the parts for, and teach the others to sing in chords. He liked music and music liked him and gave him a place, and the world was very young. Then on top of that, first off the crank-winding phonograph and later up the river from New Orleans in boats, came jazz, with horns. He got a cornet and taught himself to play it, for that was the kind of instrument it took to blast out this new thing in music. He got quite a little drunk on the excitement of it and did not want to be Douglas Fairbanks any more. His family began to worry about him, for it was one of those happy families that enjoy their group with pride and a fierce concern that it shall have the best. They sent Bix from high school to Lake Forest Military Academy, thinking to get him away from the bad balance of nothing but music. But Lake Forest was near Chicago, and Chicago was jazz then. It was as though jazz were a house that had been built just for him. And he moved in.

GEORGE AVAKIAN: Lake Forest had a liberal week-end policy, and Bix constantly found himself getting down to Chicago's South Side, where the first New Orleans jazzmen had begun to find work. The New Orleans Rhythm Kings, a fine white band, hit town that year, too. It didn't help Bix's homework, but his cornet took on a new sound while he was at the academy.

Bix naturally gravitated into the student band that played for dances and during reel changes of movies in the gym. Social life was pleasant; a nearby girls' school, Ferry Hall, provided partners for the dances. (Jean Harlow was a Ferry student about the time Bix was at Lake Forest.) The band played on a balcony which was reached by a trapdoor, and Frank Norris recalls the time that Bix was heating it up for the kids down on the gym floor and the headmaster, John Wayne Richards, poked his head through the trapdoor to call out, "Tone it down, Bix, tone it down!"

A year and a half of Lake Forest, and Bix had convinced the faculty that it was no use keeping him around any longer. Bix (who always was to have a reputation as a self-taught musician and a poor reader) continued to play cornet his own way. Not knowing that the first two valves of the horn are the principal ones, he used all three equally and habitually played many notes "the hard way." This dependency on the third valve, however, probably helped more than that. Eventually he was able to play with ease fantastic passages that would have been tough going in orthodox fingering.

Bix's apprenticeship among the New Orleans migrants in Chicago paid off in late 1923, when with a group of other youngsters with whom he had been jobbing around he landed a steady job at the Stockton Club, a roadhouse in Hamilton, Ohio. This was the debut of the Wolverines, the first good white jazz band consisting entirely of non-New Orleans musicians. For a pioneer group, they played remarkably well, and Bix made the band swing almost as much as the New Orleans Rhythm Kings (which, oddly enough, included four musicians from southern Indiana and Illinois). Those who criticize the early-jazz sound of the Wolverines from the vantage point of a quarter-century would do well to consider that they gave Bix more of a jazz setting for his horn than any group of musicians he ever worked with. Bill Priestley adds: "I know of no other band that relied less for ideas on the other bands they were hearing."

Squirrel Ashcraft, another Princetonian and a good pianist who frequently sat in with the Wolverines, points out that "the band pioneered ideas which meant so much to Bix that as long as he lived he repeated variations of things he played with them, or which other members of the band played." The tenor saxophonist, George Johnson, was especially an influence on Bix. He set the rhythm of the band, and it was from Johnson that Bix first picked up one of his most striking characteristics: a strong dependency on the whole-tone scale.

An Indiana University student named Hoagy Carmichael heard about the Wolverines that winter and brought them to the campus for a spring dance. There is a classic description, quoted by Eddie Nichols in his illuminating chapter on Bix in *Jazzmen*, of the Wolverines' arrival in an old phaeton, six musicians with beat-up instruments spilling over the sides. Even Hoagy, who hadn't heard them play, was worried, but they were a sensation and came back for ten weekends in a row. Hoagy became one of Bix's closest friends, and wrote a number for the Wolverines called "Free Wheeling," which the boys went for in a big way because it gave them four breaks to blow in every chorus. Bix changed the name to "Riverboat Shuffle."

The Wolverines had no lack of jobs that year, although there was a lull during the summer of 1924 which Bix filled in with Mezz Mezzrow's band at the Martinique Inn at Indiana Harbor, a tough mill town near Gary. The owner of the joint was a former welterweight named Monkey Pollack, who had studied English literature and later became a newspaperman. His bartender was a still stranger combination: he came from the Texas panhandle and had been both a cowboy and a rabbi. He always carried a pair of loaded pistols and could shoot dimes off beer bottles at fifty paces. Mezzrow, who was also Jewish, used to carry on in Yiddish with the bartender, just to hear him speak it with a broad Texas drawl. His boss called the ex-rabbi Yiddle, and in honor of his crack markmanship Mezz wrote a tune which the band sometimes played and sang: "Don't Fiddle with Yiddle —He'll Riddle Your Middle."

Early 1925 saw the gradual breaking-up of the Wolverines. Bix joined Charlie Straight's band in Chicago, where he could once more hear the great Negro musicians who were pouring into town. He even heard Bessie Smith, who usually toured the South, and they say he was so moved that he gave her his week's pay to keep on singing.

In September of that year Bix joined Frank Trumbauer's band in St. Louis. When Tram broke up the band in 1926 to join Gene Goldkette in Detroit, Bix went along. Goldkette had an all-star crew that was pretty expensive to keep up, and when he had to let the boys go in the fall of 1927, most of them (including Bix and Tram) went with Paul Whiteman.

Bix was still pretty much in a world all his own, although he had learned to make compromises such as clean shirts and nothing loud before midnight, please. He was good, and Whiteman liked him and paid him well, but Bix would have played for less if he had been allowed to play more.

Bill Challis, Goldkette's arranger, joined Whiteman just before Bix did. As before, he frequently wrote passages especially for Bix, either as lead horn or for ad lib solos with whatever sort of background Bix wanted. The other section men admired and respected Bix (with Goldkette, they were Ray Ludwig and Fuzzy Farrar; Whiteman usually had Charlie Margulies, Eddie Pinder, and Henry Busse, who was later replaced by Harry Goldfield) and they always made a point of helping Bix with the tough concert arrangements. But it was never enough to make up for the fact that Bix often had to sit there for an hour blowing section harmonies (or just plain sit through the Ferde Grofe productions) and when he finally got a chance to play something on his own it was over before he could really get started.

By 1929 the pace was really rough. Whiteman's radio show was packed with new tunes every week, and Bix had to work harder than ever at the aspect he disliked most. Drinking didn't help much any more, because now drinking itself was pushing Bix around even more than the commercial music. It got to the point where Whiteman had to send him for a cure, and when Bix got out of the hospital in February, 1930, he was scarcely able to return to the grind. He went home to Davenport for a while, and returned to New York, but it was obvious that he couldn't go back with Whiteman.

Challis tried to get Bix into the Casa Loma Orchestra, an ex-Goldkette unit that was just beginning to build a reputation that was to make it the prom-trotter's favorite in the early thirties. Bix didn't have much confidence in his own ability to cut the tough Gene Gifford arrangements, though Challis had done several for the band which were based on arrangements that Bix had played often. After one false start that got no further than the Plaza entrance of Central Park, Challis and Corky O'Keefe, the band's manager, drove Bix up to Connecticut to give it a try. Four nights of the constant repetition that the Casa Lomans needed to execute the precision arrangements were all Bix could stand, and he rolled back into town further off the wagon than ever.

For the first time in his life, Bix was broke. The considerable amount of money he had sent home to his sister through the years was lost in the crash; Bix had invested it all in bank stock, and the stockholders' double liability of those days wiped out all his savings. Club dates were few, but still he manged to stay on at the 44th Street Hotel. Among his companions in those days was a fellow named George Herman Ruth, who had an afternoon job with a ball club up at East 161st Street. Bix, a well-built fellow with a physique that remained robust until his final illnesses, had always been a baseball fan and had even played for the Lake Forest Academy team, as an old yearbook picture attests. His friendship with The Babe survived the fact that Bix's room was so small that Ruth had to take the door off the hinges to get in—or so they say.

Bix turned more and more to classical music and playing the piano. He frequently spent the day at Bill Challis' apartment on Riverside Drive and 81st Street, where they gradually worked out a score of "In A Mist" and some other piano pieces Bix had developed through the years. It was slow going; there was a jug hidden in the bath-tub where Challis' sister, who also lived there, wouldn't see it. But aside from that Bix never played anything the same way twice. He was very conscientious about the piano scores, though; he had a premonition that something might happen to him, and he wanted to be remembered mostly by them. The published version of "In A Mist" differs somewhat from the recording, partly because the publisher wanted a slow section just before the return to the first theme. After Bix's death, Challis also edited Bix's "Davenport Blues" in the same style for piano.

OTIS FERGUSON: I was no intimate, but I think I could say in general why he blew up. It was partly the pace, of course, and taking it too fast. He began to see little fellows with green beards walking up and down on his chest, and Whiteman sent him back to Davenport, to get squared up. He was too far gone for any working band at that time, which was 1928. At home, he came out of it. He was shaky but still good, and he jobbed around with his old friend from grade school, Larry Andrews, and watched his hand when he held it out every morning to see if it still looked as though he were waving at somebody. He had been at the top but somewhere along the line, some time or other, he'd taken a fall. And he wasn't sure in his own heart he would fit back there again, even if he stayed off brass rails. He was honestly anxious. Was it just liquor that had pulled the knife on him? Maybe it was something else too?

It was, all right. He lifted his horn over the sixty-odd dancers or the beer tables of this cover-your-expenses circuit, and the other musicians (if no one else) would shake their heads and marvel; and it was the same as in the first days when he showed up in an Indiana town where the boys had thought they were really going, and played a few sets, and as one of them reports today, a day in which he is pretty famous, "I tell you the tears stood in my eyes, I couldn't get out the next number in the book."

He stayed on the wagon and the music was as good as ever— which he proved later on the last recording date he had before he died, with Hoagy Carmichael's pick-up band. But what he couldn't see, the nameless thing that was his trouble, had got him down. First he'd wanted to be "as good" as the men out front whose music had excited him. Then he wanted to stay good, and be if possible better. This was a preoccupation to bridge the years from the rusty clangor of the Wolverines to the bright lights of the Goldkette and Whiteman shows; this and the handy gin pitcher kept him assuming that if he felt low and the road ahead was flat and lonesome, it was just a hangover, just feeling low, let's sick a hare on the hound that bit me. Actually something else had been creeping up, something he never saw clearly. He had come to the top like a cork, and he had no more place to go.

And still he had to be going, he had to travel, so completely a musician that music was in his ticket and there was no other line. He didn't go much for women. He was loyal, true, and happy in his friendships with men, even self-effacing, but his friends were, after all, musicians. It had to be music for him, and as far as he could see when he could see, he wanted neither the money, nor the place, nor the show. But what else? He dreamed of being a composer. He had written some piano pieces, and he wanted to do something even more ambitious. But what? He had no equipment, not the kind of equipment that a so-called legitimate musician acquires from study of the great body of Western music, which has had its best time in other times. He didn't know what to do, and listened with awe to Debussy records (Debussy is for some strange reason a great favorite of good jazz men), and would sequester himself and sit morosely at the piano, fingering the chords of a new music without being able to reconcile the old, which he didn't comprehend, with the new, which was in him as natural as a voice in your throat and which he had spent his brief lifetime tuning for song.

From the top of folk music as folk music, there is no place to go. Actually jazz is a folk music, but Bix had never taken time out to think of things like that: jazz was the country where he grew up, the fine high thing, the sun coming up to fill the world through the morning.

He never heard about what was troubling him and only knew it was trouble. He came back to the big time eventually, but he could no longer stay on it, he played here and there, hole and corner, but he was too unreliable now for the standard type of shows—and the big time was letting jazz go underground quietly in those days, for whatever life there had been in bands like Pollack, Goldkette, Whiteman in 1927-28 was no longer in demand by 1930, and even the great jumping Negro outfits were either breaking up or hightailing off to Europe. Bix played for dances and recordings, and went back to the bottle and was not seen in the better places; and even moped around fearing he had lost his sense of perfect pitch; but when he lifted that stumpy dented cornet at the fraction of the second after the release, for dancing or just for the record in a dead studio, it came tumbling and leaping out as complete and lovely as ever. What he could always do he could still do, from the jazz-band tone to sadness. But what he had was more than enough, and he didn't know where to put it.

Perhaps you will have to hear him a lot; perhaps you won't have any ear for the jazz music that grew up around you and in your time, and so will never hear the voice, almost as if speaking; but there is something in these records that goes beyond a mere instrument or the improviser on it, some unconquerable bright spirit that leaves no slops even in confusion and defeat and darkness gathering; some gallant human thing which is as near to us as it is completely marvelous, and which makes only just and apposite that end of a career so next to the heart of all who would like this country to be a country of happy people, singing.

GEORGE AVAKIAN: Like the stock market, Bix was riding high but shaky by 1920. He died on August 7, 1931, his health shot, all but washed up professionally at the ripe age of 28. The standard story of his death, which has been printed over and over again (as opposed to the whispers involving gangsters) is that Bix, sick in bed with a cold, got up to go to Princeton for a club date which would have been called off if he didn't show. He drove down in an open car, the story runs, developed pneumonia, and died.

Somehow, until now, no one (the present writer included) even questioned the anachronism of a Princeton dance in midsummer. One of Bix's Princeton fans, Frank Norris, who had gone to Lake Forest Academy with him ten years earlier, recalls that Bix caught a beauty of a cold at the last of the week-ends that spring, and never did shake it off. "But die of a cold? Bix didn't die of a cold," says Norris. "He died of *everything.*" Eddie Condon, who saw a great deal of Bix in 1931, confirms that Bix just gave out. "He was broke, run down, and living in one study room out in Jackson Heights. He had this cold that you or I—well, you, anyway—could shake off in a few days, but with Bix it was a case of having to stay in bed. It was the end of July, and so hot that he rigged up a couple of fans to blow on the bed. Two days of that and he had pneumonia, but good." By the time Bix got to a hospital, he couldn't have fought his way through a wet beer label.

OTIS FERGUSON: They buried the body. For those who had been around and those to come after there was something, grown in this country out of the Iowa dirt, that didn't die and could not be buried so long as there should be a record left in the world, and a turntable to spin it on.

EDDIE CONDON: I hope he isn't wearing a cap.

AL SILVERMAN

Fats

> MY FIRST DISASTROUS encounter with Fats is mentioned in this piece of Al's, in detail if not in agony. When Al says there was nobody like him, he's got him. Considering the space, Al does a competent job here, but the subject demands a book. A book? What Fats ought to have is an encyclopedia.
>
> E. C.

It is doing Fats Waller a disservice to kick off a Fats Waller story by comparing him to Louis Armstrong; but a point has to be made. The fact is, both men had much in common. Both were artists at their instruments. Both sang in a bruising nasal baritone, although Fats had less gravel in his voice and more melodic impudence. And both were consummate showmen, quite possibly the two most dynamic personalities jazz has ever produced. But Louis is alive today and his reputation still bubbles around him. His place is secure. Fats is dead some years, gone before his time, with full recognition of his large talent yet to come.

Satchmo himself would be the first to step aside and leave room for Tom Waller. "I've seen Fats enter a place," Armstrong has said, "and all the people in the joint would just rave and you could see a sort of gladness in their faces . . . honest . . . and Fats wouldn't be in the place a hot minute before he would tell them a fine joke and have everybody holding his side from laughter. Right now, every time someone mentions Fats Waller's name, why you can see all the grins on all the faces as if to say, 'Yea, yea, yea, yea, Fats is a solid sender, ain't he?' "

It should be stated at the outset that the memory of the Waller name is not altogether blighted by the twelve years he has been off the scene. There is in existence an organization called the "Friends of Fats Society," which supposedly numbers some 65,000 music lovers. The organization is run by people who are interested in selling Fats Waller records and every year there is a Fats Waller Memorial Week in which the disc jockeys of the country are urged to play Waller music. Despite the stark commercial aspect of the undertaking, here at least is a hint that Fats is remembered today.

The people who remember him most are the ones most concerned with American jazz. They understand Fats' massive contributions as a pianist and organist and composer of such durable pieces as "Ain't Misbehavin' " and "Honeysuckle Rose." Hugues Panassié has written with glowing admiration of the Waller genius. "I really believe he is the most perfect orchestral pianist jazz has ever known. Fats is also a great soloist, quite the equal of any other. No other musician has been able to reveal as he has that music is not a complicated and methodical art, but on the contrary a simple cry of love and of the relaxation coming from the heart of man. Fats is a power."

Other tributes, though more simply phrased, have said much the same thing. Jack Chrystal, who has conducted weekly jam sessions in New York for fifteen years, says of Fats, "He played what appeared to be casual piano, but no one's ever been able to equal it." About his composing genius, Fats' one-time collaborator, Andy Razaf, said it best:

"Fats," Razaf exclaimed, "could set the telephone book to music."

In his time Fats wrote the melodies to over 360 songs. Not that many bear his name today, unfortunately, because when money was needed he'd write the music and sell all rights to unscrupulous

Tin Pan Alley characters. But his name sticks out on such tunes as "I've Got A Feelin' I'm Fallin'," "Keepin' Out of Mischief Now," "Rhythm Man," "Blue Turning Gray Over You," "John Henry," "Aintcha Glad," "If It Ain't Love." He made hundreds of recordings. His records sold well when he was alive and they are selling well today, especially in Europe, where his artistry has been most keenly appreciated. A cousin of Queen Elizabeth, for instance, is said to possess the world's largest collection of Waller recordings.

When he sang, even the most banal of lyrics took on magical qualities. The words to "Your Feet's Too Big," for instance, are said to be one of the most direct and funniest declarations of non-love in popular music. The way Fats sang it there was no doubt. He'd sit at the piano, all 285 pounds of him, his ham-like hands running with surprising delicacy over the keys. Then he'd turn his head, cock his derby to a tilt, smile and wink and leer at the audience and give out with phrases like this:

"My goodness, gun the gun boats. Your pedal extremities are colossal, to me you look like a fossil . . . Your pedal extremities really are obnoxious." Then the final ad-libbed Waller touch, "One never knows, do one?"

Some of his vocal improvisations are a constant source of embarrassment to record companies today. In his record of the "Sheik of Araby," which, for some strange reason, is currently out of circulation, Fats inserted a line that went, "What's that! Get on a camel? You know I never ride between humps." And on "Spring Cleaning," another missing record, he interpolated, "No lady, we can't haul your ashes for twenty-five cents. That's bad business."

Once an exasperated recording executive said to Fats' business manager, Ed Kirkeby, "Can't you muzzle Fats?"

"Nobody can muzzle Fats," Kirkeby replied.

How could you muzzle a man whose whole life was one big ball, "one rising crescendo," as someone put it? Everything Thomas Wright Waller did he did on a grand scale. He was an enormous man with enormous appetites, and he had an enormous amount of love in his heart for his fellow man. He had a sardonic sense of humor and he would kid everyone and everything, including himself, but deep inside he was a man of compassion. Money meant nothing to him. At his peak he was earning $72,000 a year. He left only $20,000 on his death. He was a soft touch for everyone. Having a good time and looking out for his family were his only interests.

Fats stood five feet eleven, weighed anywhere from 265 pounds to 300 and wore a size 15 shoe. He could eat, drink and make love with the best of them. For breakfast he might have six pork chops or a couple of slugs of scotch, four fingers on awakening and four fingers after shaving, an elixir he referred to as his liquid ham and eggs. His capacity for liquor was simply overwhelming. When he was on a date, he'd have a quart of whisky on top of the piano so that when he was playing treble he could reach up with his left hand, and another quart at his foot, so while he beat out the bass, he could reach down and grab the jug with his right hand. Other times, his brother-in-law, Tom Rutherford, might bring in a tray of glasses and Fats would look up from the piano and cry, "Ah, here's the man with the dream wagon. I want it to hit me around my edges and get to every pound."

But he was never really drunk. Liquor merely heightened his already frightening zest for life. Although he was a devoted family man—he'd often jump dates just to get back to his St. Albans, Long Island, home to see his wife and sons—he loved to have women around. Just two days before his death, after he had finished a gruelling set at the Florentine Gardens in Hollywood, someone asked Fats how he felt. "Man, I feel awful," he said, "I need a long rest." Just then, a beautiful girl came bouncing up to Fats and said, "Hello, Fatsy-Watsy, my boy, do you remember me from Cleveland?"

Fats looked up, gaped and hollered to a waiter, "Order up some champagne."

He worked the way he lived, with the throttle full out. "He was the most prolific and fastest writer I ever knew," Andy Razaf once said. During one session at Razaf's home in Asbury Park, New Jersey (Fats had been lured there by the promise of Razaf's mother's cooking), the two turned out "Zonky," "My Fate Is In Your Hands" and "Honeysuckle Rose" in two hours.

In 1929 Fats wrote "Ain't Misbehavin'" in forty-five minutes. Fats composed his "London Suite," in six movements, in less than an hour with his manager, Ed Kirkeby, describing places and locales and Fats picking up the situation on the piano.

Once, when Waller was playing in Sheffield, England, he called Kirkeby at six in the morning. "Mr. Kirkeby, are you up?" Fats said.

"I'm up now," Kirkeby replied groggily.

"You know, Tiny and I (Waller's chauffeur) have been walkin' in the botanical gardens and the dawn flamed in the sky, the birds played me a song. Come on down." Kirkeby roused himself and went to Fats' room. Fats was in his bathrobe, playing the piano. He was drinking sherry. When he wasn't on whisky, he drank sherry. Kirkeby said, "Let's hear what you got."

Fats said, "Let's have a libation of sherry first." Then he started playing a catchy melody. Kirkeby listened a while and said, "I got it. You remember when we came over on the Queen Mary and you were talking to a gushy woman and you said, 'Honey, hush.' That's it, 'Honey Hush.'" Two hours later—and two bottles of sherry—the song, "Honey Hush," was finished and Kirkeby went back to sleep.

Fats often got inspirations like that. One time in Providence, Rhode Island, after he had played a date, he was having a late supper in a chop suey joint. Ed Kirkeby was with him. Fats began humming a tune and Kirkeby remarked that it sounded like a military march. Waller and Kirkeby went back to the darkened night club, brushed aside some chairs and charwomen who were cleaning up, broke out a bottle of whiskey and started composing. The song was named "Swing Out to Victory."

His recording sessions were even more abrupt and inspiring. Eddie Condon in his book, *We Called It Music*, has described in detail the results of one session he participated in with Waller. It seems that Condon had been hired by a record company to see to it that Waller was delivered to the recording studio at a certain date with his band. (Fats was never much at keeping appointments.) Condon, who had never met Waller, thought it was an easy way to make some extra change.

"I introduced myself to Fats. 'Earl Hines told me to look you up,' I explained.

"'Ol' Earl,' Fats said. 'Well, that's fine. How's ol' Earl? I'm so glad to hear about him. Sit down and let me get a little gin for you. We'll have to talk about Earl.'

"He was so amiable, so agreeable, so good-natured, that I felt almost ashamed of my mission; but I performed it. I asked Fats about making a record. A recording date? He'd be delighted, he'd be proud; just any time? In four days? Fine. At Liederkranz Hall? Wonderful. At noon? Perfect."

(Al here forgets to include Condon's comment on this adventure. The man had promised Eddie fifty dollars if he brought Fats in for the job. "For fifty dollars," Eddie said, "I'll bring you Herbert Hoover in a soft collar."—R. G.)

At 10:30 A.M. on the morning of the recording date, as Condon tells it, he and Fats were stretched out on cushions at Connie's Inn, where Fats had been playing, sleeping off the effects of an all-night battle with gin. Nothing had been done up to that time about getting a band together. "It's half past ten," Condon croaked to Fats. "We're due at the studio at noon.

"Fats sat up, stretched and yawned. 'That's fine! That's wonderful! That's perfect!' he said. 'Now we got to see about that band. Look around for some nickels so I can make the telephone go.'

"He went to the phone booth and made three calls. By the time we finished washing and straightening our clothes, three musicians had arrived. Charlie Gains, a trumpet-player; Charlie Irvis, a trombonist; and Arville Harris, who played clarinet and alto saxophone." (Condon was also to play banjo with the group.)

"We piled into a taxi and headed down Seventh Avenue. 'Now here's what we are going to play,' Fats said suddenly. He hummed a simple basic pattern of rhythm and melody, a blues in a minor key. When he had it memorized he explained what each of us was to do."

At ten minutes before 12, the group walked into Liederkranz Hall at 58th Street and Lexington Avenue. Condon was congratulated by the record executive for being so punctual and then he asked Fats, "Well, Mr. Waller, what is it to be this morning?"

"Well," Fats said, "this morning I think we'll start with a little thing we call the 'Minor Drag.' It's a slow number. Then we got a little ol' thing for the other side we call"—he hesitated—"Harlem Fuss.'"

The recording session went off perfectly, except that when the record was released the titles were reversed. "Harlem Fuss" was called "Minor Drag" and "Minor Drag" was called "Harlem Fuss." It didn't matter, though. *Time* later referred to the sides as one of the greatest jazz records of all time.

That's the way Tom Waller was, and there wasn't anything anybody could do about it. Fats worked almost completely by instinct. Once a young lady stopped him and asked, "Mr. Waller, what is swing?"

"Lady," he replied, "if you got to ask, you ain't got it."

Fats always had it, no doubt from the moment of his birth on May 21, 1904. There is no proof, of course, but that day must have been filled with sunshine and laughter and happiness, at least in the Waller household. You can almost picture Fats coming out of his mother's womb, that big mocking smile already fixed on his round face, saying, if he could talk, "Well, well, lookee here. A baby. My! My! My! Ain't that a killer diller from Manila!"

The Waller family came originally from Virginia and there was always music. Fats' grandfather, Adolph, was a noted violinist who had toured the South after the Civil War. His mother, Adeline Lockett Waller, played the piano and organ and had a pleasant soprano voice. Tom's father, the Rev. Edward Waller, was minister of the Abyssinian Baptist Church in Harlem, which now has one of the largest Protestant congregations in the country. The good Reverend wasn't much of a jazz buff. He wanted Tom to be a minister. "Jazz," he always said, "comes from the devil's workshop."

Adeline Waller bore eleven other children and Fats never had a very cool time of it growing up around 134th Street, but he managed to get a musical education early. He played the harmonium when he was five years old. When he was six his brother

Robert bought him a piano. He also mastered the bass viol and by the time he was ten he was playing the organ in his father's church. He was also a member of the orchestra of his grade and high school. Playing with them was more important to him than studying and when he got low marks, as he was apt to, especially in mathematics, he had a ready alibi: "There's not enough rhythm for me in algebra." He ran errands for a grocery store and pig's feet stand to earn his spending money of $.75 a week and help pay for his musical lessons. In his leisure moments he read Nick Carter novels as well as books on musical theory.

One day in 1918 when he was fourteen and attending DeWitt Clinton High (and had already earned the nickname of Fats) he was asked to fill in at the organ at the Lincoln Theatre in Harlem. The regular organist was ill. One of the great early thrills of his life as he remembered it was sitting down at the console of that ten thousand dollar Wurlitzer Grand Organ. In a short while he wearied completely of a formal education and he quit school to become regular organist at the Lincoln Theatre at $23 a week.

The next year he turned up at an amateur pianist concert at the Roosevelt Theatre in Harlem. He won first prize playing one of James P. Johnson's tunes, "Carolina Shout." That same year he wrote his first song. He was in Boston at the time, on tour with a vaudeville act, and he called the song "Boston Blues." Later he changed the title to "Squeeze Me," and it has since become a standard in the jazz repertoire.

It was while working at the Lincoln Theatre that Fats made friends with Andy Razaf. ("I used to listen to him there often," Razaf said, "and eventually, because everyone knew him and everyone was his friend, I somehow came to meet him.") Andreamentana Razafinkeriefo was the son of a grand duke of Madagascar who had been killed when the French took over the Island. He and Fats formed an endearing song-writing partnership. "One of the first things we did as a team," Razaf said, "was cash in on the vogue on West Indian songs. As soon as we got broke all we had to do was grind out two or three West Indian numbers and take them up to Mills or some other Broadway office and get a nice sum for them."

Fats worked like an IBM machine grinding out melodies. Once during World War II he wrote a song called, "Get Some Cash For Your Trash," which the Treasury Department adopted as a theme for a waste paper drive they were conducting at the time—until they discovered the song title's true meaning. Ed Kirkeby, who wrote the lyrics, best tells the story.

"We were playing in a Washington theatre and I had gotten there very early. I was sitting in the dressing room waiting for the rest of the cast to come in. Then all of a sudden, Myra Johnson, who was our femme fatale, walked in, an apparition, swinging her hips as she passed and saying to me, "Hiya, Mr. Kirkeby."

"One of the other boys watched her swivel by and hollered, 'Baby, I just want to tell you, you better get some cash for your trash.' I wrote the lyrics on paper and took them to Fats. He read it and said, 'Man, this is great.' He had the melody down perfect in fifteen minutes."

The individual who meant the most musically to Fats in the early days was the late James P. Johnson, the dean of Harlem piano players. He became Fats' first teacher in Chicago in 1920 when Fats was sixteen and Jimmy twenty-seven. "I taught him how to groove," James P. said, "how to make it sweet—the strong basée he had dates from that time. He stuck pretty well to my pattern, developed a lovely singing tone, a large melodic expression and," Johnson added knowingly, "being the son of a preacher, he had fervor."

Under the tutelage of James P., Fats became one of the most prominent pianists in Harlem, playing at parlor socials, otherwise known as rent parties, in cabarets, night clubs, vaudeville and burlesque. At the rent party, a popular way of saving a family from eviction in those days, a regular admission fee was charged and the performers got a small percentage of the take.

In 1923 Fats met Duke Ellington when he was playing a burlesque show in Washington. Later that year, back in New York, he thought he had a job for Duke so he sent for him and some of his side men: Toby Hardwick, Sonny Greer, Arthur Whetsel and Elmer Snowden. The job never materialized, so there was a lot of time for free playing. Ellington, Willie (The

Lion) Smith, James P. Johnson and Fats used to walk the streets and ring doorbells. They would get into homes where there were pianos, and they would play. All night long they would play, Duke and Fats and James P. and the Lion. "If he liked you," a friend said of Fats, "he'd play forever."

But Fats kept reasonably busy during this period. He cut his first piano rolls at $100 per roll. When he was twenty he recorded his first solo on an Okeh label. He accompanied such singers as Sara Martin, and worked in vaudeville with Bessie Smith. And in 1927 the Prodigal Son returned to the Lincoln Theatre with his own band.

All along, he was studying music seriously, first under Carl Bohm and then under Leopold Godowski. His father had taken Fats to hear Paderewski play the piano when he was eleven and classical music always had a profound influence on him. Once when he was asked who his favorite personalities were he replied, "Abe Lincoln, Teddy Roosevelt and Johann Sebastian Bach." In 1928, in collaboration with James P. Johnson, he wrote his first musical show, "Keep Shufflin'." That revue had a lovely Waller tune, "Willow Tree." In 1929 he did the score for the "Hot Chocolates" Review, in which "Ain't Misbehavin'" was heard for the first time.

After these successes, Connie and George Immerman asked Fats to do a score for the Connie's Inn show. Connie's Inn was a landmark in Harlem in the twenties. It was located at 131st Street and Seventh Avenue, a corner graced also by the Lafayette Theatre, an all-night barbershop, a rib joint and, above the inn, a barrelhouse café called the Performers and Entertainers Club. And in front of Connie's Inn marquee stood the legendary Tree of Hope, Harlem's blarney stone, a sidewalk totem pole which entertainers stroked for good luck. The story goes that once a hoofer who was out of work ran up to the tree, gave it a big smack and yelled, "Lawd, please make me a pimp, any kind of a pimp as long as I'm pimpin'. I'm tired scufflin', and my feet are too long outa work."

Fats did a show called "Load of Coal" at Connie's Inn, out of which came "Honeysuckle Rose."

In 1932 Fats made his first trip to Europe. He and a friend,

Spencer Williams, wrote over one hundred songs to pay for the tour. They planned to appear as a piano and vocal team but they were too busy wining and dining and having themselves a ball to bother with work. About the only distinction Fats earned out of the trip was playing the organ at historic Notre Dame cathedral in Paris. A friend, Marcel Dupré was organist at the time. One day he and Fats climbed into the Notre Dame organ loft where, as Fats put it, "First he played on the god box, then I played on the god box."

About three months after his arrival in Europe, Fats began to get homesick. One day he and Williams were drinking in a bar with a beautiful girl when suddenly Fats excused himself. "He said he had to go out for a minute," Williams remembers. "Well, he left a full drink so I thought he would be back. The next thing I heard from Fats was when he wired me from the *Ile de France*. 'I'm on my way home. Good luck.'"

In the next six years Fats was solidifying his reputation by his recording and personal appearances. In 1933 he was in Cincinnati broadcasting over WLW, which called him the "harmful little armful." Later he made his debut over the Columbia network. He recorded with his own group and other groups, sometimes under the name of Fats Waller and his Buddies, and sometimes using a pseudonym. The money was rolling in, but it was washing away just as fast. Fats bought himself a de luxe Lincoln Continental convertible. On a tour of the South anti-Negro gangs poured sand in the crankcase and slashed the tires. Fats made his booking agent rent him a whole pullman car before he'd continue. Like other Negro artists, Fats had his share of racial prejudices to contend with.

He had also to contend with alimony payments. The year 1938 was a year of crisis for Fats. He was maturing as an artist, yet his reputation in the United States was on the skids. There was a good reason for this—he had a distressing habit of running out on dates, partly because of domestic difficulties and partly because he was just Fats Waller and when the spirit moved him, he moved, no matter what.

Fats had taken himself a wife when he was seventeen, but the marriage never worked. He was married just after the death of his mother when it was probably a mother he needed, not a wife. A son, Tom Waller, Jr. (a music dealer in the Bronx today) came out of the marriage but it didn't prevent its break-up.

About this time, when he was playing at the Lincoln Theatre, he met Anita Rutherford, a very pretty young lady who had much more in common with Fats than his first wife. They were married when Fats was twenty. Anita bore Fats two children, Maurice and Ronald. Today, Maurice is an assistant buyer in a large New York department store and Ronald is a musician. Fats' first wife, Edith, died about a year ago but Anita still lives in the same St. Albans home that is alive with memories of Fats, in a street which could have been called Piano Row. When Fats was living, James P. Johnson owned the house on one side of him and Clarence Williams lived on the other side. Another New York pianist, Hank Duncan, lived down the street.

By 1938 Fats was sick and tired of being hounded for alimony payments by his first wife. Whenever he slipped behind, she'd have subpoena servers on his trail. It got so that he didn't care whether he earned any money or not. It was at this low ebb in his career that his management was taken over by Ed Kirkeby, who became as close to him in the remaining years of his life as any one else.

The first thing Kirkeby did was book Waller into the South for a series of one-nighters. There was little box-office response; apparently Fats was "lousy" with the customers, as the saying goes. After a couple of weeks of futility, Kirkeby brought Fats back to New York, undecided about the future.

Then he got an idea. He knew Fats had a considerable reputation in Europe, so he got hold of Tommy Rockwell of the Rockwell booking agency and said, "Send a wire and find out if there's any demand for Fats—at $2,500 a week."

"Are you crazy?" Rockwell said.

"Send the wire anyway," Kirkeby said. They received an answer the same day. It read, "Interested, when can he start?" Fats, Anita and Kirkeby sailed to Europe on August 1, 1938, booked to open first at the Glasgow Empire Theatre in Scotland.

When the boat landed at Genoch on the Clyde, the reception was a tumultuous one. As Fats walked down the gang plank he was greeted by a Scottish jazz band playing "Honeysuckle Rose." The trip to Glasgow was just one long champagne party.

Still, Kirkeby wasn't sure about how Fats would be received by the people of Scotland once he was out on the stage. He watched anxiously as Fats sat down at the piano and prepared to play. "After that first number," Kirkeby said, "I knew we had an act."

When he finished, Fats received curtain call after curtain call. The audience was wildly receptive to Fats. Finally, he stepped out in front of the curtain and said, "You've been good to me, and I want to do something for you." He whipped out a plaid beret, put it on his head and announced, "I'm gonna play 'Loch Lomond,' and I ain't gonna swing it." Just as he reached the final chord a man in the balcony hollered, "Hey, Fats, swing it." "Yah, man," Fats cried and he turned "Loch Lomond" into something that had never been heard before.

After that, it was all honey. He played a hold-over engagement at the Palladium in London then went to Scandinavia for two more weeks of concerts. Fats was really kicking up a storm in Europe. The only trouble was, so were the Nazis. It began to look like war was imminent and Fats cut short his tour and returned to the United States.

Then Neville Chamberlin negotiated his "peace in our time" at Munich and Fats, in 1939, returned for another triumphant tour, this time covering the English provinces and parts of Scandinavia. At one point he had to travel through Germany to get to Sweden. Fats refused to make the trip unless his compartment was sealed. They had to change trains at Hamburg and when Tom was forced to exit from his compartment the first thing he saw was a regiment of goose-stepping Nazi storm troopers.

The Nazis, incidentally, paid Fats a lovely compliment during the war when they referred to him as a "musical clown whose income was derived from syncopating German classical music and setting it to jazz." Such treatment was usually reserved for musicians and artists who reached sympathetic German ears.

After his European success, Fats had no trouble selling himself in America. He returned as big as he ever was, playing solo dates all over the country, composing for Broadway musicals, recording and making three movies, "Hooray For Love," "King of

Burlesque," and "Stormy Weather." One critic wrote about "Stormy Weather" that "Fats Waller lifted his left eyebrow and nearly stole the picture."

On January 14, 1942, Fats played a concert at Carnegie Hall before a packed house of 2,800. He played all the songs he had written, from "Squeeze Me" to his latest hit, "All That Meat And No Potatoes." The concert was arranged by Eddie Condon as a tribute to Fats. "When I arrived in the hall," Condon remembers, "there were more people backstage than in the orchestra. Fats' friends had dropped in to wish him luck. He had a drink with each of them."

That was the trouble with Fats. He had too many drinks with too many friends. By 1942 the whole tremendous pace was beginning to tell on him. That year his doctors told him he'd have to go on the wagon. He did, for two months, substituting soda pop and drinking it by the case. Early in 1943 he became ill and he was warned he would have to slow down or face the consequences. Later that year he wrote the melodies for a new Broadway musical, "Early to Bed." Then, in December of 1943, he contracted to play engagements in Omaha, Los Angeles and Hollywood. He got through the Omaha and Los Angeles dates but came into Hollywood suffering from a bad case of influenza. He was out ten days and then had apparently recovered and the doctors said he could fulfill his engagement at the Florentine Gardens. When he finished his date, Ed Kirkeby had all he could do to load him aboard the Santa Fe Super Chief. Fats was exhausted from an all-night farewell party and he was looking forward to spending the Christmas holidays at home with his family.

"As the train pulled out," Kirkeby remembered, "Fats sat down and said, 'Oh, man, I can't take this much longer.' 'You're not going to,' I said. 'You'll never do one-nighters again. We'll have enough from records, royalties, incomes from shows, concerts—no more one-nighters.'

"Then we went into the club car. He was approached by people all over the damn world. 'Hey, Fats, glad to see you.' And the party was on. We took some people up forward to our room. Then near midnight, I started taking off my coat, said I was going to bed. It was the only way to break things up. I woke up at 11 the next morning and I said to Fats, 'How you feel, Tom?' He said, 'Man, I'm gonna get some more shuteye.' He slept all day long, which wasn't unusual. He used to hibernate the same way at home.

"About two that morning I opened the door to the room and a gust of cold air hit me. I said, 'Jeesus, it's cold in here.' Fats said, 'Yah, Hawkins is sure out there tonight,' [a reference to the very blustery tenor sax of Coleman Hawkins]. Then about five that morning I woke up and heard a choking sound. I saw him over there in bed trembling all over. I shook him, thinking he was having a bad dream, but he didn't wake. The train was stopped at the time in Kansas City and I rushed to find a porter to get a doctor. Finally the doctor came and examined Tom and then he said to me, 'This man is dead.'"

It was December 15, 1943, and just as the Sante Fe Super Chief rested in the blackness of a Kansas City night, so did Fats Waller, 39 years old, rest too, perhaps for the first time in his life. An autopsy indicated that death had been caused by bronchial pneumonia.

The funeral was a fine and expensive one, held at the same Abyssinian Church where Tom's father had been preacher many years before. There was a crowd of 4,200 in the church and thousands more in the surrounding streets which had been blocked off. The pallbearers included Count Basie, Don Redman, Claude Hopkins, Andy Kirk, Andy Razaf, J. C. Johnson and J. P. Johnson. The coffin and sides of the pulpit were banked with floral pieces that formed a rectangle at least twenty feet in length and nine feet high. "Oh, my," Fats might have said if he had been there looking it over instead of lying in the blue casket with the mountain of flowers behind him, "Break this up children, why break this up."

The Reverend Adam Clayton Powell, now a United States Congressman, conducted the service. "Because God gave him genius and skill," Powell said, "he in turn gave the world laughter and joy for its difficult and lonely hours."

It was a gray, overcast day but Ed Kirkeby swears that just as the casket was being put into the hearse a shaft of sunlight broke through and fell on the coffin. It lasted, Kirkeby says, just long enough for the doors to shut behind Fats.

GEORGE FRAZIER

Lee

I FIRST MET tall, impeccable, dashing, sophisticated, debonair, handsome George (Gentleman George) Frazier when Pee Wee, Bobby Hackett, George Brunes, some other burglars and I were working at Sizzlin's (Eddie's word for Nick's—R. G.) He used to come in, usually single-handed, freshly sprung from Boston, and drink ale (I don't know why he didn't drink whiskey, but I think George knew why). He was a very impressive guy. He was always not only a jazz devotee, but a complete lunatic on the subject. Also, he had good taste, which he never hesitated to express in positive and declarative terms. George was always hypercritical; it had to be the best, and if it wasn't, he didn't mind who he scorched. Somebody told me once that he was fired off a Boston newspaper because his column, in which he panned the Glen Gray orchestra (then working for Camel cigarettes) ran right alongside a Camel advertisement. What I mean here is that George always had high standards and contempt for people who didn't know what standards were. Also, he was always, and is, one hell of a writer, although brevity is not one of his weaknesses. In this piece, somebody—I suppose it was Georgie Porgie Wein, the Boston impresario, had sense enough to turn him loose on Lee

Wiley. This was done as album-liner material for an album in which Lee sang some Rodgers and Hart songs. What we have, therefore, is one of the best jazz writers on THE best jazz vocalist.

E. C.

In the not overwhelmingly genteel semantics of her own profession, Lee Wiley, a tall, striking-looking woman with olive skin, corn-colored hair, and Cherokee blood, is "one bitch of a singer," which, for all its robustness, happens to be just about the sweetest, most terrific tribute you can pay a person, meaning, as it so richly does, that he or she can reach your heart with her singing. In Miss Wiley's case—as heard by me anyway—it also means that she has a voice and style that have long since made me extremely eager to go to bed with her—but in a nice, noble way, you understand. For what I am getting at is that although she sings with devastating sex appeal, she does so in an exalted way. But maybe I better amplify.

There are, you see, simply slews of girls who sing in a style gingerly calculated to arouse the male listener's interest in getting them into the feathers—girls like Sunny whatever-her-name-is and others along the same sleazy lines. But the difference is that girls like Sunny whatever-her-name-is have a kind of appeal that stimulates only the baser instincts—the you're-gonna-hate-yourself-in-the-morning delayed reaction. About them there is no possibility for the *grand passion*, no inspiration to desert your wife and put your children up for adoption. You simply want to possess them and then run, not walk, toward the nearest exit. Which is not at all the way it is with Lee Wiley, who is so unmistakably a creature of infinitely more lingering enchantment. Miss Wiley has a little thing going for her called class. And class, I scarcely need remind you, is rare enough these days.

You know what class is? Well, it is, of course, *ne plus ultra* and *noblesse oblige*, Fifth Avenue at Christmastime and a *Boss* over-and-under gun, *Tom Jones* and Delius and Humphrey Bogart in *The Maltese Falcon* and the matchless tap-dancing of John Bubbles, and so forth. But it is also like, for instance, Garbo. Like when you give the first name a miss—like, for instance, Caruso or Goodman or Bogart or Schweitzer or Ellington or Hemingway or Cartier. When you say "Hemingway," is anybody likely to give you the puzzled-look department and inquire, "Which Hemingway you talking about? Drew Hemingway or Fulton J. Hemingway or Sam Hemingway or Ernest Hemingway?" Nobody is. At least nobody I know, because in my set we mean Hemingway —just Hemingway! In my set nobody ever said, "To which Hemingway do you have reference?" or "Hemingway—who dat?" And if they did, we would have said, "C. O. Jones!"—if you follow me. Whatta hell, whatta hell—you don't know any Emily Garbos or Martin Cartiers, do you? So Wiley is Lee Wiley, and not Wiley Post or Senator Wiley or any other Wiley, see?

Anyway, Wiley is one of the best vocalists who ever lived, with a magical empathy for fine old show tunes and good jazz. Indeed, I know of no one who sings certain songs so meaningfully, so wistfully. She is, however, an artistic snob and, consequently, simply awful when (as is blessedly rare) somebody persuades her to experiment with mediocre material. When she doesn't get a lyric's message, you might just as well call the game because of wet grounds. But given a number worthy of her endowments—well, she is miraculous, as, in fact, she is here.

To hear Lee at her best, listen to her Storyville LP—the portfolio of songs by Rodgers and Hart. Not Rodgers and that other fellow (who would be Oscar Hammerstein, II, who, no disrespect intended, no Larry Hart, he). These are haunting songs —songs that have withstood the ravaging headlong rush of the years, the fickleness of public taste, and the debasement of the lyric to the nadir where we are subjected to, forgive the expression, "Be My Life's Companion." But whatta hell, whatta hell. The gratifying thing is that Richard Rodgers and Lorenz Hart (who, although dead and buried these many years, is more artistically alive than the no-talent author of "Be My Life's Companion") turned out some lovely, lovely stuff and that Lee Wiley has a superb affinity for it. To my mind, indeed, she is the definitive interpreter of Rodgers and Hart and I daresay she need fear no competition from, say, Sunny whatever-her-name-is. Can't you, incidentally, just imagine Sunny whatever-her-name-is trying to do "Glad to Be Unhappy!" But keep your fingers crossed, because Sunny's husband is her manager or something, so you can never be sure. If there were more space at my disposal, I would say a thing or two about some of those husbands who manage their singing wives—something to the effect that they thought Mickey Jelke was evil—but no matter. Moreover, it's pleasanter to talk about Lee Wiley.

About the vast art of Miss Wiley there is a sophistication that is both eloquent and enduring and utterly uncontrived. And it is about her person too, in—oh, for example, the marvelous skirts from I. Magnin's, the little white straw hat and the navy blue dress with white piping that she wore to the Stork for brunch last Easter Sunday, the apartment over the East River, and so on. This, as the vulgate has it, is only the best. I am afraid, though, that it may not be apparent to everybody, because—leave us face it— there are a lot of stupid bastards in the world. There are, for example, men ignorant enough not to be able to distinguish a Paul Stuart suit from one out of the workrooms of Brooks Brothers! And the Stuart job with but two buttons on the sleeve! Yet there are some bright bastards too—and for them the special things, for them quality, whether it be the Golden Fleece of Brooks, the charm of Mary Martin, the genius of Otto Graham, or what-not. For them the special and dedicated likes of Lee Wiley, Richard Rodgers, and Larry Hart.

It was John O'Hara, in that magnificent introduction of his to *The Portable Scott Fitzgerald,* who pointed out that if Clifton Fadiman (who had offended O'Hara by (A) criticizing his literary absorption with the brand names of clothes; and (B) calling *Butterfield-8* "Disappointment in O'Hara")—it was, I was saying, O'Hara who said that if Fadiman tried to wear Brooks clothes, he would be recognized as a spy. The O'Hara introduction may not have very much to do with Fitzgerald, but it is a masterpiece just the same—a fine, snobbish defense of taste; a brimstone condemnation of the second-rate; a lovely, bitchy reproof of Fadiman for his colossal cheek in daring to entertain views about male attire. Him with that take-me-home-for-twenty-two-fifty appearance of his, that catcher's-mitt-free-with-every-purchase style—him who looks like he forgot to take the hanger out of his jacket.) It is, in short, an introduction that pleads for the recognition of authentic art, whether it be the art of Scott Fitzgerald or of Lee

Wiley and Rodgers and Hart—the art for which I am prepared to send a box top any time.

I do not in the least mind admitting that it gets me livid when most girl singers make it big, for it is my dour conviction that, by and large, they have plenty of nothing. Lee Wiley, however, is an artist. Technically, she may leave something to be desired, but artistically, she's simply magnificent, projecting emotion with dignity and warmth, expressing nuances with exquisite delicacy, and always making you share her bliss or heartbreak. She came to New York from Fort Gibson, Oklahoma, and before very long all the right people were bewitched by her incomparable magic. There is no room here to catalogue all the individuals—that is, the prominent ones—who are Wiley devotees, but right offhand I can think of Bing Crosby, Ted Straeter, Victor Young, Louis Armstrong, and Marlene Dietrich.

Indeed, if I have any objection to Lee's singing, it is that it always assails me with bittersweet memories—with the stabbing remembrance of the tall, breathtaking-lovely Wellesley girl with whom I was so desperately in love in the long-departed November when the band at the Copley Plaza in Boston used to play "My Heart Stood Still" as couples tea-danced after football games on crisp Saturday afternoons, with reawakened desire for the succession of exquisite girls with whom I spent many a crepuscular hour listening to cocktail pianists give muted voice to "Funny Valentine," of the first time I saw "Connecticut Yankee," of—Yes, of the first years of my marriage and listening to Lee Wiley records with my wife late at night. My wife, who knew more about show tunes than any woman has a right to know, had a special affection for "You Took Advantage Of Me" and she always sang it when her spirits were high. Afterwards, when she had long since ceased to sing it, when a judge had severed what no man is supposed to put asunder, I lived for more than a year with a girl who I hoped might make me forget. She was not witty or talented or, for that matter, particularly pretty, but she was very, very sweet and she tried very, very hard, even pretending to appreciate the Wiley records that I used to play over and over again as I clutched at the past. And for a little while, indeed, it would actually seem to be kind of wonderful, with the mournful wailing of tugs in the river below and in the distance the Fifty-ninth Street Bridge stretched like a giant necklace across the night sky, as we sat there listening to the songs of heartbreak. There were even moments when I rather fancied myself falling in love again. But always such moments fled, because when Miss Wiley sings, there is nothing spurious, nothing fraudulent, nothing affected. So I would sit there and hurt more and more with the remembrance of other, never-to-be-recaptured nights in that same room. Lee Wiley can do that to you—damn her! But damn her gently, because she is, after all, the best we have—the very best.

(*A note on a session Lee once made. Among those present were a few musicians and Johnny DeVries. Johnny is a versatile guy. He's a song writer, artist, layout man, advertising executive—he knows how to do everything but abide by custom and behave himself. He had a friend in those days, a rich kid from the Philadelphia area, whom we called Toilet Head because of his habit, when loaded, of going into the toilet and pulling the chain to permit the cold water to douse his head. Toilet Head's family was worried about him; they assigned a male nurse to follow him about. Nursey-nursey was also present on this session. The recording director became overwrought at one point and kept asking Lee to sing a certain passage several times. Lee became disgusted. She said she wouldn't do it. She said it several times in rather dramatic terms, and wound up yelling, "I can't do it! I'm sick!"*

("*You're sick?*" *said Toilet Head.* "*I've got a male nurse!*"—E. C.)

CARLTON BROWN

Bill

THIS IS LIKE trying to explain what makes the universe in non-theological terms. Carlton—call him Bob—has undertaken it with courage, and has come through clean. Around our joint, we call Wild Pitch Davison The Iron Chancellor. He plunges each day for a ninety-mile commute from his house to our saloon; he's never late, never unavoidably detained either by booze or domestic matters. Or by his gum. Nobody has ever found out what Davison does with his gum while playing, but he must have some special cavity for it—something similar to a kangaroo pouch. Let's just say this about Davison: His reticence has never been so noticeable as to cause complaints. As for Bob Brown, if you want to check up on what kind of writer he is, look up a novel called Brainstorm. That'll do it.

E. C.

Wild Bill Davison, who is considered by many jazz experts and fans to be the most driving, inexhaustible Dixieland cornetist in the business, has a personal hardihood that fully matches his professional reputation. It is appropriate that he was born, on January 5, 1906, in Defiance, Ohio. Wild Bill, like his spiritual ancestor, Hickock, shows a hardy mid-Western defiance for all kinds of challenges. Not the least of these, for Davison, is the challenge of getting whisky while working. Night-club waiters do not hover solicitously around the bandstand, and there's no sense getting maimed in the crush at the bar between sets. Bill attacks the problem with characteristic boldness.

"Whisky!" he shouts lustily in his first breath after a chorus, propping his horn on his knee and giving a snap to his chewing-gum. He gets the whisky. In the course of a session that is going hell-for-leather, he is also fond of interjecting a yell of "Let me out!" or "HELP!"

Jazz-wise audiences won't let him out until closing time, and he doesn't need help in any department. Trumpeter Max Kaminsky says that Davison is the only musician he knows who can drink and continue to play well, and this has been borne out in repeated demonstrations. He is known among fellow jazz-men as one who never lets down all night long, but keeps driving the rest of them on with unflagging energy and inspiration. While waiting for his present job at Eddie Condon's elegant saloon in Greenwich Village to materialize, Bill spent his spare evenings sitting in for free at Jimmy Ryan's on 52nd Street. It was a common occurrence, when the doors were open, for Bill's throbbing cornet to revive an almost non-existent trade by dragging in a houseful of customers off the street. When, once, he was the only trumpeter to show up at a Condon Town Hall concert, in place of the usual three or four, Davison thought nothing of taking every cornet part straight through.

The power of Wild Bill's person and playing under any conditions is phenomenal. It was once written that, after a hard night of work and play, he overpowered a turkey in a cornfield outside Milwaukee by blowing a few high blasts on his cornet. Davison modestly amends the report.

"I woke up and went to take a shower," he says, "and found this great big monster in the bathroom. I shut the door on it fast and yelled 'Help!' to the superintendent. Then it all began to come back to me. There'd been a whole flock of turkeys by the road on the way home, and I'd stopped the car and got out to get me one. I did lay a few high notes on them, and I guess it dazed them a little, but the fact is I had to chase them and nab

BILL

one with my bare hands. The superintendent's wife made us a fine turkey dinner out of it."

The Pride of Defiance has had tougher things to down than whisky and turkey, either of which he can take or leave alone. There was that bad setback in Milwaukee in the late thirties, for one. Bill was having a drink at the bar where he was playing, minding his business, when a fight started among some customers. One of them heaved a beer mug which flew wide of its mark and caught Bill on the upper lip, splitting it wide open and knocking out half a tooth. This had about the effect that a couple of broken ankles would have had on Fred Astaire at the up-turn of his career.

"It took six weeks for the lip to heal so I could even touch it," he says. "Then when I tried holding the horn to it the lip just refused to vibrate. The nerves were severed and I couldn't make a sound. I got to thinking awful fast what else I could do for a living." He found that by holding the horn into a pillow he could get a back-pressure that was firm but a little yielding, and day after day, for hours at a time, he worked at it. "It was another six weeks before I could make any kind of noise come out. It wasn't much, at first, but I knew it was a start at getting back in the music business." For a long time after, he delayed getting the tooth repaired, for fear of upsetting the adjustment he had made to the injury, and he still holds his mouthpiece to one side of center, giving an added effect of nonchalance.

(There was another bad time that I told about in We Called It Music. It happened in January, 1932. The paragraph in the book said,

"Tesch [Frank Teschemacher] was working in Chicago with Wild Bill. They were driving to work in Davison's open car, which had no top. Tesch was sitting with his hands in the pockets of his overcoat. A taxicab without lights hit them broadside in front of a drugstore at Magnolia and Wilson. Tesch was thrown over the hood and struck his head on the curb. He was killed instantly."—E. C.)

Davison's life and times are interwoven with the strictly American story of hot music, and his playing—which may be heard abundantly on records, broadcasts, at concerts, night-clubs and jam sessions—has the quality of autobiography. A couple of quick quotations that he likes to insert in his solos might be called cadenzas, but anyone who has been an American boy will identify them more readily as "The monkey wrapped his tail around the flag-pole," and "Oh, they wore no clothes in those old Egyptian shows," and be able to carry on from there.

Years of hard living have aged Davison hardly at all. His cheeks are smooth and rosy and his eyes unadorned by what a mellowing actress has termed "mouse bellies." During one winter furlough in New York, the boy in Bill instigated an epic snowball fight outside of Julius' Tavern, involving a couple of jazz critics, an executive of the American Broadcasting Company, their wives, and ultimately a large slice of the clientele. Cowardly combatants who retreated inside for safety had not measured the mettle of their opponent. Davison followed with a volley of slush-balls that found their targets unerringly down the length of the bar and gave bystanders a refreshing shower. Host Pete Pesci, whose joint has gained fame and trade as a musicians' hangout, barely batted an eye.

A couple of snapshots of Bill at the age of twelve should qualify for the archives of the Institute of Jazz Studies. In both he wears his Boy Scout uniform. In one, he stands on a hill at the juncture of the Maumee and Auglaize Rivers, the site of the lookout for Fort Defiance, erected by Mad Anthony Wayne in 1794 to stand off the Indians. Young Willy's big, deep, nickel-plated Carl Fischer cornet is upraised as though ready to blow down any lingering redskins, and his stance and expression have a familiar look to those who know him today. In the other, he is standing on the steps of the Defiance Public Library, cornet at ease.

He had already worked up an embouchure by practicing on lengths of garden hose, with a funnel in one end, until he could produce bugle calls. He ran a paper route, and to help him earn money for his first cornet, his mother made up loaves of boned chicken for him to sell along the route.

"Who started me in the music business," Bill says, "was a friend of my father's who played mandolin and taught me how to finger it on numbers like 'Yip-I-Addie-I-Ay.' He'd spend week-ends at our cottage on the Maumee River, where we went fishing and my father cooked up a wonderful soup made with those big softshell turtles and Blue Channel catfish—what a deal! Last I heard of my dad he was renting boats, guns, fishing tackle, everything, out of Little Rock on the White River in Arkansas."

Davison's present loose connections with his family extend to everyone but his mother, a handsome matron who lives in Detroit. When his first impressive records came out in 1944 and hit the columns, one reviewer received a letter from Bill's brother Walter in Defiance, asking how, after all these years, he could get in touch with the wandering Wild One.

This familial elasticity began early. When Bill posed on the steps of the library, he was living in its basement with his maternal grandmother, the librarian, and his grandfather. He remained with them until he hit the road in his late teens. It may be psychologically significant that a man whose job is to make the loudest noise in a jazz band should have spent his formative years in an atmosphere of rigidly enforced quiet. When William first got to the cornet, he had to take it down to the banks of the river to practice.

"The first time I ever heard a brass band," he remembers, "was when a troop train stopped off and put on a full-dress parade. They came marching down the street to 'Ja-Da' in march time, with a little syncopation—real corny, but I thought it was the most wonderful thing in the world, with all that brass going. I kept asking the trumpet questions—how do you get all that stuff on the first valve? I would have run away from home just to clean their instruments."

If military security hadn't forced radio amateurs to dismantle their sets with the advent of World War I, Davison thinks he would now be a big man in the technical end of broadcasting, rather than a musician. His 1½-kilowatt sending station, 8FU, was active on the early ham network, with a range all the way to Rome, Georgia.

One night some years ago Bill was standing at the bar in Julius' when he noticed a soldier next to him with a patch of lightning on his sleeve, and recalled a long-unused aptitude. In vocalized ta-da-da-dat-ta-da's, he flashed the soldier a rowdy message. The soldier answered cheerfully, "Kiss mine, too," and soon they were cutting up touches on radio. Bill has a large capacity for making friends, and it is seldom that anyone is offended by his highly robust language, thanks to the explosive humor and good nature of his delivery. Seeing a bunch of cute chicks at the curb while waiting for a green light, he is likely to ask, in the tone of one requesting directions, "Say, pardon me—would any of you girls like to get married?" In more familiar circles, his query is blunter, but in the same light-hearted vein that turns away wrath.

Though music was at first a sideline with Billy the Kid, he developed it with the energy and enthusiasm which he now throws into such hobbies as collecting guns and antiques, hunting and making model boats. While still in grade school, he organized a small band in which he doubled on banjo and cornet.

"Our first job together," he recalls, "was an ice-cream social on the steps of the Methodist Church for two dollars apiece—really unheard-of dough. We knew two songs—'Moonlight' and 'St. Louis Blues.' We'd play one and then four encores of the same tune. It went over so big that we got a job to play a Presbyterian church bazaar. Then we called ourselves the Ohio Lucky Seven. By the time I hit high school, I was already a full-fledged working musician."

The Seven is not listed in the jazz books, and graduated no one but Davison to the big time. An early photograph of them, however, might almost pass for one of Bix Beiderbecke and the Wolverines of the early Twenties, now hallowed immortals of jazz. Bill sits erect, bright-eyed, slick-haired and sharp in his tux, the bell of his cornet on one knee and a banjo and slide cornet at his feet.

The Seven were so far from being in Bix's class, then, that when they were booked opposite the Wolverines once in 1924, they were glad to concede defeat and just listen. Bill soon promoted himself into such high-sounding organizations as James Jackson's Royal Jacksonian Society Syncopators and Rollin Potter's Peerless Players, and though the jazz content of these groups was undoubtedly low, they helped put Davison into the business for keeps.

BILL

"One reason I could always get jobs with bands," he says, "was that I could sing and be the comedian. I did a drunk act from Bert Williams, I remember—the one that went, 'Brother, if you craves more preachin' save a little dram for me.'"

Today, Bill frequently enlivens a performance by topping off a chorus with a bump, burlesque style, accompanied by a parodied look of being sent. In his pre-induction band at Nick's in New York, he used to team with clarinetist Pee Wee Russell, trombonist George Brunis and drummer Danny Alvin in a knocked-out routine to "Baby, Won't You Please Come Home," complete with singing, dancing, and purposely frightful stuff on combs, toy instruments, and bicycle bell. On very good nights, customers were treated to a specialty of Brunis' as an encore. George would lie on his back on the stand and let Bill or, preferably, one of the lighter members of the ensemble stand on his stomach while he played the trombone with one foot operating the slide. Brunis is the only known instrumentalist in the world who would dream of attempting the feat, and he was one of the most fitting musical companions Davison has ever had.

The Wild One's memory is as rich as his comic repertoire, and he can tell deep-dish jazz students exactly in what spot he played with whom and when. He recalls all the details of recording and broadcasting with the Chubb-Steinberg band of 1924 and '25, for instance, but none of them are as interesting to the non-jazzicologist as other memories of the period.

"That's where I did my first drinking, there in Cincinnati—gin," says Bill of a historic occasion. "Carl Clauve, the banjo in the band, introduced me to Mama Somebody's in Walnut Hill—a dollar a pint. Then Carl, Bix and myself would get together after work and go to the Hole in the Wall and play together. That was some tough joint—greatest collection of barflies I ever saw. The whole upstairs was vacant and the drunks went up there to sleep on the floor."

(*In those days Bix was having trouble with his pivot tooth. It was in front, upstairs, and it frequently dropped out, leaving Bix unable to blow a note. Wherever he worked it was customary to see the boys in the band down on the floor, looking for Bix's tooth. Once in Cincinnati at five o'clock in the morning while* driving over a snow-covered street in a 1922 Essex with Wild Bill Davison and Carl Clove, Bix shouted, "Stop the car!" There was no speakeasy in sight. "What's the matter?" Davison asked. "I've lost my tooth," Bix said. They got out and carefully examined the fresh snow. After a long search Davison sighted a tiny hole; in it he found the tooth, quietly working its way down to the road. Bix restored it to his mouth and they went on to The Hole in the Wall, where they played every morning for pork chop sandwiches and gin. It was natural for Bix not to get the tooth permanently fastened; he couldn't be bothered going to the dentist.—E. C.)

The Chubb-Steinberg band, in one of those sudden upsets common to South American governments and early orchestras, was taken over by its dancing fiddle-player, Art Hicks, and tenor-saxist Paul T. Omer, now a prominent New York lawyer. An incident of the time nicely illustrates the raiding aptitudes of pioneering band-leaders. Davison was practising in a Chicago hotel room one day when there was a knock on the door. The caller was Eddie Neibaur, leader of the Seattle Harmony Kings. He'd heard Bill touching it off from his own hotel room across the street and a block away, and tracked him down to offer him a job. Bill filed it for the future and went on barnstorming around Ohio with Omer-Hicks. Then one of their ads read: "TONITE! Direct from Cleveland and enroute to Roseland Ball Room, New York." Our boy was really going places.

"It was there and at the old Monte Carlo, under the Roseland, that I first got together with Miff Mole, Red Nichols, the Dorseys, Red McKenzie, Coleman Hawkins and those guys"— all names that loom large in the jazz fan's lexicon. "Omer-Hicks was playing against Fletcher Henderson," Bill says, reverting naturally to the fistic terminology that was used in those jazz-battle days. The band was also involved, indirectly, in a noted tussle of the times.

"We played the Earl Carroll bathtub party—not in the pit, but a one-night stand for the party on stage after the show." That was the time, in February, 1926, when Carroll served a tubful of champagne garnished with a naked girl, and all the guests dipped in. There was a little legal trouble about it, resulting in the temporary eclipse of Carroll, but the band was not hauled to the clink. It all seemed pretty proper to Bill, because the girl wore a robe up to the tub, and thereafter was fundamentally covered, and he has no feeling about the affair beyond a mild resentment that he didn't get so much as a whiff of champagne.

Bill went back to Defiance for his first visit since leaving home, and then jobbed around some more until he hit Detroit and Chicago with the Harmony Kings. He heard his first Louis Armstrong record, "Cornet Chop Suey," in Detroit, and thereafter got everything he could of his. Since then, he says, he's been sold. "I wanted to see Louis and see what kind of man could play that kind of cornet. I couldn't get enough." He got a good helping when Armstrong's first groups were playing the Sunset, the Plantation and the Savoy, and they became friends.

"There was a place called the Ranch on South Parkway where all the colored musicians went. I used to go there with Louis. I had a great big blue Packard, a seven-passenger job about eight miles long, and I used to drive Louis, Lil Armstrong and Zutty Singleton out to my place on Sheridan Road."

By this time, Bill was with the Benny Meroff band, which featured him in hot solos and held him until the early thirties. It was mainly for bucks, and quite a batch of them—up to $11,000 a year. For kicks, there was jamming with all the since-famous Chicagoans. There was the stretch of living with Eddie Condon's brother Pat, a wonderful guitarist, Bill says, who taught him a lot of right melodies and chords. Brother Eddie relates that the guys would make early-morning raids on grocery-shop deliveries, one being assigned to lift a bottle of milk, the other bread, and so on, for their breakfast.

This was in a lean, lay-off period period that may have had an influence on Bill's present habits. A friend who recently observed him as a house-guest noted that Bill was excessive about everything but food. He made a wry face at the morning orange-juice his host offered, but after fortifying it with an equal portion of whisky, managed to down it along with a couple of eggs. Otherwise, he seems generally satisfied with one square meal a day.

More than the music of that time, Bill recalls the incidents. One night a chorine impersonating a bird was being wafted through the air above the band when the wire snapped and she landed in Bill's lap. He remarked later that it was the first time a babe had used the aerial approach on him.

"If you could ring in the girl angle," he says, now that he is nicely settled in that respect, "it would make nice reading. I've often lain in bed and thought, what if I saw them all coming down the street at once. *Help!* There must be thousands. There's *got* to be."

There was a surfeit of them during those sixteen weeks of playing for burlesque at the Garrick, before the righteous citizens looked into the show—"a real foul one"—and drove it out of town.

"The girls—all thirty of them—thought nothing of stripping to the buff in the dressing-room while the band was sitting around, and we got so we didn't even look up. When the girls came out on the runway I'd blow them off the stage with some real jazz. I used to just *blast* 'em and make 'em shake twice as much." As a result of this engagement, Davison is equipped to deliver a thoroughgoing analysis of the cumulative B.O. effect of crowding forty active entertainers into a small, overheated space.

But the most memorable kicks were provided by Louis. He came back to the Savoy for a one-night stand and Bill's attendance was assured.

"I was about the only white guy there. Louis looked over and his face lit up in a big smile. He was so happy to see me he walked over with his cornet and just laid it on me—played about eight choruses right at me." The picture has not, apparently, been enhanced in the rosy light of reminiscence. During Armstrong's stay at the Zanzibar several years ago, he corroborated Bill's account of their friendship, and volunteered some unstinting praise of his follower.

Davison is not reticent about his idolatry of Armstrong or his influence on his playing. "I've heard Louis so much that I copy his tone as much as possible, and the feeling in his heart. Just to be able to make one *note* that sounds like Louis is enough to accomplish in a lifetime." Davison's admirers feel that he has practically achieved his ambition, and still has many years to go. They accord him adulation only a little short of that given Louis in his heyday, and during World War II clamored for more of his records than Commodore, limited by shortage of materials, could supply. When the news leaked out that many Davison platters were as yet unreleased, the company was deluged with advance orders for them.

From Chicago in the Louis days, Bill hit the road again, and before long the ads were reading: "EXTRA! Tonite in Person. 'The Trumpet King' Davison and his Dixieland Music. First Milwaukee appearance." He played there, at eight or ten spots, up to 1938. The name of Dianne Lee, "Blonde Bombshell of Popular Song," began to show in the early ads. She came from an out-of-town job for an audition, missed up on the appointment, and connected with Bill by chance after she'd decided to go home.

"That was it," Bill says of his first meeting with his pretty wife, who cooks a mean dish of spare-ribs and is what he would call, in his highest words of praise, "a real barrelhouse chick."

(*There has since been another replacement. Tommy Manville is not yet worried, but Davison was pressing him hard. To Wild Bull, love is a many-splendored thing.—E.C.*)

The word began to go out from Milwaukee about Bill's cornet. He got some money together and came to New York to follow up a few nibbles. That, too, was it. From there on in, minus time out for Uncle Sammy, he has been traveling with the very best jazz company, the bunch who could get chairs with any of the big commerical bands but prefer to stick together in small groups. Nowadays, after years of kicking around which are pretty well summed up in Bill's career, they're getting by handsomely at playing the uninhibited stuff that comes from the heart.

Davison had been telling friends to start buying Jap war bonds if he was drafted, but the grind of his final civilian days again revealed iron-man qualities that any army would want to enlist. He finished his first batch of twelve Commodore sides one day in the winter of '44, took his place that night in the revived Original Dixieland Jazz Band in the Katherine Dunham show, drove home to Dumont, New Jersey, snatched four hours of sleep, made radio transcriptions all the next day, played the Dunham show again, returned to the studio for an all-night session with the Dixielanders, and went directly from there to induction, just a couple of weeks shy of the thirty-eighth birthday which would have exempted him.

Bill's two-year stretch in the army did nothing to impair his ruggedness. He hit Fort Dix at the same time as his friend Dick Carey, who likes to play trumpet as well as piano. The Colonel ordered them both to play Fire Call. This and the other chores of an army bugler might sound as though they'd be kid stuff to a graduate Scout, but Bill says of bugle calls, "There's a million of them, and when I was bugler for the day, I couldn't depend on my memory for the complicated ones." A tune like "Bugle Call Rag," or any other popular one of the past twenty years, would have come to Bill as readily as his memory of what band he played with when, but when it came to his first try at Fire Call, he had to get Carey to write it out for him. Davison got a kid to hold the music up for him in the high wind, and went through it perfectly three times. The fourth time, the wind blew the music away. Davison had to fake it, and naturally, considering his background, a few hot licks sneaked in, and a little fancy vibrato—as natural to him as breathing. As it happened, he was laying this last one on some Negro troops, and it went over big with them.

After a tough grind in basic, Bill had it pretty easy in regular service. Dianne went along to Camp Patrick Henry in Virginia, and then to the redistribution center at Asheville, N.C., where she worked for the government and they had their own apartment. They made, naturally, a few of their own loose interpretations of regulations. When Bill fractured his kneecap and was in the hospital for a month, time often hung heavy. One night he and another guy sneaked out into the garden for some surreptitious drinks with their wives, and later Bill and Dianne took a ride in their car and renewed their acquaintance.

"That took some nerve," he points out—a quality in which the Wild One has never been in the least deficient. Though Bill insists that he worked hard in the army and earned it, his friends consider it an exquisite piece of irony that Cpl. William Edward Davison was awarded the Good Conduct Medal.

(Bob does not mention Bill's hobbies in this piece. The Wild Man has almost as many diversions as drinks. A few years ago he opened an antique shop, Trash and Treasures, and took to making lamps out of old horns. He was obsessed with this hobby for a long time—at least three days—and could talk of nothing else. One night while on the stand at Condon's, Bill was chattering away to Cutty Cutshall about his lamp-making project while Eddie was vainly attempting to beat off the band. Eddie finally grew exasperated. "Listen, you son of a bitch," he said to Davison, "will you quit that gabbin', pick up that lamp and play it?"—R. G.)

(Once The Wild One got out of the Army, he played around at various milk bars on 52nd Street, and in 1945 began the first of several long-run engagements at Condon's downtown Boozeteria. He's been there longer than any other trumpet man, and there have been very few complaints registered by the customers, including the ones who are stone deaf. Final note: Any way you look at him, there's nobody like him.—E.C.)

LEONARD FEATHER

Dave

IT SEEMS TO have fallen to Leonard Feather to deliver our farewell orations. Here he's talking about a close friend of mine. I described the way I met Dave Tough in We Called It Music:

"In Chicago in 1924 I was saving my dough for some of the haberdashery in Dockstader-Sandberg's on Michigan Avenue, a store so high class it eventually soared out of business. One day I spotted a new style hat, with a high crown. That's for me, I thought, when I get enough paper. The next night I worked on a date at Northwestern University in Evanston, just over the line from Chicago. A gaunt, hollow-looking kid came in, dragging drums. Something about him seemed familiar. Then I spotted his hat—he had the pilgrim's model. Damn him, I thought, he got it before I did. He said his name was Dave Tough; he set up the drums and I wondered where he would find the strength to hit them. He was behind me when we started our first number; what he did to the drums nearly drove me through the opposite wall. I turned around and looked at him. He was possessed.

"While we were having a drink between sets I said to him, 'You sort of like this music, don't you?' He nodded gloomily. 'I guess I do,' he said. 'My family doesn't understand what I'm doing. I can't get a job with a big band because they don't play this kind of stuff. I must be crazy to keep on playing it, but I do.'

" 'Where do you live?' I asked.

" 'Oak Park,' he said.

"I knew he wasn't kidding about bucking his family; Oak Park, a suburb of Chicago, was credited with being the richest village in the world.

" 'Do you go to school?' I asked. I had a feeling he ought to be at Harvard; maybe he was being kept at Northwestern so his drumming could be watched for symptoms of violence.

" 'I go to Lewis Institute,' he said. 'It's a prep school for two kinds of people—those who can't go to the best schools and those who get thrown out of them. We have a dance there once a week, with a pickup band—this kind of music. Why don't you come and sit in?'

" 'Who plays?' I asked.

" 'Almost anybody. Some weeks we have all saxophones, some weeks we have all cornets, some weeks we have three sets of drums. Only two of us are regular, myself and a kid named Benny Goodman.'

"I knew Benny; we had met at union headquarters and played pool together until we discovered both of us were after the same thing, carfare and walk-around money. After that we took on separate opponents. I had been to Benny's home for dinner—a widowed mother, lots of kids, big bowls of good food, pitch until you win.

" 'So you know Benny,' Tough said. 'He and I joined the American Musicians Union the same day. We were both in short pants; I was thirteen, Benny was twelve. He's going to Lewis Institute now. I hope the education won't ruin his clarinet playing. We jazz players are supposed to be vulgarians beyond the moral as well as the musical pale; I guess we might as well live up to what is expected of us.'

"He looked at me.

" 'Do you expect to go on playing jazz?' he asked.

" 'While I'm eating meat,' I said.

" 'Then you are a no-good drunken tramp and you'll never

get anywhere,' he said. 'Come over to the Institute and play with us. Last week we had twelve trombones and a rhythm section.'

"When we finished and I was about to leave he said, 'If you want to go to Lincoln Gardens ask Voltaire Defoe. He took me when I was small. He's a friend of mine.'

" 'Thanks,' I said. 'I can usually get in by myself.'

" 'Come to the Institute,' Tough said. 'We've never had twelve banjos.' "

Later in the book, I told about a place Dave played that was owned by Al Capone: "Its clientele was composed almost exclusively of baseball players, gangsters, and detectives. It was managed by an ex-prize fighter named Jake, who weighed three hundred pounds and who had a little brother named Joe who weighed two hundred fifty pounds. Capone, of course, was the owner. Jake was bad-tempered and moody, particularly on rainy nights, when the weather got into his battered sinuses. Sometimes he would turn off the lights at midnight, order the customers out, and take the band into the bar to play for him. He had a passion for crossword puzzles, the easy ones in the Hearst papers. One night in the bar Dave helped him with a couple of words. From then on Jake grabbed him every night and asked him all the words. If Dave got stuck Jake would reach across the table, put his six-pound hand on Dave's shoulder, and say, "Come on, think!" So Dave worked the puzzles at home in the afternoon and went to work prepared; anything else for a drummer weighing 108 pounds would have been suicide.

"One night after finishing the puzzle and grabbing a double rye at the bar Dave was hurrying to the bandstand. An inconspicuous-looking man standing in front of him didn't move. Dave put both hands against the man's shoulders. 'Get the hell out of my way!' he said. One of the boys on the bandstand looked at Dave with admiration as he sat down at the drums. 'I guess you don't care how long you live,' he said. 'Or aren't you afraid of Bottles Capone?' Bottles was Al's kid brother. Dave played the set involuntarily; he shook enough to beat the drums in perfect time. But Jake saved him; he couldn't afford to have his crossword puzzle expert damaged."

We played some ferocious joints in those days, including the Commercial Theatre, a neighborhood movie house on the far south side. The customers were just as ferocious as the place, but actually they were afraid of us. They didn't know what we were doing when we broke into "Jazz Me Blues" or "Fidgety Feet." We were supposed to watch the news-reel and play appropriate accompaniment; we seldom did. One night in the middle of "Clarinet Marmalade" I looked up and saw a French general placing a wreath on the tomb of the Unknown Soldier. Just then Dave went into an explosion on the drums. Things like that confused the customers. Later that year we discovered that a South Side kid was sitting through two shows every night and three on Saturday to hear Tough on the drums. His name was Gene Krupa.

E. C.

It was a cold, miserable January night in the brutal New York winter of 1940. The rain was coming down in sheets when my door-buzzer rang.

"Leonard," a faint voice said on the house-phone. "Let me in. I'm sick. It's Dave Tough."

Seconds later, a tiny, bedraggled figure appeared at the door—a human sponge, topped by a gaunt, weary face and eyes that seemed to see nothing but despair.

"I haven't eaten in three days," said Dave. "I don't know where I'm staying . . . I forget what happened . . . just let me lie down and rest."

He refused all offers of help, wouldn't accept any food until my girl friend finally coaxed half a sandwich into him; his face unshaven and haggard, he seemed to want nothing but companionship and solace.

It was my first meeting of this kind with Dave Tough, and it was to be by no means the last. The Jekyll-and-Hyde jazzman, who had acquired more knowledge from more books than the next ten musicians read in a lifetime, was to dodge in and out of my consciousness and my presence as he wandered in and out of the musical forefront.

I felt more than mere pity for Dave Tough, on that first encounter with the darker side of his personality; I felt a sympathy and curiosity concerning the frustrations that led him periodically to these wild, masochistic jags. I remembered reading in *Down Beat* a few weeks earlier that Dave had been warned by a doctor to "Take it easy so your ticker won't stop suddenly." Despite a critical illness, ignoring the counsel of doctors and friends, he had joined Jack Teagarden's big band.

Then he had left it, suddenly and inexplicably just as during the previous two or three years he had wandered in and out of the Tommy Dorsey and Benny Goodman bands.

It was a miracle that Dave's frail physique continually survived the beatings to which he exposed it. Perhaps the will to live was redoubled in him because he wanted so much to live as a musician, and perhaps even more to express himself as a writer, a man of slowly and deliberately acquired culture.

Whatever the reasons, his condition apparently failed to prevent him from passing the physical examination in 1942 when he and Artie Shaw decided that Dave would be the right drummer for Artie's Navy band—though there were many rumors at the time that Artie must have sneaked him in in his duffel-bag, all ninety pounds of him.

It was during the first year after he rejoined the civilians that Dave Tough enjoyed his greatest glory in the music world. As the rhythmic cornerstone of the Woody Herman band that caught fire with "Apple Honey," "Northwest Passage," and "Caldonia"— the band that brought swinging big band jazz to a new peak—he was a hero to a million fans.

On big band records with Woody and the small band sides with Chubby, Flip, Bill Harris, and his other Herman colleagues, Dave was the Little King of the drums, the man with the cymbal that wouldn't quit and the little afterthought bass-drum tag that lent the Tough personality to every swinging performance.

Dave was a dapper little man during that Herman era, neatly dressed, sober, smiling, possessed perhaps of a greater sense of belonging than had ever before been his. And then suddenly the balloon burst.

It happened somewhere down South, in the middle of a set— some kind of a fit, they said, an agonizing experience for those who watched it as it was for him who suffered it. Again, Dave disappeared; days later John Hammond found him sitting on a sidewalk in some Alabama town and supplied him with the fare home.

So Dave was no longer with the Herman herd, but *Down Beat* readers knew enough of his work in the band to elect him the No. 1 drummer in the 1945 all star band, and again the following year.

But during that time Dave was undergoing a terrible psychological ordeal. Not only was his personality split between the desires to write and play, but now the musical world itself had undergone the fission into what were then two armed camps.

Bop had arisen, Dixieland was on the defensive, and Dave found himself in the position of the liberal who is at home with neither Communists nor fascists.

One week he would be working with Charlie Ventury or Bill Harris at the Three Deuces, with two or three boppers in the band; he would come over to my table and complain sadly that he wasn't keeping up with the times, that he knew nobody liked his work, and that he would never be able to play like Max Roach. The musicians' assurances of confidence never seemed to convince him.

Then Dave would cross the wide gulf into Dixieland and would find himself working at Condon's. He left the club, telling *Down Beat* that George Brunis played the trombone with his foot, that it sounded the same as when he played it with his hands, and that Wild Bill Davison et al were "dead jazz" characters.

Davison then denounced Dave as "Little Bludgeon Foot," assailed his attacks on Dixieland and called him, with supreme contempt, the Dizzy Gillespie of the Cymbals.

It was the beginning of the unhappiest era for Dave. There would be spells of security, then periodic binges when he would be found staggering along some dark street, homeless and distraught. And every time he came home, his wife would be waiting there as ready as ever to forgive, to forget and to rehabilitate.

Little Casey Majors, as small of stature as Dave, himself, had been a chorus girl at the Grand Terrace in Chicago, and she had made Dave's life her own for many years, enduring all the heartaches, nursing him through every breakdown.

One of the last times I saw Dave, he called again from downstairs. "Leonard, I need two dollars to buy some flowers—I'm going out to Newark, back to Casey."

I had Dave come up, glanced at him, gave him only enough for the tube to Newark but called the florist to arrange a credit for him. I was worried where temptation might lead him if I acted otherwise.

I remembered the time, a few weeks earlier, when I had opened my front door to find him lying outside. Too weak to stand up and ring the bell, he had collapsed and fallen asleep.

Dave got home to Casey that time. I knew it, because a few weeks later I saw him and Casey at the Royal Roost—Casey trim and petite, Dave as demure as a bank-teller, bespectacled now, drinking Coca-Cola. Dr. Jekyll had happily returned; but he was not to remain long.

Dave's last days were divided between visits to a veterans' hospital in Jersey where he was an out-patient, and jobs that vacillated from Dixieland to bop.

One cold December night I met him up at Pete Rugolo's apartment, his mood quietly desperate, his speech thick. "I'm giving it up for good, selling my drums. Help me to get work as a writer, Leonard."

Again, as on that night in 1940, he refused every offer of food. We left together; he said goodnight and Pete and I left him, protesting that he was all right, walking along 45th Street.

A week later the news reached the Kenton band backstage at the Paramount, where Dave had dropped in frequently to chat with Shelly Manne. The news was that somebody had found Dave's body in Newark. He had been trying to go home again to Casey, but had stumbled and broken his skull on the sidewalk.

They held his body in the morgue three days before anybody knew it was David Tough, 41, of Oak Park, Illinois. The late David Tough—the World's Greatest Drummer to so many, the world's unhappiest man to some who knew and loved him.

Write a book about Dave Tough? Sure, he'd make a book, this pint-sized man who could swing a king-size band, this little guy who crossed the style line in his music and the color line in his marriage and the line between Austin High School and the *Saturday Review*, this magnificent musician who never quite made up his mind what he wanted, whose problem was not alcohol but the forces that drove him to it; this weak little Tough guy whom so many in the music business will never forget.

Sure, he'd make a great book; for in so many ways, Dave Tough's life would be the story of Jazz and the story of the 20th century. If only fate had granted Dave the time to write it himself.

(At the funeral, Casey asked me to say a few words about him. That sort of thing is entirely out of my line, but I was touched and proud and pleased to do it.—E. C.)

GEORGE FRAZIER

Pee Wee

THIS ONE COULD be twice as long as the book. There are more stories about Pee Wee Russell than he's got seams in his face, and most of them are printable. Most of them are reprintable, in fact. For example, there was the time during the ASCAP-broadcasting networks fight when I was asked to assemble a group of Chicago musicians for The Chamber Music Society of Lower Basin Street, an NBC program allegedly devoted to hot music. I got Dave Tough, Joe Sullivan, and Pee Wee.

We assembled for rehearsal in an NBC studio in the afternoon of the day we were to broadcast—Pee Wee, Dave Tough, Joe, and myself. Two ASCAP tune sleuths came to me and asked for the names of the numbers we were to play. The first was a piano solo by Joe, one of his own compositions. The sleuths listened to it and agreed it did not belong to ASCAP. The second number was to be a blues by the quartet; I had instructed Pee Wee, who was playing the only horn in the group, that he was to go along with the story that this was an original composition of mine, untitled and unscored. I told this to the sleuths. They looked dubious. We played it for them, Pee Wee improvising while the rest of us gave him background.

"It sounds all right," one of the sleuths said when we finished, "but how do we know that he"—pointing at Pee Wee—"is going to play it on the broadcast the same way he played it just now? He hasn't a score to go by."

I took him aside and spoke to him confidentially.

"Don't you know about Pee Wee Russell?" I asked. "That's what he's famous for. He has a very retentive mind. Once he has played a thing he never varies it; he repeats the same notes time after time. It's considered one of the most remarkable musical accomplishments in America."

The sleuth nodded. "I remember now," he said. "I knew he was famous but at the moment I couldn't recall why."

That night on the broadcast Pee Wee, who is utterly incapable of playing anything in even approximately the same way twice, gave a fresh improvisation of the blues. When the program was finished the tune sleuth shook hands with me.

"That Pee Wee is surely a remarkable man, isn't he?" he said. "He played it tonight exactly the way he played it this afternoon." He sighed. "If we had as little trouble with other musicians as we had with him," he said, "our jobs would be easy."

Later that year Pee Wee and I went out to Chicago for a job at the Brass Rail. Pee Wee stayed with Josh Billings and Slim Kurtzmann. Both of them had given up their old instrument, the suitcase, and Billings was working days as a lithographer. While he slept at night, Kurtzmann borrowed his car and drove to the Brass Rail to meet Pee Wee and take him home. They stopped along the way each morning and shopped at a milk wagon. One morning they found the wagon in front of a large apartment house. The driver was in the building; they waited for him to appear, getting sleepier and more thirsty. Finally they decided to take a few quarts and pay the man the next day. Someone saw them as they drove away, took the license number of the car, and telephoned the police. As the two sat in the kitchen of the apartment drinking the milk the doorbell rang: Kurtzmann answered it, a glass of milk in his hand. He opened the door and two detectives walked in. Half an hour later the thieves were in the Chicago Avenue jail. They got word to me and I telephoned Uncle Dennis.

"Why did they want to drink milk?" he asked. "If it was liquor it would be easier to straighten it out; a man can understand the need of another man for a drink of whiskey at half-past four in the morning, but not milk. Well, I'll do what I can."

By the time the case was called at nine o'clock that night everything was arranged. Pee Wee was a pathetic sight as he stood before the magistrate. He was still wearing his band uniform—tuxedo trousers and a tan jacket. He had neither shaved nor slept in twenty-four hours; he was hungry and he needed a drink. The magistrate stared at him. Pee Wee, always shy, dropped his eyes.

"What do you do?" the magistrate asked.

"I p-p-p-play the c-c-c-clarinet," Pee Wee said.

"See that you stick to it," the magistrate said. "Don't let me ever again hear of you drinking milk. Case dismissed."

Then too, there was the time when Pee Wee and Bix were playing together, after the breakup of the original Wolverines, at Hudson Lake, Indiana. They lived in a cottage near the lake with the rest of the guys in the band. There were three bedrooms, a kitchen, a living room, a tired grand piano, and no housekeeper. The place was always a shambles. The only commodity kept in sufficient stock was a local whiskey, purchased in large quantities for five dollars a gallon from three old-maid hillbillies who lived five miles away. Barefoot in a cabin with a brother they were all past sixty and asked no questions.

Bix and Pee Wee were without a car. It bothered them; they couldn't visit the old maids when they wanted to. One day, having received some pay—usually they owed it all—they went to LaPorte to buy an automobile. There were several secondhand Model T Fords available but Bix had notions of grandeur. He found a 1916 Buick which could be had for eighty dollars. It ran around the block well. "This is it," Bix said to Pee Wee. "Wait until the guys see us with this. We won't have to ride with them anymore, they'll be begging to ride with us." Pee Wee was dubious, but he agreed.

They drove back to the lake and hid the car in a side road. Just before starting time that night they sneaked off, got into it, and drove to the pavilion. As they reached the entrance and caught the attention of the boys on the stand the motor stopped. It refused to start; the owners had to push it to the cottage. Next day they got it going and decided to visit the old maids. They took Charlie Horvath's wife with them—Charlie was managing the band for Goldkette. They got to the cabin, bought a jug, and started back. Half way home the Buick went dead. They had to find a farmer and hire him to tow it by horse to a garage. Sitting in the car they nibbled at the jug; they arrived at work, loaded, at eleven-thirty. A surprise awaited them. Goldkette was there; he had chosen this one night of the whole season to visit the band at Hudson Lake. "Is this the way things always go—the cornet and clarinet players drunk and mad and missing with your wife?" he asked Horvath. "It's their birthday," Horvath said. He could think of nothing else.

The car was delivered next day at the cottage. "Park it in the backyard," Bix said to the man who towed it from the garage. It never ran again. It had a fine mirror and the owners used that while shaving. Ten years later Pee Wee was driving to the coast with the Louis Prima band; he detoured to reminisce at Hudson Lake and found the cottage. The car was still in the backyard, on its wheels but groggy with rust. Pee Wee pointed it out to the Prima boys. "I own half of that," he said.

If I keep this up, this piece will wind up longer than Frazier's, which is a short one to begin with. It doesn't tell many stories about our friend, but it tells who he is. Pee Wee is, as George says, jazz.

E. C.

Jazz is a lot of things, but there are a lot of things that it is not. It is Pee Wee Russell's clarinet and Louis Armstrong's trumpet, but not Tommy Dorsey's trombone. It is the silvery notes that spilled out of the bell of Leon Bismarck Beiderbecke's cornet in Paul Whiteman's band, but not the pretentious, over-arranged band itself. It is the occasional brief, heartfelt chorus by Bobby Hackett of Glenn Miller's ensemble, but never the Miller ensemble. It is the music that was being played in New Orleans just after the turn of the present century and in Chicago during the resonant nights of the coonskin-coated era known as the '20's. It is the band that Benny Goodman had around 1936, but not the band he has today. Because jazz is a lot of things, but blariness and screeching and pretension are not to be numbered among them.

You just don't teach people about jazz. Either they like it (and when they like it, they like it deep down inside of them) or they cannot tolerate it. Because jazz is like a lot of other things. It is like spinach and a foggy night and the poetry of T. S. Eliot. It is something that you heard once upon an enchanted night and that you will remember until the day you die. It is something eloquent and deeply stirring.

What you have today is, with rare exceptions, no longer something fresh and vital and completely sincere, but an out-and-out commercial venture. You have Ellington, of course, and he is always miraculous, and you have Basie too, and he is no slouch, and you have some others. But for the most part, you have the Dorseys and the Millers. It is swing, maybe, because swing is commercial and always mechanical, but please don't think it's jazz.

Jazz is a small band improvising on a good old tune like "Jazz Me Blues" or "Way Down Yonder in New Orleans." It is fire and drive and gimme the ball and the hell with the signals. It is, finally, a man named Pee Wee Russell, who is fifty and a clarinetist of no mean ability. He is tall and spindly, with patent-leather hair and a long, seamed face that reminds you of a clown's. He is scarcely what you would call an impressive-looking man. But that is before he takes his clarinet to his mouth and begins to play. Then he is one of the most eloquent men on the face of the earth. It is an aged clarinet that he plays and it is kept serviceable only through the judicious use of rubber bands, but in Pee Wee's hands it is an instrument of surpassing beauty.

He is no virtuoso and his tone is breathy and squeaky, but you forget these shortcomings when you hear the bliss and the sadness and the compassion and the humility that are there in the pattern of the notes he plays. He is always but a step ahead of the sheriff and you won't find his name in Dun and Bradstreet, but he is always jazz. He could be affluent, if he would but accept any one of the jobs offered him in big bands, but he doesn't like affluence that much. He plays what he feels and there are no confining arrangements to imprison his imagination. He is playing for the sheer joy of playing and not because a leader is paying him a fat salary. His life and his hard times and the stuff he dreams up on his clarinet are in the true jazz tradition. He is everything that Glenn Miller and Tommy and Jimmy Dorsey aren't. He is jazz, and the best too.

He has been playing for a good many years now and behind him lies some of the most exciting jazz on records. But no matter how often you hear him, he is always superb. He closes his eyes and there seems to be torture written in the lines of his face, but the music that comes out of his clarinet is beautiful. It is music for the ages. You won't hear it on any sponsored radio program and you won't find it in a plush night club, but that is of no moment. It is jazz and it is either for you or it isn't. If it is, you are fortunate indeed. If it isn't there is no point in trying to change your views. Because jazz is like spinach, and Pee Wee is like nobody but Pee Wee.

EDDIE CONDON

Turk

One day in the spring of 1955 I backed into the Commodore shop for a word with Jack Crystal, one of several brothers-in-law of the management. Swallowing my modesty, I inquired how, or if, the old Eddie Condon releases were moving.

"Eddie Condon releases?" Jack snorted. "If I didn't know you were Eddie Condon, I'd say 'Who is Eddie Condon?' Turk Murphy is stirring up the commotion these days, uncle."

All I know about Trends in Musique Moderne is what I read in the collected spasms of Nat Hentoff. This was something Nat hadn't dusted; not in my ken, anyhow. "What does Turk Murphy do?" I asked. "Wrestle?"

"With a trombone," said Jack.

"Where's he from?"

"California."

"That's enough for me," I said, and told him how I'd got entangled with Gerry Mulligan, a stir-trimmed kid from California who plays fireplug (bass saxophone), at the Newport Jazz Festival in the summer of 1954. "This Mulligan played very advanced music," I told Jack. "He was so advanced he was out of sight of himself. If that's California jazz, I may join Kostelanetz in protest."

Jack explained that there actually are two types of California jazz: the intellectual type, played by such fellows as Shorty Rogers, the Mulligan boy, Chet Baker, old Red Norvo (traitor!) and others. They might be described as *avant-garde* bop, with liberal doses of classical music and nonsense.

"Then," said Jack, "there is San Francisco jazz, as played by Turk and a few other bands."

He put on a record, and I listened. The selection was "New Orleans Joys," by Turk Murphy and his Jazz Band. Jelly Roll Morton was playing this number in the city of the same name back before 1920. When I was no taller than the banjo I used to play, the "Joys" was already forgotten. The Turk Murphy band had no drums; I could hear a tuba, a banjo and a washboard. This was music right out of the Museum of Natural Surprises.

"San Francisco jazz, eh?" I said. "It took that music nearly forty years to get there. At this rate, San Francisco ought to be enjoying a pronounced mambo swell around 1994."

Jack went on to say that all San Francisco has been smitten by this creaky style of jazz, and that several bands are playing it, including a couple led by old-timers who were in New Orleans when the music was far ahead of its time.

"Play some more," I implored, and Lou Blum, another Commodore brother-in-law, stepped in and twirled a flock of LPs. They included "Barrelhouse Jazz," "The Music of Jelly Roll Morton" and "When The Saints Go Marching In," all by Turk Murphy and his Jazz Band (Columbia label); Bob Scobey's Frisco Band in three volumes (Good Time Jazz label); "Dawn Club Favorites," "Originals" and "Rags," all three by Lu Watters' Yerba Buena Jazz Band (reissues on Good Time Jazz label of old West Coast labels); and a couple of volumes of Kid Ory's Creole Jazz Band, also on Good Time.

"This is a good representative selection for anybody who wants to hear how Crescent City music sounds when it's been transplanted to the Golden Gate," Lou Blum said.

"Well," I said, "you don't have to be an authority to know it's less than modern."

Some of the tunes in those LPs were: "Down in Jungle Town," "Santa Claus Blues," "Sweet Substitute," "Big Fat Ham," "Wild

Man Blues," "The Pearls," "New Orleans Blues," "Oh! Didn't He Ramble," "Canal Street Blues" and "Workingman Blues." As I listened I could imagine I was back in the Lincoln Gardens in Chicago listening to Joe Oliver's band, fresh up the river from New Orleans. I used to stand around drinking in that band's music with my lower jaw scraping my plus-fours.

Not all the numbers were from New Orleans. Some were old Barbary Coast specialties ("Ace in the Hole" and "Silver Dollar") featuring vocals by Clancy Hayes, a fellow who doesn't need too many lessons. Others were old vaudeville tunes, such as "Evolution Mama" ("Don't you make a monkey out of me") and "I Wished I Was in Peoria." The latter, which Billy Rose wrote while he was still a shorthand champion, is the plaint of a captain on a ship that's going down. That city is now one of the biggest distillery centers in the U. S., which must prove that the captain was gifted with foresight.

"After two hours of this, I'm almost ready for some bop," I said. "Well, not quite *that* ready."

Aside from the age of the selections, the most impressive thing about those records was that everybody seemed to be having an old-fashioned good time. All the tunes moved right along without hesitation. I found this particularly remarkable in the case of Kid Ory's band, which is mainly composed of very old old-timers—New Orleans originals, in fact. Most of these bozos are so old you have to credit them for being able to stand up. You can say this: they may not be much on tone, but they sure have one hell of a walk.

I was puzzled when the records were over. "I can understand Brubeck, Rogers, Mulligan and those kids trying to go forward," I said to Lou and Jack, "but what would make relatively young guys like Turk Murphy and Bob Scobey want to go back?"

"Murphy is in town," said Jack. "Ask him."

This seemed sensible. Murphy was in the middle of his first evangelical coast-to-coast tour, and I caught him in Toots Shor's between Philadelphia and Boston. He turned out to be a husky guy with a stir-trim, and looked somewhat the way Fred MacMurray might have if he had stuck to the music business. I asked him to tell me how he and his pals started San Francisco jazz.

"Understand this," I said, "I've only been in San Francisco once for one day only, and I couldn't see anything for the fog. Wild Bull was along, and he couldn't see much either."

"Where'd you play there?" Turk asked.

"Guest concert at a place called Hambone Kelly's," I said. "It was no crib. It's—"

"Hambone Kelly's was my old hangout," Turk said, the mist of reminiscence seeping into his eyes. Then he began to talk. If I can just untangle my notes, most of which I jotted down on some old Taylor wine labels, I'll reveal what Turk imparted. . . .

His name, for reasons known only to his parents, is Melvin Alton Edward Murphy. Until he was of voting age he had a speech defect so severe he couldn't get out an entire sentence. Today he can sing the lyrics to "I Wish I Could Shimmy Like My Sister Kate" and still remain his natural color. Jazz helped him overcome his difficulty. I always knew jazz had therapeutic values.

Turk was nicknamed while playing on all possible teams in high school at Williams, California. He came from a family to which music was no intruder. His grandfather had been a fiddler for prospectors during the gold rush and also had played in the Hangtown, California, Silver Cornet Band. His father played cornet and drums and at various times had bands similar to the one Turk leads today.

When Melvin was eleven, his father presented him with a cornet and turned him over to grandfather. The old man taught him a lot of those old Barbary Coast shouts—pretty rough stuff for a lad.

After high school Turk went to Stanford and dematriculated after one semester. By now he was playing trombone, an instrument more in keeping with his heft (at thirty-eight, he still looks capable of staying a round or two with Firpo). He began using his trombone in such bands as those of Will Osborne, Mal Hallett, and other unmentionables. Their music, designed for people who had never heard anything better, made him think wistfully of the old barrel-house, the sinful songs he had learned at grandpa's knee.

Most of Turk's energy in those days was expended in and around the San Francisco area. When the music he played for a living weighed too heavily on his nerves, he would quit for a while and work as a plumber or electrician. Around 1937 he dropped into a place one night and heard a band led by a fellow named Lu Watters, who played trumpet. The band consisted of a rhythm section, four brasses and three reeds that, Turk explained, never played together.

Watters was not satisfied with this band. He wanted a smaller one and he, too, was tired of playing music he didn't like. His tone was not unlike Louis Armstrong's, and he knew oldies, like "Melancholy Blues."

Turk was delighted to find a blood brother, but he and Lu did not join forces immediately. There was still the problem of making a living. To solve it, Turk went to Lake Tahoe, Nevada, to lead a band that played behind Sally Rand. Despite the scenery, this engagement soon turned out to be even less rewarding than sliding around with Will Osborne. Turk returned to San Francisco and sought out Watters, and the two of them began to think about organizing their kind of band.

"Nobody was working at King Oliver or Jelly Roll Morton music then," Turk said. "We figured it would be a do-or-die proposition."

Both Lu and Turk had large collections of records made even before the Victor dog began staring into that horn. Turk unearthed other old tunes, and the older they were the happier he was. He consulted the Library of Congress, old musicians and students of folklore, files of long dead publishing houses—and finally he had a basic library which would have delighted his grandfather.

The next problem was to find some sympathetic cohorts. There was a fellow around named Paul Lingle who could play every ragtime piano number ever written, plus a few he'd ragged up himself. He joined. So did a tall clarinet player named Bob Helm, who had been playing in pit bands literally since the age of eleven. Then came Clancy Hayes, the banjoist and singer. Bob Scobey operated the second trumpet. Other proselytes came in.

When I first heard this band on records I remarked that it was plain that these boys hadn't rehearsed in separate rooms. Turk verified the statement.

"The band was very carefully planned," he says. "We rehearsed almost every night during the last half of 1939 at a place called The Big Bear, in the Berkeley Hills."

They rehearsed every night from one A.M. until seven or until physical tolerance took over. They played that old-time stuff and added their own ideas, so that what came out was not totally a carbon copy. Pretty soon they decided that if they performed in public their music might draw some fans as well as vegetables; they figured their stuff was so old that at least a few people might think it was the newest thing.

The band was called Lu Watters and The Yerba Buena Jazz Band. Yerba Buena, Turk explained to me, was the original name of San Francisco; these guys were determined to be authentic even in the geography department. They played a few scattered engagements for a local hot-music society, and in December, 1939, they opened at The Dawn Club, located in Annie Alley.

This room had a capacity almost like that of Carnegie Hall, and a good thing. Kids from Stanford, California, and other surrounding academies found out about the music and before long it was difficult to get on intimate terms with a glass of beer in there.

To say that the band and its music was a sensation would be like saying that Marilyn Monroe will do.

This first success did nothing to quell Turk's quest for authenticity. He heard that Mutt Carey and Kid Ory, two of the foremost old-time New Orleans guys, were living in musical retirement in Los Angeles. They were working on a railroad, and they were so old even the railroad was ready to retire them. Turk made a pilgrimage and hauled old Mutt back upstate with him.

Mutt Carey's first whiff of the Dawn Club came one Saturday night when the seams of the place were being strained as usual.

"When Mutt heard the music," Turk said, "he got a look on his face as though he'd seen a ghost. We asked him to sit in, and he sort of hesitated. Nobody in the audience knew he was the great Mutt Carey—I doubt if most of those kids had ever heard of him. We played 'Dippermouth Blues,' and he took the old traditional cornet chorus. When he finished, the people went nuts for twenty minutes. I looked at Mutt—and there he stood with the tears streaming down his face. Then he played and played and played all night long."

Mutt is dead now, but some of the other old boys are still very much alive. Kid Ory's band is playing up and down the west coast, and so is one led by the veteran George Lewis. The late Bunk Johnson came out of retirement in 1942, went out to the coast and made some records with the Yerba Buena Band (they are still available on the Good Time label).

For a time, San Francisco was like Chicago in the twenties, when jazz first came up from New Orleans. There was a real boomeringer, with bands springing up all over. World War II put the Yerba Buena Band in drydock for a time, but Turk managed to play with compassionate friends whenever he got home on leave from the Navy.

The boys reopened at The Dawn Club in 1946, and a year later they started their own place, Hambone Kelly's. To get this one running, Turk got his plumber's tools out of moth balls and went to work on the pipes himself. In a way it was like Old Home Week for him: Sally Rand had formerly played there. The boys cleaned out the feathers and set about making the barn—it was 10,000 feet square—into a fitting monument to their prehistoric music. The place was so big, several members of the band lived behind the bandstand and a few in rooms upstairs.

They opened on June 13, 1947. That was a Friday, but they had nothing but luck. By then jazz was so firmly implanted in San Francisco, even Pierre Monteux didn't flinch when it was mentioned. Hambone Kelly's turned out to be almost too small for the mobs. I remember when Davison and I went there for our guest shot the crowd was as thick as the fog.

That period lasted two and a half years. Hambone Kelly's closed on New Year's Eve, 1950. Meanwhile various members of the band had drifted off to start their own outfits; Bob Scobey had formed one, and Turk decided to try it as a leader. Some quarrels had developed; they always do when people not only play together but mingle with the customers together and even live together. The rear of a bandstand can get to be quite a crowded place. Lu Watters retired and is said to have sold his trumpet.

According to *The Record Changer*, a magazine for jazz scholars, when last heard of Watters was running a restaurant.

The *Changer* did not say whether or not there was a jukebox present.

Still, the movement went on. Today San Francisco jazz is stronger than ever. According to George Avakian (of Columbia Records) it hasn't even reached its peak. Today there are nearly a dozen bands playing the old-fashioned music in the shadow of the big bridge.

When Turk finished telling me all this, he got up. "Eddie," he said, "when are you coming out to San Francisco again?"

"I've given up commuting," I said to him.

That's all I know about San Francisco jazz. But I also know this: whether you like it or dislike it, there's a rapidly expanding number of people who prefer it to the strange discords the Brubecks and Mulligans are playing these days. In fact, there's a growing number of people who prefer it to anything. The popularity of the various records proves that, and the large crowds who turned out to hear Turk on his coast-to-coast tour constitute supplementary evidence. As far as San Franciscans themselves are concerned, it's a toss-up between the music and the cable cars, and it looks as though both of them are there to stay.

# THREE:

THEY CALL IT MUSIC

Note: Never mind what I call it.

                                                           E. C.

MARSHALL STEARNS

Rebop, Bebop, and Bop

IN JULY, 1954, I did a piece for This Week on Marshall Stearns, who may very well go down in history as one of the most important jazz lovers of all time. We have decided to reprint most of it here, first because it contains a good deal of information about Marshall available nowhere else and second because it calls attention to the increasing interest in jazz on the part of the intellectual community:

I visited Marshall Stearns the other day at his Waverly Place duplex in Greenwich Village. Stearns is tall and loose-jointed, with a sober visage behind dark-rimmed spectacles. He is an Associate Professor of English at Hunter College, an expert on medieval literature: Harvard Sc.B. '31, Yale Ph. D. '42. Special interest: Chaucer. Extra-special interest: jazz. In addition to teaching English at Hunter, he lectures on jazz at the New School for Social Research and New York University.

"People always ask me, 'What's a Chaucer man doing fooling around with jazz?'" Stearns said. "They seem to think it's a joke. Well, it isn't. Chaucer and jazz are quite similar: they both swing, they both have the same punch, vitality and guts. Why, they're not far apart at all."

For years, Stearns has been trying to get people to take jazz seriously as an art form. He defines jazz as "improvised Afro-American music, with strong European influences." Some people might disagree with this definition. Nothing could be more pleasing to Stearns. He is never happier than when he is surrounded by people wrangling over jazz. "We had twenty-eight down here last Friday to listen to records," he told me. "One argument lasted until four in the morning. Wonderful."

As a step toward organizing jazz discussions, Stearns six years ago inaugurated an annual Roundtable on Jazz at Music Inn, Lenox, Mass. The Roundtable is held at the conclusion of the annual Tanglewood festival. Musicians come and play, singers come and sing, and students of jazz come and listen—and, of course, argue. Out of the Roundtables has come a more serious, permanent project—The Institute of Jazz Studies, Inc., of which Stearns is one of the founders, the president and executive director.

The Institute, Stearns told me, has a five-point program. It aims to assemble a complete archive of recordings and literature on jazz and make it available to students. It will sponsor trips by scholars to collect data on the history of jazz. It will publish material on jazz, and it will work out a series of jazz courses on a university level. Finally, it will go on sponsoring the Roundtables. The Institute is non-profit.

Producing a letterhead, Stearns pointed to the list of the Institute's Board of Advisors. It included such disparate names as Louis Armstrong, Stan Kenton and Artie Shaw; Stuart Davis, the painter; Ralph Ellison and Langston Hughes, writers; Monroe Berger, Willis L. James, S. I. Hayakawa, Lorenzo Turner and Melville J. Herskovits, college professors. "Herskovits, the anthropologist, was one of my sponsors when I applied for a Guggenheim fellowship to write a book on the history of jazz," Stearns told me. "So was Duke Ellington," he added, smiling.

The book was published in the spring of 1956. Stearns hopes it will be regarded as the first scholarly work on jazz. He believes passionately that the recent academic interest in jazz is long overdue.

"After all," he said, "it's our only native American music. You could say, too, it's the only art form that ever originated in

America. Charles Seeger, former head of the Pan-American Union music division, said once that our music history will be done largely in terms of popular music. It's true. Jazz is a prime force in our popular culture, and I'm interested in trying to evaluate its effect.

"And," Stearns continued, warming up, "I'm not the only one. S. I. Hayakawa, the semanticist, is going to do a study of the semantics of jazz. Dr. Maurice R. Green, of Roosevelt Hospital, is working on a study of the psychological implications of jazz in our society; Tremaine McDowell, head of American civilization studies at the University of Minnesota, has incorporated jazz material into his courses. For the purposes of my book, I've had to get out of English and into anthropology, sociology and even psychiatry."

Stearns now led me on a guided tour of the headquarters of the Institute, which is in his own spacious living room, a room the size of a small concert hall. The ceilings are eighteen feet high and the entire right-hand wall is covered with paintings by Stearns' wife, Betty. The left-hand wall is dominated by huge shelves which reach almost to the ceiling. The shelves contain Stearns'—and the Institute's—record collection.

"We've got about ten or eleven thousand here," Stearns said. "I've been trying to get a sample of everything ever recorded— everything from the music of the American Indian up to classical stuff, and excluding both."

Stearns keeps the Institute's files in several large cabinets. As he pulled out drawers, I saw folders headed AFRICA, BLUES, GOSPEL SINGERS, JAM SESSIONS, LINDY HOP, MUSIC: HINDU, JUG BLOWERS. One cabinet is completely devoted to original photographs, another to letters and diaries of jazz musicians.

"Been collecting this stuff since I was a boy," Stearns said. He said he was born in Cambridge, Massachusetts, in 1908, son of a Harvard graduate whose father was a Harvard graduate. The father, an amateur singer, bought him a set of drums when he was thirteen ("To keep me off the streets"). He began drumming along with recordings, then took up a guitar, and finally graduated to C-melody saxophone. He played in small bands around Cambridge but gave up his musical career and followed his father to Harvard.

After graduation, Stearns went to Harvard Law School for two years, was bored, and switched to Yale to take up medieval literature. All this time he had been soaking up all the jazz and folk music he could listen to and developing his record collection. While at Yale he began writing for Down Beat. His first article was a blast at the big, organized heavily-arranged commercial bands. It ran under a headline that said:

YALE AUTHORITY HAILS DECLINE OF SWING

Stearns taught at the University of Hawaii for two years ("Not much jazz out there"), then spent four years at Indiana University and two at Cornell, not to mention his Penn State stint. Inevitably, he came to New York City ("More jazz here") and, after a year out to work on his Guggenheim, began teaching at Hunter. Few of his students there, he believes, know of his interest in jazz. However, George N. Shuster, the president, does know—and approves heartily.

As Stearns' concern with jazz has broadened, his preoccupation with English has not precisely narrowed, but it is obvious that in the arena of his interest, literature is no longer at ringside. He speaks enthusiastically of his night lectures on jazz at New York University. The courses attempt to present a non-technical introduction to jazz and to survey the entire panoramic history of the music. "We go from the birth of jazz in New Orleans right up to the stuff they're playing over at the Bandbox," Stearns said, "—from Jelly Roll Morton and 'Wild Man Blues' right on up to Lionel Hampton and 'Flyin' Home.' Musicians come down and play for us some nights; other nights we have records. And after class, we often take field trips to clubs to study the stuff on its native heath."

Stearns feels that these classes, and others which are coming into being at other universities, and the work of the Institute, may ultimately aid jazz in attaining its rightful position. "The trouble is," he said to me, "that so few people have ever taken it seriously, possibly because it started as the music of a persecuted minority. But it is one of the few original American phenomena, and it's

REBOP, BEBOP AND BOP

my deep conviction that it's a very vital part of our culture." His eyes became warm.

"Sooner or later," he said, "people will give it the attention it deserves."

R. G.

When an eager undergraduate once demanded, "What is jazz, Mr. Waller?" the great pianist is said to have growled: "Man, if you don't know what it is, don't mess with it!" And the land that gave birth to jazz has followed Fats Waller's advice. During the twenties, when famous European musicians were writing enthusiastically about this new American music, the hostile attitude of our own composers and critics was typified by Gilbert Seldes' comment: "I am on the side of civilization." It is a matter of record that the first reasonably competent book on jazz was published in Belgium in 1932; the first good book by an American did not appear until seven years later.

Yet during the forties, the moralists of the lunatic fringe who periodically announce that jazz is the cause of juvenile delinquency and the common cold were not having the same success in hitting the headlines. Somewhere along the line a battle had been won and jazz had become an accepted sound, if not yet accepted music, in America. There was even scattered talk of jazz as a native art-form, to be classed with chewing gum, Mickey Mouse, and the skyscraper. In fact, even the most confirmed critics of jazz seemed to be adjusting successfully to the new environment, when suddenly jazz itself erupted into a civil war which split its own ranks and gave new hope to those who had said it would never last. The center of attention seemed to be a new kind of jazz, successively known as "Rebop," "Bebop," and finally just plain "bop." When this volcano eventually subsided, the landscape of jazz had completely changed. What had happened?

Fortunately, the brief but busy history of jazz music gives us a clue to bop. The most recent material comes from an unexpected source: the anthropologists who have investigated the music of the West African coast. It is from this area that a large number of Americans of Negro ancestry trace their descent. Although the anthropologists are waging their own private wars over the question of how much African culture has survived in the United States, it is clear that many of the communal, improvisational, expressive, and rhythmic qualities of African music can be found today in jazz.

We can now safely say that as far as rhythm is concerned African music, far from being crude or barbarous, is actually the most sophisticated in the world. There is some harmony and quite a bit of melody in this music, but its use of complex rhythms is outstanding. Indeed, as the German scholar with the improbable name, Erich M. von Hornbostel, has stated: "The syncope, an African commonplace, is a European achievement." (By the word "syncope," Hornbostel probably meant what the jazz musician calls "off-beats.") Perhaps it should be added that Hornbostel is the grand-daddy of the musicological anthropologists and/or anthropological musicologists—the terms seem to be interchangeable—who helped make it possible for us to place jazz in its proper context musically. The work is being ably carried on in this country by Professor Melville J. Herskovits and his department at Northwestern University.

The "drum choir," or trio of drums, supplies the rhythmic heart of African music. These drums are of very different sizes; the biggest drum with the deepest voice is always called the "Mama" drum, while the smaller drums are know as the "Papa" and the "Baby" drums. The most amazing feature of the drum choir, however, is its use of mixed meters, or polyrhythms, in which two or more separate rhythms occur at the same time. On top of this, the melody frequently adds a few rhythms of its own.

To the European or American ear, accustomed to two simple rhythms, played one at a time—the 4/4 of the march or the 3/4 of the waltz—African music sounds like static during a thunderstorm. We have been so completely conditioned by European music that our ears reduce the steady and undifferentiated beat of a clock, for example, to the 2/4 rhythm of "tick-tock, tick-tock," and we tend to reduce everything we hear in the same way, from the clicking of the wheels of a train to the complicated tempos of modern compositions. Yet the average West Coast African thinks nothing of matching a 5/4 beat with an already established combination of 6/8, 4/4, and 3/4 rhythms. There is probably some truth to the story that when a one-cylinder gasoline engine, with its intermittent explosions, was imported into the Belgian Congo, the natives crowded around in pure ecstasy, fascinated by the unending rhythmic complexity.

Many top-notch symphony musicians, rehearsing a score in which the tempo shifts back and forth from 4/4 to 7/4, will furrow their brows with concentration and move their lips as they count to themselves. Some of them have told me afterward that they had no idea of how the music sounded as a whole. On the other hand, African drummers have been known on occasion to accent every fifteenth beat simply because they felt it that way at the time—and they certainly do not count on their fingers. Again, I have seen the facial expression of a modern composer, famous for his scoring of intricate rhythms, change from pleasure to amazement and finally to something like helplessness as he listened to a record of African drumming.

Of course, the musics of the world are many, and African music is by no means the only one with rhythmic complexity. Yet it is difficult for us to realize, since we are hardly aware of any other, how highly specialized our Western music really is. Classical music has developed harmony (among other things) to the highest degree but it has very rarely made use of the complex polyrhythms we find in Africa—the classical music of the late nineteenth century, for example, has rhythm but comparatively speaking little or no rhythmic variety. My point is simply that, viewed in true perspective, African music not only can stand securely upon its own merits but also, because of its relationship to jazz, can be regarded as an important influence in American music.

Jazz did not spring full-blown from the head of Jelly-Roll Morton in 1902, as that masterful pianist loudly proclaimed, but its birth is still something of a puzzle. We do know that wherever the Negro migrated—North America, Cuba, Central America, the Caribbean, or South America—he influenced the music of the region deeply and more or less uniformly, according to the receptiveness of the culture in which he found himself.

The Negro's celebrated sense of rhythm, it should be remembered, is not instinctive but rather an unconscious pattern handed down from generation to generation by means of examples, attitudes, and points of view. When Baby Dodds, the New Orleans drummer, recalls that his great-grandfather "talked" on the drums in the African manner and when he actually remembers some of the rhythms his great-grandfather played, we have a significant though rare example of the African heritage being handed down explicitly from person to person.

African music adapted itself quite easily to the Latin-American countries and today is found nearly intact in some areas. The special drum rhythms for various gods which existed in Africa were transferred to Catholic saints in Cuba, Haiti, and Brazil. The African snake god, Damballa, was in certain localities identified for better or worse with St. Patrick. And the entire process was aided by the rhythmic flair of Latin Americans and their generally tolerant attitude toward questions of skin color.

In the United States, on the other hand, African music hit a series of high hurdles. The Protestant religion had no saints to whom the ritual drums of Africa could be readapted. Again, the Negro was surrounded by music in which polyrhythms were practically unknown, where there was no syncopation to speak of, and where the melodic accent fell monotonously on the same beat, in the trudging manner of the widely-used Moody and Sankey hymnal. And finally, it was forcibly impressed upon the Negro that he was inferior and that all things African were worthless.

In part because of these very obstacles, and perhaps because Catholicism was the official religion in New Orleans until the Louisiana Purchase of 1803, it was in that city, around 1885, that a new music was forged, far greater than any of its component parts. For New Orleans, with its Latin colonial background, was a musical melting pot *par excellence*. Combined with the surviving elements of African music were the melodies of French, Italian, Central European, and Spanish music (both popular and classical), the simple rhythms of Scotch-Irish folk music and German brass bands, and the elementary harmony of Protestant hymns. (To this mixture, some hardy theorists have added the music of the American Indian and the Chinese laborer.) An echo of almost any European music can be found in jazz—yet the combination is unique.

The question is, of course, how and to what extent did the specifically African heritage survive? Although New Orleans was notorious for racial intermixture, social distinctions along economic lines (except for a small group of Creole aristocrats) tended to be hard and fast. Poor people were virtually thrown together in a ghetto, although a line of musical communication ran to the wealthy Creoles of color, and an intense feeling for the common interest sprang up. A great number of fraternal and benevolent organizations were founded, similar in many ways to the African secret societies, and the Negro became a lively contributor with an established audience.

Social life revolved around these organizations and many of them had their own bands, without which no picnic, river-boat excursion, parade, or funeral was complete. Music offered one of the few paths for the individual to fame and fortune, but it also mirrored the life of the entire group. It is probably no accident that as this music matured it was characterized by an ensemble style of collective improvisation, in which each player followed his own bent within the limits of an established rhythmic and harmonic pattern—the musical equivalent of a fact in the life of its creators, as well as a definite part of its African heritage.

There were other, more specific influences at work. Although holiday celebrations by the slaves were frowned upon and the manufacture and sale of drums discouraged, the slave-owners sometimes permitted dancing—after work. We now know that the slave-owners had reason to fear revolt, and they sometimes considered dancing an effective safety-valve. In time, dancing became a pathway to white approval though it never abandoned the complex rhythms of the African dance.

Certain historical accidents helped too. After the Civil War, the pawnshops were flooded with brass instruments discarded by returning Confederates bands, and these instruments became readily available to the Negro at low cost. The fact that he could not afford orthodox instruction led him to develop his own vocalized style, with an African quality of expressiveness. And there was Storyville, the world-famous red-light district of New

Orleans (created by ordinance in 1897), which symbolized the easy ferment of the times and which lent a sympathetic ear to any man's musical invention.

Instead of dying out, the African musical heritage in New Orleans went underground. European melody, harmony, and even instrumentation prevailed, but the elementary rhythms of Europe slowly suffered a sea change. Although the prevailing tempo was the simple ¾ of the hymn or march, polyrhythms kept popping up—especially in the improvised melodies. Combined with other less tangible factors, a gradual readjustment took place until today we take the rhythmic suspensions of jazz for granted in our dance music.

From the turn of the century to about 1940, however, jazz assimilated more and more of the European musical tradition. There were temporary exceptions when jazz dipped back into the reservoir of Afro-American vitality for inspiration, but in the main line of development the ensemble style of New Orleans gave way to a succession of solos which, in turn, gave way to written arrangements. During the prosperous twenties, the size of the bands increased and with it, the importance of the arranger. As musicians acquired an improved technique, the emphasis tended to be put on written composition and not on improvisation.

Rhythmically speaking, jazz almost stood still for forty years, though it gradually won wide acceptance and became a part of the giant entertainment industry. A few of the big bands did not abandon the sources of their music, however. Duke Ellington and Count Basie, for example, developed a kind of rhythmic streamlining which managed to make clean and satisfying music out of some of Tin Pan Alley's worst tunes. Basie's rhythmic amortization of that miserly piece of pie-in-the-sky, "Pennies from Heaven," released in 1937, testifies to the sham-destroying humor and basic healthiness of jazz. His orchestra is the nearest thing we have to a big-band ancestor of bop.

By 1940, jazz—then renamed "swing"—had achieved a comparative equilibrium and a large public (peace to the bobby-soxers) which enjoyed, understood, and supported what it heard. Among the extreme enthusiasts which jazz seems to attract, there were antiquarians who wanted to go backward and revolutionists who wanted to go forward. The antiquarians had the advantage, for their objectives had long ago been achieved. Yet the musical sky was clear and serene and gave no indication that storm clouds were gathering—or that the greatest musical revolution since the birth of jazz itself was about to take place.

The public really heard about bop too late in the day, when the bop costume—heavily-rimmed glasses, goatee, long cigarette holder, and beret—had become over-publicized and treated as a joke. This new form of jazz—based on comparatively complex rhythms and dissonant harmonies, and rejecting many of the hallowed customs of jam-session etiquette—was nearly buried in bewildered press releases. Even the fad among Negroes for adopting Mohammedan names, which had the practical value of making discrimination more difficult (and may have begun with the small number of West Africans who had been converted by the Arabs long before they were brought to this country), was linked indiscriminately with bop. These symptoms of revolt, however, served only to obscure radical experimentation in the music itself.

Although the seeds of bop had been planted long ago, they blossomed during the second world war. Because of the enormous demand for music, dance bands were able to experiment and make a living at the same time; because of the scarcity of musicians, boys in their teens landed good jobs with first-rate bands. These youngsters were eager, flexible, and bent upon developing a style of their own. During the same period, in an atmosphere of restless rebellion, a great migration to the North was taking place and time itself seemed to be speeded up. In the jazz jargon, "Things were groovy, man!"

After the war, some of the older idols of jazz, having spent the intervening years in the Army unhappily wedded to military bands—or sometimes in the guardhouse—returned to find a music they never blew. Jazz musicians were already split into warring camps. From the early days in 1940 at Minton's up in Harlem, when a small group of pioneers had dreamed up weird modulations just to scare the uninitiated musicians off the stand during a jam-session, the breach had widened. Today, the split is almost a matter of age alone: musicians over thirty are inclined to criticize bop, and musicians under thirty tend to praise it enthusiastically.

The current state of affairs is indicated by the harsh comments of Louis Armstrong, the acknowledged king of pre-bop jazz. Louis makes it a rule to speak no evil of any music or musician, but the day arrived when he could no longer restrain himself on the subject of bop. Referring to "boppers," Armstrong swung from the ground up: "They want to carve everyone because they're so full of malice, and all they want to do is show you up, and any old way will do as long as it's different from the way you played it before. So you get all them weird chords which don't mean nothing, and first people get curious about it just because it's new, but soon they get tired of it because it's really no good and you got no melody to remember and no beat to dance to. So they're all poor again and nobody is working, and that's what that modern malice done for you."

Since Louis Armstrong is endowed with a fine musical intelligence, his objections deserve to be taken seriously. Take his last point first: there is no doubt that bop, which made good money for a while, cut down on the earning power of the older musicians. There is also some truth in Armstrong's charge that bop is merely a novelty. Boiling over with revolt against tradition in general and musical convention in particular, bop is often dominated by the desire to be different. A trifling shift in the musical amenities illustrates the point: ten years ago, a musician at a jam-session would nod his head as he neared the end of his solo to forewarn the man who was to follow him; more recently, the bopper starts a new chorus and stops short, leaving his successor to pick up the pieces. I have seen this trick unnerve an oldtimer.

Other more technical innovations seem, and perhaps are intended to seem, maliciously wrong-headed to the older generation. The bopper often remains silent precisely where the traditionalist would be blowing his heart out, only to fill the customary pause with a cascade of notes executed at breakneck speed. Another reversal of the usual jazz procedure, paralleled by the bop musician's use of "cool" instead of "hot" as a word of highest praise, is the tendency while taking a solo to lag tantalizingly a fraction of a second behind the beat. To a devotee of the older Dixieland style, who is accustomed to having most of the melody fall on top of the beat, the effect is nerve-racking, but to the initiate the result can be one of relaxation and even restraint. The point, of course, is that these surface symptoms indicate something that has taken place deep in the heart of bop.

When Louis Armstrong complains of "them weird chords which don't mean nothing" he has put his finger on the most obvious innovation of bop. In terms of harmony, jazz has developed along the same lines as classical music, but more recently and rapidly. It still lags behind. Today bop roughly parallels the period in classical music which followed Wagner and Debussy, and ninths and the augmented fourths (jazz musicians call them flatted fifths) appear over and over again in the solos as well as the accompaniments. Bix Beiderbecke, the legendary "young man with a horn," whose preoccupation with Debussy was echoed by the unusual intervals in his solos, may be a remote ancestor of Bop. The effect on the ear of the older generation today, however, is not altogether delightful, and for years Dizzie Gillespie, the dean of bop trumpeters, was forced to clown and pretend to be playing "screwy notes" in order to obtain any hearing at all.

Melody, in the sense of a tune meant to be whistled, has disappeared from bop, and Armstrong's objection here is well taken. Yet bop is paradoxically traditional insofar as most of its numbers are based upon the chord progressions of standard and familiar tunes (with "I've Got Rhythm" and the "Blues" especially favored). The original melody, however, cannot be heard; bop consists of variations upon themes which are never stated, although the performers are well aware of them. A complex melody played in unison in the first and last choruses is substituted for the original tune, with which it would harmonize if you could manage to whistle the original at the same time. Often the new melody attains a limited popularity of its own.

Armstrong's criticism that bop has "no beat," or rhythmic drive, also goes straight to the heart of the problem, and it affords a clue as to why older musicians are often unable to play bop.

The rhythm has become much more subtle and complex. The late Dave Tough, one of the few older drummers who survived the transition, remarked ruefully: "I had to forget everything I ever learned before I could put on that new musical look." He admired Max Roach, one of the foremost drummers of bop, and pointed out that he could never anticipate when Max was going to "drop a bomb," although it always seemed right afterward.

On first hearing bop, the traditionalist usually objects, "If that drummer would quit banging that cymbal, I'd be able to hear the bass drum." As a matter of fact, there isn't any regular bass-drum beat to hear. The heavy "chugg-chugg" of the rhythm that Armstrong knew, with its incessant floor-shaking "boom, boom, boom, boom," has disappeared. The 4/4 beat is heard in the flexible and melodic accents of the string-bass alone. This is the reason for the mistaken notion that you can't dance to bop. You can, but it takes a rhythmically educated ear.

The key percussion instrument in bop is the cymbal, which dominates the rhythm with a continuous, flowing accent that changes phase to fit the counter-rhythms suggested by the soloist, while the bass-drum marks special accents and contributes "explosions" to punctuate the performance as a whole. When the off-beat interpolations of the guitar and piano are added, the result in the best of bop is a light and delicate rhythm, closely integrated with the improvisation of the soloist.

The bewilderment of first-rate jazz musicians when they first heard bop is illustrated by Dave Tough's story of how he and a gang from Woody Herman's band dropped in on the Gillespie-Pettiford group on 52nd Street in 1944. "As we walked in," said Tough more in wonder than anger, "these cats snatched up their horns and blew. One would stop all of a sudden and another would start for no reason at all. We never could tell when a chorus was supposed to begin or end. Then they quit all at once and walked off the stand. It scared us." A year later, the Herman band was blowing its own version of bop.

The process of assimilation makes a fascinating study, and its conflicts are most dramatically illustrated in the solos of the great musicians of the thirties—like Benny Carter, Coleman Hawkins, or Benny Goodman—who have had the courage to attempt the new idiom under the critical scrutiny of a younger generation. For example, after flatly condemning bop in print, Benny Goodman admitted that he couldn't play it, and finally had a change of heart and organized a bop band. To judge from his playing, he doesn't seem to like it.

Meanwhile, the cliches of bop, watered down almost past recognition, are beginning to appear in the arrangements of dance bands all over the country. And one thing is certain: jazz will never be the same. Many years hence, a few of the more simple melodic twists of yesterday's bop will turn up in the accompaniment to a hit-parade tune played by Guy Lombardo and his Royal Canadians. As of that moment, bop will be revolving in its grave.

As the shouting and the dissonances die, it may be that bop's greatest contribution to jazz is rhythm. Why it should have happened is as difficult to explain as the birth of jazz in New Orleans, but one major source can be documented: Afro-Cuban music. In a literal sense, jazz went back to the good African earth for rhythmic inspiration when Dizzie Gillespie, the pace-setter in bop, borrowed a conga-drummer from another orchestra and featured him in his own band. It was the beginning of a trend.

As early as 1940, Gillespie had listened carefully to the rhythms of Mario Bauza's Afro-Cuban band. (It is worth noting that Bauza was one of the first musicians who understood what Dizzie was trying to play. Bauza had been with various jazz bands, and it was Bauza who got Dizzie his early job with Cab Calloway.) Later, when the legendary Chano Pozo arrived from Cuba, already famous as a composer and virtuoso drummer, Dizzie heard him and hired him on the spot for his Town Hall concert of 1947. Pozo broke up the concert.

Chano Pozo was born in Cuba, though the musicians who grew up with him there say that his grandparents were born in West Africa. In Cuba, Pozo belonged to the Nanigo Secret Society, an African cult whose members speak only in a West African dialect. He never learned English, but that did not interfere with his inspired drumming. Backed by the Gillespie band, he could hold a large audience entranced for half an hour, while he sang in a dialect full of African phrases and played incredible rhythms on a many-voiced conga drum. The impact was so tremendous that at one such concert at Cornell a woman literally screamed and fainted.

Pozo helped bring the Gillespie band to the peak of its performance, made a few records that are now hard to get, and a year or so ago stepped in front of several slugs from an automatic pistol in a bar on 111th Street and Lenox Avenue. The murderer was brought to justice; it was the third and last time that Pozo was shot at. With a rhythmic background that he had dreamed up himself, Pozo made one record before he was killed which, when slowed down to half-speed, closely resembles a recording of the Bini tribe made in West Africa by the Straus Expedition and dramatically illustrates the origin of his music.

Pozo's influence on jazz drummers was direct and electric. Max Roach, for example, goes out of his way to say that he was fascinated by Pozo. Teddy Stewart, the regular drummer with Dizzy Gillespie, who had to take a back seat while Pozo was in the limelight, admits it gave him an inferiority complex but insists nevertheless that "Pozo was the most!" Apparently, Pozo's African rhythms had something in common with the experiments of the bop drummers and, what is more, showed them the way to new and limitless possibilities.

Pozo was by no means an isolated phenomenon. Later, when Stan Kenton decided that jazz rhythms were too monotonous, he borrowed the entire drum choir from Machito's orchestra to furnish a background for his great recording of "The Peanut Vendor." Thereafter, Kenton used the Afro-Cuban drummer, Carlo Vidal. At one time or another, Gene Krupa, Woody Herman, Jerry Wald, and the King Cole Trio employed Afro-Cuban drummers.

On the other hand, Bop musicians have played with Afro-Cuban bands. Machito and his orchestra performed at the Royal Roost on Broadway, also known as the Metropolitan Bopera House, along with jazz musicians like Howard McGhee, Charlie Ventura, and Brew Moore as soloists. For years, of course, jazz musicians have played in Afro-Cuban bands and jazz drummers have played dates with various "Spanish" bands in Harlem, but here the two streams met and merged.

The most successful blending of this kind took place in a recording of "Mango Mangue" by Machito, featuring the solo saxophone work of the greatest bopper of them all, Charlie Parker. The harmony of Machito's accompaniment is elementary, but the rhythmic background is superb and plays a fascinating counterpoint to the rhythmic suspensions in Parker's solo. Parker heard the tune exactly twice in the studio before he made the record. When asked about it, his eyes lit up with pleasure and he exclaimed: "That Afro-Cuban rhythm is real gone! I like to play with those drummers—man, it's so relaxed." Where Parker, who was born in Kansas City, picked up his superb sense of timing and his affinity for African rhythms is another unanswered question among the many which concern the specifically American elements in jazz.

The fashion of featuring Afro-Cuban drummers with jazz bands is on the decline. In fact, the entire band business is on the skids at the moment, and band leaders, in an attempt to please everybody, are holding their bands down to rhythms that even the visiting firemen can follow. As Machito says of the crowds who come to dance to his music at the Palladium on Broadway, and there is no audience with more rhythmic sophistication, "We cannot play that Afro stuff so many; the dancers, they get lost."

At the same time, bop developed harmonic as well as rhythmic complexity, and a conflict arose between the two. It became increasingly difficult to improvise along the new harmonic lines without stumbling over the intricate rhythms, and vice versa. The emphasis is thus upon technique, and there are very few musicians who are able to relax and allow their invention to flow freely while playing bop. This fact alone would account for the scarcity of first-rate exponents of the style.

The musical revolution is practically over. A lot of bad music —unorganized, meaningless, and exhibitionistic—has been played and recorded under the banner of bop. That was inevitable, yet the total effect was not unhealthy. Bop established a precedent for openminded experimentation and led jazz musicians toward a better technique, a broader understanding of musical theory, and, above all, a keener appreciation of rhythm.

The reasons why jazz is still a neglected art in the land of its birth are many and mysterious. The hostility of the classical music-lover, since he is in the same general field, constitutes one of the most serious problems. Carefully conditioned in a different idiom and unacquainted with the best parts of jazz, the classical musician often fails to realize that jazz is a separate and distinct art form and must be judged by separate and distinct standards. Jazz should not be likened to musical architecture, as classical music quite rightly is, but rather to the projection of sound *in time*. The mistaken notion that jazz is a perversion of classical music is of course the sheerest nonsense.

There are other, less tangible factors blocking an appreciation of jazz. One is a kind of snobbery, or worse. Before the Army and Navy forced the closing of Storyville, New Orleans' red-light district, on November 12, 1917, the famous madam, Willie V. Piazza, observed: "The country club girls are ruining my business." The country club girls have done much—by accepting it only in its most watered-down forms—to ruin jazz. Actually, the milieu in which jazz was born is quite humble, frequently disreputable. Jazz originated as a music of, by, and for the people, and as a dynamic art it is continually returning to the people who make it and dance to it. Further, jazz is a potent force in debunking the myths of Fine Art and the social pretensions of the Concert Hall. To allow that jazz should be granted a role in the world of art leads to disconcerting questions about who is really cultured in our society, and to admit that a persecuted minority is able to produce a real art is to imply that the individuals in this group are gifted enough to play a more important part than that of second-class citizens.

When the great Swiss conductor, Ernst-Alexandre Ansermet, heard the clarinetist Sidney Bechet at London in 1919, he wrote with admiration and wonder: "What a moving thing it is to meet this very black, fat boy with white teeth and that narrow forehead, who is very glad one likes what he does, but who can say nothing of his art, save that he follows his 'own way,' and when one thinks that his 'own way' is perhaps the highway the whole world will swing along tomorrow."

Today the avant-garde of jazz is still very much alive, even though it flourishes for a time under the far from flattering name of bop. This music is the sharply outlined reflection of the musicians who play it and, especially, of the environment in which it is played. Born in protest, both social and artistic, and cradled in contradiction, Bop mirrors the pace, complexity, and confusion of the times—frequently with too much accuracy for comfort.

RICHARD O. BOYER

Bop: A Profile of Dizzy

WITHOUT STATING IT *in so many words, Richard O. Boyer has caught the flavor, spirit and meaning of the bop rebellion, its musical and sociological aspects, in this wonderful piece. Boyer wrote it for the New Yorker in 1948, but even without updating it is still fresh. Some of the bopsters' language has changed, Dizzy's bell now points toward the sky, and Bird is no longer with us—aside from all that, the situation as Boyer describes it is much as it was seven years ago.*

Dizzy Gillespie, a spirited, copper-colored Negro trumpet player and band leader, who has a light-timbred voice that sometimes squeaks into falsetto and who has a tendency to jump up and down in a stiff, straight line when pleased or excited, is one of the founders of a new school of jazz music, called bebop. He is also its best-known practitioner. The music, which the knowing refer to simply as bop, has shaken the world of jazz. Its proponents praise what they call its weird and beautiful chord progressions, whereas its opponents declare that it is meaningless dissonance. Dizzy, who erupts into mirth rather unpredictably and is almost always cackling and prancing about when he isn't playing his trumpet, bursts into mysterious laughter when he is asked about the dispute. Arguments over bebop have, on occasion, ended in violence, and that aspect of the phenomenon enchants him. "We was blowin' in Les Ambassadeurs, most exclusive night club in Paris," he recalled not long ago. "Two Frenchmen were sittin' at the same table and all of a sudden, Lord-a-mercy, they begin poundin' each other! Yeah! Real murder! 'You call that music?' one of them says, and then bam! bam! bam!" Dizzy doubled his fists and smote the air. "They let each other have it," he said, and almost collapsed with laughter.

Dizzy is a husky young man with the chest development of a middleweight boxer and the bandy legs of a cowhand. When he blows his trumpet, his cheeks pop out as round and hard as if they were distended by billiard balls, while his neck, size 16 during his softer passages, leaps to size 20 when he rears back and really blows. His followers, both white and Negro, often affectionately declare that Dizzy is "it," that he is "real crazy," "a bitch," and "a killer." The bebop people have a language of their own. They call each other Pops, Daddy, and Dick, their expressions of approval include "Cool!," "Gone!," and "Bells, man!," and they use the word "eyes" oddly, as in "Have you eyes for a sandwich?" and "Have you eyes to go uptown?" Many of the Negro adherents of bebop are converts to Mohammedanism; others take a subsidiary interest in psychoanalysis and abstract art. Dizzy's male fans, most of whom are in their late teens or early twenties, express their adoration for Gillespie by imitating him. They try to walk with his peculiar loose-jointed, bow-legged floppiness; try to force their laughter up into a soprano squeak; wear blue berets and shell-rimmed spectacles, as he does; smoke meerschaum pipes, as he does; and assiduously cultivate on their own lower lips replicas of the tuft of hair that Dizzy wears on his. Gillespie, in the words of one of his admirers, "is usually a-hollerin' and a-whoopin' and a-jumpin'," but there is method in some of his antics. He knows that his slightest mannerism of action or dress may be reproduced on an international scale. A few months ago, in St. Louis, he was photographed with the bottom buttons of his shirt, by chance, unfastened. After the picture appeared in a jazz-music magazine, beboppers, as both practitioners and lovers of the music are called, began leaving their shirts partly unbuttoned. Last winter, Dizzy took his band to Europe on a concert tour. In Paris, he happened, he says, "to blow on an old, beat-up horn" that he had borrowed. The next day, young French bebop trumpet players were mutilating their horns to make them resemble his. "They thought they get my sound if their horns were beat-up," Dizzy explains. When Dizzy is on the road, he is sometimes forced to sleep in an overnight bus, and he then turns up rather rumpled for an engagement. As a result, no true bebopper will ever have his suit pressed. Many of Dizzy's fans are too young to grow the Gillespie beard. A Fifty-second Street night club at which he was appearing recently did what it could to remedy this deficiency by passing out little tufts of hair that adolescents could, and did, paste to their lower lips. One bebopper has a dog that wears Gillespie spectacles and has been trained to grip a meerschaum pipe.

Bebop's more articulate partisans sometimes call Dizzy the Abraham Lincoln of jazz, asserting that he and his colleagues have freed it from a weak banality of using a complicated, irregular rhythm and strange new chord combinations featuring altered intervals such as augmented fifths and ninths. One of the more erudite aficionados has described bebop as "sophisticated, highly literate, and immensely cerebral." Beboppers enrage players of traditional jazz by murmuring, "How can you play that sticky stuff, man?" To the layman's ear, bebop is cacophonic and episodic. Gil Fuller, a young Negro arranger for the Gillespie band, once said that comparing New Orleans or Dixieland jazz with bebop is like comparing "a horse and buggy with a jet plane." The old jazz was characterized by four beats to a bar, with the first and third accented; in bebop, the beats are present, but they are almost always so thoroughly disguised that they seem not to be there. The rhythm instruments—drums, bass, and piano—often attempt the complex figures that are being played by the brass, and the rhythm is at best oblique and merely implied. The music, difficult to dance to and sometimes called "head music," to indicate that its appeal is to the intellect rather than the emotions, is frequently loud, aggressive, and defiant. Such is the bitterness that bebop has stirred up in the jazz world that some of its detractors say that the new music is a product of heroin, cocaine, and marijuana, a charge that Fuller, a college graduate of impeccable morals, denounces as "a gross and gratuitous libel." Upon hearing the solos of Bunk Johnson, Sidney Bechet, and even Louis Armstrong, regarded by their admirers somewhat as the Cathedral of Chartres is by medievalists, the beboppers shudder as convulsively as if someone were rasping a fingernail down a blackboard. "How can they play that square stuff?" they ask. This, of course, from the classicist's point of view, is sacrilege, and makes for exceedingly hard feelings. The beboppers occasionally describe themselves as progressives and their opponents as reactionaries. They call themselves "the left wing" and their opponents "the right wing." Friends of the older music call the beboppers "dirty radicals" and "wild-eyed revolutionaries." Boppers are proud of the men who have gone without jobs and meals rather than play music that outraged their convictions, and speak indignantly of "the underground." Until a few years ago, it seems, some beboppers had to play in private, because most jazz fans took such a strong dislike to their work.

Dizzy doesn't like to remember the days of the underground. He even refuses to admit that he was a martyr. "I went for the new music because I dug it that way," he says. "From the first, I felt it was my kick." Bebop began to take form in 1940. As late as 1946, the public revealed such an antipathy to the bebop of Dizzy's band that saxophonist Charles (Yardbird) Parker, another founder of the genre and then a member of Dizzy's outfit, had a nervous breakdown. The band was appearing at a Hollywood night club run by a man named Billy Berg. "They were so hostile out there," Dizzy says. "They thought we were just playing ugly on purpose. They were so very, very, very hostile! They were really very square. Man, they used to stare as us so tough!" Then he erupts into his extravagant hilarity. A bebopper from New York walked into Berg's during Gillespie's tenure there. "Why does it have to be such a fight?" Dizzy asked him despairingly. "Why are people so square? If I ever get back alive to the Apple, I'll never leave it." Gillespie's men, feeling that they were in enemy territory, conversed in whispers at Berg's, and they rented a dingy basement where during off hours they could play their music without fear of being overheard. It was about this time that Parker, an extraordinary performer on the alto saxophone and the composer of some fifty bebop pieces, decided to relax in a sanitarium. "It's too tough a kick for me," he said.

When Gillespie did get back alive to the Apple, where he opened at the Spotlite, on Fifty-second Street, his luck began to turn. More and more of the younger jazz musicians were being attracted to bebop, and their enthusiasm was spreading to a growing segment of the public. Although bebop is by no means preeminent in the field, a half dozen of the big name bands occasionally play it, or commercial modifications of it, many disc jockeys are using Gillespie and other bebop records, and such respected old-timers as Duke Ellington, Count Basie, Barney Bigard, Teddy Wilson, and Billy Eckstine have declared it an important development of jazz. Dizzy and his band have little trouble getting engagements now, and they work steadily, playing theatres, concerts, night clubs, and dances. For dancing, he says, he has to "compromise," giving his music enough regularity of beat to make it possible to dance to. He does some fifty concerts a year, at Carnegie Hall and Town Hall, at Symphony Hall in Boston, at the Academy of Music in Philadelphia, and so on. Last year, after he grossed $6,400 at a Carnegie concert, Variety headlined its story on the event "Wham Coin for Jazz 'Longhairs.'" The bop movement has spread to Europe—especially France and the Scandinavian countries—where Dizzy's records bring as much as twelve dollars apiece and where leaders of jazz bands play them over and over in an attempt to score the complex arrangements for their own bands. The European popularity of bebop, which its more chaste adherents prefer to call modern, or progressive, jazz, has been accompanied by the shattering of certain friendships. Hugues Panassié and Charles Delaunay, perhaps the foremost authorities on jazz in France and once old friends, are no longer speaking. Panassié, it appears, is a square. Naturally, American beboppers say, Delaunay can have nothing to do with him.

Bebop, according to its pioneer practitioners, is a manifestation of revolt. Eight or ten years ago, many Negro jazz musicians, particularly the younger ones, who were sometimes graduates of music conservatories, began to feel, rightly or wrongly, that the white world wanted them to keep to the old-time jazz. They held the opinion that the old jazz, which they called "Uncle Tom music," was an art form representative of a meeker generation than theirs. They said that it did not express the modern American Negro and they resented the apostrophes of critics who referred to them, with the most complimentary intent, as modern primitives playing an almost instinctive music. A lurid and rococo literature grew up around jazz, the work of writers who were delighted by the idea that this music began in New Orleans sporting houses, which was a notion that, whatever its merits, aroused no responsive spark in the younger Negro musicians. Among the dissidents was Gillespie. "That old stuff was like Mother Goose rhymes," he says. "It was all right for its time, but it was a childish time. We couldn't really blow on our jobs—not the way we wanted to. They made us do that two-beat stuff. They made us do that syrupy stuff. We began sayin', 'Man, this is gettin' awful sticky.' We began gettin' together after hours at Minton's Playhouse, on a Hundred and Eighteenth Street." Another who attended the after-hour sessions at Minton's was Thelonious Monk, a sombre, scholarly twent-one-year-old Negro with a bebop beard, who played the piano with a sacerdotal air, as if the keyboard were an altar and he an acolyte. "We liked Ravel, Stravinsky, Debussy, Prokofieff, Schoenberg," he says, "and maybe we were a little influenced by them." Fuller, a graduate of New York University's school of music, dropped in at Minton's now and then; and Joe Guy, a trumpet player, and Kenny Clarke, a drummer, played there for a while. Perhaps the strongest influence, though, was Yardbird Parker, who had never heard of Schoenberg and says that he developed most of his ideas about bebop on his saxophone in his mother's woodshed in Kansas City. "Bebop is what I brought from Kansas City," he says. Fuller's comments on the new music are more general. "Modern life is fast and complicated, and modern music should be fast and complicated," he says. "We're tired of that old New Orleans beat-beat, I-got-the-blues pap." It was at Minton's that the word "bebop" came into being. Dizzy was trying to show a bass player how the last two notes of a phrase should sound. The bass player tried it again and again, but he couldn't get the two notes. "Be-bop! Be-bop! Be-bop!" Dizzy finally sang.

There are devotees of bebop music who believe that the Monk, as Thelonious is sometimes called, had more to do with the origin of bebop than Dizzy did. There is a certain coolness between the two men, and their relations are rather formal. Not long ago, they happened to meet on the street. "Thelonious, you murder me," Dizzy said graciously. "You're it. You're a killer." Not to be outdone, the Monk gravely replied, "Dizzy, you're real crazy. You knock me out." A few months back, the Monk appeared at the Gillespie apartment, on Seventh Avenue, in Harlem, at four-thirty in the morning and asked to be allowed to play the piano. "I would have let the Monk in, but my wife wouldn't let me," Dizzy says. Thelonious will not accept that excuse. "Dizzy should be the ruler of his own household," he says severely. (The Monk is as unorthodox in his conduct as in his music. He eats only when he is hungry and sleeps only when he is tired. He may eat five meals one day and none the next, and may go two nights without sleeping and then take to his bed for two whole days.) There are other points of dispute between the two artists. The Monk claims that the blue beret, the bebop beard, and the horn-rimmed spectacles were his idea; Dizzy says that it was he who identified them with bebop. The Monk believes that bebop should have a strong and regular beat, but Gillespie favors irregularity. "What would you do if your heart beat irregular?" the Monk once asked Dizzy. "The steady beat is the basic principle of life." Thelonious, like many other beboppers, is intensely interested in the basic principles of life. He will take nothing for granted. Some weeks ago, riding in a taxi, he suddenly demanded of a companion, "What makes this car go? I mean *really* go? What *is* going, anyway?" His friends often say, "The Monk is deep."

Dizzy feels that most bebop musicians have extended their basic thinking to the outer world, and that many of his friends have broken down under the strain. Some, he says, have such seethingly complex personalities that psychoanalysts compete for the chance to work on them, without charge. One of his colleagues, he reports, paid two hundred dollars for a painting by

Dali. "He lives in a little cubbyhole of a room," Dizzy says, "with a strong-box in the center. He's got the Dali all locked up in it." Many Negro boppers like to pretend that they are Arabs. Thelonious sometimes forgets that he was born on West Sixty-third Street and announces that he is a native of Damascus. Another bopper, a native of Georgia, tells people that he was born in Madagascar. Dizzy appreciates this flight from harsh reality, and occasionally even joins it himself. Now and then, he wears a turban when he is abroad. "People in Europe see me on the street and they think I'm an Arab or a Hindu. They don't know what I am. Sometimes Americans think I'm some kind of a Mohammedan nobleman. I like to pretend I don't talk English and listen to them talk about me." The large number of bebop-pers who have become Mohammedan converts want to escape from their American environment. The drummer Art Blakey has taken the name of Abdullah Buhaina and insists that his friends call him that. Orlando Wright, a tenor saxophone, is now Gonga Mussa, and Edmund Gregory, alto saxophone, is Sahib Shahab. McKinley Durham is Abdul Hamid, Howard Bowe is Sulayman Rasheed, and Walter Bishop, Jr., is Ibrahim Ibn Ismail. All of them, though unmistakably Harlem, are extremely serious about their new faith. They read translations of the Koran, study Arabic, which some of them can even write, and proselyte un-ceasingly. Neither Dizzy nor anyone in his band is a convert, but other bands that rehearse, as they do, at the Nola Studios, on Broadway in the Fifties, are full of them. Some months ago, Dizzy and Fuller went to a rehearsal of one such band. At sundown, the Mohammedan beboppers stopped playing, laid their trumpets and saxophones aside, knelt on the floor, and bowed in the general direction of Queens and Mecca. Dizzy's eyes filled with tears. "They been hurt," he explained, "and they're tryin' to get away from it."

"It's the last resort of guys who don't know which way to turn," Fuller said impatiently.

"East," said Dizzy. "They turn east."

Gillespie sometimes says that he owes everything to his trum-pet. With it, he says, he expresses his "soul," won his wife, be-came a success, and once saved his life. This last happened four years ago, when he used the instrument to beat off six sailors who attacked him early one morning in a Harlem subway station. "In a fight," he says, "you can't use the bell of the horn, because it may bend. You must be very, very, very careful not to use the bell. Use the valves. Then what you *hit* will bend." Dizzy emphasizes this advice with a cackle of laughter. He won his wife ten years ago, after she had heard him play in a Washington theatre.

"Trumpet's the best part of a man," Dizzy says. "Nothing comes before that horn. Every hour, you must practice. Day or night, you got to keep blowin'." He sometimes plays his horn in bed at four in the morning, to the intense annoyance of his wife and other tenants of the large apartment house in which he lives. When he gets up, at two in the afternoon, he reaches again for his horn and tries out a few ideas before breakfast. "I blow so much," he says, "that the acid in my hand sweat wears a hole in my horn." He has worn out six trumpets in the last eight years. He remembers with particular tenderness one he had in 1939, when he was blowing with Cab Calloway's band. "Never got sound out of a horn like that," he says. "The valves were a little sluggish, but the sound was really a bitch. I loaned it once to Freddy Webster. Freddy had the world's greatest sound." One time, an officer of the law tried to take it away because Dizzy was behind in his installment payments. "I fought that man off like a tiger," Dizzy recalls with satisfaction. Despite his devotion to his horns, he is always leaving them in taxis. "I never worry about it," he said recently. "I know the horn will come back. A few weeks ago, I came uptown from Fifty-second Street and left my horn in the taxi. The driver goes back to Fifty-second Street and says, 'Some guy left a horn in my cab.' Before he could say anything more, ten guys said, 'It's Dizzy Gillespie's.' "

In the 1947 poll conducted by *Metronome*, a magazine devoted to jazz music, Gillespie was voted the outstanding trumpet of the year. He has a dazzling technical virtuosity, according to his colleagues, and a great deal of feeling in his phrasing. "He can play two chord changes to the average man's one," Fuller says. "He's prejudiced, though. He is suspicious of slide trombones. And he really doesn't like saxophones. If he had his way, he'd make his whole band trumpets." Several weeks ago, Dizzy was sitting at a restaurant table describing his way with a horn. "You got to get your moods," he said. "You got to get your chords. You're thinking all the time. Say I want to make a B flat on the first valve. I'm liable to make a C and I'm liable to make an A flat. My fingers would be the same for all three, but my lips are different. That's why you've got to have a good mouthpiece. I got a mouthpiece I'm in love with. Wouldn't trade it for a Packard. It's specially modelled for my lips. Guys are always askin' me, 'How do you get from a B-minor chord to an A flat?' They always talk about my attack. 'What is that?' they say. 'I'm playin' the same notes, but it comes out different.' But you can't teach the soul." Dizzy ran his fingers up and down the tablecloth, as if they were punching the valves of a trumpet. "You gotta bring out your soul on those valves," he said. He laughed uproariously, and, suddenly changing the subject, said, "My wife's the world's greatest fighter against dirt and disorder. Look, if I move a glass from here to here, she knows it and tells me to put it back." His voice was full of admiration.

Dizzy suffers a good many enthusiasms, mostly aroused by seeing someone else do something or display something that he suddenly realizes he wants to do or have more than anything else on earth. Noticing, on one of his trips to Europe, the ship's captain using a pair of binoculars, Dizzy knew no peace until he had a pair himself. For several months, he went around New York wearing the binoculars on a strap. Now and then he would peer through them and murmur, "There's so very, very, very much I want to see!" Once, the driver of a taxi he was riding in rolled a cigarette, and Dizzy was not content until he, too, was rolling his own. If he meets someone with a fancy pipe, lighter, or cigarette case, he immediately wants one like it, and as a result he has a remarkable collection of these articles. He also has a weakness for unusual hats. A year ago, playing in a small Pennsylvania mining town, he saw a man wearing one of those miner's caps with a little lamp set in above the peak, and bought it from the fellow. He wore it everywhere until a friend pointed out that, as head of the beboppers, he was morally committed to his blue beret. "Why can't they get the miner's caps?"

Dizzy replied. "I like the light on it." He finally made the sacrifice, but it was not easy. Before the advent of bebop and the beret, Dizzy, playing with a band touring England, wore for a time a British regimental bear-skin busby with a strap under the chin. When he was in Paris last winter, he was charmed by the Russian Cossack hat of a night-club doorman. He bought it and occasionally wears it around the house. A short time ago, calling on a jazz musician named Eddie Barefield, he picked up a book on Barefield's desk. It was a history of Egypt, by Breasted. "Say!" Dizzy burst out with a terrible urgency. "Where can I get one of these things?"

Wherever Dizzy goes, he brings with him a great deal of pleasant noise, most of it laughter. Many of his friends also laugh inordinately. A peculiar etiquette governs their meetings. When Dizzy meets a friend on the street, both men are apt to stop some twenty feet apart and stare at each other for two or three seconds, as if they cannot believe their eyes, and then simultaneously explode into overwhelming laughter, as though they find each other irresistibly and excruciatingly funny. Dizzy usually raises a weak hand and points helplessly at his friend while he whirls on his right foot, swinging his left in an arc and turning his head and his laughter over his right shoulder. The meetings of other bebop musicians are also stylized, but Dizzy has gone a little further than most in elaborating the technique.

Dizzy, formally known as John Birks Gillespie, was born on October 21, 1917, in Cheraw, South Carolina. He says Cheraw is "very, very, very small. Ha! Ha! Ha! Oh!" His father, who died when Dizzy was ten years old, was a bricklayer, and there were nine children in the family. "My father treated my mother good," Dizzy said not long ago. "He got my mother real expensive stuff. I was scared of him, though. When he talked, he roared. He was a real man. He didn't have a voice like this." Dizzy ended the sentence in a falsetto. "I got a beatin' every Sunday morning." He exploded into mirth. "At school, I was smart, but I didn't study much. I'd fight every day. Ev-er-y day I'd fight. I was all-ways bad, you know."

The elder Gillespie was the leader of a local band, and to prevent its members from hocking the instruments he kept them all in his home. The Gillespies had a piano, too. As a result, Dizzy can play the trombone, piano, and drums almost as well as he can play the trumpet. Sometimes, when a member of his band is late for a job, Dizzy fills in for him. When Dizzy was fourteen, his prowess on the trumpet was known as far as Laurinburg, North Carolina, and because of it he received a scholarship to Laurinburg Institute, a Negro industrial school, where he studied theory and harmony under an instructor he remembers only as Shorty Hall. He went out for football, too, because, he says, "they ate better at the training table." In 1935, when his mother moved to Philadelphia, a few months before his class graduated, he left school and went with her, but on a visit to the Institute last year he was given his diploma and football letter at a special ceremony.

Dizzy was, he says, a real country boy when he arrived in Philadelphia, carrying his trumpet in a brown paper sack. He played with several Philadelphia groups. It was there that he began to be called Dizzy, a name given to him by other musicians, who felt that somehow or other it was more appropriate than John Birks. In 1937, when he was twenty, he came to New York, where he immediately landed a job in a band led by a man named Teddy Hill. Between that time and 1946, when he formed his own band, Dizzy blew with the Ellington, Calloway, Eckstine, and Earl Hines bands. With his own and other bands, he has made a hundred and twenty-five records earning about twenty thousand dollars in royalties in the last eight years. His band usually gets between seven hundred and fifty and a thousand dollars for a dance and around fifteen hundred dollars for a concert. Dizzy pays his men twenty dollars a night. His agent gets between ten and fifteen per cent of the take, and then there are travelling expenses. Dizzy usually nets between a hundred and fifty and two hundred and fifty dollars on a dance. He hopes to make twenty-five thousand dollars this year, which would be the best he has ever done.

When Dizzy is not on the road, he spends much of his life shuttling between the dirty, crowded streets of Harlem and midtown Broadway. His three-room, sixth-floor apartment is often crowded with friends. In the summer, when the windows are open, the cries of children in the streets provide an insistent background to the conversation. Sometimes Dizzy is bothered by the congestion of his apartment, and then he dashes outside to laugh and chat on a crowded street corner or to seek refuge in a dim, crowded saloon. Mostly, however, when he leaves his apartment he is going downtown. He generally reaches midtown Manhattan at three in the afternoon. His band usually rehearses between four and six at the Nola Studios.

On a recent afternoon, Fuller was reheasing the band when Dizzy and a non-musical friend arrived. The band is made up of Ernest Henry and John Brown, alto saxophones; Joe Gayles and James Moody, tenor saxophones; Cecil Payne, baritone saxophone; Dave Burns, Elmon Wright, Willie Cook, and Dizzy himself, trumpets; Clarence Ross, Jesse Tarrant, and William Shepard, trombones; Teddy Stewart, drum; Luciano Gonzales, bongo drum; Nelson Boyd, bass; and James Foreman, piano. All of them are young, several of them are war veterans, only a few affect the Gillespie beard and beret, and most of them dress in floppy, loose-fitting clothes. When Dizzy walked in, the band's brassy clamor was so loud that Fuller, who was trying to tell the players something, could not make himself heard. He finally put his fingers in his mouth and whistled a piercing blast. "I wish you'd play it like it's written," he said wearily when there was silence. "What's happening? The music's right in front of you. I'll tell you what I'll do. For you no-readin' cats, I'll add another bar, make it four instead of three. I'll change it to what you're actually playing."

The band began again. "The men are hard to discipline!" Dizzy yelled over the uproar to his companion. "They're always addin' something! They won't play anything like it's written!" Fuller whistled again, and the band stopped playing. He seemed irritated. As he began to talk once more about the music, one member of the band started clowning. "What you doin' now?" Fuller said to him. "Floor-showin'?"

"I ain't floor-showin'. Ain't no one here to see me."

"It's a real drag to bounce a guy," said Fuller, who does most of the hiring and firing for the band, to Dizzy's friend. "It's a real draggy job to be the guy who bounces a guy." He paused, and then, raising his voice, said menacingly, "Trombones and trumpets, look! Don't use cup mutes ever again. Cup mutes make a trumpet sound like a saxophone. If there's sax parts, don't use cup mutes. No cup mutes unless it's for brass alone. Let's do this one more time from the top, gentlemen."

Dizzy started playing, and the band really came to life. Even when it was at its loudest, his trumpet was clearly audible. His neck and cheeks swelled until it seemed as if something would have to give way. After a while, he began using his horn as a baton, his head thrown back, his mouth open, the tuft of beard trembling in the breeze he was stirring up. Presently he started walking up and down in front of the band, each jouncy step and each exaggerated motion of hips, legs, head, and shoulders in time with the music. "I lead with my whole body," Dizzy says proudly. He uses his body with comic effect. He will interrupt a motion, hold everything until he gets a laugh, and then go on with the interrupted motion. Not all Gillespie music is an exercise in volume. Some of it is quite melodic. When his band is playing, Dizzy likes to sing such peculiar bebop lyrics as this, from "Oop-Pop-A-Da," written by a man named Babs Brown:

> Oop-pop-a-da
> Bli ah bu du la
> Be bli bop
> Oop-pop-a-da
> Bli ah bu du la
> Be bli bop.

Fuller and Gillespie have written a large part of the library of bebop music. After a rehearsal, they often have supper together at a Forty-eighth Street delicatessen and then go up to an office Fuller has on Broadway, overlooking Duffy Square, to do some composing. On this particular day, it was dark and rainy when they and Dizzy's non-musical friend reached the office. They did not immediately turn on the lights but stood at a window and looked down at the glare of Broadway. A large electric sign on the other side of the street flashed on and off, and the silent room jerked back and forth from light to shadow. The office is in a building filled with studios, and from one of them came the faint sound of a piano. Across Broadway, above a shooting gallery, is a sign reading, "America's Hall of Femmes." Dizzy was reading it aloud when the telephone rang. He answered it as Fuller switched on the lights. Dizzy hung up and said, "It was Leonard Feather. He wants us to write something Swedish. For the Carnegie Hall concert." He cackled. Feather is a jazz pianist and author who usually acts as master of ceremonies at Dizzy's concerts.

"Why Swedish?" Fuller asked.

"Why not Swedish? Anything wrong with Swedish?" Fuller didn't answer. "Publicity," Dizzy said. "Feather says he can get the Swedish Ambassador there if we write something Swedish." Another reason for writing something Swedish, Dizzy said, was that he was very popular in Sweden. "Had a sellout in Stockholm my last trip."

"Well, let's get going," Fuller replied. "I gotta get home early." He sharpened a few pencils, took some music paper out of a desk drawer, and sat down before an upright piano with the air of a plumber about to tackle a nasty job. "How long shall it be?" he asked in a tired voice.

"Three movements, eight minutes," Dizzy said. He was rigging up an electric recorder. Dizzy uses this while composing, so that he can play back his ideas.

"What shall we call it?" Fuller asked.

"'Swedish Suite,'" Dizzy said. He began shouting into the recorder to test it. "Wah! Wah! Wah!" he bellowed. "You long-armed, big-nosed, no-good bastard." He pushed a lever and the machine bellowed, "Wah! Wah! Wah! You long-armed, big-nosed, no-good bastard."

"Let's get goin'," Fuller said. "I gotta get home to the wife." He played a few chords, then said, "Let's put a new melody to that."

"That's so common," Dizzy objected.

Fuller tried something else. "How about giving me something for this?"

"That sounds like a lullaby rhythm. I'm trying to get a theme like—like—well, sort of something that portrays the Swedish people."

Fuller played a few more chords. "What kind of people are they? Happy? Sad?" He played some mournful chords.

"That sounds too Latin," Dizzy said. "When we first got there, it was cold as a bitch. Freeze the drops on a polar bear's nose. There was snow up there." He began singing. "Bah! Bah! Bop-pity bah! Bah! Snow! Snow! Snow! Very, very, very cold!" He stopped, then said, "We could work that up." He put his hands on the keyboard, and Fuller got up and let him sit down. Dizzy played a phrase or two. "We gotta get a general sound in our mind, and after that we can get the notes." He hummed another phrase, then sang, "Steamship comin'! Big white steamship comin'! Toot! Toot!"

"That whistle is pretty sour," Fuller said. "Don't know as I like that whistle." However, he began setting it down on paper.

Dizzy went on playing, punctuating his music with eerie bursts of vocal sound, and now and then Fuller wrote something down. Once, Dizzy said, "See, man? Can't you tell Sweden is cold? I'll give that to the trombones."

"Let's make it a B natural," Fuller said.

Dizzy repeated one passage several times. "Oh, that sounds good," he said. "Trumpets there, you know."

Fuller continued scoring. Presently he said, "O.K. Six bars. Better put that extra bar in there. Give me the notes. Just play 'em any way." Dizzy played a long passage, and Fuller wrote it down.

Three hours later, the "Swedish Suite" was completed. Fuller stretched and yawned. "Lord-a-mighty, what a day!" he said. "I gotta get home to the wife."

"It's *cold* music," Dizzy said, cackling. "Bah! Bah! Boppity bah! Bah! Snow!"

LAWRENCE W. MC MASTER, JR.

A Conversation with Dave Brubeck

THE YEAR 1955 may be known in the future as the year jazz and religion got together once again.—R. G.
Not for me, it won't. It was the year I was fifty and the saloon was ten years old.—E. C.
As a matter of fact, jazz and religion have never been far apart. Consider the wonderful Mahalia Jackson and her gospel songs. Ever since the bands began playing those post-funeral marches in New Orleans, and ever since congregations found out that God could be praised joyfully, the beat and the beatitudes have lived peaceably together.—R. G.
That was mainly in Negro churches.—E. C.
I'm coming to that. In 1955, a group of young ministers around the country began trying to show people that jazz, which had some sinful origins, wasn't at all sinful of itself. The Rev. Alvin Kershaw appeared on a television program and answered some questions about jazz to the delightful accompaniment of $32,000. But before Rev. Kershaw ever showed the country the color of his collar, a Presbyterian minister of Oxford, Pennsylvania, named Lawrence W. McMaster, Jr., had been linking jazz and religion on a CBS Sunday morning TV show called "Look Up And Live."

A CONVERSATION WITH DAVE BRUBECK

What follows is the script of a show done by Dave Brubeck, one of the foremost exponents of the modern school, and the Rev. McMaster, in which they discuss the relationship of their businesses.—R. G.

McMASTER: You may recall that about six weeks ago the Reverend Alvin Kershaw, assisted by a different combo than we have with us today demonstrated the close relationship between religion and jazz . . . pointing out that "Jazz helps us to be sensitive to the whole range of existence, and that's the nub of religion . . . to be properly aware of the majesty of life." Well, today we continue with that theme. You might call this the "Theology of Jazz, Part Two" . . . the progression of this unique art form from its humble beginnings to a point where it has achieved its greatest freedom of expression . . . and, therefore, the greatest degree of innovation. Do you go along with that, Dave?

BRUBECK: Yes, and I'd even go one step further. Jazz is one of the few art forms existing today in which there is this freedom of individual expression without the loss of group contact. You have a sense of freedom and also a sense of togetherness.

McMASTER: That's a point I'd like to delve into later, Dave, but first there's something I'd like to find out. I quote from *Time* Magazine:
"Pianist David Brubeck has been described by critics as probably the most exciting new jazz artist at work today. In five years Brubeck fans have grown from a small West Coast clique to a Coast-to-coast crowd."
Dave, what's the secret?

BRUBECK: Larry, actually there's no secret involved. Today's jazz reflects the American scene . . . the hopes, dreams and frustrations of our generation. The closer you can come to that sensitive spot which makes the individual tick, the greater the bond you create between the player and the listener. That's our primary aim—not to play a standard, familiar piece, but to convey a mood . . . a feeling which flows back and forth from the guy on the stand to the guy in the front row . . . and the rows behind him. Do you catch?

McMaster: Yes . . . up to a point. Suppose you demonstrate that technique for us, Dave.
Brubeck: Sure thing.

(Brubeck and his boys played a number here, presumably "The Old Rugged Cross Romp."—E. C.)

McMaster: So that's how it's done.
Brubeck: That's how it's done this time. It doesn't necessarily mean it'll be done that way again. We use only one rule: Everything we play is superimposed on the one before it. If you don't goof, you're obliged to keep going farther out all the time.

(Obliged?—E. C.)

McMaster: Well, Dave, just as there are probably as many concepts of a given piece as there are musicians, so are there as many variations of theology in this world as there are concepts of God and truth. But the basic theme is the same. Just as it is in music. You do start and finish each piece with a familiar arranged tune, don't you?
Brubeck: That's the paradox in jazz. A certain amount of arrangement is necessary. The arranged familiar theme is the skeletal framework . . . the foundation on which we build. All jazz musicians start with a given theme. It's the degree of departure and method of departure which makes one musician differ from another.
McMaster: You depart from the melody then . . . the theme . . . but the basic rhythm, the beat remains the same.
Brubeck: Not necessarily. In the early days of jazz they only improvised on the melody. Gradually musicians began to improvise on the original harmony as well, making it dissonant and thus creating a completely different feeling. Now we're also improvising rhythmically . . . distorting the rhythmic line . . . say, putting in three notes where there were only two. If we may, Larry, we'd like to say all this with music.

(Dave and his boys then said it again. I'll say this for them, they may keep time irregularly, but they keep it. I sometimes wish they'd give it away.—E. C.)

A CONVERSATION WITH DAVE BRUBECK 225

McMaster: This is what a music critic said about you in *Time* Magazine: "Brubeck picks up an idea and toys with it. He ripples along for a while in running melodic notes, builds up a sweet and lyrical strain, noddles it into a low down mood, adds a contrapuntal voice, suddenly lashes into a dissonant mirror-inversion ..." What does that mean, Dave?

Brubeck: Well, all that means is that we use ... that the arrangement ... hanged if I know. If I'm going to do any communicating, man, I'd rather let my music talk for me. After all, that's a universal language and needs no explanation.

(Except to us squares.—E. C.)

McMaster: I'm glad you said that, because in asking my question I had a point to make ... The point is that both among the musicians and the critics jazz has developed a jargon all its own ... a language that is becoming more and more difficult to understand ... and is increasing their difficulty in communicating with the world outside. To my mind it is only tending to create a barrier between the musician and the layman. The same is true in the church too. It kind of has a jargon all its own ... a ritualism that may look and sound lofty and impressive, but goes way over the heads of many laymen. It seems to me both fields ... music and religion ... have to learn to communicate more clearly ... then a couple of the biggest barriers will have been done away with. Okay, now that we're communicating with each other again, what's the next example?

(The next example was Einsteinistic to me, and for all I know, Einstein may have written it.—E. C.)

McMaster: That's great. Hearing you play is really to demonstrate how far jazz has progressed since its early days in New Orleans.

Brubeck: And yet in New Orleans is where it all started ... a kind of combination of cultures, the fusion of which produced this uniquely American art form. There was the African influence ... the drive, the beat. Then via French New Orleans, from Western Europe, came the harmonic sense, the tonal structure, the instruments employed. Today, in addition to these primary influences, there are the newer influences, of contemporary serious composers—Barton, Stravinsky, Milhaud and others. We've taken the foundation of the past, so to speak, and set upon it a loose structure without doors and windows, so that anyone who wishes may enter and take part. . . . There has got to be interplay. A jazz group is simply no good unless everyone cooperates.

McMASTER: That's a good maxim in all walks of life . . . a good way of running the world. Freedom of individual interpretation . . . accompanied by universal cooperation.

McMASTER: You've heard it now . . . the music of liberation. Complex but free, it flows along completely unrestrained . . . and yet is held together by a firm foundation . . . a core called an arrangement. This is progress . . . learning by past experiences and applying the knowledge toward a fuller life, a greater understanding of our fellow men, a greater tolerance for others who may arrive at their conceptions of God and truth in regions different from our own.

The past is like a rear view mirror on a car. If you drive carefully, observing safety rules, you must refer to it to see what's going on behind. In driving as well as living, on highways as well as every other pathway of our existence you should, you must do both . . . look back and look ahead. Progress should have no limit . . . and the future can be rich and fruitful if we have learned from the past . . . from our successes as well as our mistakes and failures. And if progress is to have no limit, there is but one way to insure it . . . and that is to insure the freedom of the individual, the freedom of expression, the freedom to explore, create, originate and improvise according to his conscience . . . providing only that his freedom does not impose on someone else's freedom.

This is why we've coupled religion and jazz . . . the two mediums of communication which speak a universal language . . . and need no interpreters to touch the soul of man. Both mediums, so different and yet so much alike, have many valid reasons for welcoming this progress—jazz, in creating a common conversation . . . in building a community and fellowship of voices . . . the church in ever trying to bring man closer to God. Dave Brubeck mentioned earlier that in jazz they have taken the foundation of the past

and set upon it a loose structure without closed doors or windows, so that anyone who wishes may enter and take part. Speaking for myself, this concept can and should also apply to religion. For two thousand years the church has been building a foundation of truth—that which God has chosen to reveal to man. Upon this solid, firm foundation we should start building a newer structure . . . new rooms with doors wide open to receive all men who wish to enter and take part. For the truth doesn't belong to us alone, nor to any particular denomination, sect or creed, but to all men.
BRUBECK: That was well said, Larry.
McMASTER: Thank you, Dave. I didn't mean to deliver a sermon, but so long as I have we might as well close with a hymn . . . not the conventional familiar paean of praise, but the spontaneous, unrestrained tonal conversation of jazz, which too can truly be an act of worship.
BRUBECK: Right.

(Dave then did it again.—E. C.)

McMASTER: Thank you, Dave. I enjoyed being on this program with you. I learned something.

(So did I.—E. C.)

BRUBECK: Me too, Larry. We both got something from each other. I'd like to do it again sometime.
McMASTER: I hope it's soon . . . and by then I trust we'll both have further progress to report—you in your medium and I in mine.
McMASTER: As Browning said: The ability to progress is one of God's gifts to man.
"Progress—man's distinctive mark alone.
Not God's and not the beasts', God is, they are;
Man partly is, and wholly hopes to be."

LEONARD FEATHER
ROBERT GEORGE REISNER

Bird

THE CHARLIE PARKER legend was in the making long before he died at the age of thirty-four in the spring of 1955. Along with Dizzy Gillespie, Lester Young, Thelonius Monk and others who played in Minton's, the Harlem cradle of bop, he is regarded as one of the creators of the new jazz—perhaps the foremost of them all. Bird had a following not unlike that of Bix Beiderbecke: there were fans, Robert Reisner says, who would listen to nothing but his work, and even went so far as to taperecord his solos off records in order that their enjoyment of their idol could not be interrupted by the intrusions of other musicians. After his death people went around New York chalking BIRD LIVES on walls and subway kiosks. Bird died in the apartment of a friend, a baroness who sent his body to the city morgue; the circumstances were mysterious, and may never be cleared up until Reisner's book is published. For these reasons, we have decided to include two pieces about this remarkable man.

E. C. & R. G.

Leonard Feather is a pleasant exception to the rule that states that all jazz scholars must be fairly obnoxious. For more than twenty years, Leonard has been writing about jazz, supervising record sessions, conducting radio programs and promoting the music in various ways. He also has found time to play a little piano. In one of my early newspaper columns I wrote, "The idea of my doing a record column is purely ridiculous . . . something like asking Leonard Feather or some other jazz scholar to sit in with our band." Leonard got on the telephone and said, "Just ask me." I did. He came down and sat in; none of the customers left. There isn't space here to list all Leonard's accomplishments, but one must be mentioned: The Encylopedia of Jazz, published in the fall of 1955. Leonard spent nearly ten years compiling information for and writing that work, which ought to be a permanent addition to everyone's jazz library.

Leonard's piece on Charlie Parker is not, as I know he will admit, a definitive one; it is a cursory accounting of the saxophonist's life as seen by a sympathetic friend. It was done originally for Melody Maker, the London newspaper.—E. C.

LEONARD FEATHER: What kind of man was Charlie Parker? The answer is a complex one. Parker was a man who loved his music and his instrument, yet often was without a horn to play; a man who at one point in his career had a fortune within his reach, yet went around in raggedy clothes borrowing dollars; a man who under the influence of dope, created some of the most embarrassing scenes ever witnessed in a night club, yet who, when he felt right, was a polished, reliable performer and a smooth-tongued, witty master of ceremonies; a man who loved several women passionately, many casually, his children tenderly, yet neglected ever to send a letter, or a cent for support, to the mother who had struggled to raise him.

To his death, he was an incorporation of inconsistencies.

My happiest memories of Charlie, the years of our closest friendship, go back to the couple of years after his return to New York in the summer of 1947. He had spent seven months in Camarillo State Hospital in California, was mentally healthy again and ready to resume a career that had been wrecked by narcotics.

With his resonant, well-controlled voice and courteous, deferential manner, Charlie impressed many who knew him then as a suave, articulate human being, capable of great emotional warmth.

He was married to a lanky and lovable girl named Doris, a former hat-check girl in one of the clubs where he had worked. Doris, who is about six feet tall, seemed to tower over Charlie. For a while they appeared to find happiness in normal pursuits.

When my wife and I went down to the beach with them, Charlie was content to eat hot dogs, drink a glass of beer and talk about music, politics and mutual friends. For a while it seemed as though he had adjusted himself to a life he had never previously known.

But that was his basic problem: the normal was abnormal for Bird. As he told me at that time: "I was introduced to night-life when I was very young—and when you're not mature enough to know what's happening, you goof.

"I began dissipating as early as 1932, when I was only twelve years old; three years later a friend of the family, an actor, introduced me to heroin. I woke up one morning, very soon after that, feeling terribly sick and not knowing why.

"The panic was on."

The panic, said Charlie, took eleven years out of his life. He didn't know what hit him; he was a victim of circumstances, a high school kid who didn't know any better.

"I was missing the most important years of my life," he said. "The years of possible creation."

This was the Charlie Parker who wandered in and out of a series of bands in Kansas City, Chicago and New York. While his style matured and became the subject of excited talk among musicians his body and mind wasted away.

By the time he got out to the West Coast in the winter of 1945-46, he was unable to pay for clothes or rent, living from house to house until somebody put him up in a converted garage.

"What made it worst of all was that nobody understood our kind of music out on the coast. They *hated* it, Leonard. I can't begin to tell you how I yearned for New York."

As his craving for and dependence on dope grew worse, he developed violent tics. On the night of July 29, 1946, his limbs and muscles jerking and twitching uncontrollably, he went to a recording studio on a session organized by Ross Russell of Dial

Records. He was only able to struggle through two sides before he left.

That night he set fire to his hotel room and ran down into the lobby naked and screaming. Russell helped with the arrangements in sending him to Camarillo after his arrest, but to his dying day Parker never forgave Russell for releasing "Lover Man," recorded on that disastrous night and a shamefully unrepresentative example of his work.

He was bitter toward Russell, too, for using up scraps of incomplete masters, alternate takes, and other devices that enabled two or three times the original value to be coaxed from his Dial recordings.

When Charlie left the hospital, he could hardly wait to get to New York. "As I left the Coast," he told me, "they had a band at Billy Berg's with somebody playing a bass sax and a drummer playing on the temple blocks and ching-ching-ching-ching cymbals —one of those real New Orleans-style bands, that *ancient* jazz— and the people liked it! That was the kind of thing that had helped to crack my wig."

After the arrival in New York and a comparatively serene stretch, leading his own combo around Fifty-second Street and living in a small but comfortable apartment with Doris on the lower East side of Manhattan, Charlies began little by little to deviate again. His chaotic, off-and-on relationship with Billy Shaw was typical of his business affairs; on many occasions Shaw, after swearing he'd never again have anything to do with Parker, would resume booking him—and on the first booking, Charlie would show up an hour—or a whole day—late!

Doris was as loving and patient a wife as ever lived; but Charlie drifted away from her. Eventually Doris, convinced that her task was hopeless, moved to Chicago, and the new light in Bird's eyes, a beautiful, petite brunette named Chan Richardson, grew brighter.

Charlie drank more and more in a desperate attempt to stay away from narcotics, while still avoiding the terrors of sober reality. He wound up in a hospital after a violent ulcer attack.

Visiting him there, I heard him tell me that he would follow the doctor's orders, because if he resumed drinking it would be fatal. That was several years and several thousand drinks ago, though from time to time, with Chan's loving help, he would make an effort to stay straight, perhaps for her sake and for the sake of their two little children, Baird and Pree.

Acclaim and recognition had reached him by now; first he won an *Esquire* award and then, from 1950 on, the *Down Beat* poll every year, as well as victories in *Metronome* and foreign publications. But it often struck me that there was a deeply seated, perhaps unconscious, sense of rivalry with Dizzy, and that he may have resented the extent of commercial success encountered by his fellow bop pioneer and quondam partner.

When he started recording for Norman Granz, who gave him his first chance to record with strings—the only modern jazzman then to have done so—it seemed that a new and important career might lie ahead. Charlie talked excitedly to me about the string albums, enthused about Jimmy Carroll's arrangements and about the new horizons this idea might open up for him.

This probably resulted in another frustration, for the string ensemble was too big to be booked into any but a handful of night clubs; moreover, some of the more narrow-minded jazz fans reacted poorly to the music, claiming that Charlie was "going commercial."

His confidence, never strong, was shaken again—another good excuse for seeking oblivion.

(One of the places Bird played during this period was a small café in Pittsburgh. I was out there doing an article on Ezzard Charles, who was then heavyweight champion of the world. Charles had been dying to go and hear Bird, but after we were in the place fifteen or twenty minutes he grew restive and wanted to leave. We listened to one set and took off. Outside, Charles said, "You ever see anybody so sad in your life? That man's killin' himself."—R. G.)

Most of the time, then, Charlie just led his own quintet from club to club, with Red Rodney or Kenny Dorham or Miles Davis and a rhythm section. His career never seemed to be going anywhere in particular; his relationship with Birdland, the club that had been named after him in 1949, was always stormy, though many times, after being banned from the premises "forever" as a result of some wild scene, he would be booked back in because the club needed somebody to fill up a blank week.

Because a primary sign of heroin addiction is the wasting away of the body, Charlie continued to look "healthy" by the standards of earlier years. He had come back from California with his weight up from 127 to 192 lb. Gradually, though, the extra weight became excess weight, the weight of bloated alcohol-induced fat.

He grew more careless in the way he dressed and was criticized for walking into a job looking like a tramp.

He worked less regularly and began to lose a little of his desirability in the eyes of club owners, not so much because he had lost any box-office appeal as because they could never be sure when he would show up.

Then, two years ago, little Pree, his daughter, died suddenly of pneumonia. The shock was almost too much for both Charlie and Chan to take. The next time I saw him he was in the audience at Basin Street. He came over to our table, knelt beside me and stayed there in a crouching position for at least ten minutes, talking about nothing in particular, not wanting to sit down, not wanting anything but to talk to someone he felt was a friend.

It was then that I felt Charlie Parker wanted to die.

The events of the next few months showed a pattern of apparently intentional self-destruction. Birdland reluctantly agreed to let him work one more week there, with a string group. Charlie created a shocking scene, insulting the musicians, and announced that he was firing them there and then. After which, he slumped into a chair on the bandstand and fell asleep.

That night Chan was awakened by the sound of Charlie's cries of agony. He had swallowed iodine.

The suicide attempt seemed at first to have been a blessing in disguise, for Charlie was taken to the psychiatric ward at Bellevue, where a doctor took a sincere interest in his case. Soon after, Chan and Charlie rented a home in New Hope, Pennsylvania, an hour or two from New York. Charlie arranged to take the train in every day and go to the hospital for psychoanalysis. He stopped drinking.

On October 30, 1954, Bird played in an intimate concert at Town Hall. It was the last time I heard the real Parker, the brilliant Parker in complete control of every faculty. Backstage, afterwards, he talked like a new man, with renewed confidence. It seemed beautifully appropriate that his home now was in New Hope.

What happened after that? Where, when and how did he go off the rails again?

All I know is that the visits to the analyst gradually stopped, the drinking began again, and he spent less and less time at New Hope. The turbulent life with Chan came to a definite and final break.

Charlie had long since given up the pretence of holding a combo together. He merely went from town to town, fronting local rhythm sections wherever he could be booked.

He had parted finally with Shaw and was being booked by the Gale office, who persuaded Birdland to give him one more chance, if only to help him wipe off his heavy debt to the musicians' union—the AFM—incurred by his summary firing of the string section there the previous September.

Charlie was booked in for two nights only—Friday and Saturday, March 4 and 5. He was to appear in an all-star quintet with Kenny Dorham, Bud Powell, Art Blakey and Charlie Mingus.

I was there on the first night and stayed for one set—which was one too many. Mingus announced Bird, but he refused to take the stand. After finally and reluctantly mounting the platform, he engaged in a long and clearly audible argument about tempos and tunes with poor, sick Bud Powell, who was clearly even worse off than Charlie and in no condition to understand what was being said.

Charlie played a few desultory notes and marched off the stand in high dudgeon. Later, persuaded to come back, he stood there at the end of the set, after Bud had left the stand, and called his name out loudly over the microphone, slowly, about ten times. The tension was terrifying; mayhem or murder seemed imminent.

Later I heard that a friend ran into Bird between sets, around the corner at Basin Street, with tears streaming down his cheeks. "It's so wonderful to see you," Parker said. "I need to have some friends around, to see some kind faces. Please, please come over to see me."

Later still, after another hassle on the bandstand at Birdland, I was told that Mingus had said, over the mike: "Ladies and gentlemen, please don't associate me with any of this. These are sick people." And, to Charlie, he added: "If you go on like this, you'll kill yourself."

Three days after the Birdland fiasco, Charlie was at the hotel apartment of a friend, a Baroness, when he complained of difficulty in breathing. She sent for the hotel doctor, who advised immediate hospitalization. Parker refused. He stayed on in the apartment and was treated by the doctor several times, the Baroness said later.

Then, on Saturday, he started to watch an hour-long programme which featured the Dorsey brothers. While he was laughing at one of the acts in the show, his laughter turned into laboured breathing—and he collapsed. He died within a few minutes.

The Baroness had the body shipped to Bellevue, where it lay, apparently unidentified, for a full forty-eight hours before the news came to light. On Sunday night she was seen chatting with Art Blakely and other friends at the Open Door, a boppers' hangout in Greenwich Village, evidently telling them nothing of what had happened at her flat the night before.

After the newspapers broke the story, all kinds of complications set in. Birdland said a big benefit would be held for Chan on April 3; Chan said she wanted no part of it.

Ultimately a great memorial concert for the benefit of Bird's children (he had a teen-age son, now in the Army, by a long-forgotten marriage) took place at Carnegie Hall. Hazel Scott, a sincere and objectively motivated admirer, played a major role in organizing the evening. Scores of artists, including many who owed Bird no musical debt and many more whose styles clearly revealed that they did, came to pay homage.

This spontaneous concerted reaction, the desire to express their respects, reminded me of those days, not so far off, when Charlie was engaged in his fiercest struggle for the recognition that ultimately was his. We were talking about classical music and he had cited his interest in Schoenberg and Stravinsky, had played me records of Debussy and Shostakovitch.

"You know, Leonard," he said, "life used to be so cruel to the musicians, just the way it is today. They say that when Beethoven was on his death-bed he shook his fist at the world because they just didn't understand. Nobody in his own time ever really dug anything he wrote. But that's music."

Charlie Parker lived a life of mental torment and physical agony; he could find peace only in death. Let us hope that despite the years he spent fighting the prejudices and malice of those who could never understand, he died knowing that all over America, and all over the world, there were countless hundreds of thousands who did.

We are lucky to be able to print the material that follows. Robert George Reisner, Curator of the Institute of Jazz Studies, became a friend of Bird through his jazz session promotions around New York. Soon after Bird died, Reisner began work on a biography which as we go to press is still in the research stage. Nevertheless, he has kindly given us permission to use some of his material, provided we emphasize that it is still in rough form. This we are delighted to do, for these notes, comments and anecdotes give a more rounded picture of one of the most colorful figures jazz has ever produced.—E. C. & R. G.

ROBERT GEORGE REISNER: I first met Charlie Parker on a rainy night in 1953. I had just emerged from a party on the lower East Side in New York. It was around 12:30 A.M., and I had walked about a block when I saw a large, lumbering, lonely man walking kind of aimlessly. I recognized him and was amazed and thrilled; but what the devil was he doing in this poor neighborhood, walking by himself, soaked by the rain?

"You're Charlie Parker," I said; "I'm Bob Reisner, what are you doing by yourself?"

He smiled the big warm brown smile, and I felt so good; lives there a man with soul so dead who is impervious to hero worship? "My wife is having a baby and I'm kind of walking off my nervousness and waiting to call back." I walked around with him and remember asking him where he lived and he said in Avenue B. He sensed my wondering why a guy of his tremendous reputation lived in such an out-of-the-way poor section. "I like the people around here," he said; "they don't give you no hype."

It was a year and a half later that I saw him under very different circumstances. I had launched a series of jazz sessions at The Open Door on West Fourth Street in the Village. A great deal of know-how and navigation in the cool world was afforded to me by Dave Lambert, the great bop singer and arranger. He was a great help in setting the aesthetic policy, and he often suggested line-ups to me. One day he staggered me by saying, "How would you like to feature Bird next Sunday? I asked him, and he said he would like to play in your place."

"I'm running to the printer right now to make posters reading 'Bob Reisner presents CHARLIE PARKER,' " I said.

"No, Bob," Dave corrected. "Make it 'Bob Reisner presents BIRD'—just 'BIRD' in large letters."

Bird and the guys got scale plus, and a percentage of the house for him, and he packed them in. It was a lovely beginning to what was to be the first of many sessions featuring him. Sessions filled with arguments between us . . . As I look back now they are funny, but then they were far from humorous. We yelled at each other but always made up the next day, and though I swore never to let him work for me again I knew that if he just honored me by asking me to let him play, it was my cultural duty to do so. Bird was one of the most difficult of individuals to get along with that I have ever met. His suavity, cunning, urbanity, charm and general fiendishness were too much. He could butter up a person, lull him into position, and then bang—a great betrayal. I have seen managers quit on him in succession like horses shot from under a general . . . Like the comedian who wants to play Hamlet, Bird fancied himself a business expert and virtually assumed command of the Sunday sessions in which he appeared. He was pretty shrewd about it . . . One night a person came up to me. "Is that Charlie Parker playing?" he asked naively as Bird's fingers were flying over the keys. "No," I replied bitterly, "he's not playing, he's counting the house."

. . . Yet he was an untrammeled spirit, rebellious—he felt he could not be bought—when he played free or for a few friends. One night he disappeared and I found out later that he wandered across the street to another place called The Savannah Club and played for a few drinks.

One evening . . . people were drifting in, in goodly numbers. Parker had them enthralled, glued to their seats. No one ever danced; they just sat drinking in the sound. At intermission Bird was walking around, smiling, shaking hands, checking with me on business details. Suddenly I heard music from the bandstand, and when I looked I saw two men, one with guitar and one singing—cornball junk, tourist stuff, phony jive, "Get your kicks on Route 66." I could hear slight groans from the cognoscenti. I went over to the stand. "Gentlemen," I said, "you're superb, but not for this audience."

"Man, don't bug us in the middle of our number," one said.

"I'm manager here," I countered.

"Charlie Parker hired us," they countered.

"Are you sure?"

"Ask him."

I walked away to where Bird was. "Charlie, you didn't hire those guys on the stand?"

"Yes, I did."

"The audience is reacting unfavorably," I said, "and I'm throwing those idiots off."

"If they leave, I do," he said. I was stymied at this. I knew that Bird's taste in music was very catholic, that he dug classical music and that when in a car he always turned on the radio to pop music, even hillbilly, but this was really bad. I just sulked. After a few moments he came over to me, put his arm on my shoulder and said pleasantly, "You fool, you just don't understand business. We're full up. These cats are so bad that some of the audience will leave. We need a turnover."

"Bird," I said, "you're a supreme con man—such a hype on this audience that loves you!"

"Bobby," he said, "bread is your only friend."

Bird had such fierce beauty in his playing. In describing his greatness, trumpeter Howard McGhee once said, "Whoever the musician is who plays with him, he feels he's playing shit next to what Bird is putting down." I . . . felt that the opposite was true, too. Bird made and drove and inspired average musicians to excellences they never dreamed they could muster.

The one word which is used most often by musicians in describing Bird is "soul." Bird had so much soul. They forgave him his trespasses when Bird felt evil . . . because they knew he poured so much soul into his art that it must have created an imbalance at times.

Charlie Parker in the brief span of his life crowded more living into it than any other human being. He was a man of tremendous physical appetites. He ate like a horse, drank like a fish, and was as sexy as a rabbit. He . . . was interested in everything. He composed, painted, loved machines, cars, and was a loving father. He liked to joke and laugh. He never slept but subsisted on little cat naps. Everyone was his friend, delivery boys, cab drivers—and he died in the apartment of a Baroness. No one had such a love of life and no one tried harder to kill himself, but try as he did it was hard to tear down that magnificent body. "Bird has disintegrated into pure sound," I heard one musician say. . . .

He never refused a challenge. If you dared him to play Russian roulette with you, he would. He was a thrill seeker. It was a delight for him when a friend of mine, Bob Benson, invited him for a motorcycle ride. It was his terrible curiosity, his hunger to encompass all experience that was to be his ultimate ruin.

No one messed with Bird's music. He went his own way and his way was right, so says every modern alto player, so say even the Hollywood big band studio arrangements. He went on a summer excursion boat up the Hudson one day and was frolicking with a group of Polish people; out came his horn and there was Bird playing polkas for them. One of his ambitions was to study under Paul Hindemith at Yale. There was so much he wanted to do. How much further he would have gone in his musical explorations it is impossible to say. Perhaps not too much, because the miracle of Charlie Parker is that he seemed to have sprung full-grown from the earth. His style seems to have been fixed from the beginning. Hear him on early Jay McShann records such as "Hootie Blues," "Dexter Blues" as far back as April, 1941, and from out of the solid Kansas City jump beat emerge the free-flowing eloquence and idea-jammed notes . . . Bird said his first model on the saxophone was Rudy Valle. Another person who taught him much was Buster Smith, and his first major influence was Lester Young.

Bill Graham says of him, "He could borrow a horn, anybody's horn, and it would always come out his sound, it didn't matter if it was a thin or thick reed, he could make a trombone sound like an alto." One night when a key fell off his instrument, he broke a spoon and fastened a part of it with chewing gum and tape and blew the rest of the evening.

Charlie's sense of the surrealistic was sharp. His escapades are legion. One day he was astride a horse in the middle of New York and attempted to ride into Charlie's Tavern. A few nights later, dressed in T shirt, dungarees and broad canvas suspenders, looking just like a Kansas farmer with a toothpick in his mouth, he stood in front of Birdland.

Oscar Pettiford says, "In 1943 I met Bird in Chicago . . . I was with the Charlie Barnet band and we were playing the Capitol Theatre. Bird was with the Earl Hines band playing at the Apollo. Diz was in the band too. I got word that I could be in a session with Bird and Diz. I walked two miles carrying my bass without gloves in ten below zero weather. It was a fine session."

Bird never seemed to have a union card. He didn't stay in town long enough. There's an 802 regulation that says a musician must wait in town six months for his card. For the first three months he may work at a steady job with union approval as long as he is in town. Bird was always broke and he would have to work out of town to make quick money. He continually borrowed. Dizzy and Oscar always allotted part of their pay to him. They never expected it back; never got it; nobody ever did. One musician said, laughing, "To know Bird you got to pay your dues . . ." He was so likeable that you didn't mind being generous with him.

Pettiford relates a strange incident that occurred two days after Bird's death. Pettiford was sitting in Charlie's, a famous musicians' hangout, when the owner came over to him and said there was a pigeon sitting in the vestibule. He didn't know if the bird was sick or tired or what. Pettiford brought it in and the bird stood on a table, making himself at home. It was not hurt at all. Oscar called for a photographer around the corner to come and take a picture. The bird posed with a saxophone strap around its neck and a saxophone on the table. I cite this story to show how everyone who was touched by the spirit of Parker felt that the quality of the man's creative genius was something unearthly, metaphysical. Several people told me that at the Carnegie Hall Memorial Concert for Bird, when they were playing a composition of his, "*Now's the Time*," a white feather fluttered down from the ceiling.

FOUR:

THE SALES CONVENTIONS

CONDON BELIEVES THAT if a band is composed of more than seven or eight congenial souls, it is no longer a band but a sales convention. His abhorrence is partly due to his ears, he has said, but it also may be dimly connected with an experience he had in 1936. As he related it in WE CALLED IT MUSIC:
". . . Artie Shaw had a string sextet. His playing impressed George Gershwin, and Artie found himself booked for a run at the Paramount Theatre. He organized a full band for the date, with Wettling on drums. Just before the opening his guitar player went to a hospital with appendicitis and I replaced him. The band wore uniforms and ugly brown suede shoes. At one point in the performance I had to stand up, put my right foot on a chair, and play a sixteen-bar solo. Otherwise both my feet were hidden by the music stand. Wettling's right foot was hidden by his bass drum; his left was visible to the audience. We wore the same size shoe, and since each musician had to buy his own uniform and acces-

sories, we shared a pair of the brown suede atrocities. George wore the left one, I wore the right one."

This may not have turned Eddie permanently against large organizations, but it unquestionably helped. Whenever we've had big-band records to review, he has fidgeted and made remarks about the "blood-relative" sound. Some idea of his general contempt for big-band music may be gleaned from his habit of calling the Sauter-Finegan Orchestra "the Sauteed Fingers mob." In his more rational moments, he will admit there is a place for the big band—preferably, some place where he isn't. To him, there can be no more tolerant attitude. When it is pointed out to him that on occasion, at Town Hall and in his own saloon, he has led jam sessions (he calls them "ham sections") of as many as fifteen or sixteen musicians, he parries by claiming that although the bands may really have been big, they didn't sound big and they certainly weren't organized. Thus, in order to get this section into the book, I had to read most of the pieces aloud to him. He listened with the same monumental patience he exhibited one night when I somehow persuaded him to go with me to Birdland. He was interested primarily because the articles are all about people he has known over the years. "I'll let you read me stories about those big outfits," he said, "on one condition: don't make me listen to any of them." So:

The minute this book is in print we will get complaining letters, all demanding to know why we haven't included material on Jimmy Lunceford, Chick Webb, Woody Herman, McKinney's Cotton Pickers, Jean Goldkette, Paul Whiteman, Fletcher Henderson, Cab Calloway, Bennie Moten and numerous others. My excuse is the same as for all sections. These are the good ones we managed to find. Happily, the pieces are primarily concerned with enormously popular and influential bands, so the majority of our readers may be more pleased than annoyed.

R. G.

RALPH J. GLEASON, MURRAY KEMPTON

Two Views of Duke Ellington

DUKE ELLINGTON IS not merely a jazz landmark, he is a land mass, a whole continent, an enduring geographical entity. As in the case of Louis Armstrong, we first had decided not to include him because there already has been so much about him, including a brilliant three-part profile in The New Yorker by Richard O. Boyer and a biography by one of the more indefatigable of the older critics. Then we came across two newspaper columns which presented views of Ellington as he is today.

Ralph J. Gleason's piece first appeared in his column in the San Francisco Chronicle. Murray Kempton's slightly more pessimistic job was done as part of his work for the New York Post. We are presenting both exactly as they ran originally; Kempton wrote us, "These are daily pieces, and I think it's a little dishonorable to tinker with the transient; it should stand with all its faults. . . ."

RALPH J. GLEASON: One of the favorite indoor sports of the jazz aficionados in recent years has been to complain about the Duke Ellington band. For twenty-five years Duke was unique; his fans broke through the bitter departmental lines in jazz collecting and included lovers of every style associated with the word.

But since the great exodus of stars, which began with Barney Bigard and Cootie Williams and continued through Johnny Hodges and Sonny Greer, his fans have been so busy griping they haven't had time to listen.

And they should have. Ellington's strongest point has always been his living compositions. Standard Ellington warhorses like "East St. Louis Toodle-Oo" and "Mood Indigo" have been rewritten and rewritten constantly to include the talents of new men and eliminate the spots that called for the peculiar abilities of former sidemen.

Everytime a new musician joined the band there was a new sound. But the fundamental, viscous, flowing rhythm and deep lush tones that characterized Duke in music have remained.

Naturally, the memories of yesterday are sweeter than the facts of today—they always have been. But Duke's music is every bit as good right now as it ever has been and it is singularly stupid for his long-time friends and fans not to listen to it.

Would they have him always sound the same, always say the same thing? Do they?

Recently, Duke made two magnificent broadcasts, heard here over KNBC and originating in a Chicago night club, the Blue Note. There were many new tunes, many revisions of old ones, but through it all there was the wonderful Ellington sound and the promise of great things to come.

We may well be witnessing the dawn of a new Ellington age that will be even better than the past. Some evidence of this seems to have influenced the country's jazz critics as they just voted him top band in the *Down Beat* poll. More specific evidence was contained in those two broadcasts and in a new Capitol LP album, "Premiered by Ellington."

In this LP, as in those broadcasts, Duke demonstrates again that his is the greatest single talent to be produced in the history of jazz. His music has always been geared to a standard that is above dating. It has maintained an astonishing level of excellence over a quarter of a century and I would like to predict that a quarter of a century hence, Duke's music will be studied in the schools and critics will grant him his true place beside the great composers of this century.

In the Capitol album, for instance, tunes like "My Old Flame," "Stormy Weather," "Flamingo" and "Cocktails for Two" are played so magnificently and with such excellent solos that if these were the first Ellington versions of the tunes there would be no question of their value.

They sound different from the original recordings, naturally, bec? ;e Duke and the band have changed since then. But they are solid evidence that the great Ellington talent is unchanged; and it is a talent that has been making musical history in unpretentious fashion all his career.

Today's band may well be, as Duke says it is, the best he has ever had. It is truly a fine band. Young musicians like Clark Terry, Britt Woodman and Jimmy Hamilton have as much to say as their predecessors and they say it with authority. Harry Carney continues to make all other baritone saxophone players seem feeble by comparison and Duke, of course, is ageless.

Ellington's music is deceptive. Jazz has always depended on the personality of musicians and thus has had an individualized flavor. Duke has always written for the instrumentalists at hand and right now he has some of the greatest ever. They are making a major contribution to jazz and all other music today. They deserve as wide an audience as they can get.

MURRAY KEMPTON: Edward Kennedy Ellington, who is such a piece of royalty as to be almost degraded by the press agent's title of "Duke" closed at the Apollo in Harlem last night. He began in Harlem in the Twenties, glittering in his white dinner jacket at the old Cotton Club, where all the appointments seemed silver and gold, except, of course, the dressing rooms of the performers.

Percy Grainger said once that Edward Ellington was our only original musical mind. There are white musicians still rich from the larceny of Ellington's old ideas. To Europe, Ellington, Louis Armstrong and William Faulkner are our seminal cultural figures. A Los Angeles art gallery has just asked him to send one of his paintings to hang with the work of Dwight Eisenhower, Winston Churchill and other distinguished amateurs.

Yesterday Ellington and his orchestra were playing accompaniment to a balloon dancer. She worked in a net and took off harmless stuff here and there. Ellington is the most courtly of men; he brought her on as if she were Audrey Hepburn; but he forebore to watch her.

His act closed with five boys calling themselves The Flamingoes, whom Ellington introduced as fresh from "a uh, ah, triumph on records." They offered "September Song"; the white singers make their living, thieving old Negro breaks; the young Negro singers are so desperate to imitate the white manner that you would think the history of American music had ended with the first vocal on "Indian Love Call."

The Ellington band remains what it will always be, the finest there is, impeccably precise and clean of limb, because Ellington still flies the old high standard. Yesterday, it was on stage an hour and a half; for maybe ten minutes, among the coloratura males, with the balloons and the comedians, it was allowed to play music. Edward Ellington was otherwise a master of the shabbiest ceremonies.

He sat afterwards in the stars' dressing room at the Apollo, where his guests could spread themselves on a sofa with its stuffing out, next to a wall of dirty sick green. When you are a Negro, even an Ellington, your backstage is a railroad flat.

Twenty years ago, the Ellington band would sit onstage and play for an hour with never a cheap interlude. Now the theater managers, like the rest of us, are afraid of perfection unvarnished; they must surround even Ellington with his inferiors. *What ever else happens, he will not cheapen his band.* "But it's a lot of loot to keep those guys to just sit." The long, reverent afternoons playing note after note of great jazz are over. "You can't do it at popular prices any longer," says Ellington. "You can only do it at concert prices." They allow him only echoes.

He plays college proms where the committee asks for the soft, the smooth and the suave. Sometimes, in Iowa or Minnesota, he finds a college crowd that likes the music that made him what he is. "It's a gasser," he says. "Out there they're hip to us. They know what we're doing."

And then, for a little while, the Ellington band is free to play with what its delicate master calls its old texture. He ran through all these things with pride undiminished and a kind of pleasant resignation and someone said how sad it was that the music business had come to this even for the tallest of its giants.

"A long time ago," said Edward Ellington, "I decided that that type of complaint has no future."

He stood up then and got ready to resume his place as background for the balloon dancer. As his guests went away, he gave one of the chicks an affectionate pat on the cheek. He was smiling. "Nothing ever got me into trouble," said Edward Ellington, "but my good taste."

He will be on the road all the way until June, playing the many places where they want the smooth and the suave and the very few places where they still want the old Ellington texture. We live in a time when the best can only masquerade as the less good, and where our Picassos must paint *Saturday Evening Post* covers or lay down the brush.

JOHN HAMMOND

Twenty Years of Count Basie

IN THE EARLY thirties it was sometimes tough to get even people who had no money to listen to our music. Thus John Hammond was a phenomenon. He was a kid from a family that had never known a trump shortage, and he'd gone to Hotchkiss and Yale. He had a stir-trim and unlimited enthusiasm. We didn't understand him, but he understood us. One night he took Joe Sullivan and me up to his house. I'll tell you what kind of house it was by saying that the flats of people named Astor, Kahn and Vanderbilt were nestling nearby. The place looked like something Cedric Gibbons might have done for an early-thirties movie about the rich. John apologized for it. "I'm getting my own place downtown soon," said he. He led us into the salon, which had a Steinberg that would have pleased the most exacting classicist. Several hundred people could have congregated there for tea and Mozart. Sullivan felt as though he probably should have washed his hands. Then John disappeared up the stairwell, and lowered a microphone from what must have been at least the sixteenth story. Joe sat down at the piano. I think I took out the porkchop and attempted some assistance. There was some rustling audible in the shadows: Beethoven's ghost. Presently John reappeared, the usual grin in command of his features, and asked if he could get us something.

Visions of twenty-five year-old Scotch dancing before our eyes, we admitted that we might not refuse a taste. John summoned a member of the male entourage, who vanished briefly and returned with a tray.

He brought us milk and cookies.

Later on, when John finally did get his own place, there was a noticeable absence of butlers, milk and above all, cookies. But the enthusiasm was still present, as it is today. John's middle has widened a bit but he still looks much the same. And he acts much the same, for he's kept pace with the newest developments. At Newport in the summer of 1955, his applause for the Modern Jazz Quartet was as unrestrained as his excitement over Pee Wee Russell.

But John has never been a mere enthusiast. He has always been an active force behind the scenes. I don't believe another soul, the NAACP officials included, has done as much for the Negro in America—not just the Negro jazz musician, but the Negro, period. It was John who first persuaded a hesitant Benny Goodman to appear in public with Negroes on the same stand. It was John who argued certain club owners in New York and other cities into hiring Negroes as a matter of policy.

John first began writing about jazz in prep school. He did a great deal for the music in England by contributing to various musical publications put out over there, and he was one of the most frequent contributors to the early Down Beat. We asked him for a couple of his earlier pieces, but they were nailed into a barrel on MacDougal Street, he said. He then sent us the piece that follows. It appeared in Down Beat in November, 1955. It's a survey of Count Basie's career when Bill was just celebrating his twentieth anniversary. It's written from the inside. In the thirties, whenever an argument would come up about who played what on which record, John could always settle it by saying, "I know it was so-and-so because I was in the studio at the time." And he always was. Here's John.

E. C.

There may be many areas of controversy in jazz today, but there is one fact that is conceded by almost everyone—critics, musicians, and fans: Count Basie has the greatest band in the business. From the hipsters to the traditionalists, not even excluding the kids who like "rock 'n roll," all get some kind of a message from the Basie entourage.

But 18 years ago, when the Basie orchestra was even more inspired than today's superbly disciplined group, there was only an occasional critical voice raised in its behalf, and the public was mainly concerned with the activities of Benny Goodman, Tommy Dorsey and Artie Shaw, to name only a few. This year Bill Basie is celebrating his 20th year as a bandleader, and it's been a tough struggle all the way.

My first encounter with Bill Basie was in 1932, when he was playing second piano in Bennie Moten's band one week at the Lafayette Theater in Harlem. He had just made his first records with the Moten band, among them "Prince of Wails," "Moten Swing," and "Lafayette," and his presence in the rhythm section made a great group out of one that had been only mediocre before.

In a little speakeasy called Covan's right behind the Lafayette's stage door, Basie used to relax between shows and occasionally sit down at the piano. It was then that I found out that he had been around New York for years, playing in Harlem night clubs, in June Clark's band in a 14th Street dance hall, and accompanying such blues singers as Clara Smith and Maggie Jones. Once in a while, Fats Waller had let him play the pipe organ at the Lincoln Theater on 135th Street, but a good part of the time there was no work at all.

Moten's band never returned to New York. The one theater engagement had been a flop, the depression showed no signs of lifting, and Moten was never to record again. It was not until late in 1934 that I heard the name Basie again, from the lips of Fletcher Henderson.

When Coleman Hawkins left the Henderson band in 1934, to go on a European tour as a soloist, Fletcher started to talk about a little group he had heard in the west headed by Basie. He told me that this band was the greatest he had ever heard, and that he would like to take it over intact. He didn't, of course, but he did send for its tenor saxophone, Lester Young, to replace the incomparable Hawkins.

I'll never forget the day that summer when Lester came into

the rehearsal at the old Cotton Club and took his place in the sax section, which included Edgar Sampson, Russell Procope, and Buster Bailey. Lester was his incomparable self, but the whole band was horrified at his sound. It wasn't like Hawkins! Henderson bowed to the will of the majority, hired Chu Berry, and sent Lester back to Kansas City.

Basie had taken over the Moten band in 1935 after Bennie's death, and late in 1935 settled down with it in a little Kansas City joint called the Reno Club. The Reno had nickel hot dogs and hamburgers, nickel beer, and whiskey for 15 cents. It also had a floor show, complete with chorus line and three acts. The "scale" for the musicians was $15 a week and the hours were from 8 'til 4, except on Saturday, when it was twelve solid hours from 8 to 8. It was a seven-day week, naturally, and nobody got rich, least of all the club owner.

It seems almost unbelievable, but the Reno had a nightly radio wire over the local experimental station, W9XBY. You had to have a radio set capable of receiving police calls to tune in the station properly, but the transmitter was powerful enough to be heard in Chicago, and occasionally I was able to get it on my car radio in New York, around 3 A.M.

The first time I heard a Basie broadcast was in December, 1935, when I was in Chicago to attend the opening of Benny Goodman's new band at the Congress hotel. The group comprised three rhythm, three reeds, and three brass, and it almost made me forget the star-studded Goodman personnel. Jones and Page were on drums and bass; Buster Smith, Jack Washington, and Lester Young were the greatest reed section in history, while Joe Keyes, Lips Page, and Dan Minor were on trumpets and trombone.

Basie became almost a religion with me, and I started writing about the band in *Down Beat* and the *Melody Maker* early in 1936, even before I had heard it in the flesh. I was scared to venture to Kansas City lest I be disillusioned. But my first night at the Reno in May, 1936, still stands out as the most exciting musical experience I can remember.

This Basie band seemed to have all the virtues of a small combo, with inspired soloists, complete relaxation, plus the drive and dynamics of a disciplined large orchestra. Charlie Parker considered

Buster Smith, the lead alto, as the greatest of them all and the man from whom he learned the most. Pres of today is a mere shadow of the genius of the 1936 Lester Young. Lips Page was a consummate showman, stylist, and section man, while Basie, Jo, and Walter worked as a team which has never since been equaled. At the piano, Bill had an uncanny ability to spur the individual musicians to heights they had never before known. Twenty years later he still has the same quality.

In June of 1936 I enticed Willard Alexander of MCA to K.C. to hear the band. Willard, who had been the managerial genius behind Benny Goodman, was bowled over by Basie, Jimmy Rushing, and the whole unit, but he was less than sure about how the other MCA executives would react to an uninhibited nine-piece colored band, without a library, uniforms, showmanship, or even decent instruments to play. It was a couple of months before Willard could persuade such skeptics as Billy Goodheart and Jules Stein that there was a market for a good colored band, and by that time it was decided that Basie should enlarge his group to the Goodman size (five brass, four reeds, and four rhythm) so that it could play the larger dance halls and theaters.

Despite the signing of a contract with MCA in the fall of 1936, Basie was by no means on the road to success. Just before rehearsals started with the enlarged band, Joe Glaser signed up Lips Page to an exclusive contract. Joe, one of the canniest of agents, had caught the Basie band and was convinced that Lips was the only commercial element in the whole unit.

Although Brunswick, with which I was very loosely connected, was all ready to sign Basie to a 5 percent royalty contract, Jack Kapp dispatched his brother Dave to the Reno with a contract for Decca. Dave was the first full-time recording man to see Basie, and when the magic figure of $750 was mentioned, Basie could not resist signing "that piece of paper."

It was probably the most expensive blunder in Basie's history. Upon later reading the contract he found that the $750 was for 24 sides by the full band, without one penny of artists' royalty, and that he was tied up exclusively for three years. It was typical of some of the underscale deals which record companies imposed upon unsophisticated Negro and "country" artists. When Basie finally reached New York I brought the contract to Local 802, and Decca was forced to write a new one which would at least conform to union minimums. But they were unable to make Decca give artists' royalty, and as a result all the biggest hits like "One O'Clock Jump," "Swinging the Blues" and "Woodside" were made for flat scale.

One night in October, 1936, after a battle of music with Duke Ellington, the Basie entourage piled into a new Greyhound bus en route to Chicago for the MCA-booked engagement at the Grand Terrace. It was a 14-piece band, including the vocalist Jimmy Rushing, who received a sidesman's scale, and there were some new faces added to those at the Reno. Buck Clayton, just returned from Lionel Hampton's band in California, had replaced Lips. Buster Smith had no confidence in Basie's future, and Couchie Roberts was his alternate. Herschel Evans was an addition on tenor, George Hunt on trombone, Claude Williams on guitar, and Tatti Smith on third trumpet.

The Grand Terrace in Chicago was a strictly jimcrow establishment on the south side, not unlike New York's Cotton Club. It boasted a pretentious floor show, with a specially written fancy score, and an owner with a reputation for an ungovernable temper. The Basie-ites arrived, took one look at the complicated arrangements, and collapsed. Ed Fox tried to cancel them out after the first rehearsal and swore mighty oaths at Willard Alexander, who was safely in New York.

Willard, for one, was anything but worried. He had booked Basie into the club for the sole purpose of its nightly coast-to-coast radio wire, and it was of no concern to him that the band crucified the show score night after night.

Fletcher Henderson's band had just vacated the Terrace's bandstand, but he did everything possible to help the Count. He gave Basie dozens of his arrangements, as well as much-needed encouragement. Most of the well-heeled patrons of the club hated Basie's music, but a few of the chorus girls loved it, and the word began to circulate in Chicago that the band was "different" and exciting. The airtime helped, even though imperfect intonation and unfamiliarity with the new arrangements were painfully evident and audible.

During that Chicago engagement I did my first recording date with Basie. Because of his disputed Decca contract the session had to be secret, but in November, 1936, four sides came out on the Vocalion label under the mysterious title of Jones-Smith, Inc. It was the very first record date for Lester Young, Jo Jones, and the trumpet player, Tatti Smith, and I will always remember it as the smoothest date in history: three hours of blowing without a breakdown or even a clinker. "Shoe Shine Boy," "Evenin'," "Boogie Woogie," and "Lady Be Good" were made by the five men that day, and they are still in the catalog today.

Last month, some 19 years later (*This piece appeared in* Down Beat *in early November, 1955—R. G.*), Jo Jones was making a Vanguard date out in Brooklyn. Halfway though the session there was a loud knock on the door, and Basie walked in. Nat Pierce solemnly got up from the piano, Basie sat down, and with Walter Page, Jones, Freddie Greene, Lucky Thompson, Emmett Berry, and Benny Green, made an even greater "Shoe Shine Boy" to commemorate the first recording of the original rhythm section.

The rest of Basie's history is pretty well known. Willard Alexander continued to have faith in the band despite its uncertain New York reception at Roseland, the ignominious flop at the William Penn hotel in Pittsburgh, and the puzzlement of Harlem audiences the first time the orchestra played the Apollo and the Savoy. With the acquisition of such men as Ed Lewis on first trumpet, Earl Warren on first alto, Harry Edison, Freddie Greene, and vocalists like Billie Holiday and Helen Humes, the band took on a polish and confidence that made it hard to resist.

With the release by Decca of "One O'Clock Jump" in June of 1937 Basie became a popular favorite. His band of that era was infinitely more subtle and intoxicating than the one he is known by today. Its roster of soloists was unparalleled: Buck Clayton, Harry Edison, Dicky Wells, Benny Morton, Vic Dickenson, Earl Warren, Lester Young, and the great Herschel Evans. It may not have achieved the consistency or precision of a Goodman, but it rose to heights no other jazz group has ever reached.

After World War II Willard Alexander left MCA. To his everlasting regret, Basie stayed with the agency, and the band floundered for the next three years, finally breaking up in 1949.

The present band was assembled in 1952 with many notable soloists and, this year, the superb Joe Williams on vocals. Basie has had his first record hit since 1941 in "Every Day," and the future never looked brighter.

A few days ago, Bill and Catherine Basie were at my house listening to records and tapes. I started to play some old Fletcher Henderson sides cut in the '20s. Basie knew every note of the arrangements and had memorized most of the solos.

"Fletcher had the greatest band of them all," Basie said. "And you know one thing, John? He was the only leader in the business that ever went out of his way to help me. Without those arrangements he gave me in Chicago there's no telling what would have happened to my band."

There is talk now of sending Count Basie and his orchestra on a trip to Russia and her satellite nations, under the auspices of the state department. If this should happen, you may confidently expect a new era of international good will.

(*Characteristically, John has failed to mention his own part in the progress of the Basie band. In Pittsburgh, one of the musicians lost his reason for a time; John saw to it that he went to a sanitorium until he was well. It's too bad that we couldn't get Bill Basie to do a piece about John—R. G.*)

BENNY GOODMAN

That Old Gang of Mine

HERE IS THE story of the King of Swing's first band, which many consider the greatest "white" band ever organized. Benny put down his story with my assistance just about the time the movie called "The Benny Goodman Story" was first being shown around the country. We spent several evenings together; Benny searched his memory, and I tried to capture the essence of his conversation. Then I spent a couple of weeks talking to musicians and old acquaintances who had been involved in the formation and subsequent activities of the band. The story as it stands is more realistic than the movie.

R. G.

"Pops," said one of the boys, "do you remember the time we were riding through the mountains on our bus, and you, your brother Harry, Helen Ward and Vido Musso got to tellin' stories, and the bus driver laughed so hard he ran the bus off the road and nearly killed us all?"

"And what about that time at Nuttings-on-the-Charles," said another, "that ballroom near Boston, on the pier out over the river? The band got to rockin' so good and the people were stompin' so hard the manager was afraid the whole ballroom would go into the river, and he called the police and made some of the people leave."

"Remember the opening at the Paramount in New York?" somebody added. "The kids got so excited they came up and danced on the stage, and they had cops on duty *inside* the theater."

"Pops," said Hymie Schertzer, "it's been a long time. Why, it's been twenty years."

It was July 1955, and we were standing in the recording studio at Universal-International, getting ready to record the sound track of "The Benny Goodman Story." The band was not exactly the same as the Benny Goodman band of 1934-'38, but most of the old sidemen were there: Gene Krupa, Harry James, Ziggy Elman, Hymie Schertzer, Babe Russin, Chris Griffin, my brother Irving, Allan Reuss, Murray McEachern, Lionel Hampton and Teddy Wilson. Some of the heads were grayer now, and some of the faces had been lined and sculptured by passing time.

Twenty years have elapsed since I got that old gang of mine together . . . twenty years since we were jolting along in a bus on 400-mile overnight hops to one-night stands, eating in roadside grease traps, staving off exhaustion to play our music for ever-increasing crowds. Somebody tagged our music "swing"; I never knew exactly who was responsible, but I remember that I felt uneasy about it. I thought "swing" was a fad word, and that it would die out and leave me stuck with it.

It didn't die out. It captured the country. To the press and the public, I was "the King of Swing," and the nation was my kingdom.

That was some band. The brass had a hard, biting attack, the saxophones were warm and rich and gutty, and the rhythm pounded with an insistent solidity. It was a loose band, very relaxed, yet utterly precise. As saxophonist Art Rollini said recently, "Everybody seemed to think as one man; we all did the same thing at the same time."

Like all big dance bands, mine had a constantly fluctuating personnel. A pal of mine, Jim Maher, once made a list of saxophone men who'd played in bands of mine between 1934 and the present. It came to 95 men he was sure of, plus about 15 others he and I thought were on records, or 110 in all. But the band I think of as the best and the one that stayed together longest during the time when the country was really swinging, lined up like this:

Gordon (Chris) Griffin, Harry James and Ziggy Elman, trumpets; Murray McEachern (or Vernon Brown) and Red Ballard, trombones; Hymie Schertzer, Vido Musso (or Dick Clark), Toots Mondello, George Koenig (or Bill DePew) and Art Rollini, saxophones; Jess Stacy, piano; Harry Goodman, bass; Allan Reuss, guitar; Gene Krupa, drums; Helen Ward (later, Martha Tilton), vocals.

I've had many groups since but I've always regarded that one with a special feeling. It gave me some of the best times I ever had, and some of the worst: times when I was so close to total exhaustion I could scarcely remember my own name, but moments of genuine exhilaration, too.

It all started in 1934, when I was twenty-five.

For most of my life—since I was thirteen—I had been a professional musician, and when I could I played the music I had learned in Chicago, where I was born: jazz, the improvised, creative music originated by Negroes and usually played by small groups. Although jazz wasn't often a paying proposition in those days (we used to play it in our spare time), with the help and encouragement of a young, well-to-do jazz fan named John Hammond I did make a few records in the early thirties with men I liked and respected. The records got a good reception, especially among musicians. They led to several more record dates for me, and also led me to think seriously, for the first time, about organizing a big band to play my kind of music.

Nothing much came of my thinking for a while. I was playing in radio, making a pretty fair living. I'd brought my mother, sister and two brothers to New York from Chicago, which added to my responsibilities. Also, I wasn't quite convinced that the public was ready for the kind of band I dreamed of leading. Then, that March of 1934, my brother Harry, who was playing with Ben Pollack, told me that Billy Rose was thinking of opening a new night club. Naturally, he would need a band.

Oscar Levant, who was working with me on a radio show, introduced me to Rose and I began rounding up some men. I had definite ideas about how I wanted my band to sound. First, I was interested only in jazz—I wanted to create a tight, small-band quality, and I wanted every one of my boys to be a soloist. The band had to have a driving beat, a rhythmic brass section, and a sax section that would be smooth but with lots of punch.

When I had the best men I could get I started rehearsals. I didn't just ask for good musicianship; I insisted on it. I've never been a particularly patient guy where music is concerned. When somebody let me and the band down, I got sore and let him know it. Nothing less than perfection would do: I lived that music, and expected everybody else to live it, too.

However, the band I had in mind was not the band Billy Rose had in mind—not at first, anyhow. We auditioned for him one afternoon, and he was far from impressed. He said, shortly, "Let you know," and turned to something else. I was discouraged and disappointed; by that time I had become excited over the prospect of having my own band, and I'd been counting on getting the job.

Someone must have put in a good word for me; soon afterward, word came that we were hired.

When we reported for the first rehearsal with the show, we found that Rose seemed to have dug up every last old-time vaudeville act that wasn't working at the time. There were roustabout tumblers, dogs, a trampolin act, a fire-eater, and several production numbers with girls. My boys' spirits picked up when they saw the girls, but fell as soon as we started playing the music for the show. We were terrible. I don't know why, but we couldn't seem to work our way through that score.

Rose came over to me and said, "It doesn't look like you can play the show."

I looked at my boys, ready to tell them to pack up their instruments.

"I tell you what," Rose said, "you'd better play for dancing, and we'll let Jerry's band play the show." (Jerry was Jerry Arlen, brother of composer Harold Arlen.)

So we had the job. Yet, even though Billy Rose's Music Hall was a success from the beginning, the same could not quite be said for the band. Most of the customers liked the jugglers, but they didn't understand what we were trying to do. The band kept getting better and better, but instead of dancing, the crowd just sat and pounded their feet in rhythm. Still, I kept hoping. I was still working in radio during the daytime hours, and one evening I had a broadcast with Leo Reisman's Orchestra that made me late for work at the Music Hall. The boys started off without me, and they were playing when I walked in. I remembered thinking: *Gee, this gang sounds pretty good.*

Two days later we got our notice.

I was about ready to give up the band. Then a fellow named Joe Bonime walked in and changed everything. Joe worked for an agency that was lining up bands for a big three-hour dance-music show that was to go on the NBC radio network in the fall. Joe wanted to know if I would be interested in playing for some of the people at the agency—sort of an audition for an audition.

"Fine," I said, without stopping to consider that we had hardly enough orchestrations to show what we could do. Playing for the Music Hall dancers had been a cinch. Our numbers, except for the few arrangements we could afford, were made up as we went along and consisted of improvised solos by various members, with the rhythm section behind each soloist. So, on the night that Joe showed up with his friends, I was a little panicky. My problem was to let them hear the handful of special arrangements and get them out before they realized that we had exhausted our repertoire.

We never sounded better than we did that night. The band played with real authority, and when I shot a glance at Joe and his colleagues, I could see they were eating it up. Then we came to the last number in the book. Sweat was pouring off me; I didn't know exactly what to do, so I decided to bluff it.

"Act as though this is the end of the set," I told the boys.

We finished the number, stood up, and walked off. The boys went down to Fifty-third Street to their favorite hangout, a confectionery where there was a pinball machine, and I went over to Bonime's table. Luck was with me.

"Sounds pretty good," Bonime said. "You'll hear from me." He and his party left.

Time passed. Nothing happened.

The call came when I had just about given up hope of hearing from them. NBC was going ahead with its "Let's Dance" program, featuring the bands of Kel Murray (for sweet music), Xavier Cugat (for Latin American) and—Benny Goodman!

Now there was a series of hasty conferences. The first problem was to get some arrangements. The great Negro leader Fletcher Henderson had more or less broken up his band the year before. He was looking for work, and was only too happy to begin developing a book for our band. He charged us only $37.50 per arrangement! As I recall, the first things he did were "Sometimes I'm Happy" and "King Porter Stomp." We also got some other arrangements, but Fletcher was the man who really made our band, by arranging popular tunes in the same style he used for hot numbers, which we called killer-dillers.

To get used to playing the book, we played some dates around town. The band was shaping up, but it still wasn't anything like the way I wanted it to sound. The rhythm, especially, wasn't right. Our drummer was merely adequate, and a couple of new men we tried didn't seem to add anything. The man I really wanted, Gene Krupa, was in Chicago, playing with Buddy Rogers at the College Inn.

John Hammond, the young jazz bug who'd helped me earlier, was still enthusiastically lending a hand, and he went to Chicago to try to corral Krupa. He happened to hit Gene on a night when Rogers, who was versatile but not much of a jazz man, was working out on about eleven different instruments. Gene was having a sad time, but for various reasons he didn't want to change jobs.

"This is going to be a real jazz band," John urged. "Think of the kicks, Gene, playing jazz every night."

About then Buddy Rogers picked up another instrument and prepared for a solo.

"I'll come," Gene said.

Now we had everyone we needed, I thought—and then the producer asked what I was going to do for a girl vocalist. I thought immediately of a girl we'd auditioned for the Music Hall job. Her name was Helen Ward, and she was a New Yorker not too many years out of high school. I had offered her the Music Hall spot, but she then had a job with Enric Madriguera and wasn't inclined to leave. This time she said yes. At the same time, she put me in touch with a fellow named George Bassman, writer of "I'm Getting Sentimental Over You," which our rival-to-be, Tommy Dorsey, had adopted as his theme. Theme-writing evidently was a specialty with George. He took Von Weber's "Invitation to the Dance," made it into a jazz arrangement, and called it "Let's Dance," after our NBC show. It's been my opening number ever since.

We got our closing theme one day when one of our trombonists, Red Ballard, introduced me to a young fellow and said, "This kid's got a tune I want you to hear." The tune was "Good-bye," and the kid has since become pretty well known for his compositions and arrangements. His name is Gordon Jenkins.

We made our debut on the "Let's Dance" show in December, 1934. We were all pretty nervous, but I couldn't help feeling that we were going over pretty well. The mail that began pouring in a few days later confirmed that opinion.

(I went to see Benny at the studio one night when he was broadcasting. He was wearing a stovepipe and tails. "Hello, Eddie," he said.—E. C.)

The show, which was broadcast in New York City from 11:00 P.M. to 2:00 A.M. each Saturday night, was to go for twenty-six weeks, and with each succeeding week we gained more assurance. Fletcher kept turning out inspired arrangements, and we found another excellent arranger who knew what we had in mind, Edgar Sampson, who was with the Chick Webb band ("Stompin' at the Savoy" and "If Dreams Come True" were two of Edgar's tunes).

We began playing more and more one-nighters around the New York area. We still weren't big enough to command much money—some of them we jobbed for $200 or a little more. And some of them were disasters. Once I hired a bus to take us up to Binghamton, New York. It was in mid-winter, but that bus would have had trouble making the run in July. Two hours after we were due, we were still twenty miles out of town. The manager had hired an all-girl band to fill in for us, but we finally dragged in and played the job.

Yet we were moving along. Our success on the radio got us a record contract, and our first two sides, "Dixieland Band" and "Hunkadola," had a pretty fair initial sale for a jazz record. We hired Bunny Berigan, one of the all-time greats on the trumpet, and for piano we got Jess Stacy, whom John Hammond had found in a run-down Chicago saloon. Willard Alexander, our booking agent, began lining up a summer road tour. I was full of excitement: it looked as though my theory was right. There seemed to be a real audience for our music.

It all came to an end abruptly. The sponsor of "Let's Dance" didn't pick up the option, and when our twenty-six weeks were up, we were finished on the air.

But Willard was optimistic. "I've booked you into the Hotel Roosevelt," he said, "for two weeks."

I couldn't believe him: Guy Lombardo was the regular band leader at that spot.

"The change of pace may appeal to the customers," Willard said.

The Change of Pace did not appeal to anyone. We even drove the waiters out. The few customers who had the courage to remain sent caustic, complaining notes up to the bandstand—I still have several in my collection of souvenirs.

(George Simon reviewed the band in Metronome. He raved about it. But by the time the magazine came out, the closing papers had been served.—R. G.)

Despite the Roosevelt fiasco, we started out on the road tour Willard had arranged. Because we weren't prosperous enough to afford a bus, we traveled in three or four automobiles. The first stop was Pittsburgh, for a week's engagement at a theater. The reaction was fair. In Columbus, Ohio, we did a little better, but not much. I began to wonder what had happened to all those radio listeners who'd written us fan letters. None of them seemed to turn up, either, in Toledo, or at a couple of Michigan dates we played. We had two good days in Milwaukee, principally because it was handy to Chicago—which has always had its jazz fans. But even Milwaukee was not very good.

Then came Denver, and near desperation.

We were booked into Elitch's Gardens, perhaps the best-known place of its kind in the Rockies, for four weeks. We should never have been booked there for four minutes. The instant we started to play, the manager came ranting out of his office, demanding to know why we were making all that noise. People were getting their money back.

That first evening was just about the most humiliating experience of my life, up to that time. Next morning I went in to see the manager. He suggested that I get my boys to play waltzes.

"I hired a dance band," he said.

I bought some stock arrangements and gave them to the band. That night we hit upon a pretty good idea. Helen Ward played fair piano, so she sat down and she, Gene Krupa, my brother Harry on bass, and guitarist Allan Reuss accompanied Bunny Berigan on a couple of sets of the schmaltziest waltzes ever heard even in Denver.

The manager appeared again, "Look here, Goodman," he said, "I'm paying for a full band!"

I got Willard on the telephone. "We're laying a bomb," I said.

"What do you want to do?" Willard parried.

There was only one possible answer. Thus far the cross-country tour had been mainly a bust. I had been wrong: the country simply wasn't ready for the kind of music I wanted to play. On top of that, the band's spirits were really low. I drew a breath. "I guess I'll have to give it up," I said. But even as I said it I knew I wouldn't.

Somehow we finished out the Denver job, waltzing it up and playing slow, sticky stock orchestrations. The next stop was Salt Lake City, where the crowd was moderate in size and in applause. Then came Oakland, California. We got there about an hour before the scheduled starting time, asked directions, and headed immediately for the dance hall.

As soon as we got in sight of the place, I knew there'd been a mix-up in our bookings. The street in front of the auditorium was solidly packed with people. I was utterly disgusted, and was all set to send Willard a furious wire about the mix-up.

"Imagine him making a mistake like this," I muttered.

A guy was shaking my hand. "How do you like our turnout, Mr. Goodman?" He was the manager.

It was impossible for me to believe that so many people had come to hear us—I was still sure they had us confused with some other band. We set up our instruments sort of warily, half expecting the other band to walk in the door.

When the manager finally opened the doors to the public, the crowd surged inside and jammed up tight against the bandstand.

I thought: If it's a mistake, it's a mistake. I might as well make it a real mistake.

I called for "King Porter Stomp," one of Fletcher's real killers.

That number started off with Bunny Berigan playing a trumpet solo, the saxophones and rhythm behind him. Before he'd played four bars, there was such a yelling and stomping and carrying on in that hall I thought a riot had broken out. When I went into my solo, the noise was even louder. Finally the truth got through to me:

We were causing the riot.

What was even more amazing, the fans seemed to get wilder and wilder as the night wore on. I was positive it was a fluke, and that we'd just had the good luck to be booked into a jazz-mad town. But a few days later, at the Palomar Ballroom in Los Angeles, the same thing happened. When we beat off "When Buddha Smiles," it was the Oakland riot scene all over again. We'd been scheduled for four weeks, and stayed seven—breaking all records, if you please.

Later on, I figured out what had happened. Our NBC show had been broadcast from 11:00 P.M. to 2:00 A.M., New York time. That meant it reached the West Coast (skipping Denver, I imagine) between 8:00 and 11:00 P.M. or at the best possible time in which to develop an audience. So, when we got to the Coast, they were ready for us.

In the words of the late Fats Waller, the panic was on. After our Palomar job we started back East, playing one-nighters to terrific crowds, doing phenomenal business, for a new band. Willard booked us into the Congress Hotel in Chicago for three weeks. The Congress was known as a dead room; nobody had ever done much business in it. We stayed eight months, playing to near capacity every night. Everything we tried seemed to click. We were offered a radio show and our records were selling so fast that the dealers couldn't keep them in stock.

To me, the Congress was important for another reason. It was there that we broke through the color line.

We had been playing some Sunday-afternoon concerts to standing-room-only crowds, and after the second or third I had the idea of bringing Teddy Wilson out from New York to appear with us. My acquaintance with Teddy went back several years. But I had never realized how really fine he was until one night at a party at the home of Red Norvo, the xylophonist, who was then married to Mildred Bailey. Somebody had asked Teddy to play at the party, and I'd liked his style so well I hadn't been able to resist picking up my clarinet. Teddy and I began to play as though we were thinking with the same brain. It was a real kick. A couple of days after that I had one of the first recording jobs with my "Let's Dance" band, and I asked Teddy to come along and make some records with Gene Krupa and me. We cut "Body and Soul" and "After You've Gone"—two sides I still think of as ranking with the best I ever did.

The trio records were selling as well as those of the big band, and some of the more knowing fans at the Congress were asking me when I was going to bring Teddy to Chicago. I was hesitant, at first; I didn't know but what some bigots might raise a fuss over different-colored men playing on the same bandstand. But Negroes had been my constant musical companions for years. They had been well received. Somebody had to take the step.

I wired Teddy to come on out.

When he arrived, I was even more worried. At the same time I felt sore when I considered the possibility that some people might object. Negroes were the ones who had found this kind of music I loved; why shouldn't Negroes have the same chance to play it as my white friends and I had? At our next Sunday concert at the Congress I stepped to the microphone and announced the Trio. Gene got behind his drums; Teddy came out and sat down at the piano. We started to play. There were no objections. In fact, there was nothing but tremendous acclaim for Teddy's masterful playing, and from then on he was a regular member of our organization.

About a year later, in Hollywood, some of us went to hear a kid who'd been described as a fantastic drummer. He was playing at a place called the Paradise Cafe on Central Avenue, and when he wasn't drumming he was working out on a novelty instrument called the vibraphone. We closed the doors that night, and he and I and some of the boys jammed until daylight. Then we went to the studios and he, Teddy, Gene and I made the first Benny Goodman Quartet records. I need hardly add that his name was Lionel Hampton. A few months later, when I was back East, I sent for him—and he, too, became a regular. When Gene left me in 1938, Lionel took over on drums for a time. By then, so far as I was concerned, it was as natural to have a mixed band as it was to play jazz.

In bands I led in later years, I always had several Negroes as sidemen and featured soloists. I didn't do it, I must point out, because I was trying to prove something. I hired Negroes because I wanted the best musicians I could find.

Looking back, I consider the addition of Teddy and Lionel one of the high spots in my old gang's collective career. But then, almost everything that happened in those swing-happy days was a high spot. Soon after we went from the Congress back to California, we made our first movie, "The Big Broadcast of 1937" (actually, we made it in 1936). In the spring of 1937, we opened first at the Hotel Pennsylvania in New York and then, almost simultaneously, at the Paramount Theater. Then we got a radio show, the "Camel Caravan." Our friends said it was that show which made us into an institution. Wherever we went from then on, we played to enormous crowds.

On a date we played at the Lincoln Colonnades, a ballroom in Washington, D.C., the crowd was so heavy that police had to help the band into the hall. Dwight Chapin, our man-of-all assignments, nearly went crazy setting up the instrument stands on that job. As soon as we began playing, there was another complication. In walked Fats Waller, fresh from finishing a show at a local theater, and ready for what he always called a "ball." Fats, one of the jolliest men who ever lived, seemed forever in mortal terror of running short of cheer. Therefore he always carried his own supply, usually in a suitcase which was complete with collapsible drinking cups. He came in with the suitcase, plus every one of the six or seven boys in his band, plus two or three admiring girls for each of the boys—and, because there was no other place to sit down, they all came up on the stand and sat down with us. Fats broke out his suitcase and began distributing his cheer. The boys were relaxed, to put it mildly.

As the months went by, it became necessary to make some changes in the band. Bunny Berigan left me and I replaced him with Sterling Bose. On a date at the Steel Pier in Atlantic City, Bose became ill. Then I heard of a kid with the relief band who played pretty respectable trumpet. His name was Ziggy Elman. He didn't show me much in the band he was with, but when I asked him to sit in with us he nearly blew us off the stand. I guess he must be one of the most powerful trumpet players who ever lived.

In the summer of 1936, in California, we made the first major change in the saxophone section. Dick Clark got sunshine-and-orange-juice fever and decided to stay out there, so we needed a tenor soloist in a hurry. Someone heard of a kid playing with a little combination down at Balboa Beach, and we went down to hear him.

The combo was soso—except for a piano man with some ideas, named Stan Kenton, and the tenor man, a thickset, tough-looking young Italian. I invited him to come around the next evening and sit in with us. He showed up while we were in the middle of our arrangement of "Honeysuckle Rose," and I beckoned to him to take a chorus. He took twelve. The crowd was excited, but their reaction was nothing compared to mine: I jumped right off the stand. When I got back on, I told him he was hired.

Vido Musso was his name, and he became to us what Yogi Berra is to the Yankees. He had been born in Italy and had been brought to this country when he was quite small, and what with moving around here and there, he hadn't acquired much formal education. That didn't worry me; I had finished only one year of high school. But what did bother me was his lack of formal schooling on his instrument.

Because Hymie Schertzer was in charge of the saxophone

section, I asked him to run through some of the arrangements with Vido. Later on, I asked Hymie how the new man was working out.

Hymie took his cigar out of his mouth and stared at it. "Well," he said, at length, "we got through the first eight bars of 'When Buddha Smiles'."

Vido couldn't read music.

I was in a quandary. He was too good a soloist to let go, but on the other hand, a man who couldn't read could have hurt a section as precise as ours.

"What's the trouble?" I asked Vido.

"Benny," said he, "it ain't the notes, it's the rest-ess."

I've since thought that that remark, in Vido's appealing broken English, won him his permanent job. I decided to keep him. He faked the section parts, and did it remarkably well. And, little by little, thanks to the patient Hymie and the conscientious Art Rollini, Vido learned his section parts. He even learned to read, eventually.

Vido was an extremely good-natured fellow. His mangling of the language always broke us up. One day he came to work with a fearful boil on his neck. The next day it was gone. "I had it glanced," he said, "and the doc put some easy tape on it."

There was a lot of horseplay in that band, usually with Harry James and alto player George Koenig as ringleaders. Harry and George were the ones who organized the airplane caper when we were making Hollywood Hotel. There was a dollar-a-ride airport nearby, and when the director called for the band he learned that the boys had got tired of waiting, and were riding around in the sky. Whenever we played an amusement park, Harry would disappear between sets to try all the rides.

But on the whole we were also an extraordinarily conscientious crew—the boys were always on time for rehearsals, and they seldom complained about the long hours. Most of them, in fact, were perfectionists. Gene was constantly getting new tomtoms, trying for sounds that would completely satisfy him. Harry, Ziggy and the other brass men kept experimenting with horns. I was always a nut about looking for good clarinet reeds. But I wasn't nearly so finicky as Vido Musso. He used to break as many as 100 new saxophone reeds before he found one that suited him.

Our concentration and hard work paid off—we were popular not only among the swing-crazy kids, but among the intelligentsia, too. The literary set took us up. Clifton Fadiman, the distinguished book critic, did two scripts for our "Caravan" radio show. He was succeeded by Robert Paul Smith, the novelist. Robert Benchley appeared with us on the program, and he introduced the band to a group of writers for The New Yorker, including S. J. Perelman and E. B. White. They used to show up at the Madhattan Room of the Hotel Pennsylvania in New York every Saturday night.

Faithful as they were, they couldn't compare to Lord Nelton, an Englishman who developed a most undignified passion for our music. Lord Nelton came every night, always sat at the same table, and always ordered champagne. He listened quietly enough while we played our regular numbers, but when we played "One O'Clock Jump," which Count Basie had given us, he seemed to be seized by devils. It got to the point where he had to hear it every night. If we forgot, Lord Nelton's rich accent rang out across the floor.

"I say, Goodman," he would call, "it's one o'clock—aren't you going to play the 'Jump'?"

(Bud Freeman contributed this Lord Nelton story, which is one of an anthology Bud is compiling about His Worship. My favorite concerns the time Lord Nelton went to hear his friend Ray Noble rehearsing a new band. He arrived for rehearsal every day for several weeks. One day Bud, during a break, asked him how he liked the group. "Frankly, Freeman," said Lord Nelton, "I've never heard it—but now that you mention it, I'm going to listen!"—R. G.)

The kids, however, were our most constant followers—or pursuers. At the height of what the music magazines called "the Benny Goodman era," it was very difficult for me to appear in public. Kids used to try to get into cabs with me, and even though I used to take off my glasses to keep from being recognized, they followed me everywhere. It was very tiring, but when I remembered that the kids had made us what we were, I tried to be as polite as possible—and most of the time, I must admit, I enjoyed it.

The big kick came with our Carnegie Hall concert. The funny thing was, I was opposed to it in the beginning. Win Nathanson, who was then doing some publicity for us, had the idea, and he had to do some talking to get me to agree. "We'll die there," I kept saying. "You'll be great," Win said, and Willard Alexander agreed.

(*Benny was actually so worried over this job that at one point he urged the managers to bring in a comedienne to tell some jokes.*— R. G.)

Seats for the concert began selling about a week before the date—which was January 16, 1938—and the day before, when I went to get some tickets for some relatives of mine, I had to get them through scalpers. Yet I still couldn't believe that we would be a success. I was nervous about the whole thing. Just before we were ready to go on, the stage manager asked me how long we wanted for intermission. "How much time does Toscanini take?" one of the boys asked. That helped break the tension. Then Harry James looked out at the audience and the hall and made another remark that broke us up. "I feel like a waitress on a date with a college boy," he said.

We went on and, with very little formality, started to play "Don't Be That Way." The shout that went up from the crowd was the same one we'd been hearing in dance halls across the country, and we knew we had them. The noise continued until we played our final number, the fifteen-minute version of "Sing, Sing, Sing." During that one, some of the people started to dance in the aisles and had to be restrained.

In the months after the concert, the gang began breaking up. In Philadelphia, on a theater date, Gene decided to leave. The late Dave Tough, an old pal of mine from my Chicago days, came in to replace him. Then Harry James got the leader bug, and decided to try to make it on his own. Teddy soon followed suit, and so did Lionel. The band, as a whole, stayed together for about two years, until I developed a slipped disk and had to lay off for a spell, but I suppose the original, dyed-in-the-wool fans are right when they say it was never quite the same.

People have asked me what made that band so good. There are several answers. First, there was the wonderful book that Fletcher, Edgar Sampson and Jimmy Mundy wrote for us—big-band arrangements that gave the soloists a genuine chance for sustained individual expression. Second, we had outstanding musicians. Third, there was the collective feeling we had. We knew we were doing something nobody else had done. We were all bound and determined to show the public that jazz was a healthy form of expression, not just a passing fancy on the part of some kids. We were dedicated; that's the only word for it.

The best way to explain it is to tell what happened the night we finished playing at Carnegie Hall. We had played for three solid hours, and had had perhaps the most remarkable reception ever accorded a swing band—in the most remarkable place. That should have been enough; most musicians would have gone home to bed, secure and happy in their triumph. Not my boys. About half the gang went up to Harlem to hear Chick Webb playing a battle of music with Count Basie's band. The rest took their instruments and went out and jammed in a room until daylight.

That was the way it was, with that old gang of mine.

(Whenever I see Benny I remember the winter in Chicago when jazz was fairly new to the world and we were, too. I had a girl named Barbara whom I'd met at a lake the summer before. She came from a family that never had any worries over empty refrigerators, and when I knew her she was between finishing schools. The family wasn't exactly wild about their little girl playing nosey-nosey with a banjo player. Put it this way: her mother couldn't stand me, and I was equally impressed. Barbara and I, back in Chicago, took to having clandestine meetings on street corners. Everything was going along all right until winter came. I had a jacket that was fairly presentable, a halfway decent pair of tights, but no overcoat. Benny, in those days, had some overcoat connections—a sister was in the business, or some other relative. Of course he always had a coat. It was just my size. He and I would meet over at musicians' headquarters, he would give me the coat, and I would sail off to meet Barbara. It was a tubular coat, a perfect fit, and I always thought that if Barbara's mother could only have seen me in it, she might have got over her prejudice against banjo players. Benny's grown a lot today, in biceps as well as in finance. I certainly wouldn't want to meet any girls in one of his coats now.—E. C.)

GEORGE T. SIMON

The Real Glenn Miller

GEORGE T. SIMON *was an editor of Metronome magazine for twenty years, or long enough to take root and flower as one of the foremost authorities on jazz of all kinds, but especially big-band jazz. He was the first to review the Benny Goodman band when it played its initial engagement at the Hotel Roosevelt, and he was on hand at the inaugurations of the careers of many other leaders. Perhaps no one (with the exception of John Hammond, of course) has had George's intimate backstage acquaintance with so many people in the big-band business. Therefore he is best qualified to write on the late Glenn Miller, who was one of the most successful of them all. He was also a close personal friend of Glenn's. This piece may be a little biased, but it's authentic— and it shows, as well as anything that's ever been written, what can happen to a guy who gets mixed up in the commercial scene. Reading it makes it easier to understand that Artie Shaw, by tossing up his career and hurling himself off to Mexico, may only have been doing what came naturally.—E. C.*

The news hit me a few hours before Christmas, 1944. I was just starting down the stairs of the subway at Broadway and 50th Street when I saw those headlines:

GLENN MILLER MISSING IN ACTION

I bought the paper and read the complete sketchy report, about how Glenn had taken off in a plane on December 15th to go to Paris and how he hadn't been heard from since and was presumed to be lost. Of course it didn't give the complete story. Even today nobody knows the complete story. There's a lot to it that the newspapers couldn't print. That's because they never knew the real Glenn Miller.

I knew him. I knew him well. I was with him when he organized his first band. I was with him when it played its very first job as a substitute band at the Hotel New Yorker and I was with him the night he fronted his civilian band for the last time in a theatre in Paterson, New Jersey. I was with him in the Army too. But I wasn't with him overseas.

Why I was left behind, after having been a member of his outfit, I'll never know. I was thinking about that as I walked through the snow that Christmas Eve, after getting off the subway in Greenwich Village. They were singing carols, as they always do, in Washington Square, and I thought maybe the spirit of Christmas might soften the shock of that short newspaper story. It didn't. I could only feel the spirit of Glenn Miller. Intensely.

I was back here in the States, still in the Army, making V Discs, no longer a part of the greatest morale building effort of the war. This had been Glenn's big dream when he had enlisted; it was now in the process of completion. He was intensely proud of it, proud of the soldiers who formed this great venture. Glenn was a man of intense likes and dislikes. He was a man of snap judgments. He was intuitive. You were either on his list or off it. I think that above all he admired honesty. He couldn't stand even a hint of fakery. The phonies in the music business knew it. They learned to stay away from him.

As he became more successful Glenn, in one sense, lost some self-respect, as he felt himself losing a portion of a quality he admired so much in others. He told me about it one day backstage in his dressing room in the Paramount Theatre. "I don't quite know how to handle it," he said. "I'm really beginning to be one helluva ——. I can't help it, though. So many people are asking me to do so many things and I really want to do some of them, but I just don't have the time. It's murder. I find myself doing things I'm ashamed of doing, and yet I know people would never understand if I told them just the plain, simple truth. I'm not the kind of a guy I really want to be."

Glenn was practical, extremely so. He knew what he wanted and knew how to get it. In the Army, one of his big concerns was to provide inspiring music for marching. With the help of Ray McKinley and Jerry Gray, he produced some great marching versions of standards like "St. Louis Blues" and "Blues in the Night," which his band played for the AAF cadets in training during reviews on the New Haven Green. The reaction, which I witnessed while beating a street drum, was invariably immense. The cadets always marched ever so much better, alert and spirited.

But there was a major in charge of the training program who didn't approve. It all wound up with a showdown in the post commander's office. The major was vehement, as vehement as any West Pointer, steeped in Army tradition, could be. "What sort of junk is this, anyway?" he complained. "What is this jazzed-up music doing in the Army? We've been playing straight military music for years, and we've been turning out some pretty fair soldiers. After all, we won the last war, didn't we, without any of this jazz music!"

Glenn eyed the major scornfully, so I'm told, then emitted this thoroughly cutting and convincing reply. "Tell me just one thing, Major. Are you still flying the same planes in this war that you flew in the last one?"

The band continued to blow "St. Louis Blues" and "Blues in the Night."

Practical common sense had prevailed in Glenn's civilian days. At first perhaps, he had organized his band so that he could express himself and his music—the way it says he did in the picture of his life, *The Glenn Miller Story*. But once he had achieved success, his was strictly a practical, dollars and cents approach. His dance band was, I always felt, primarily a business and secondarily an art form.

One incident, more than any other, convinced me of this. Glenn called me one day at the office and asked if I could hurry on down to the Victoria Barber Shop, where he was getting a shave and a haircut, and where he knew we wouldn't be interrupted by phone calls, etc. (He used to transact quite a bit of business in that chair, by the way.) As soon as I arrived, I sensed his enthusiasm. "How would you like to write my story?" he asked. I was knocked out. Here was a story I felt I really knew, a man I really knew, a cause I really knew. I'd watched him struggle for everything he believed in and now that he had the greatest band in the world I figured there'd be a great angle to his story: how a musician fights for his ideals, sticks with them through great hardships, and emerges triumphant! What a great object lesson for every honest, aspiring musician.

"I got the title already," exclaimed Glenn from behind his lather. "Listen: 'My Dance Band Gave Me $748,564!'" I'm not sure of the exact figures. They were somewhere in that vicinity. Immediately my enthusiasm waned. I sensed that this wasn't to be a music story. It was to be a business success saga. I think the incident indicates rather aptly just how Glenn did feel about the importance of his band and his success.

I suspect that one of the reasons Glenn had asked me to write his biography was loyalty. I'd been his staunchest supporter in print since the very beginning, so much so that I used to take quite a ribbing from other leaders and musicians because I insisted from February of 1937 on, when the band first started rehearsing, that this would be the country's next number one band. Glenn always remembered.

Of course, it was loyalty, in a much larger sense, that prompted him to make the most fateful decision of his life. That was when he decided that he wanted to enlist in the Army so that he could play for the men overseas. Glenn's love of his country was amazingly unselfish. He never would have been drafted. He could easily have remained at the top of his profession, perhaps playing in camps and even taking a safe trip overseas, and everybody would have looked upon him as a loyal, war-effort aiding citizen. But from the start he felt that wasn't enough. His burning ambition became to serve his country first-hand.

This ambition received numerous restrictions in the Army, however.

Frustrations hounded him in every phase of his Army career. For the first year he did little more than desk work. He had all sorts of plans for organizing great dance bands throughout the Air Forces, but other Army men had had all sorts of other plans which they had been following for years and years, and they didn't relish the innovations suggested by this new captain.

Finally, after more than a year, he got what he wanted: a complete unit, composed of topnotch musicians, which he could mould into a great marching band and an equally great entertaining unit. This he did, on the Yale campus in New Haven, Conn., starting in March, 1943. Even there he was restricted by men like the major who didn't approve of his style of marching music.

Glenn's big ambition was to go overseas, but several times, when he felt he and the band were all set to make the jump, another brand of red tape would hold him back again. By the time he broke the leash well over a year later, and more than two years after he had enlisted, the strain was beginning to tell on him. To me and to others who had known him over the years, he had changed in many ways.

He was much more serious in every way. Matters that he used to pass off lightly assumed too much importance. As time wore on, he became more and more G.I. I always had the feeling that he hated the cleavage that existed between officers and enlisted men, that he never knew quite how to reconcile the two different relationships between him and men he had been pals with in civilian days but who were now, rankly speaking, in a lower strata. He became so strict at one point that he ordered, without offering any explanation, every musician in his outfit to shave off his mustache. For several of the brass men, especially, this meant great hardship, for they had been used to blowing for years with their mustaches on. With them off, it meant almost new embouchures and looks.

As a matter of fact, some of the musicians looked pretty ridiculous, especially to those who had known them with their mustaches on for many years. I doubt, though, if Glenn thought it humorous.

So upset was he in those days, that, I'm afraid, he retained little of the great sense of humor that was once his. I think that if he had been able to look at life a little more lightly, he might well still be with us today.

I'm referring to the circumstance surrounding that last flight. Don Haynes, his close friend and manager and AAF assistant, wrote me in part a few months later as follows: "Regardless of all the rumors, there's been no trace of Glenn, the other passenger (a Colonel attached to the VIIIth Air Force), the pilot, or the plane, since that foggy Friday afternoon I alone saw them off (15 December) . . . Glenn took the trip that I was to make—decided to the day before—and as I had made all the arrangements, it only necessitated cancelling the orders that had been cut for me, and getting orders cut for him. I brought the outfit over three days later (after having been 'weathered in' for two days) only to find that Glenn had not arrived. Our trip was uneventful, but not his."

Glenn hated to fly. Why he decided at the last minute to sit in for Haynes on the plane nobody knows. Perhaps it was his sense of duty. Perhaps it was because of the same frustrations that had been plaguing him throughout his Army life. He wanted to get things done, and so, rather than have somebody else hop over to Paris to start things going for his band, he may have decided that he wanted to do it, himself. Whatever the cause for his wanting to go may have been, I still feel that if he had retained his sense of humor he might have resisted the dare which, so I'm told, he accepted that foggy Friday afternoon.

All the AAF Transport Command planes had been grounded. But that colonel and Glenn were all set to go. From all I can gather, Glenn was kidded into going. A less frustrated, a better adjusted man could have taken the purported riding about his fear of flying in his stride. This Glenn did not do. He accepted what amounted to a dare to take off with the colonel and the pilot in a general's small plane on an uncharted flight under obviously unsafe flying conditions. They took off. Nobody knows what happened after that.

The Miller sense of humor was one of the first things I noticed about the guy. The first time I saw him was in 1934 when he played, as a member of the Dorsey Brothers Band, at Nuttings-on-the-Charles just outside of Boston. He sang the last of several verses of his own comedy song called "Annie's Cousin Fanny," and

THE REAL GLENN MILLER 281

this studious-looking man looked even funnier than the other musicians as he sang.

Even when Glenn was struggling with inferior musicians in his early band, trying desperately to keep a band together, his sense of humor was still in evidence. On his first trip he was having a tough time trying to find a drummer he liked. His band had always been plagued by bad rhythm. But, he wrote on October 12th, 1937 from the Hotel Nicollet in Minneapolis, "we are getting a new drummer (thank God) in a couple of weeks . . . about two hundred and fifty pounds of solid rhythm—I hope. This boy we have is pretty bad and MacGreggor says outside of being a bad drummer he has a quarter beat rest between each tooth which doesn't enhance the romantic assets of the band . . ."

Another part of the same letter seems strangely prophetic in the light of future events. "I don't know just where we are going from here—I guess no one else does either. We are hoping for some sort of a radio set-up that will let more than three people hear us at a time. If this drummer only works out there will be nothing to stop us from now on. (Barring mishaps of course.)"

Few people in those days were enthusiastic about Glenn Miller and his musicians. In fact, things were very tough.

The Minneapolis band was the second of three, Miller editions. The first had been a combination string quartet-jazz band which had been organized solely for making a set of Columbia Records and which was never heard from again thereafter.

Edition #2 was organized in 1937, after Glenn had left Ray Noble's wonderful band, which he had organized for the English leader on assignment. It had been a stellar crew. Glenn and Will Bradley were the trombones. Charlie Spivak and Peewee Erwin played trumpets. Bud Freeman and Johnny Mince were among the saxes. Claude Thornhill was the pianist; George Van Epps the guitarist.

Assembling groups was nothing new to Miller. He had helped the Dorsey Brothers put together their great outfit of the midthirties by bringing over several musicians, including Ray McKinley and Skeets Herfurt, from Smith Ballew's fine band. And who had organized Smith Ballew's fine band? Glenn Miller, of course.

Before then he had done both studio and jazz tromboning. His first name band had been Ben Pollack's, for which he arranged and played. He had also been an important arranging and playing penny among the numerous Red Nichols coins which made so many great jazz records in the early thirties. Most of the jazz greats blew with the crew. On records it was listed as "Red Nichols and his Five Pennies." I recall one of the first talks I had with Glenn. I asked him about the Five Pennies. The records had always sounded amazingly rich for so few musicians. "The labels said 'Five Pennies'—that's right," said Glenn. "That's all they mentioned. But there were always a few playing behind curtains or something," he added wryly.

Glenn let me in on his big secret one day at our house while we were playing records. "I'm going to start a band," he confessed. "And if you can help me find some young, good musicians, I'd appreciate it. Right now all I have is a theme song." He had written "Moonlight Serenade," based on a Schillinger exercise, and the men in the Noble band were all raving about the song. At the time it was called "Now I Lay Me Down to Weep," and it had a set of beautiful lyrics by Eddie Heyman (all of which I still remember, in case Eddie is reading this). Later on some publishers convinced Glenn that it should have a more grandiose title, if it were to serve as his theme, so he had Mitch Parrish write lyrics to "Moonlight Serenade."

The first man Glenn hired (on a tip from John Hammond) (*who else?*—E. C.) was Hal McIntyre, whom we found in Meriden, Conn., after a trip through a snowstorm. Hal wanted Glenn to take on some of the other men in his band up there, but they didn't suit Miller's tastes, so Mac became the band's first musician, himself.

Back in New York Glenn held many rehearsals, often aided by several of the many studio musicians who admired and liked him so much. Chief among these were Spivak (then Glenn's closest friend) and saxist Toots Mondello. On Miller's first record date (for Decca in March, 1937) he had to use mostly studio men. Spivak, Mannie Klein and Sterling Bose blew trumpets; the saxists had George Siravo (the arranger), McIntyre and Jerry Jerome, while the rhythm section boasted the late Dick McDonough on guitar and pianist Howard Smith. (There was also a drummer named George Simon.—E. C.)

The band's first date, a relief session at the New Yorker Hotel, was heard by the late Ralph Hitz, who owned a chain of hotels. He was greatly impressed, hired the band for several dates, on one of which, the Roosevelt in New Orleans, the group broke all records for that room.

In the late Fall the band came back East, playing at the Raymor Ballroom in Boston, where it had its first coast-to-coast air-shots. Until that date, the band had not found a set style. Glenn was experimenting constantly. One day he remembered that happy accident that had occurred in Ray Noble's band. Glenn had been voicing Pewee Erwin's trumpet as lead above the saxes. The musician who replaced Erwin had a more limited range and, so that the arrangements shouldn't be a total loss, Glenn reassigned Peewee's trumpet part to a clarinet. The new sound was pleasant.

Glenn remembered the pleasant sound and, despite opposition from advisers, dropped the guitar from his band and added a fifth sax. That was the start of the now famous Miller style.

But it didn't do him too much good in those days. He had trouble in his band, mostly with drinkers. The morale was very low and when Glenn's wife, Helen, was stricken with a severe illness, his spirits reached the depths also. By the middle of January, 1938, Glenn had had enough. He disbanded and went back into the studios, even playing trombone in Tommy Dorsey's band for a while.

Glenn had learned a lesson. No more prima donnas. No more problem musicians. With just four hold-overs (McIntyre, close friend Chummy MacGreggor, bassist Rollie Bondoc and trumpeter Bob Price) he started Edition #3 two months later. From Detroit he brought in the tenor saxist he considered "the greatest of them all!"—Tex Beneke. Booker Si Shribman was now one of Glenn's managers, and he found work for the group. One of the jobs was the Paradise Restaurant in New York (later Bop City), which it played several times. During one of the band's return visits to Boston, Glenn heard two sisters, Betty and Marion Hutton, singing in Vincent Lopez's band. Glenn could have hired either. He chose Marion, because he felt she was more mature, because her personality seemed to fit the clean-cut, All-American approach for which Glenn always strove.

But despite improved morale in the band, it still wasn't making it. It tried very hard, but the frequent Paradise engagements were a drag, because the band had to play three shows a night, and, after running through them, the guys seldom had lips left for their broadcasts.

By February, 1939, the band had hit another low. I accompanied Glenn on a trip to North Carolina. Everything went wrong. On the way back he had made up his mind. Band-leading was not for him. He was going to chuck it all again, he told me, and return to the studios.

But then came March 1st, 1939. The band was rehearsing that afternoon in its usual spot, the Haven studio on West 54th Street. It was Glenn's thirty-fourth birthday. And then somebody brought in the news. The Glen Island Casino, which had sprung such bands as Casa Loma, Ozzie Nelson, the Dorseys and Charlie Barnet had decided it wanted Miller's for the Summer season. And Frank Dailey, after hearing of the pick, decided to book the band for the period prior to Glen Island.

From then on it was all up, including everybody's spirits. Glenn prepared many new arrangements. Some he wrote or sketched himself. Others were produced by young Bill Finegan, fresh from New Jersey, who always remained Miller's particular pet. Later on Jerry Gray, who had been writing for Shaw, also joined.

Success had come at last. Success had come to one of the really great dance band leaders of all time—for my dough, the greatest all-around leader of all time. Personally, I've never known any man who knew so exactly just what he wanted, and what's even more important, knew exactly how to get what he wanted.

Many of us still wonder what Glenn would be doing if he were with us today. Paul Dudley, the radio-TV producer and writer, who served with Glenn overseas and who became a very close friend, told me recently that Glenn had great plans for the future, plans that went much further than just fronting a band. He wanted to do even bigger things, for more people, to expand in his recording, publishing and other activities.

It never happened, of course. But, whatever he had in mind,

I'm sure that whatever would have happened would have been another great credit not only to a wonderful leader and person, not only to those closely associated with him, but also to the music and to the country to which Glenn was so intensely devoted, with a devotion which, had it been a little less intense, might never have taken him away from us.

(I knew Glenn Miller mainly in Plunkett's, a speakeasy at 205½ West Fifty-Third Street in New York. The room was sixteen feet long; the bar was two feet shorter. There was a small back room with a few chairs and tables; off it was a stand-up icebox in which I often changed my clothes. It was already a musicians' hangout when Tommy Dorsey first took me there. In the telephone book it was listed as the Trombone Club, in honor of Tommy. All sorts of business was transacted there; the telephone rang constantly, bands were organized at the bar, and everybody drank. Those who were working bought drinks for those who were not working. I'll say this for Glenn: when he was working, he never failed to buy. Everything George Simon says about him is true. One hell of a guy. He had to be: didn't he give Bobby Hackett a chair in his band? Hell of a guy.—E. C.)

RICHARD ENGLISH

The Battling Brothers Dorsey

RICHARD ENGLISH WROTE *this piece about Jimmy and Tommy Dorsey in 1946. Since then, both contestants have hung up their gloves, but the odor of arnica lingers on.*

E. C.

The Glen Island Casino in Westchester County, New York, is the Gettysburg of the danceband industry. There on May 30, 1935, which is still referred to in the trade as Separation Day, the famed Dorsey Brothers orchestra blew up right in the faces of the astonished patrons when the Dorseys, already loud legends in their own time, had one of their most violent partings. With the Dorsey brothers no parting is final, but all are violent. Today, James Francis Dorsey and Thomas Francis Dorsey have become, by going their separate ways, two of the nation's all-time box-office attractions in a business where you don't grow old, you just drop dead.

To jazz historians who already know how these Pennsylvania coal miner's sons have become to the $100,000,000-a-year band business what the Fisher brothers are to the car industry, the facts of that parting are strictly hallowed. Jimmy and Tommy, taking

THE BATTLING BROTHERS DORSEY

turns leading their band, had highly opinionated ideas as to how each piece should be rendered, and the pay-off came when they found themselves involved with "I'll Never Say Never Again."

Tommy, leading, took the band into the piece a lot faster than Jimmy, who was about to take a cornet part, felt was proper. "Let's do it right or not do it at all," Jimmy said bitterly.

Tommy, certain that Jimmy had added a slight raspberry on his horn, shouted, "All right, we won't do it at all!" and in midchorus departed for his home in New Jersey. That's all, brother.

From that day the highly competitive name-band business found itself neatly sliced down the middle by two brothers who weren't giving an inch to each other or anybody else. In the same battle-royal style that the neighbors around Shenandoah, Pennsylvania, would have once dismissed as "only Dorsey's kids at it again," they have in the past five years grossed $6,201,000 between them. With 20,000,000 records sold, they have become full-fledged picture stars and two of the top-paid radio bands, and have averaged $18,000 to $25,000 a week on theater dates.

Now, at an age when most men are hoping their jobs will prove steady, the Dorsey brothers have become so much of a national institution they are about to have their lives committed to celluloid. With no false modesty they know their screen biographies offer more than the usual glossy material. Up the hard way, with one year's high school between them, they matured in the Jazz Age of F. Scott Fitzgerald and hot music. In their twenties their records were collectors' items. Coming from the wrong side of the tracks in a mining town, they have proved it can still happen here. Hollywood could ask no more. Only a log cabin is missing.

(That movie, incidentally, was called "The Fabulous Dorseys." It was different from other movies about the band business in that the Dorseys played themselves. A producer, I understand, operating on the theory that nobody would accept the Dorseys as the Dorseys, tried to get Jimmy to play Tommy and vice versa. He was overruled.—E. C.)

"There was always this bickerin' between them," Tess Dorsey, their mother, says proudly. "Tommy was always a great one for pushin', and Jimmy for takin' his own sweet time. They both always got where they were goin', but they had to do it their own way." At seventy-one, their mother is still the rallying point of the Dorsey clan and, although born in this country, speaks with something like a brogue. Cheerful and stout, liking nothing better than a good laugh or a little cry, she commutes between her home in Pennsylvania, Jimmy's home on the Coast and Tommy's New York penthouse. A big woman, she has Tommy's jaw, glinting glasses and quick zest.

"And the Lord knows he's got my gift o' gab, too," she says. "Jimmy's always been the shy one—like his father, rest him. Sometimes I say to him, 'Jimmy, does it hurt you to talk?' and he'll say, 'Now, mom, you do enough talkin' for the two of us,' and he's right. When they were still tykes growin' up in Shenandoah, Pennsylvania, Jimmy was always more for the playin' than talkin'. Mr. Dorsey used to have a band on the side, and by the time Jimmy was ten he was playin' cornet solos. And Tommy, who was too little to sit in with the grownups, hustled through the audience sellin' pictures of Jimmy at ten cents apiece."

It was three years after Tess Langton married a thin quiet coal miner named Thomas Dorsey that Jimmy first attracted local attention by being born on Leap Year's Day, February 29, 1904. His father, earning $10.20 a week in the mines, was a self-taught musician known to the neighbors as The Professor, who made a little extra money playing in lodge bands and giving music lessons at fifty cents an hour. Scarlet fever had left him blind in one eye and deaf in one ear since infancy.

In those days, every little town, lodge and church had its own brass band, and Professor Dorsey, as the neighbors called him, was often coaching five bands at a time.

On November 19, 1905, the squalling baby who was to become Tommy Dorsey, That Sentimental Gentleman of Swing, was born. Strikes were cutting each year's pay checks, and their father swore in that quiet, half-deaf voice of his they were going to be something besides miners.

"When they was only six and five," Tess Dorsey says, "their father was learnin' them on the cornet like they were grownups. He wanted they should amount to something and he didn't give them or himself any rest. He'd be teachin' them at night, all tired out from workin' in the mines, himself, and I'd say, 'Ah, Tom, they're but lads!' And he'd shout, 'Tess, you mind your own business. I want my lads to go somewhere! They got me to teach them; and I didn't have nobody!' "

There was a third Dorsey child, Mary. She was the only one on whom any money was wasted for lessons. Not content with her being a singer, her father saw that she was taught piano, trumpet and saxophone. She couldn't wait to grow up and forget the whole thing. Not so with the boys. With the chance of a licking always around the corner, they learned all the wind instruments and how to read and transpose. Still in knee pants, Jimmy was on saxophone and Tommy on trombone, the reed and horn that were to bring them a fortune, and chosen by their father because of their great commercial possibilities.

They were already displaying that every-man-for-himself trait that was later to dismay the whole band industry. "Always squabblin', they were," Tess sighs now. "If it wasn't music, it was somethin' else, and first you knew, the fists were flyin'. What with their practicin' and the fights over how they should play what, there was never any peace in the house." Jimmy was growing more and more silent and shy, like his father, but he took no back talk when it came to music. And Tommy, always 'hustling, had already branched out for himself at the age of ten, opening a store in the parlor.

"Taffy candy, he sold," his mother recalls. "I made tiny little pans of it to sell at a penny apiece, and he was always gettin' kids in to eat it. But it wasn't until he was thirteen he got big ideas, and took to sellin' canned goods, groceries and sugar. He was Tommy even then, goin' out and buyin' himself a fancy brass scale that cost seventy whole dollars. I kept tellin' him he didn't need it, but he had made up his mind, and get it he did."

Now of an evening they were also sitting in with their father's orchestra, playing waltzes, plain and fancy quadrilles, square dances and two-steps at Gorman's Hall. And one night Mr. Dorsey came home with a strange, quiet look in his face and said, "Tess, it's a proud day when I can't be playin' with my own sons any more. They're gettin' too fast for me."

Jimmy was working as a blacksmith's helper in the mines that year, having had a brief exposure to high school, an ordeal Tommy managed to skip altogether. When the sledge slipped in Jimmy's hand one day, hitting the blacksmith instead of the shoe, the brothers hurriedly agreed it was time to leave town. Grabbing several other teen-age hot shots, they dubbed themselves Dorseys' Wild Canaries, and took off for a Baltimore amusement park.

It was Carlin's Park, 1922, and the leaders, eighteen and sixteen at the time, received $285 a week for the whole orchestra. Twenty-three years later, grossing $1,600,000 a year between them, they were still to look back on that roller-coaster arena with all the nostalgia of old grads.

Now forty-one, Jimmy Dorsey has a delicate face, dark hair, gentle blue eyes, and is one of the band business' foremost silent worriers. Shy and vastly determined, he keeps his own counsel. He is unassuming and he lays it on the line, letting the chips fall where they may. He is a quiet perfectionist who often wonders mildly what all the shouting is about. He can, and will, as Tommy says proudly, "play any other saxophone right out of town." Having no intention of going from pick and shovel to pick and shovel in one generation, his one extravagance is hand-painted ties, which, at forty dollars a copy, depict his golden saxophone and the hit songs which he has made famous. He likes playing golf and remembering old times, like Carlin's Park in 1922.

Sitting backstage, a small man in a blue suit, he looks more like a bank teller than a great hot saxophone. Nowadays his band leans more to the mellow side, but, given the occasion, he can still blow the man down. One of the nation's great theater attractions, he has a quiet concern for all comers that the rest of his company finds highly restful. He travels in comparative loneliness, with only nineteen musicians, his secretary, road manager, arranger and property man along for company, and his dressing room is usually deserted except for himself and The Champ. The Champ is Al Joslow, Jimmy's closest companion, and once a good featherweight out of Philadelphia. Handy man, pal and masseur, he left Philly with three shirts on a rush call from Jimmy four years ago, and has not been home since. He still speaks well of it, however.

"The Brother and I were but from hunger in those days," Jimmy says. Both Dorseys have the abstract habit of referring to the other as The Brother. "I was eating shore dinners until I couldn't see straight. But we were having such a fine time in Baltimore it never did occur to us that sooner or later the amusement-park season would end. We came home without any dough, but wearing derbies, strictly a couple of men from the big town."

He does not add that Tommy attracted some comment by falling asleep on the stand each night around eleven and, when awakened, caused no end of hard feelings by suggesting it was time the dancers went home anyway.

A big man with the juke-box trade, Jimmy Dorsey stays up there by the cool calculation with which he works over every new record. He can stand anything but sloppy musicianship. Let a man start blowing a few clinkers and J. D. is right in there, drilling the man the way his father used to.

(What English forgets to mention here is that Jimmy is also one of the greatest raconteurs now breathing. One night Gehman and I went down to Hotel Pennsylvania to watch the brothers close out an engagement. Jimmy said, "Did you guys hear about Tommy at Princeton?" We hadn't, but we did. Tommy Dorsey, Jr., was a sub on the Williams football team, and Tommy went down to Princeton to see him play. Sitting next to Tommy was an old Williams grad, complete with flask and spirit. Tommy was glum throughout most of the game, for Tommy, Jr., was kept on the bench. Finally he was sent in, and his name was announced on the loudspeaker. Tommy sat up, full of fatherly pride. The old Williams man peered at him closely.

"That your boy, there?" he inquired.

"Yes, sir," said Tommy, "that's my boy."

"You the bandleader?" the o.g. asked.

"Yeah," Tommy said, trying to keep his mind on the game.

"What fraternity's he in at Williams?"

"I don't know," Tommy said.

"What do you mean, you don't know?"

Tommy's well-known Irish was rising. "I don't know," he said. "I knew once, but I forget."

"Why don't you know?" the Williams pest persisted.

"Listen," said Tommy, "why the hell should I know?"

"Why," said the old grad, "I've got all your records!"—E. C.)

In the war years, both Jimmy and Tommy met their vast record audiences face to face. Between them the brothers played almost every camp, hospital, Navy base and bond show in the nation. And each time in the great uniformed audiences there were thousands who had known them only through records, caught in some juke-box joint.

Jimmy has a fourteen-year-old daughter, Julie Lou, a pretty wife, who, as Jane Porter, was Miss Detroit of 1925, and a rambling house in Toluca Lake, California. He would much rather be with them than, as he puts it, "going around being slightly famous." In contrast to Tommy, he likes to write music himself, "It's the Dreamer in Me" being one of the hits on his ledger. A J.D. family evening is frequently spent listening to platters, and he is secretly relieved that his record collection includes none of the Scranton Sirens', the band that fell heir to the Dorsey brothers' spot when Baltimore folded.

"Brother," he says, "when the Sirens rendered a piece it stayed rendered. Hannah Williams, just a kid then, sang with that band long before she ever thought of being a Broadway star. Then I caught on with Jean Goldkette's jazz band in Detroit, and that was our start in the big leagues. I got them to hire The Brother, too, and we were in business. They had some great men in that band, the kind you can't forget. There was Frankie Trumbauer on C Melody sax, Bix Beiderbecke on cornet—he sparked the music business for sure—Fuzzy Farrar, Don Murray and Tommy and I in there trying to break even."

With their own careers on the upbeat, they presently departed for New York. Came then brief tours of duty with Vincent Lopez and Paul Whiteman, and they found themselves in demand for the big new radio bands. Professor Thomas Dorsey had trained them well, for in the next year half the young musicians who hung out at the jam sessions at Plunkett's on Fifty-third Street were trying to play in the style that came so naturally to the brothers. They sat in on the Metronome All Star record session, and concert men like Andre Kostelanetz kept complimenting them.

(As a footnote to the Glen Miller piece, I mentioned the existence of Plunkett's. The same system, everybody-drinks-with-

or-without-trump, prevailed at the Onyx, another famous 52nd Street spot. One night I walked in there and found Jimmy Dorsey and Jerry Colonna at the bar; Joe Helbock, the proprietor, was mixing drinks for them. I wasn't making enough to have my shoes half-soled.

"We'd like to ask you to join us, Eddie," Dorsey said solemnly, "but we just decided on a new system. Each night one person will buy all the drinks; tonight that person is you."

"Fine," I said. "Joe, ask the boys how they'll have their water, hot or cold."—E. C.)

"The big-money days in music had just blown in, nobody was being cozy with a buck, and every kid in New York was eating his heart out trying to play like Duke Ellington and Louie Armstrong. There was so much money around that even I got to Europe—J.D., who never saved a dime."

He still speaks of success and money as if he were a stranger there himself. Yet in 1941 his band grossed around $450,000; in 1942, $500,000; in 1943, $525,000; in 1944, $625,000; and in 1945 he bettered that figure. After his overhead and before taxes, Jimmy gets about a third of that money for himself. His picture salary with band is $100,000; a week of one-night stands brings in more than $25,000. In 1942, when five of his records sold more than 500,000 platters apiece, his royalties were $100,000.

He set the all-time location high for dance bands—the Frolics Ballroom in Miami paying him $9000 a week. Theater dates average around $19,000 a week, and radio shows pay him an additional $2500 a week. A wealthy oil man in Houston, Texas, wanting Jimmy's band for his son's twenty-first birthday party, chartered two planes and flew them from the Hotel Pennsylvania in New York City to Houston and back in thirty-six hours. The cost, $10,000.

But back in those days a $100,000,000-a-year band business was something that couldn't possibly happen. It took a war to bring that about, and the Dorseys were having enough troubles of their own without looking around for any outside wars. With two highly dissimilar brothers working under high-pressure circumstances, there was a growing tension. But it was still some time before Gettysburg.

"You know how The Brother is—always in there pitching," Jimmy explains. "He keeps saying, 'Let's get going,' while we're working in the pit band at the Capitol Theater. It was a seventy-piece outfit and the next thing you know, we're promoting half the boys to sit in and make a record for us—our first one. Finally we get it all worked up, but we got no leader. 'How about getting the guy who leads the band during the newsreel?' The Brother says. So we get this guy, and he does a swell job. Then he is all upset when the record comes out with the label, 'Was it a Dream? by the Dorsey Brothers Concert Orchestra.' Nobody had thought to put his name on it—Eugene Ormandy. Imagine doing that to the Philadelphia Orchestra."

It was the late Glenn Miller who kept after the Dorseys to form their own dance band. With mutual misgivings—Jimmy didn't want to be a leader and Tommy had been warned he was too hotheaded to handle a baton—they finally struck out on their own. In the trade, that band is still referred to as the Dorsey Brothers Finishing School. In it were Bob Crosby, Charlie Spivak, Bud Freeman, Ray McKinley, Bunny Berigan, Ray Bauduc and Miller, all of whom soon had their own bands.

The Dorsey Brothers orchestra's skyrocket career was as brief as it was glorious. It is still remembered on two scores: one, they got their first radio contract and, after paying off their sidemen, not being content except with the best in the business, they lost nineteen dollars apiece with each show; two, their father, listening in back in Shenandoah, turned to Tess Dorsey and said, "You know, Tess, the boys are getting so they execute better all the time."

A quick forty, Tommy has graying hair and gray-green eyes that, with his highly polished glasses, are as much of a trade-mark as his famous trombone getting off on "I'm Getting Sentimental Over You." His tone, like his life, is broad as a house. A fast man with a dollar, generous, quick-tempered, he has an adding-machine mind and a musician's lip. For the last eight years his band has always been in the first three on any band poll. When his Irish flies up, you could drive nails with his eyes.

He stays up until five A.M. rehearsing his band after closing hours at the New York night club that is gladly paying him $6000 a week. Then, with a record date at a crisp one o'clock, he bursts around his apartment with all the assurance of a man who can play a trombone that makes you feel as if you were nine feet tall and six feet wide. He has a son and a daughter by his first marriage and is now married to Pat Dane, striking brunet starlet of the Andy Hardy pictures. With T. Dorsey every night is Saturday night, and he affects others the same way.

"It's no secret The Brother and I had more fights than newlyweds," he relates. "We're so different we can't help it. Take that band of ours, there was always factions in it, with us on opposite sides of the fence. I'm a guy who wants things to come off right, always in there for a Sunday punch. Jimmy didn't care much what happened, as long as the music was right."

Known in the band business as being very sudden in the brain department, Tommy can take a song and, by giving it that commercial flourish known as the old switcheroo, make it into an overnight success. He was one of the first leaders to have his sidemen start backing up tunes with an off-beat chorus behind the singers, and he was always itching to be on his own. When the Dorsey Brothers band blew up at the Glen Island Casino in an explosion that rocked the industry from Tin Pan Alley to the Celluloid Coast, he was.

The Dorsey Derby, a two-horse race to be top man with the public, started as of right then. The band trade immediately chose up sides, and Tommy, burning with a desire to "catch The Brother," whipped up a band of his own, opening at the French Casino in New York City. The cause of brotherly love was not further served when Jimmy, opening in the Roseland Ballroom a few blocks away, was billed as "The Original Dorsey Band." Throwing off voltage at all hours, Tommy let out one persecuted cry and promptly set out on a revolutionary path of becoming a name leader.

He ignored the chance to play it safe in a steady job and took his band on the road, aiming smack at the campus trade. "What a clambake that was," he recalls, "playin' every one-nighter we could get. That first year we made sixty colleges. But when we did catch a location date at the Lincoln Hotel in New York City, we had a following started. We were getting a lot of radio time and the college kids we'd played for took to drifting in."

Even with that first band Tommy went in for a more driving combination than Jimmy featured. To this day they can be playing the same tune the same night, and Tommy will play it fast, Jimmy slow.

Where a job with Jimmy has a high professional life expectancy, musicians come and go with T. Dorsey with the regularity of commuters' trains. He has two good tough reasons for that: "I couldn't have got where I am if I'd kept the band I had in '36. A dance band's like a ball club; they were great then, but couldn't win a pennant now." And then, with cold self-analysis, "Besides, I need boys with me who stand out. And when they get that good, they soon go out on their own. I need those standouts for the simple reason that the trombone isn't as exciting an instrument as Goodman's clarinet or Harry James' trumpet."

(See how it was with Tommy? Always looking for an argument. He could have got himself a few with that statement.—E.C.)

Tommy had barely got his own band together when he came up with a smash record, "The Music Goes 'Round and 'Round." It sold 67,000 platters, and he followed it with two more hits, and there he was, breathing right on The Brother's neck. Now, coming into the stretch, when Tommy played a theater date, Jimmy couldn't wait to top his figure; when Jimmy had a smash record, T. Dorsey didn't rest until he had bettered it. Though it is true they still spoke and smiled slightly on meeting, they were certainly giving each other lots of space.

There was a very rugged similarity in the dates they played, prices received, and how they both shot so rapidly into what had only recently been the private playgrounds of Rudy Vallee, Benny Goodman and Guy Lombardo. Loud cries urged them on from all sides. Music Corporation of America booked Tommy's band, and General Amusement Corporation handled Jimmy. The strenuous rivalry between the agencies did nothing to pour oil on the water.

Now the band business was slipping into high gear, and Jimmy started clicking off smash records with Latin-American backgrounds, his vocalists, Bob Eberle and Helen O'Connell, knocking off "Amapola," "Tangerine" and "Green Eyes." That gave him an industry lead in the South American markets that he has never lost and, at the same time, baled plenty of hay north of the border.

And Tommy was right behind him, pushing with his own vocalists, Joe Stafford, Frank Sinatra and Dick Haymes. "I'll Never Smile Again," with the aching Mr. Sinatra, and half a dozen other records were in the 500,000-to-1,250,000 bracket.

Sinatra, who was to create an entire new public with his bobby-soxers, is a Tommy Dorsey discovery. Styling his breathing from Tommy's trombone, he worked hard for his success. "It was funny about that sigh routine," Tommy says, "but we worked that up while he was in the band. Playing theater dates, he'd come out to do a number, and some little mannerism would make some kid down front sigh. Well, I noticed it, see, and coached the band that the minute a kid sighed, we stopped everything and the whole band sighed back in chorus. That needled the kids into keeping it up."

It was during this time that the widely heralded Dorsey reunion at the Hotel Astor took place. Tommy was playing there, and Jimmy, in town for a theater date, dropped in to pass the time of day. Tommy took exception to certain friends of Jimmy's in the party, and the next thing both of them were on the floor, giving each other what-for. The tabloids built this up to black eyes being exchanged, and what would have passed in Shenandoah for a simple exchange of pleasantries became a *cause celebre*.

That driving race between the Dorseys tapered away on July 12, 1942. On that day the quiet old coal miner, who had been so determined that his boys were going to get someplace in the world, passed away. Tommy and Jimmy made up at his funeral. Their mother wanted it that way, and that's the way it is.

(Thank you, National City Bank.

A good many things have happened since English wrote this piece. For one thing, the Dorseys are reunited professionally. Jackie Gleason may have been responsible; beginning in the fall of 1955, they went on TV with a Gleason production known as "Stage Show." The band was billed "Tommy Dorsey and his Orchestra, featuring Jimmy Dorsey." When I saw them last, both had switched to a permanent milk diet. Things were a little different in the old days. In We Called It Music, I recalled an incident that occurred in Plunkett's that went this way:

'One day Tommy came in during the afternoon. He had a radio program in half an hour. "I'll have to drink in a hurry," he said to Jimmy. "I need a shave."

'"Maybe you need a drink more than you need a shave," Jimmy suggested. Not Jimmy Dorsey—Jimmy the bartender, a practical man, a non-drinker.

'Tommy looked in the mirror. "I need a shave," he said. "I'll have to skip to the barbershop."

'Standing quietly down the bar was Tommy O'Connor, a former wrestler with gnarled fingers and an eighteen-and-a-half-inch neck. He was from the Dorsey home town in Pennsylvania.

'"Nothing of the sort, Tommy," he said. "You'll not have to stir from this place."

'"I need that shave," Dorsey said.

'"It so happens that I myself am now in the profession you intend to patronize," O'Connor said. "I am a barber."

'He reached into a vest pocket and took out a straight razor.

'"It will take but a minute," he said. "Jimmy, run some of that draught beer."

'Jimmy ran some beer and O'Connor shook some salt into it. A fine head of suds formed. O'Connor scooped the suds off and put them on Dorsey's face.

'"Put that bar rag around his neck, Jimmy," he said to Plunkett. "I don't want to soil his shirt. Now, Tommy, just lay your head back and relax."

'In a few minutes it was over and Dorsey, stunned, bleeding, but shaved, was standing upright with another drink in his hand.

'"Just one more thing, Tommy." O'Connor said. "Give me a shot of that gin, Jimmy." He poured the gin over his hands and rubbed Tommy's face.

'"Finest after-shave lotion in the world," he said.

'Dorsey finished his drink, had time for another, and left for Radio City in excellent condition.'

He's using Aqua Velva today, and he's still in good condition. And so is Jimmy.—E. C.)

RICHARD GEHMAN

Lionel Hampton

MIKE HALL, THE press agent, introduced me to Lionel Hampton, his client, in mid-1953. Mike thought I could get a magazine piece out of him, and I did too. I spent three or four uproarious nights with Hamp in Philadelphia in June, and for the rest of the summer I kept running into him: at Ephrata, Pennsylvania; at Hyannis, Massachusetts; at Revere Beach, Massachusetts; and in New York. Presently I had so much material I didn't quite know what to do with it all. I made an outline—that is, I started to make one, but before I was half-finished I had nine pages. I sent this out to two or three magazines, hoping for a go-ahead. They all said about the same thing: "We think Hampton is a wonderful character, but we don't feel that he will appeal to our readers." Around that time the editors of Nation's Business were buying a good many off-beat pieces; I had sold them one on muzzle-loading shotguns, and another on smoked fish. Also, George Frazier had sold them his recollections of the Benny Goodman band. I sent my outline to Paul McCrea, the managing editor. He held it ten days and returned it with a note that will stand in my memory as the strangest I ever received from any editor. It said, "You know very well this story is not for us, but we like it anyhow. We don't know what to do with it. We'll put it up to you. Search your conscience. If you want to write it, go ahead; we'll buy it. If not, don't and we'll forget the whole thing." I wrote it and they published it.

"Nation's Business?" Hamp howled. "Man, what a gas!"

MEMO TO THE A.E.C.: If experiments in peacetime applications of atomic energy are lagging, get in touch with a bandleader named Lionel Hampton. Although Hampton, or The Hamp, as he prefers to be called, knows little about the technical aspects of nuclear power, he probably could explain it in his own language, a species of hipstertalk that would baffle a physicist. There is no question that The Hamp knows the fundamentals of atomic energy, for he possesses power potential which rivals that of cobalt.

Hampton's prodigious energy alone has enabled him to become one of the most successful bandleaders in the world. The big-name band business reached a peak in the late '30's and has been declining since. Most of the leaders—Fred Waring, Horace Heidt—have stayed on top by using choruses, production numbers, and having their musicians put on funny hats. The straight, musicianly bands, particularly those that play hot, have found the going rough indeed. The big Negro bands have had more trouble than the white ones, because there are fewer places where they can play. Unless a band gets a good series of stands at hotels, and makes records, and gets plenty of air time, and knocks off a contract for a television show, it has no hope of getting into the upper brackets—unless, of course, it is led by Lionel Hampton.

(*This piece appeared in July, 1954. Soon afterward, the big-band business got better.—R. G.*)

In 1953 Hampton grossed more than $1,000,000. He did it without particular benefit from record sales (he does not make many records and he has never cut a really big hit, except for his theme, "Flyin' Home," a steady seller over the years). He did it without any plush hotel engagement. He did it simply by dint of his appalling energy. In 1953 he played more than two hundred one-night stands, including a back-breaking forty-day tour of Europe.

(*Since then, Hamp has made three trips to Europe.—R. G.*)

Before taking his band to Europe, The Hamp made "a little swing through the South." In ten days he and his boys played ten cities. Some days they jumped five hundred miles. The schedule becomes doubly frightening when you consider that the Hampton organization travels exclusively by chartered bus. In the middle of that southern swing, Hampton's booker, Joe Glaser, called him up and told him he was arranging the jaunt to Europe.

"Solid, man," said The Hamp. "But remember—I won't go by boat, and I won't go in the big metal bird."

"How the hell will you get over, man?" Glaser demanded. "They want you the most."

"If they want me that bad," said The Hamp, "let them figger it out."

Later, Glaser and Hampton's wife, Gladys, a handsome lady who acts as her husband's manager, talked him into flying. Not the least of their arguments was pointing out that, when they returned, their chartered plane could zoom into Idlewild airport with the whole band blaring "Flyin' Home." The idea appealed to The Hamp, whole loves spectacle almost as much as he loves to eat. Once, in Washington, D. C., playing a concert on a barge, he concluded a rendition of the theme by having his five frontline saxophonists dive into the Potomac, uniforms, instruments and all. Frequently, when the band is swinging into a frenzied sixteenth or seventeenth chorus of the number, Hampton will lead them off the bandstand down to mingle with the dancers.

There is no other big band in existence like Hampton's. For one thing, it is a well rehearsed group composed of young men who idolize their high-powered leader. The boys jump like the old Count Basie band that came out of Kansas City in the '30's, and few bands have ever touched that one. It has a rock-solid beat, an insistent rhythm produced by the drummer, the piano man, and the guitarist and bassist, both of whose instruments are electrified, plus the drums that Hampton plays.

It has a brass section that goes high enough to shatter glasses; it sounds more like a marching band than one designed for dance music. The brass helps the rhythm by playing figures. Then, too, it has a saxophone section that is as rich, full and warm as the reeds in the old Jimmie Lunceford band, with which at one time none could compare. Finally, it has The Hamp himself, a virtual virtuoso, as one fan has described him. The Hamp plays hot, hard, whaling vibes, as he would say; but he also plays delicate, highly imaginative stuff.

Hampton's band enjoys itself while in action as few other bands do. The seventeen men prance all over the stand as they play. A trumpeter leaps down to play figures with the saxophones, the piano player works standing up in sheer exuberance, and Hampton himself plays both drums and vibes in nearly every number. He also leads, not with a baton but with his body, throwing himself about like a dervish. He juggles drum sticks and hurls them into the audience; he tap-dances and turns somersaults. The only time he is still is when he is crouched over the vibes, and then the stillness is only relative: He bounces up and down in rhythm, singing to himself in a sort of half-chant, half-grunt. Invariably, the audience and band take up this curious sound and sing along.

Audiences everywhere react violently to this pounding, compelling performance. I once saw the band get the crowd in the Uptown Theatre, a Philadelphia house in the Negro district, rocking so that the floor actually swayed up and down; the following week I observed 3,000 staid Pennsylvania citizens, dressed in their Sunday best, dancing like wild men in the Ephrata American Legion Park. Hampton draws huge crowds wherever he goes, and it is no exaggeration to say that he goes everywhere. In 1948 President Truman was asked what band he wanted to play for his inaugural ball. "I want the band that plays at the crossroads of the country," he said. Hampton was hired by unanimous choice of the committee. Four years later, he was honored again by being selected to play for President Eisenhower's ball. A friend, hearing of this, asked him why he accepted, since he had been a Stevenson partisan. "Why," said The Hamp, "it's 'cause I want to bill myself, 'Lionel Hampton—Stumped for Stevenson and Stomped for Ike!' " At the ball, Hampton posed for a picture with the new President. His musicians were not awed by the occasion; they saw no reason to hide their natural exuberance.

(One said to another: "Man, who's the cat diggin' The Hamp?" —R. G.)

One hour on the stand with his boys leaves Hampton soaking with perspiration. Yet, more often than not, when the evening's work is over, he will go out and seek equally strenuous diversion. Once, after playing a two-hour show at the Philadelphia Uptown, he asked a friend to accompany him to a nearby night club, The Tropical. "Man," Hampton said, "there's a little chick about 16 years old plays tenor saxophone with that band, and man, how she blows! Oh, she just blows, and blows, and blows!" When The Hamp walked into the club, a mighty cheer went up. He sat down and ate what, for him, was a snack: two large fried chicken sandwiches and a double order of shrimp chow mein. Then, unable to contain himself, he got up on the stand with the six-piece, all-girl band. While he played daemonic drums, the girls knocked themselves out; the little tenor chick blew and blew and blew. The frenzy in the club was worse than it had been at the Uptown. Hampton's fresh suit was a dripping rag within fifteen minutes. He jammed with the girls until the club closed at two, and then went to an after-hour club, where he played drums, danced, and sang until after five A.M.

On Hampton's nights off in New York, he heads for The Embers, a night spot where jazz musicians and their admirers gather. He is not there fifteen minutes before he gets on the stand with the players. When The Embers closes, at four, he likes to round up a group of the boys and find a place where they can go on playing for the rest of the night.

On the town, Hampton is the personification of conviviality. He keeps his friends in an uproar with his nervous, restless energy, and with his colorful, peculiar language, which he calls "spectacular vernacular." The layman needs a hepcat's dictionary to follow The Hamp in ordinary conversation. One day he was trying to explain some of the words to a friend who had asked him exactly what hep means. "You don't say hep any more," Hampton said. "It means aware, or sharp, but you don't say it, man. The word now is dap. You want somebody to know a man is sharp, is au reet, you say he's dap. Must come from dapper. Same way, you don't say a cat ain't nowhere any more, meaning you don't like him or don't want him around. What you say is, he's jailhouse. If you got jailhouse eyes for somethin', it means you don't dig it, means you don't like it or don't understand it. If a cat's a lover, you call him a Continental. If a cat plays a good solo, you say that cat's whalin'. If a cat says, 'Let's go get a beer,' and you say, 'You got one,' that means you're agreeable to it. It means you got eyes for it."

On the front of The Hamp's instrument van is lettered "WATCH YO' NOSE, HAMP." This is a legend he had put up for his own benefit. It comes from another expression he favors. A man, or cat, with his nose open is a man taken by surprise. He explains, "I always try to watch my nose. I always keep it closed."

Most jazz musicians lead a private life consistent with the supercharged music they play. The Hamp is an almost unbelievable exception. Away from his music, away from the jam sessions, he is a sober, serious, conscientious, even scholarly man, leading a quiet, meditative life. He has been married for twenty years to the former Gladys Neal, who was once a Hollywood dressmaker for Joan Crawford and other stars. The Hamptons live in a modest apartment on West 138th Street in New York, along with two parrots, one named Cackleface. Mrs. Hampton goes on the road with her husband to most engagements, driving either a scarlet MG, the horn of which plays the first sixteen bars of "Flyin' Home," or a gray Jaguar, the horn of which plays the harmony. The Hamptons are active crusaders for the rights of their race and for humanitarian causes. Perhaps no other bandleader plays so many benefits. He has a six-inch stack of citations and a trunkful of plaques, but he is proudest of the honorary doctorate he received in the spring of 1953 from Allen University in Columbia, S.C. He does not confine his good works to his own race; he has been cited by the Catholic-Youth Organization in Indianapolis, and by the National Jewish Hospital in Denver.

It is good public relations, of course, to appear at benefits and to back good works, but in Hampton's case there is an extra dimension of sincerity. He is devoutly religious. Wherever he goes he carries a leather case containing a Bible and Mary Baker Eddy's "Science and Health and the Key to the Scriptures." He was converted to the faith by a man named Till Tom, whom he met while playing with Benny Goodman at the San Francisco Exposition. "Till Tom told my wife and me how God had helped him become a leadin' concessionaire around the town," Hampton recalls. "At

LIONEL HAMPTON 305

that time I was goin' into the band business, and I decided to dedicate myself to God." Today Hampton is so dedicated that he occasionally preaches small sermons to his friends and musicians. "I'm in church right now," he sometimes says in his dressing room. "My head is clean and I'm not doin' nothin' to provoke God." He prays constantly for world peace. "If each day we'd all thank God for bein' alive," he has said, "there'd be such a tremendous bellow go up to Heaven that God'd be pleased and all this fightin', all this chaos, all this trouble'd disappear, like the night disappears into the dawn."

Hampton drinks only beer, smokes very little, and has, according to his intimates, only one vice: he eats like a mastodon. One morning I looked on in mingled fear and awe; he put away what was, for him, an average breakfast. This consisted of one double order of Yankee clam chowder, one order of cold salmon complete with hard boiled eggs and other garnishes, a mixed green salad, a Spanish omelet, a dish of fried potatoes, an order of corn fritters, six slices of whole wheat toast with butter and jam, and two pots of coffee. "Man," said he, "I was the hungriest." Despite his unusual intake, he never seems to gain weight. He stands around five feet, eight inches and weighs about 170. He is convinced that his job keeps his weight down.

Oddly enough, and appropriately enough, Hampton was taught to play drums by a nun. He was born April 20, 1914, in Louisville, Ky. His father had been an entertainer, but was disabled during World War I. The parents were separated when he was small, and he was taken to Birmingham by his mother. After a few years there, she moved to Chicago. At that time there was what Hampton describes as "a juvenile crime wave" in the city, and his mother sent him to a Catholic school for boys in Wisconsin. It was there he met the nun, whose name he does not remember. "She was strict," he says. "I wanted to play the skins lefthanded, and she'd take the sticks and beat my knuckles. Man, she was a hard nun."

Hampton attended St. Monica's and St. Elizabeth's in Chicago, meanwhile joining a newsboy band sponsored by *The Chicago Defender*, the colored newspaper. There was never any question in his mind as to what he would be when he grew up. When he was in his early teens he met Les Hite, who had a band that played dates around Illinois. Hite decided to gig to the West Coast, and Hampton went along. Later his aunt, Miss Anna May Bell, went there to look after him. Hampton and Hite played in several bands together (after the latter broke up his own organization). These included Paul Howard's Quality Serenaders, and the band of Reb Spikes, who billed his combo as "The Major and the Minors." After a time Hampton wound up in the group at a Culver City night club operated by Frank Sebastian.

Louis Armstrong, whom The Hamp had heard many times in Chicago when he was making jazz history at The Sunset, came to Los Angeles and agreed to make some Columbia records. He needed a band to accompany him on these sides, and someone suggested the orchestra Hampton was playing with. At the studio, just before the date, Hampton began noodling around on the vibes, an instrument he had never touched before. "Say, Pops, that sounds fine," Armstrong said. "Let's put it on the record."

Hampton met Gladys Neal and married her soon thereafter. At the urging of his wife, Hampton, who had finished high school in Chicago, went on to study music at the University of Southern California, playing odd jobs at night. One day Hite appeared and announced he was taking a new band up to San Francisco. The new Mrs. Hampton didn't want her husband to go, and Lionel reluctantly turned down the job. In order to gain steady employment, he formed a nine-piece combination and took it into the Paradise Club in Los Angeles.

Jazz addicts everywhere heard that there was a man playing wonderful vibes and drums there, and packed the place. Among them, one day was John Hammond. (*People reading this book may get the notion that John invented jazz. He almost did.—E.C.*) Hammond brought Benny Goodman to hear Hampton one night. Goodman, unable to contain himself, got up on the stand, and he and The Hamp jammed until dawn. The next morning they went to the Victor studios, where Goodman had a recording date. With Teddy Wilson, the pianist, and Gene Krupa on drums, Benny and Lionel cut "Moonglow" and "Dinah." The records became jazz classics. Three weeks later, Goodman wired Hampton to join his band.

It was an unprecedented step. Goodman had been employing Teddy Wilson, also a Negro, right along, but it was now his intention to present two Negroes an integral parts of his organization. The conservatives in the business gave themselves over to head-nodding and tsk-tsking. "You'll never be able to play the South," some said. "We'll play it," said Benny, "and we'll get away with it." He was right. The first engagement was the Texas Centennial. It was the first time white and colored musicians had ever worked together on the same stand there, but the crowd stood and gave the band a ten minute ovation.

The Goodman-Hampton association produced some of the finest "chamber" jazz ever recorded, such classics as "Vibraphone Blues," one of Hampton's own compositions, which included the famous line,

"If the blues was whisky, I would stay drunk all the time."

Goodman encouraged Hampton to front his own recording orchestra. For such sessions, The Hamp had the pick of the country's jazzmen. Harry James, Chu Berry, Johnny Hodges, Cootie Williams and many other top sidemen sat in. This series of discs, all of which sold fairly well, led Hampton to believe that he might be successful fronting his own band, but he was reluctant to quit Goodman.

Goodman made the break himself in 1940, when severe attacks of sciatica caused him to disband his orchestra temporarily. When Harry James and Gene Krupa both took out their own outfits, Hampton followed suit. Backed by Goodman, he got together a band composed of youngsters. Unlike the bands of James and Krupa, it was no mere showcase for his own talent. It was an integrated musical unit and, at first, it was almost a total failure. Hampton made the mistake of taking it on an initial tour through the South. His account of that trip is pure horror. He and his boys played dates wherever they could get them, often for as low as $150 per night. They traveled by car and station wagon. Often they were unable to get places to sleep, and frequently they went hungry because roadside restaurants would not admit them. Several men deserted the band. From time to time Hampton himself was all but ready to give up.

Then, finally, they reached New York after months on the

road. They were booked into the Apollo, a cradle of Negro talent. The audiences went crazy, and Hampton knew he had arrived. Since 1943 The Hamp has been riding high. And there is no indication that he will stop, as long, as he puts it, as he keeps his nose closed.

WHITNEY BALLIETT

Kenton: Artistry in Limbo

THIS IS TAKEN *from a record album review Whitney did for the Saturday Review in the spring of 1955. There have been longer pieces on Kenton the man and Kenton's bands, but we are including this one because it is actually an economically-phrased compendium of big-band jazz influences and categories. It's too bad this book isn't wired for sound, so the Kenton records could be heard as Whitney describes them. But Whitney makes a serviceable substitute.*

Stan Kenton got started officially as a bandleader on Memorial Day 1940, when he opened with a thirteen-piece group at the Rendezvous Ballroom in Balboa, California. The music, already indicative of things to come, was relentless and heavy-booted, with a staccato, two-beat attack which resembled in intent, if not execution, the style of the Lunceford band of the time. Perhaps it was persuasive because it was rhythmically overpowering, for by the summer's end, Kenton had built a staunch following on the West Coast and considerable speculation about his "new music" in the East. Kenton's second period began in 1944 after he had been East, and although the band was defter and less aggressive, it was not much different. The third era, 1945-46, illustrated what is now known as the band's principal style—a big reed section securely rooted with a baritone saxophone, a metallic-sounding, inflexible rhythm section, and driving, ear-rending brass teams, all of which are piled up, block by block, into granitic masses of sound. By this time the organization, which had also perfected a sophisticated and impeccable technique, had already split the popular-record buying public insolubly into Kenton-lovers and Kenton-haters.

The next two periods extended from 1947 to 1951, years in which Kenton turned restlessly to his "progressive jazz" and "innovations in modern music," using, in addition to his own works, the compositions and arrangements of Bob Graettinger, Pete Rugulo, Ken Hanna, Neil Hefti and Shorty Rogers. The music itself moved cumbersomely between the funereal pseudo-Bergian orchestrations of Graettinger, mood music performed by a forty-piece band with strings that was perilously close to the boneless wind of movie music, and immense jazzlike frameworks that are constructed about scintillating section work and occasional soloists. The last era, which brings the band up through 1955, was more or less of a deflation to the mid-Forties period, and revealed a clearer jazz feeling than the band had ever before had.

It is impossible not to be impressed by Kenton's very aural bulk, by the sheer sinew and muscle that have gone into the music's making. It is not impossible, however, to remain almost completely unmoved. Kenton's music, in spite of all the organ-like talk that has surrounded its "progressivism" in the past ten years, fits roughly into the tradition of the silvered semi-jazz bands of Larry Clinton, Glen Gray, Glenn Miller, the Dorseys, and Ray Anthony. This tradition, although kneaded from time to time by the energy of Bunny Berigans and Bobby Hacketts, is parallel to, and quite different from, that of the genuine big jazz bands cradled by Fletcher Henderson and Duke Ellington, and maintained since by Goodman, Lunceford, Calloway, Basie, and Woody Herman. Kenton does not fit easily into the white-collar jazz of the former tradition, however, for he tried with the help of extracurricular seasonings, in his fashion to combine the two movements into something new. This he did, in part, by allowing many soloists ample space within glistening limousines of sound that, in the end, tended only to stifle and stiffen whatever potentialities for jazz there was on hand. He also created, as a result of purposely and confusedly trying to be a kind of musical refractor of his times, a self-conscious music that was caught—strident and humorless—somewhere between the pseudo-classical, jazz, and popular music.

Nevertheless, Kenton's sounds and furies have, partly through accident, had certain positive effects within jazz. His various bands have been rigorous training grounds for many of our best younger musicians, particularly those who have gone on to fashion in the past few years—in probable revolt—the sleek, evasive, small-band parlor jazz of the West Coast. His pelting about of words like "progressive" and "innovation," together with the uncompromisingly modernistic tenor of his music, have helped prepare the mind of the public for the work of the true futurists like Gillespie, Parker, Monk, Powell and John Lewis. And, finally, he has inadvertently defined, like the Thomas Wolfes of other art forms, the possible wastelands of his own medium, thus performing the negative service of showing many jazzmen where not to tread if they would further their art.

Kenton says in the epilogue to a recent album called "The Kenton Era" that "it is too early yet to attempt to ascertain whether our efforts over the years have contributed to the developmen of the world's music." It is not, of course, for—as is apparent in that album—his music has just about come full circle. It now deserves, then, a prominent place in that fascinating museum where the curiosities of music are stored.

(*Every Kenton record sounds to me as though Stan signed on three hundred men for the date and they were all on time. Music of his school, in my view, ought only to be played close to elephants and listened to only by clowns. Nevertheless, you've got to admit that Stan knows how to take charge of a band. Even if some of his boys can't read, the audience is never aware of it. It's a real accomplishment to take that many men and make them sound ruly. Give Stan "A" for discipline—E. C.*)

ARTIE SHAW

The Rehearsal

A MUSICIAN WE KNOW, upon hearing that Artie Shaw had written a kind of autobiography (he called it "An Outline of Identity") entitled The Trouble with Cinderella responded, "Why doesn't he call it The Trouble with Artie?" We can't answer that question, but we do know that Master Shaw has had his share of trouble in his day—if you call Lana Turner, Kay Winsor, et al. trouble, and if you were Artie you probably would. At the same time he has managed to play some music between and during marriages. He also has done the above-mentioned book, which Dr. Robert Lindner called "a fascinating and important cultural document." We have taken Chapter Forty-one of this book because it gives an excellent picture of what goes on at a big-band rehearsal. Artie preceded this chapter with a quotation from Vergil: "This is the task, this is the labor."

It's late at night—around one-thirty A.M.

We're in a big dark basement. Piles of junk are lying around here and there. Huge steel columns support the weight of the building overhead—and directly above us is the polished dance floor of the Roseland State Ballroom, a public dance hall in

THE REHEARSAL

Boston, Massachusetts, located about a block from Symphony Hall.

Over at one end of the basement there is a piano, a set of drums, a cluster of music racks, a scattering of brass instruments and saxophones and clarinets, a guitar, a string bass, a number of straight-backed chairs standing around in random groups. A naked electric bulb hangs from a wire. There's no other light. Huge shadows dapple the dirty floor, sprawling in grotesque patterns.

Now we hear footsteps echoing on the stairway leading down here, and in a moment a Negro boy of twenty-one or so appears in the pool of light shed by the naked bulb. He starts arranging music racks and chairs into a kind of formation.

Four music racks down front, each with a chair facing it.

Three racks behind these chairs, each with its chair facing it.

Behind these three more racks, three more chairs.

The drums are set carefully to the right of this chair-and-music-rack formation, in the space between the formation and the piano, which he has hauled into position some six or eight feet over to the right of all this.

Now he sets one other chair into the space between the drums and the piano, somewhat forward of both. He picks up the guitar, carefully lays it on the chair, and sets a music rack in front of it.

The string bass lies between the drums and the piano, behind the guitar chair. The Negro boy puts another music rack down in front of where the string bass lies, a chair next to that, another chair behind the drums, still another at the piano.

He goes around setting trumpets, trombones, saxophones, clarinets—each on its own chair. The front row of four, saxophones and clarinets; the next row back, three chairs, three trombones; the last row, one trumpet for each chair.

There's one more music rack, a taller one; this goes down in front of everything, toward the middle of the whole formation.

Now there is a tidiness about the whole setup, a kind of order, a neatly arranged pattern in what was just a short while ago a collection of assorted objects.

Only one thing is missing now.

The Negro boy goes up the stairs, and presently we hear footsteps again, this time many footsteps—and in a few moments men come straggling down the stairs.

They're young fellows mostly—ranging from eighteen to twenty-five or so. They're of every type and description; blonde, brunette, sandy-haired; short, tall, and in-between; thin, stocky, even fat. Some wear slacks and sweaters; others plain business suits. Some smoking, talking, kidding around with one another; others silent and alone.

They mill around aimlessly for a few seconds. One wanders over and picks up a trumpet; he blows it tentatively, quietly, then louder; finally a cascade of brassy sounds comes blasting out of the horn. A thin boy takes up a saxophone and plays a few arpeggios, the sounds competing contrapuntally with the blaring of the trumpet. Neither pays any attention to the other; each is intent on what he is doing.

Gradually others pick up instruments. The drummer sits down and tests the sound of a cymbal. He shifts his chair, puts his foot on the bass drum pedal and gives the bass drum a few loud thuds, He taps on the snare drum, then starts twisting the key that controls the snares, taps again, twists again, taps again, until he is apparently satisfied with what he hears. He bangs out a long roll on the snare drum, crescendoing to a loud crash on a huge cymbal dangling from a metal arm fastened to the rim of the bass drum. Now he puts down the sticks, lights a cigarette, and sits there dragging on it and staring somberly off into the darkened end of the basement.

By this time everyone has taken up an instrument. They are all at it now. It's bedlam. The blaring of trumpets, brassy, shrill, now and then ascending to a shriek, alternates with and overlaps the lower-pitched blatting of trombones resounding in the stuffy air; and over and through all this come the rippling scales of squawky-sounding alto saxophones, the sonorous throatiness of tenor and baritone saxophones. And far, far underneath—at occasional momentary ebbs in the din—there is the gurgle of the piano, the plunking thud of the guitar, the booming resonance of a string bass being plucked at random alternating with the wheezy scraping of the bow across the heavy strings.

A dark-haired boy of twenty-six or so comes down the stairs

THE REHEARSAL 315

and strides over to the tall music rack down front. He looks around, then turns and yells over his shoulder into the darkness, "Hey, Gate! Where the hell's the music?"

The Negro boy shuffles back into the light. He says something but you can't hear him for the various instruments barking, screaming, groaning, chuckling, rippling, each clashing against and over the rest and flooding the whole place with noise.

The dark-haired boy nods and waits quietly while the Negro goes over to a heap of battered-looking fiber cases lying over to one side, opens one, picks out a large, queer-looking fiber container, brings it over to the dark-haired boy's music rack, and opens it up like a book. Now we can see the contents—a thick stack of tattered, dirty music manuscripts, with ink notes and pencil marks scrawled all over the pages.

The Negro has gone off into the darkness again; in another moment he returns, dragging a high stool which he sets in front of the dark-haired boy's rack. He goes off to one side, opens up a small instrument case, takes out a collection of sawed-off black wooden pipes, fits them one into the other, adds a mouthpiece and a bell-like piece of black wood to each end of the assembled collection, and thus transforms the whole into a clarinet. This he brings over and hands to the dark-haired boy, who takes it, removes the shiny nickel-plated cap from the mouthpiece, blows several notes, then lays it down on his music rack across the ink-scrawled manuscript pile.

He sits on the stool now, shuffles through the stack of music for a moment, carefully holding on to the clarinet meanwhile, and finally, having selected a piece of manuscript from the pile, lays it out on top of the pile. He stares at it intently for ten or fifteen seconds.

All the time, the din is growing louder and louder as the various musicians keep blasting and rippling up and down the scales—here a long, loud ripping burst of shrillness exploding out of the bell of a trumpet, there a throaty scattering of notes from one of the saxophones, answered by an angry bellow from a trombone, all punctuated by the crash of cymbals, the burbling of the piano, the smacking thud of the brass drum, the booming reverberation of the string bass, the plinking of one thin, delicate guitar sound now and then peeping through the thick jungle of sound.

Suddenly the dark-haired boy puts down the piece of music he has been examining, and shouts mildly, "O.K., fellas—let's go!"

No one pays any attention.

"Come on—let's go!" he yells again.

One or two of the musicians stop now, but most of them keep blowing, tinkling, smacking.

"*Hey!* Come *on.* Break it up—let's get going, what do you say?"

There is a general slackening-off of noise and a general drift toward the chair-and-music-rack formation. The noise dies down more and more, and finally diminishes to almost silence, except for an occasional sporadic blast, as if someone had had a sudden afterthought at the end of a long and heated discussion.

"Come on, fellas—what the hell, we don't want to be here all night. Let's go, huh?"

And now there is only the sound of chairs scraping plus a certain amount of familiar small talk as the musicians take their places. These boys have been together a long time and know each other well—as people do who live together, travel together in broken-down buses and jalopies, share rooms in cheap hotels and tourist camps, eat together in diners and roadside hamburger and hot dog stands, work together in dance halls and amusement parks, barns and arenas, through month after month of barnstorming, one-nighters, occasional split-week or week stands, and an endless procession of rehearsals like this one now about to start.

"Yeah, yeah," grins one, "I hear you talkin'. Next time you get the broads, you're such a killer with the chicks."

"O.K., I will," says another, "At least they won't be dogs like these ones you come up with."

"Hey—throw me a straight mute, will you, Gate?" one of the trumpet players yells over to the Negro, who is quietly dozing over in a corner. "All right, all right," he mutters, laboriously getting up and going to another large fiber packing case, rummaging around in it, then picking up an aluminum mute and tossing it over the heads of the saxophones and the trombones, to the trumpeter, who catches it and places it in the wire-and-metal mute rack beside his chair.

THE REHEARSAL

"Get out number seventy-eight," the dark-haired boy calls out. There is a rustling as the men reach into their music-books. A slight delay, as one trombone player mumbles something or other about not being able to find his part. "Here, George," he says, handing half his music to his neighbor. "Go through that, will you? Guess it got mixed up on the job tonight." His neighbor takes the pile of music, they both start thumbing through it, until suddenly the first boy says, "O.K., O.K.—I got it." He takes back the rest of his music, puts it back on his music stand, spreads out the piece he has been looking for.

"All set? Everybody got seventy-eight out?" asks the dark-haired boy now.

No one says anything.

"All right," he says. "Now look. Over at letter C, where the saxes come in under the brass and then saxes and trombones take it by themselves—see where I mean?"

The men look at their music.

"Let's just run that part down and I'll show you what I mean," says the leader.

He sets a tempo by tapping rhythmically with his foot. There is complete silence now, except for the foot-tapping. Tap, tap, tap, tap, tap, tap, tap, in regular rhythmic intervals—and then, over the tapping and in time with the tapping, he counts off, one number for each of two pairs of taps—"one," tap, "two," tap—and suddenly the musicians hit it at "letter C" at the point where count "three" should have come if the leader had gone on counting. Only now, instead of disorganized blaring and screaming and gurgling and groaning and bellowing and tinkling and thudding and plunking and plinking and booming, there is the sound of instruments fused in an organized, rhythmic pattern, brass blending into a sectional choir, floating over the rhythmic fusion of drums, piano, bass, and guitar, and resting lightly on the trombone-and-low-saxophone base. At last, the trumpets break off in abrupt cessation, the saxophone-and-trombone mixed-choir carry on above the rhythm-pulse in a low-voiced blend so interwoven that it is hard to tell which is saxophone and which trombone. The tune is an old one, of early jazz vintage, "Someday Sweetheart" and at a certain point in the music, just before the melody soars to a high note, the leader cuts in with his clarinet, plays a crisp fill-in phrase, and suddenly takes his clarinet out of his mouth, shouting—"O.K.—hold it, that's the spot I mean."

The music straggles on for a moment, then raggedly peters out. The men look up quietly.

"See that place where we just stopped?" the leader says. "Right before letter D, where the brass goes off by itself away from the sax section—see where I mean?"

Several men nod, and one says, "Right there at a bar before D, you mean?"

"That's it," says the leader. "Now, you see what happens there? George and Les are doubling melody, and it comes out too heavy against the rest of the horns. What it should sound like is a heavy, thick chord—but all I can hear is that one melody voice. Come down a little in there, can you, George—and you too, Les. The rest of you blow up to them a little more. Let's see if we can't get it sounding like a thick blend, rather than just a melody with the rest of the voices accompanying. O.K.? Let's hit it again."

Once more the foot-tapping, then counting and tapping together, and once more the whole band hits it, and once more they're stopped at the same place.

"That's a *little* better," says the leader this time. "Only I think you can come down still more—Les and George only. The rest of you are about right now—just Les and George down a bit. Let's go—same spot."

Tapping again, then tapping and counting. Once more the same music. Once more the stop.

"That's got it," the leader says.

A couple of men start blowing their horns now. "Hold it, will you?" the leader shouts over the noise. The men seem not to hear. "Hey! Chuck!" the leader yells now, at one of the men, who puts his trumpet down. "George!"—and the other one puts down his trombone and looks up.

"Come on, let's quit fooling around and get this one over with," says the leader, mildly, now that he can be heard.

Silence.

"I want to hear another spot in the same piece," the leader goes on. "Over near the ending, about six or seven bars after letter L—

where the whole band is supposed to build up to a big loud peak." Turning toward the drummer, "I think you'd better come in under that with a rim shot, Cliff, just to kind of accent it and underline the whole thing."

The drummer looks down at his music. "You mean that spot where the brass goes—" he sings a phrase and looks up questioningly. Several of the men grin. The drummer has a strange goaty voice, and his singing of the phrase has an odd sound, but he seems unaware of anything funny.

"Yeah, that's it," the leader says. "Mark it, will you? Sixth bar after L, fourth eighth-note of the bar."

"Who's got a pencil?" the drummer asks, looking around. The piano player hands him a stub of a pencil, he takes it, starts to make a mark on his music, and suddenly looks up. "Say, Art—what about the high-hat cymbals in that spot?"

"What do you mean—what about the high-hat cymbals?" asks the leader.

"Well—when we hit that spot I'm on high-hat, and now if I take both sticks to make the rim shot I'm going to have to get off the high-hat to do it."

"Well?"

"Won't that sound kind of empty? I mean, the beat'll sorta come to a pause, won't it?"

"The whole thing shouldn't take more'n a split second at the most," says the leader. "And by that time we've got enough of a beat going to keep it right up there. Anyway, can't you make the rim shot with one stick?"

"Well, O.K."

"Let's try it and see," and the leader starts tapping again. Tapping, counting-tapping, and the band smacks in once more, this time a different sound altogether. They come to the spot, the drummer smacks his rim shot, the leader nods at him and waves the band to another ragged halt.

"That's it," the leader says to the drummer. "It needed that."

The drummer shrugs, "I guess so."

The leader nods.

They go over several other short sections of the same arrangement, and finally that one is put back into the pile of music. Another piece comes out and the whole process begins again—the same process we've just seen, with slight variations. After an hour or so, a sense of vague restlessness begins to permeate the whole group; the leader says, "O.K., fellas—take five."

The men lay down their instruments, get up, one or two stretching and yawning, light cigarettes, wander off in groups of twos and threes, talking, joking, laughing.

The leader sits on his stool, smoking and shuffling through the pile of manuscript on his music rack. Five or six minutes later, he looks at his wrist watch and shouts, "O.K., let's go, fellas. We've got a few more to run down before we start taking the new ones."

"What new ones we got, Art?" one of the saxophone players asks as he sits down.

"Couple of things—one original and a new arrangement of 'Man I Love.' "

"What's the matter with the one we got on 'Man I Love?' " another musician asks.

"Don't like the way it sounds," the leader answers abstractedly, shuffling through the pile of music in front of him.

He calls out another number, the men get out their parts, and they go through the same process as before. An hour or so later, another five-minute rest, then another hour or so of the same polishing-up rehearsal, and now it is three-thirty A.M.

At this point there is still another five-minute break. During the break two more people come in. The short, stocky one is the arranger, the other the band manager. The arranger is carrying two large manila envelopes. He comes over to the leader, who now gets off his stool and stretches lazily.

"Hi, Art," the arranger says.

"Hi, Jerry," says the leader.

The band manager is talking to the men over at one side of the band setup. He looks harassed. He is trying to explain about the time of departure for tomorrow night's job. The men are asking various questions about the bus, how much time it will take to get to the job, why they can't sleep longer and get started a little later, and so on and so forth, with everybody in on a discussion which grows more and more heated (since everyone has a different idea of what is the best way to handle the thing) until in the end the

THE REHEARSAL   321

band manager hollers impatiently—"All right, for the love of Pete —shut up, will you, you guys? The bus leaves from the front of the goddamn hotel at two-thirty, and that's that. Anybody who doesn't feel like making it can get there his own way—period."

Grumbling, muttering, a bit of griping—but the matter is settled.

Meanwhile the leader and the arranger have been looking over the two freshly-copied new arrangements. They go over various parts of the music and then, the five-minute break over, the leader turns to the band manager. "O.K., Ben—get the boys together so we can get started on these."

The men have wandered off, some of them upstairs, others to the toilet, still others outside for a breath of fresh air. The air in here is now heavy and thick with shifting planes of cigarette smoke floating and eddying in the light from the one naked bulb.

The band manager goes off and returns several minutes later herding the men back down like a sheep dog worrying and snapping at the heels of a flock.

Everyone is finally seated in his place again, the new music is passed out, and this time the rehearsal starts in earnest. Note by note, measure by measure, phrase by phrase, section by section, chorus by chorus, the two new arrangements are dissected, explained, argued about, thrashed out, understood, played over a couple of times for good measure, numbered, and put into the books. Some hours later, when it is all over, the leader says, "O.K., fellas—that's it. See you tomorrow."

"So long," some of the men say. Others are busy putting their instruments away, getting their music numbered and put away before leaving the setup to be broken down by Gate, the Negro bandboy.

The leader hands his clarinet to Gate, says goodnight to him, and goes off with the arranger and the band manager.

Within five or ten minutes, they are all gone except Gate, who shambles tiredly from chair to chair, picking up music and putting the folders together into the fiber trunk in which they are carried from place to place as the band travels around the country. He folds up the collapsible music racks with the initials A.S. on them, breaking down the whole setup he put together only a few hours back. Once finished, he switches off the one dangling bulb, shuffles off by the light of a small pocket flashlight, and climbs wearily up the stairs.

In the morning he will be back to gather up all the paraphernalia and transport it to the bus before the men are picked up.

For tonight, one more rehearsal is over, and to Gate it's all part of the day's work. Right now it's time to catch some sleep. . . .

There you have some idea of what this part of the job is all about. Just what *has* been accomplished?

Well, the band has learned a little more about several arrangements that were already in the books, which they will now be able to play that much more smoothly on tomorrow night's job. Besides that, they have two new arrangements which will be played in public tomorrow night for the first time—and these, if they still sound all right after a week or two of playing and re-rehearsing and polishing, will be kept in the books as a regular part of the band repertoire.

So much for rehearsals, then, and the part they play in the development of an organization of this kind. What else is necessary—what else is required? After all, we're aiming at the top. What other problems are we going to have to solve before we can get there?

Are they all musical problems?

Because if that were the case, all we'd have to do to make a successful big time bandleader would be to look around and find a good musician, a fellow who can play his own instrument well and/or arrange the music for his band so as to make them sound good—and there we'd be. . . .

(There is just one thing missing in this story. Mezz Mezzrow should have come in to deliver a few arrangements.—E. C.)

MAURICE ZOLOTOW

One Night Tour

AFTER NEARLY TWENTY years of chronicling the eccentric doings of people in the entertainment world, Maurice Zolotow is by now almost as colorful a Broadway figure as any of his subjects. Maurice is a suffering writer; that is, he puts himself through unspeakable torment in researching his stories, then spends several masochistic weeks pummeling his material into shape. That is why he is one of the most successful of the magazine reporters. His pieces are so full of interesting, acutely observed facts, they always seem much shorter than they actually are. The story that follows came after Maurice had joined Bobby Byrne's band and traveled with it about a week, covering 1,491 miles in seven states. The trip was made in wartime, and when Maurice sent us this story, he said he thought it might seem dated. It is, but only in one respect: Bobby Byrne's band is no longer in existence, and Bobby has gone back into studio work. Otherwise, conditions are exactly as Maurice described them. Musicians earn more today, but they work just as hard as the boys in Byrne's band did.

R. G.

Bobby Byrne, a youthful trombonist and band leader, pointed to a huge, red National Trailways' bus. "That," he said, "is where we will eat, dress, live and amuse ourselves for six weeks. We'll also try to sleep. I can't sleep in busses." He shrugged his shoulders. "If a swing band could make out playing location jobs in hotels or theaters all the time it would be swell, It's hitting the road, five or six months every year, that beats you down to the socks."

The bus, a mastodon of automobiles, was parked by the back entrance of the Saylor's Lake Pavilion, near Stroudsburg, Pennsylvania, in the Pocono Mountains. "Of course," continued maestro Byrne, smiling sadly, "we have to make time on this job. The reason we will have to stick pretty close to the bus is that we're booked for one long jump after another. I guess we can consider ourselves lucky we have no really inhuman jumps on the program. The union recently passed a law saying no band can travel more than four hundred miles a day between engagements. Too many accidents on the road."

He didn't go into details, but I remember that Hal Kemp had been killed in California while racing to a ballroom. In recent months serious accidents had happened to the bands of Tommy Dorsey, Charlie Barnet, Jack Teagarden, Sammy Kaye. In 1939 there were sixty-one accidents to musicians on the road; in 1940 there were seventy-eight; in 1941 over a hundred. I had joined Byrne and his orchestra at Saylor's Lake to see exactly why the one-night tour is considered about the most dangerously unpleasant job in the entertainment industry today.

The pattern of a musician's life on the road is simple: play, and ride on, play, and ride on. No time for leisurely eating or sleeping, no shower baths. In and out of a town before you can have suits pressed or shirts laundered. You don't stop long enough to date a girl. You have to make time on this job. You have to stick pretty close to the bus. This is the pattern of your days and nights: you sit on a narrow, wobbly bandstand (this isn't the Hotel Pennsylvania in New York, brother) and you blow into a trumpet or pound a drum for five hours and after that you stick pretty close to the bus for maybe ten hours and then you sit on another narrow wobbly bandstand and blow into a trumpet or pound a drum for another five hours. And you don't get tired. You smile all the time and play hot. You must never forget you're making rhythms for the kids. You're entertainment, the only flesh-and-blood entertainment thousands of rural communities experience since minstrel shows and vaudeville disappeared. You have to be young and strong and bursting with rhythm and very much in love with the freedom and independence that comes with being a good jazz musician to be able to stand this life, and to enjoy this pattern.

The Byrne band began its tour at Saylor's Lake, and when the bus pulled in it found another orchestra bus parked near the Pavilion. Inside, arguing with the promotor, Andy Perry, was another well-known maestro named Russ Morgan. (A chap who hires traveling "name" bands is always called a promotor in the trade even if he owns six ballrooms.) Morgan was red-faced and angry.

"Listen," he cried, "it says here in my contract that I'm due to play here, Wednesday, tonight. What gives here, anyhow?"

Promoter Perry, who looks like Shemp Howard the movie comedian, swallowed and stammered. "We expected you Saturday, Russ. I spent two hundred bucks advertising you for Saturday, Russ. I got posters in Allentown, Stroudsburg, Bethlehem, Easton. You think I like this mix-up?"

"It says here in my contract," said Morgan, "that I'm due to play here Wednesday."

"They can't do this to me," moaned Perry. "I got no band for Saturday."

"On Saturday I will hit Cincinnati," said Morgan.

Byrne took me aside. "You see," he whispered, "everything happens on the one-nighters. Hotel jobs—fine. Theater jobs—great. One-nighters—trouble. I got a contract calling for me to play here tonight. Anyway, they have my band advertised." Byrne stealthily signaled to his musicians, who had already donned their gray flannel uniforms in the bus en route from Atlantic City, and, while Morgan was arguing with Perry, Byrne's men took the stand and started playing. Eventually, Morgan took himself and contract off, calling curses down on his booking office. Morgan has good cause to dislike one-night tours. He has been on the road for fourteen months, and during this time his first child was born, and the father has never been in New York and still doesn't know what his eleventh-month offspring looks like. . . .

From 8 till 2 A.M., Byrne and his fifteen musicians were on the stand playing hot and fast and loud. At eleven-thirty they got a thirty-minute rest period. During the intermission I asked Les Reis, whose father was one of the founders of the Reis underwear empire, why top-notch musicians run all the nervous and physical risks of a barnstorming expedition. Reis, the road manager of the band, explained it this way: "A location job is like a storekeeper buying merchandise, and a one-night tour is selling it. We just finished twelve weeks at the Hotel Pennsylvania, but we didn't make a nickel. Actually, it cost us about $400 a week to play the Pennsylvania. We received $1,750 a week from the hotel. We paid out $1,550 in salaries to the sidemen and vocalists. We spent another $600 every week—commissions to our booking agent, arranger's and copyist's salaries, office rent, press agent and so forth. We know it's a good investment, however. At the Pennsylvania, we had an NBC wire—we did four nationwide broadcasts a week, we built up a demand for Bobby Byrne. Now, we're going out to cash in on this demand. On this tour we will receive as much as $1,200 for a single night—almost as much as we received in New York for a whole week!"

Our conversation was interrupted several times. Once, by a plump and pale-complexioned chap who plays trombone in the band. He sauntered over and shook his head thoughtfully. "No?" asked Reis. "No," replied the trombonist, whose name is Jimmy Emert. Reis explained that Emert's wife was expecting a baby. Emert, naturally, hadn't wanted to make the tour but he couldn't find a replacement in time. "Every time there's a break," said Reis, "he makes a long-distance call to New York. They haven't taken his wife to the hospital yet. It's a tough setup for Emert."

A few moments later, Jimmy Palmer, one of the two vocalists with the band, dashed up, his face trembling. "They can't find it anywhere," he said. "Joe looked all over the bus. Nothing doing. I'm positive I gave it to that dumb bellhop in Atlantic City. I told him to park it in front of the bus and Joe would take care of it."

"Did you see him put it outside?" asked Reis patiently.

"No," said Palmer, swearing under his breath, "but I told him to take it down and Joe would take care of it."

"He lost his suitcase," Reis explained to me. "He hasn't got a thing to wear. He's wearing a shirt he borrowed from the drummer.

Excuse me, I am going down and see if I can locate the missing suitcase."

Promptly at two in the morning, the band played its closing theme, a fragment of "Danny Boy," and Joe Slater, a husky Negro who has been playing nursemaid to bands since he was with the Mills brothers, awoke from where he had been sleeping beside the bandstand on a drumcase. The musicians deftly folded their instruments and plodded downstairs. Joe started "breaking down." The music stands were pressed flat. The $20,000 worth of arrangements gently placed in small valises, no bigger than overnight bags. Soon, there was nobody left on the stand but Slater, smashing baggage, and maestro Byrne, playing a chord progression on the piano while Dick Skinner, guitarist and arranger, wearily listened. Bobby wanted Skinner to incorporate the progression into a new arrangement. Slater noisily wedged the music stands into boxes, the bass drum and snare drums and cymbals and the other traps into their cases. In less than an hour, the band was packed, and Slater, without any other help began to lug the boxes downstairs and place them in the bus.

Downstairs, the musicians were impatiently waiting by the door of the bus. The bus was closed and the shades drawn. Dorothy Claire, the girl vocalist, was changing out of her evening gown, a glittering costume of yellow and brown, with lace and rhinestones. On a one-night tour the bus is everybody's dressing room. Miss Claire changed in ten minutes. Then, while she went outside, the musicians clambered up and changed out of their uniforms.

Dorothy is a tiny blonde girl, whose face is lively and whose voice tingles. Off duty, she wore blue slacks and a blue striped sweat shirt. She told me she had left the hospital only a week before. An appendicitis operation. "My doctor would kill me," she chuckled, "if he knew I was jumping around the country on an ol' bus. I'm supposed to be in bed, con-va-lesc-ing." She wrinkled her uptilted button nose. "I can't sit still, not when the music plays my song and I should be singing it, I can't be resting and listening to somebody else sing my song on the radio. I can't sit still." She didn't. She sang every night, slept on the bus, ate with the boys, never complained once. Her side, where she had a slit eleven inches long ("it was a hard operation—my appendix was in the wrong place") ached all the time but she never talked about it. Canaries can take it.

A little after three-thirty, the band was ready to roll. Reis was the last to enter the bus and he carefully counted off, to make sure nobody had been left behind. It was a ritual he never omitted. Then he told the driver to push off. Driver Cliff Hamilton, forty-eight, who has been driving chartered busses for musicians for twenty years, shifted the gears into first and we rolled off through the Poconos. Gradually, we hit a sixty, seventy, seventy-five mile an hour clip. . . .

Three hundred and seventy-five miles to make tonight and tomorrow. To Norfolk, Virginia. We have to make time on this job. Play, and ride on, play and ride on. The bus careened around curves, snapping your neck awake if you tried to sleep. It swung in and out of traffic, passing slower vehicles. Time to make. The men sat in the bus talking slowly and in murmuring tones. They were too worn for laughing or shouting. All the laughing and shouting was in the instruments . . . Until the lights in the bus were put out, Dorothy Claire had a make-up kit on her lap. She was slapping cold-cream on her face, wiping make-up off with tissue. Palmer and Dick Farrell, the drummer, talked about some girls they knew in Norfolk, Virginia. Johnny Martell, one of the best solo trumpeters in the business, rubbed unguent on his upper lip where a small sore had developed—lip sores are the occupational disease of a trumpeter. Byrne, given a double seat for himself according to the leader's prerogative, placed a blinder over his eyes. Then he twisted himself into an S and tried to sleep. Bob MacDonald, third trumpeter, sat in a back seat and looked quite depressed. Abe Siegel, bassist, yelled for an aspirin. The bus roared louder as it turned out of a mountain road and merged into Route 113. . . . "This is the last one-nighter for me," mused Mac-Donald aloud. "I'll be in the army on September 2. I hope they put me into one of those army dance bands. What'll happen to me if I can't practice? I used to hate one-nighters like hell, but now it feels good, even staying up in a bus all night feels fine. I wish this tour could go on forever. Suppose they don't let me touch a horn for two years?"

Tony Faso, second trumpet and the youngest member of the

band, leaned across the aisle and slapped MacDonald on the shoulder. "Solid, solid," he said happily. For Faso, a seventeen year old boy from Brooklyn, it was the first one-night tour, the first job with a big band. Faso used to play in a parochial brass band at the Church of Our Lady of Hope in Brooklyn. A few months ago he was "discovered" when he sat in on a Sunday afternoon jam session at the Hickory House on Fifty-Second Street. Tony has the drive, hoarse vibrato and imagination of the born swingster. He plays every note on his trumpet as if he had only one more note to play. He is loud and raucous and his notes drive into your body like hypodermic needles. Tony has never been away from Brooklyn before. He was thrilled by everything on the trip, the tobacco plants growing in Carolina, the hot rolls served at breakfast, the barefoot farm kids. "It's a big country," he said, staring out of the window as the bus rolled toward Philadelphia. Miss Claire, finished with her toilette, tied a bandana around her head and tried to compose herself for sleep. MacDondald joined Palmer and Farrell in the discussion about girls. Byrne sat up abruptly and said, "Where are we? Why can't I learn to sleep on busses?" Nobody laughed. In the back of the bus, Siegel, Matthews, Skinner, Usifer and Martell started gossiping about music. In the night, when the bus lights are out, all you can do is talk. Who is playing with whom, so-and-so is in bad with Local 802, too bad about Gray Gordon's band busting up, did you hear Benny Goodman's got a new drummer, who, big Sid Catlett, they say Mildred Bailey's new record is solid. Gradually, the conversation drowsed. One by one, the heads sank down, bodies tried to relax, they tried to loosen tense muscles, numbed fingers, paralyzed lips. As soon as they sank away, the bus made a sharp turn or the glaring headlights of another bus shone through the windshield and they abruptly awoke. They smoked many cigarettes instead of sleeping. How can you sleep sitting up, anyway? One or two of the boys tried to make a bed of the pile of luggage in the rear. A fine mattress a layer of suitcases makes. They all tried to sleep. Except Tony Faso. Faso stared out of the window, full of wonderment. MacDonald tried to sleep, but couldn't. He stared out of the window, but in a different way, morosely. Palmer and Farrell continued to talk about girls. Emert stared up blankly. "I'll phone New York in the morning," he said. "Maybe they've taken her to the hospital." Nobody can sleep. The bus hit eighty miles per hour. Play, and ride on.

The bus slowed down, easing through Philadelphia at a paltry sixty miles per hour. I sat down next to Gerald Yelverton, who plays second sax, and hot clarinet. Yelverton, who is from Montgomery, Georgia, is a slender lad with intense blue eyes and a slow, thoughtful manner of speaking. He doesn't drink, smoke, or go with girls. During the entire tour he sat immovable in his seat and read religious books. He was studying a work on theosophy by Mrs. Annie Besant. Yelverton discusses the higher realms of Being with the facility of a divinity student. I asked Yelverton about the hazards of one-nighters.

"Last year," he drawled, "we were playing a date at the Peabody Country Club in Salem, Massachusetts. They told us to park down the road a piece, and it was right near the club's fairway. As I was getting out, somebody sliced a drive that came right for me. I tried to jump but the ball hit me on the right side of the head. Concussion. My left arm was paralyzed two days. I was in the hospital for six weeks. I had to pay my own doctor's bills and hospitalization. And the feller who hit me, he didn't even stop to say I'm sorry, he just picked up the ball and went on playing. I don't like one-nighters."

Slater, who had overheard us, chimed in with an incident that occurred in West Virginia. Part of his job is sitting up and talking to the driver to keep him from falling asleep. He was talking to the driver, one chilly, snowy night, when he suddenly felt the bus slipping backwards as it tried to climb a mountain. It had begun to hail and the sleet had evidently packed down into an icy carpet. The driver was stiff with panic.

"Without thinkin'," said Joe, "I lep' out and pick up a rock an' prop up a back wheel. Lucky the bus was teeterin' back so slow, otherwise we be playin' in Gabriel's band."

Everything happens on the one-nighters because you have to make time. Time is the essence of a musician's life. He beats it on the bandstand, he makes it on the road. He never finds it for himself, though. On the road there is no time for any personal diversion: no movies, no bowling, no tennis, no biking, no dates, no dancing, not even drinking. (One drink and you're bawled out. Two drinks and you're fired.)

Toward morning several of the boys started a poker game, for nickel and dime stakes. They planted a suitcase in the aisle, and propped a saxophone case on the suitcase. It's not the steadiest table, but four or five can play comfortably. At night there is nothing to do but talk or try to sleep. By day, you can at least play poker. Seven of the boys uncomfortably joined the game. The others talked. Musicians really talk the way they're supposed to, they talk their own brand of the Richard English-language. When they see a pretty girl they shout, "Dig the chick." When they liked a Tommy Dorsey recording of "Yes, Indeed," they heard in a roadside jukebox, they said, "It kicks a long distance." Anything good is "solid." Anything old and worn-out is "beat."

The poker game continued till nine when the bus arrived at Salisbury, Maryland. Emert raced out to phone about his wife. The others went for coffee. "Ten minutes for breakfast," Reis announced. They returned before the time was up and stood around the bus restlessly. Clarinetist Yelverton climbed in and sat down. He began reading the book by Mrs. Besant. Palmer, aided by Joe, searched for his suitcase. Finally, he discovered it under a seat. Dorothy brushed her hair. The driver and Reis argued about mileage and tolls. Reis wanted the driver to escape a toll-bridge because tolls are paid by the band. Emert returned and shook his head. The bus started rolling.

We reached Cape Charles, Virginia after noon and boarded the ferry for Norfolk. On the ferry, I asked Byrne, who is only twenty-three and has been a professional musician for eight years and a maestro for two, how musicians stood the tribulations of such a tour. Bobby is a handsome, clean-cut boy, who looks very clear-eyed and innocent, and who plays a full, warm, quivering style of trombone that is second only to Tommy Dorsey's (and Tommy is fourteen years older). Bobby said, "I got a tough musical education. I guess every musician has the same type of upbringing. This is no job for softies."

Bobby received his physical hardening at the hands of his father, Clarence Byrn, former United States Army bandmaster who is now head of the music department at Cass Technical High

School in Detroit. A believer in stern military discipline, even where music is concerned, Mr. Byrn put Bobby to learning the piano at two, and had him mastering the flute, piccolo and harp before he was six. When he started blowing a trombone, Bobby's arms were so short he could only reach fifth position on the slide. (There are seven positions.)

This was Bobby's program when he was a kid: up at 6 A.M. and practice till 6:30. Breakfast till 7:30. Practice from 7:30 till 10:30. Half hour to rest. Practice from 11 to noon. Lunch. From 12:30 till 3:30 he attended Cass, and, for a change, studied music in one of his father's classes. Practice from 4 to 6:30. Dinner till 7:30. Rest till 8. From 8 to 9:30 he returned to Cass and rehearsed with the school orchestra. While Bobby was learning the trombone, men like Goodman, Dorsey, Miller were already making jazz history in the nineteen twenties. Byrne is the first of the new generation of swing men, who have grown up since 1933. At sixteen, Bobby was already good enough to take Tommy Dorsey's place when Tommy left the Dorsey Brothers Orchestra and Jimmy Dorsey took over. At twenty-one, Bobby stepped out with his own group.

When the band arrived at Norfolk, Jimmy Emert phoned New York. He shook his head. "Nothing happened yet," he said, vacantly, "but it should happen any hour." The boys looked hot and white and weary. It was already 4 P.M. and by the time they checked into a hotel it was after five, because the bus cruised all over Norfolk looking for a hotel with room for sixteen musicians, two singers, one road manager. All the big hotels were packed—Norfolk is a boom town. So there was little sleep before or after dinner.

The band reached the New Casino Ballroom at Virginia Beach toward 9 P.M. The musicians felt discouraged when they saw the bandstand—a small square stand, on which they had to uncomfortably squeeze themselves. The Casino was a few steps from the ocean, and the damp air made it impossible to tune the instruments. The piano was hopeless, said pianist Louie Carter. Drummer Farrell said his pet peeve is playing near water: "The damp soaks into the skins and you can't keep a drum in tune." The microphone was impossible—it gave the singers a severe shock when they accidentally touched it with lips or nose while crooning in. An emergency call went out to Joe Slater to lug out the band's own mike and p.a. system from the bus. Quickly, Joe began to set up a new mike, amplifier, and loud-speaker. Under these conditions the boys played spiritlessly for several hours, not being helped by a lady who sat on the edge of the stand and every time Bobby's slide folded out she thought it was funny to gently push it back. Everything happens on the one-nighters.

But it was amazing how, after a few hours of playing, the piston-pounding rhythms acted like a tonic and the brass section came alive and sloughed off its weariness and began to play as ecstatically as if it had a week's rest. In fact, toward the shank end of the evening when all the dancers suddenly stopped moving and circled around one couple, a curly headed youngster grinning from ear to ear who was whirling about with a loose-limbed serious girl, the band caught the spirit and refused to bring "Sometimes I'm Happy" to an end. The shaggers kept on gyrating, inventing variations of hops and skips and torso undulations, and the band played chorus after chorus of "Sometimes I'm Happy"—twenty-eight choruses in all, a matter of some thirty-five minutes. They forgot warped strings and sea damp drums; they just played for the sheer tingle of it. You had to see it, in order to believe that boys without sleep could get all that music out of their worn bodies.

They returned to the hotel in Norfolk at 4:30 in the morning, and Reis paid the men their salaries in his room. They snatched two hours of sleep and were up at 8. Play, and ride on. One hundred and seventy miles to Wilson, North Carolina, for the annual Coronation Ball of Wilson's famous Tobacco Exposition and Festival, which celebrates the resumption of tobacco auctions. The band played in the New Planter's Warehouse—86,500 square feet, and by 11 P.M. every foot was packed with the sons and daughters of the tobacco aristocracy—everybody from Durham to the eastern seaboard was on hand, nearly 10,000 strong. Mayor Bill Daniels. who likes swing, sat near the bandstand so he could enjoy the rhythms at close quarters. At one point, he grew so moved that he came up to Bobby and suggested several request numbers. (That wouldn't happen in New York. Can you imagine our Mayor coming to the Hotel Pennsylvania and asking for "Sweet Sue"?) But even a sympathetic Mayor can't prevent a band on the road from having its troubles. Without any warning, the lights went out! The band played in pitch darkness for ten minutes. Then, presto! the lights came on. Then, another blackout. This time Bobby fished out a searchlight and flashed it on the singers when they took a chorus. After the fourth blackout, however, the lights came on and stayed on. They played till 3 A.M.

Emert phoned New York before the bus left Wilson. No change in his wife's condition. Play, and ride on. Two hundred and fifty miles to Washington, District of Columbia, where the band played for two cruises on the S.S. Potomac along the Potomac River. One cruise went from 8:45 till midnight, and the other from 12:30 till 3:30. Now, even the dancers on the floor could see the bandsmen were tired, eyes bleary and red-rimmed. You could see that if you looked, but if you just listened and danced you couldn't have told the difference. On the "S.S. Potomac," which was hot and stifling and crowded with 2,200 slightly hysterical jitterbugs, was the worst bandstand of all, it was no more than ten feet wide and the men and instruments were literally wedged in. Abe Siegel, who has been barnstorming with big bands for close to ten years, vowed this was the worst bandstand he had ever encountered. But they played on, and the jitterbugs danced. For six solid hours they played, and by the time they were ready to leave Washington they were ready to drop. Farrell, the drummer, had sweated so hard that the seat of his flannel trousers had softened and then dropped off like rotted wood. Now the whole band would have to wear brown slacks with their gray coats.

They were on the road again at dawn, en route to Bridgeport. Dorothy Claire rubbed cold-cream into her cheeks. Road manager Reis figured out mileage. Two saxophonists and three brass men organized a poker game. Yelverton gently cleaned his clarinet with a handkerchief, and then he read a pamphlet. Siegel read *Down Beat*. Emert yelled out to the driver, "When do we stop for lunch? I got to call New York. Maybe I'm a father already." Tony Faso was staring out the window, wide-eyed at the passing landscape; he was thinking his own thoughts and smiling a little to himself, smiling proudly. Farrell and Palmer talked about some girls they knew in Boston. Nobody slept. By some miracle it seems that you can get by without sleep on a one-night tour.

FIVE:

JAZZ STORIES

In Season in the Sun, Wolcott Gibbs' amusing play of several seasons ago, a character obviously drawn from the late Harold Ross happens to come upon some pages of the manuscript of a novel his star writer has been working on. "It looks to me as though George is going out of his way to write a novel," he says. Most novels about jazz read as though their writers deliberately took pains to annoy their poor readers. There is no denying that writers have overlooked jazz—or perhaps that the wrong writers have looked at it. Somehow, most fiction with jazz as its theme just doesn't ring true. There have been notable exceptions to this statement, however, and we have collected some of them in the following section.

R. G. & E. C.

JAMES JONES

The King

JAMES JONES NEEDS no introduction to Frank Sinatra fans.

From Here to Eternity didn't give any delinquents any ideas they already didn't have, but it may have taught them something about honor and decency, a lesson even non-delinquents could use almost daily.

This story of Jim's is pretty obviously based on the return of Bunk Johnson. Jim demonstrated in his first book that he knew a bit about jazz and had a feeling 'for it, and in this one he proves that he wasn't faking the first time. The kids in here remind Condon of his own boyhood days, except that he never permitted his parents to be as lenient as the ones in the story. He simply said "Good-bye" and went off with Hollis Peavey and his Jazz Bandits. These kids have more respect and less fun, and may indicate to the sociologists that Americans are growing up. Or growing dull, which may amount to the same thing.

There is a story behind our acquisition of this story. Gehman read it first in Playboy, a reading habit he may have to explain to his wife, and urged that it be included. Condon agreed that it ought to be in. We wrote to Jones and asked permission, and as an added inducement, offered a free evening at The West Third Street Slenderella.

"I'd love to spend a free evening at Eddie's when I get to New York," Jim wrote back. "Whoopee, etc., etc.!"

Then he had a thought.

"But," he said, "does Condon know how much I can drink?" We don't know that. We do know he can write.

E. C. & R. G.

When we met Willy Jefferson, "King" Jefferson, our band had already been following his progress for over five years. His records used to cause more argument in our band than Stephen Grappelly's Hot Four and the question of whether the violin ought not to be morally disqualified as a jazz instrument. All we had to do was to put on some of King's records and listen to that trumpet and we would end up by bringing in everybody from Panassie and Rudi Blesh to Dave Dexter, Jr.

Our whole band were juniors in high school when they were combing the backwoods of Louisiana looking for King. The next summer, when Bob Rhynolds of US Records finally found him, our band was playing its first booking away from home ground as a truly professional outfit. We manufactured schmaltz for ten weeks in the pavilion at Seraphan Lake upstate for the dancers. Our high school music director led the outfit. We had to put up with him because he got the job for us. He was friends with the owner and also had the soft-drinks concession. We came home from there sick of Guy Lombardo, but with our minds made up to all go together in a body to the same university so we could continue to develop our band as a unit, in spite of the parents.

Bob Rhynolds was already making plans then to record Mister King. He started collections, via *Down Beat* and some others, to buy King a new horn and some teeth. And he wrote a couple of articles about him for *Down Beat*, telling how at sixteen the old man had played second cornet with Buddy (King) Bolden's Band; how, when they finally carted poor Buddy off to the nut ward, he had apprenticed himself to Freddy (King) Keppard, Buddy's successor; how later, while slow-developing Joe (King) Oliver was still earning his feed as a butler, he had organized the Trip Eagle

Band and with it won himself the title of third King in that dynasty which would die with Joe Oliver in a Savannah poolroom cleaning spittoons. And how finally, when they closed down Storyville in the First War to protect the virtue of the soldiers and sailors, he had disappeared off with a circus band and not been heard from since, mainly because after his horn got busted up in a fight at a dance and the rest of his teeth started to go he was forced to retire to the New Arcadia ricefields where he had started, without the money for a new horn, or for new teeth. And there he stayed for twenty years, until this letter from Rhynolds addressed in care of the New Arcadia postmaster found him, still working in the ricefields.

The story caught the public's imagination, and the response was terrific. A lot of people who were not even jazz fans sent in money for him. Our band would have sent in ten bucks on that horn and them teeth ourself if we had not been so short of cash.

Bob was writing King regularly, because King was giving him the dope about the early days for his book *Jazz-babies*, which was why he contacted King in the first place, but now this other of recording him had taken hold of him, and he published King's thank-you letter in *Down Beat*. King wrote he was very pleased and proud over the response, and that he was excited over the prospect of being able to play again for the audiences of the world, whom, King admitted, he had not even expected would even remember him. He said maybe his hair was gray but the only thing old about him was his clothes. And he was waiting eagerly for the chance to play for all the good people who were helping to get him his teeth and his horn.

By the time the Rhynolds records, which were to create such a stir, finally reached the market, our band had graduated and were playing our second big summer job, at Edmond's Point in Ohio. Our drummer's uncle owned the amusement park there. He talked to the pavilion owner. Edmond's Point was a summer resort on Lake Erie but not of the class of Russel's Point or Cedar Point and they only had the name bands in on the weekends. We did the playing the other four nights of the week.

It was our drummer's mother, together with two of the mothers of our reed section, who had hatched the idea to write the drummer's uncle and appeal to him. They did that after the band had declared itself about to embark for Chicago to seek a summer playing job somewhere down around the vicinity of South State Street.

Actually, it was not nearly as bad as it sounds. Our drummer's uncle hardly ever bothered to check up on us. We could buy all the bottles we wanted. And our two cabins were off by themselves on a spit, so that after we knocked off from work at midnight we could go home and play our own kind of music and jam to our hearts' content without waking up anyone. And of course, we had our records and player.

We bought the Rhynolds records as soon as they were out.

You have to remember we were all serious about the future of jazz music in general, and our own in particular. Coupled to this was the fact that they were important historically. They were the first cuttings ever to be made of King Jefferson's legendary trumpet, and they would provide a lasting link between the lost music of Buddy Bolden and King Oliver's old acoustical recordings from the days of Dreamland and Royal Gardens. We held great expectations for them.

Well, what we heard, sitting there on that screen porch looking out over Lake Erie, was a style of trumpet that was rawer and coarser than any we had known existed, including our own grade school efforts when we first got our horns. Gutty wasn't the right word for it at all. Armstrong played gutty trumpet, with a high polish and technical refinement of guttiness. This trumpet had no polish. It was as unpolished as our bass man's fingernails he had never learned to stop biting. King Oliver's cornet might occasionally sound antiquated to modern jazz ears—mainly because of the old acoustical-type recordings—but always it had a sensitivity of tone and precise originality of phrase that nobody, not even Armstrong, could beat, though he might tie it. This trumpet didn't have that either. This trumpet sounded as if a man whose reflexes had forsaken him was fumbling and choking to get half-remembered things in his head out through the mouth of his horn. And to complete it, there was not a single original phrase in the whole collection of sides. The numbers were all traditional old New Orleans numbers, and the trumpet's treatments of them were the same old trite treatments, solos so ancient they had beards, so hackneyed we all knew every note before it came out the horn. And yet, with all the faults and blunderings, you couldn't deny that there was power in the trumpet, a strong emotional power, that hit you hard.

All this was a pretty big lump for our musical natures to swallow and digest. We were disciples of men like the early Hawk, and Jimmy Archey, and Pops Foster, and Art Hodes, and old Sidney Bechet, mostly men whose music had grown and smoothed out and changed since they left New Orleans. And here we were being asked to appreciate a man whose music had not changed since around 1910. But we made it. Not all in one day, naturally. But by the end of the summer we were ready to admit he was almost as good as Bob Rhynolds maintained he was. Maybe the opinion of the public in general had something to do with it.

Even our reed section who disliked him (led by the saxes, naturally; but also reinforced by the bass and piano) argued against him theoretically, rather than personally. By that I mean, they too had accepted him as a permanence, as a big man in the field who would have to be reckoned with. They would have only sneered at a third-rater, not argued.

The critical opinion didn't agree any better than our band did. Some of the critics, who had previously lauded Bob Rhynolds' re-discovery of King, were frankly shocked and disillusioned, they said. The Opinions ran all the way from the prophecy that King Jefferson would immediately sink back into the obscurity he deserved, to the prophecy that King Jefferson would immediately rise to the top and remain there for good, above Armstrong. Several writers feared King would give jazz the *coup de grace* of cacophony. Others maintained jazz had at last reached the long-awaited fulfillment of its golden promise.

Whatever effect the argumentative reviews had on King himself when he read them, they certainly didn't hurt his popularity any. The general non-jazz public went wild over him. King and his band began to get more engagements in New Orleans than they could handle. A couple of record store owners in L.A. made a trip clear from California to record him under their own label. Another guy, from Pennsy, drove all the way down to New Orleans to record him himself. Before long King was recording right and left, for just about everybody but the big companies.

Our band enrolled en masse in James Millikin at Decatur that fall, majoring in Business Administration, a concession made to our various parents in return for the right to enroll in a body, and continued to follow the Cinderella Story from up there.

For that was what it was. We could see it in the change in our own band. The college kids, instead of asking for swing a la Goodman or Dorsey, at the dances we played, wanted to hear New Orleans a la King Jefferson. It was hard on our saxes, and the bass and piano, but the rest of our people thought it was great.

In the spring King appeared in Frisco with a series of Rudi Blesh jazz lectures, as a sort of living example. He played to an overflow crowd and told them the story of jazz in his own words, and of his happiness at finding so many good people who still liked his music. The critics' Greek chorus immediately swelled in volume, some pointing out that the story of jazz King told wasn't anywhere near the truth, while others pointed out that music in King's soul made him use words like a poet.

Then a small group of rebels, led by Bob Rhynolds naturally, voted him into third place in the *Esquire* Jazz Poll, and he was in.

In January of our sophomore year he played the Jazz Poll Concert from New Orleans. That spring Sidney Bechet brought him up to play with his band at the Savoy in Boston. That didn't last long, but King had stopped off in New York for a sensational jam session at Jimmy Ryan's that made all the trade papers, and appeared on Condon's coast-to-coast program. That fall he and his old band opened at the Standish Casino on the lower East Side. They were an immediate sensation. *Time, The New Yorker, Mademoiselle, Vogue, Esquire,* and the New York papers ran pics and stories on them. *Collier's* ran a full length feature on King and he was interviewed over the local radio stations. At the Standish he was pulling them in, not only the jazz fans but the general public.

Actually, it didn't happen all that quickly. There was a time lag of over a year of hard luck in there, but looking back you tend to forget that. When King went out to Frisco our band were still freshmen at Millikin; when he opened at the Standish we were juniors. But looking back on it it still seems it all happened in one long breathless rush.

Maybe that is because the popularity, when it did come back, came so hard and so strong that it was as if it were not fickle and had never faded, but had instead kept right on growing. New York had taken him into its arms with all its enthusiasm for what is new, and the out-of-towners asked to go to the Standish the first place, when they got in. And in the newspapers he was The King.

Our band was having its own troubles all through that time. It was all right for us during the school year, what with the dance jobs, but during both of those summers the only jobs we could get were dances at the local Moose, Elks and Country Club, and some weekends at Lake Lawler right next to home.

It was the same thing the next year, too, the summer after our junior year at Millikin. The home-rule was, if we couldn't get a regular-paying job playing, we had to work. And when the band wanted to try Chicago on its own again, the parents set their collective foot down on that.

When we went back to school our senior year, we had what amounted to a signed ultimatum. If we could not get the band established as a self-paying proposition during the summer after we graduated, then we would all come home and go into various businesses. Our bass man had an uncle who owned a couple of newspapers in Connecticut, and he promised to use his pull to get the band a job there for the summer, but after that we were on our own. Our parents were financing us for that one summer. We all knew how that would end.

It wasn't much of a deal, but it was all we could get.

The first thing we did when we got our bags unpacked in Stamford, where the job was, was to take in New York. There were only five of us, the others were coming to Stamford in another car and hadn't got in yet. In New York we headed straight for Fifty-second Street. Bechet was playing at Jimmy Ryan's, and we went straight there, without even stopping to look at the strippers' pictures down along The Street, and we did not come out till they closed at four in the morning.

We had hit town on a Saturday night and Ryan's was crammed. There was a fog of beery breath and tobacco smoke that burned your eyes, and so much screaming you could not hear yourself think and had to concentrate hard to even hear Bechet any at all. It was wonderful. We stood at the bar to save money. We were dressed right, cardigans and drapes, double-Windsors and spread collars, and pretty soon some of the cats there had swept us in and we were arguing Mezz Mezzrow, musician versus writer.

We had the best time we'd ever had in our lives. The first time of anything only happens to you once, in your life, I guess.

Maybe there was something significant in the fact that we went straight to Ryan's, to hear Bechet. We did not even consider going to the Standish Casino. King Jefferson was still playing there.

When we left, one of those cats yelled to be sure and come down for the jam session tomorrow.

We knew all about the Jimmy Ryan's Sunday afternoon jam sessions, of course. I mean, we knew they paid the players. And we knew they charged a buck and a half. We knew sidemen didn't just bring their horns down and sit in. In other words, we knew they were commercialized. But we also knew—how well—musicians had to earn a living, too. And hick strangers from the Middle West don't get into the apartments of featured strippers. Or of unfeatured strippers.

We got there early Sunday. The instruments weren't set up yet. A couple of the featured artists were floating around accepting drinks from the cats. The rest weren't there. We bought our tickets, and went across the street to Johnny's Tavern to do our drinking. We had already learned that trick last night. The rest of the featured artists were over there where rye is thirty-five a shot. Ryan's were having Pete Brown on alto, Ed Hall on clarinet, Jerry "Wild Bill" Bailey trumpet, Baby Dodds drums, Pops Foster bass, and somebody else on piano and guitar. By the time we had our drinking done, they had all sifted out and gone back across the street to work and you could hear them clear outside as we crossed the street to Ryan's.

It was during the second break of the afternoon that we saw King Jefferson standing at the bar. We were on our way out to Johnny's to have a drink. King was talking to Baby Dodds about Punch Miller, and we stopped to listen. It was a minute before we noticed Baby was embarrassed and trying real hard not to be constrained. King had his trumpet case under his arm.

"Is Punch Miller in town?" one of us asked.

The King swung around so hard he almost fell over. He was real drunk. "You know old Punch?" he asked eagerly.

"Naw," one of us said. "Just his music. We got some of his records."

"Yeah, he in town. I just telling Baby."

That was when we noticed Baby was gone. He had moved down the vacant bar and was talking to some cats at the other end.

"So you boys know old Punch," King said. "Whyn't you go look old Punch up."

"We don't know him," one of us said. "We just—"

"Here. I give you his address," King said. "He be real glad to see you boys. Old Punch is down and out. He on his uppers, and he sick. That's nowhere to be, not in this New York town." He wrote the address on one of Ryan's cards and handed it to the nearest one of us. "I just telling Baby about old Punch. You go see him."

"We don't know him," one of us said. "We just—"

"Why don't you put your name on it, too, King?" the one who had the card said. "I'd like to have it."

The King's eyes kindled. "You boys know me? Sure, I sign it. Here. Gimme that card."

"Hell yes, we know you," one of us said.

"You ever hear me play?"

"Just on records."

He nodded. "You boys stick around. I going to play here, pretty soon. They didn't ask me, but I going to anyway." He shook the trumpet case at us. "They don't ask ol King no more to these jam sessions. But I just come down anyways. I see you boys." He went off down the bar toward Baby Dodds and the talking cats.

"I'm going to keep this card," our bass man said, shaking it at us, as we crossed the street to Johnny's. "I'm going to keep it forever." He put it in his pocket carefully.

"It don't belong to you," our trumpet man said. "Belongs to the whole band."

"Like hell," the bass man said.

We argued about the card over our series of rye-highs in Johnny's Tavern, without reaching a decision, until we heard them start up again across the street, and then went back over there.

There wasn't any mimimum at the Sunday sessions and we got bottles of beer and moved down to a table as close to the band as we could get. They were already gone and going strong on "Nobody's Sweetheart," with Wild-Bill-Bailey punching out the drive in that surcharged style of his.

King Jefferson was standing in the passageway around the left of the stand to the men's room with his trumpet in his hand. He would play a few bars, low, along with them, and then he'd stop and reach up and pluck at Baby Dodds' shirt sleeve. Baby would look down at his drums embarrassedly until he couldn't any longer, and then he'd look down at King and frown and shake his head and say something, and then smile, with that constrained look of trying not to look constrained on his face embarrassedly. It was bothering his playing. King didn't even leave him alone when he was on his solo choruses. He kept it up all through the set, but Baby never got mad.

Once we saw Wild-Bill-Bailey lean over and say something to the colored guitarman and they both shook their heads and laughed disgustedly. When the set was over, Wild-Bill climbed down and cut out quick. So did Baby and Pops Foster. King Jefferson lingered around the stand, after they were all down, and blew little bleats on that exquisite trumpet as if he were warming up his lip. He would blow a bleat and look around and grin and nod his head and then blow another bleat.

When we came back from Johnny's Tavern and refreshments, they had already started the fourth set and King was standing in the passageway at Baby's elbow again. Finally, about the sixth or seventh set, we came back from Johnny's and he wasn't there any more.

When the jam session was over and Ryan's deserted, we crossed the street to Johnny's Tavern through that almost unbearably melancholy, lonely twilight New York has, to do some drinking and decide where to go for the evening, and to argue some more about the card. We were still sitting at the bar there when King Jefferson came in with his trumpet case under his arm.

He didn't seem to be any drunker. But he wasn't any soberer. He remembered us.

"You boys come on and have a drink with old King."

"Sure," one of us said. "It'll be a privilege."

"We'll be proud to," another of us said.

We seemed to kind of fall into it, the way all the rest of them did, except Wild-Bill-Bailey, humoring him. You couldn't help it.

"Let me show you boys my horn," he said, after we had been served the drink. He got the case down on the floor and squatted by it and lifted the horn out lovingly. It was a beautiful trumpet, inscribed to him. He showed us the inscription.

"They gimme that horn in France," he said. "Las year. They know real music over there. That Mr. Panassié, he a fine man.

"You boys heard my band?"

"Just on records, King," one of us said.

"No, that's my old band. I mean my new band. I got me almost all new boys."

"We've been meaning to hit the Standish, King," one of us said. "But we only got in town last night."

"You don't want to hear it," King said. "Don't come down there. They all good boys, you understand. I like my boys. But they just don't play old King's kind of music. And all the people come they want to dance, not hear old King's kind of music. Have to play dance music. Most all my old boys lef' me. They getting better jobs, see? That's all right. That's fine. You know I the man brought Buddy Ferrill back? He working in a lime kiln in that great old city of New Le'ans. You know Buddy Ferrill?"

"Sure. On records," one of us said. "Bob Rhynolds says he's the greatest jazz drummer ever lived."

"No he aint. Baby Dodds is." The King's eyes kindled. "You boys know Bob Rhynolds?"

"We just read about him," one of us said. "We never met him."

"He my good friend," King smiled at us proudly. "Bob Rhynolds my old buddy." He put the horn back into its case lovingly and looked at it and then rubbed the bell with a piece of flannel and closed the case. "I got to go, boys. Got to go to work pretty soon."

We all stood up. "We'll be down and see your band later on tonight, King," one of us said.

"You don't want to see my band. It a good band. They all good boys. But they aint like the old band, and they never going to be. Old King wouldn't lie to you. I can tell you boys know good jazz. Don't you boys come down.

"Boys," he said, "I'd like to pay for this drink. But thas all the money I got." He turned his pants pocket out; there was seventy cents in change in it. "I made a lot of money in this town, but I spending it just as fast."

"That's okay, King," one of us said. "We'll get it."

"I surely thank you boys," he said. "You boys write Bob Rhynolds, you tell him old King asking after him. I be seeing you boys sometime."

We watched him leave, the trumpet case tight under his arm. Then we paid for his drink.

Bechet was off that night and Ryan's had some other band so we ended up at Bop City. Louis Armstrong's All-Stars were playing at Bop City, and we had heard a lot about their young bassman, Arvel Shaw. He was as good as they said, too.

I guess it was about a year or so later—anyway, we were all back home, in business—that there was a little piece in *Down Beat* that said King Jefferson was anxious to hear from any of his old friends across the country or people who had seen him play and he would answer any letters faithfully. The address was New Arcadia, Louisiana.

That was the first we'd heard about his not being renewed at the Standish, and it shocked us. We'd always thought of him as a perennial. The five of us who'd met him agreed to write him a long newsy letter, but something else came up before we got a chance to do it, and we figured a lot of other people, people he knew really well, would write him.

It was probably a year after that, maybe two, before *Down Beat* mentioned him again. They gave him a double column spread and used his picture, his best one, the one that was on his first Victor album. It was a good writeup. I had read the obits for both Fats Waller and Johnny Dodds, and it was as good as them.

A lot of us musicians felt his death, personally. I remember I was sitting in the Rec Hall poolroom on the Square, when I first read it. It was Tuesday and the new issue had just come in up at the newsstand. I had taken my morning-break-for-coffee at the store and used it to beat it over and get my copy. Tom Myers, our old band's bassman, and I always took our morning breaks to get our copies when they came out and read them in the Rec Hall with a bottle of coke, where it was quiet. Other mornings we would go to

Adams's Drugstore and have coffee at the fountain like the other peasants.

Tom came in from his father's insurance office just as I finished reading it. Tom had already seen it on his way down from the newsstand. Both of us felt pretty somber, and we sat and talked about him so long we were both late getting back to work. We both felt the world had lost something pretty important, a piece of jazz history. No matter what the critics said, he had been important, a big man, a landmark. He was a great jazzman. Tom said he still had the signed card the King had given him that time at Ryan's, had it with his music stuff somewhere.

"It ought to be worth something some day, don't you think?"

"Sure," I said, "I don't see why not."

"You going to be to City Band practice tonight?"

"I don't know. Marcia's been having trouble with the baby. She's been sick. But I'll try and make it."

"How's the other one?"

"The boy? Oh, he's over it already."

"You ought to make it if you can."

"I'll try," I said.

"—You know, we met a great jazzman, when we met King Jefferson," Tom said, as we left.

"We sure did," I said. "There won't be no more like him."

SHELBY FOOTE

Ride Out

JAZZ RUNS THROUGH most of Shelby Foote's work that deals with contemporary scenes, and it would not be surprising if some day he put his talents to a full-length novel about a jazz musician. This is such a long story it could almost be called a short novel; indeed, it was called a short novel in a paper-backed collection. In that one, it was longer. The full length version appeared in Foote's novel, Jordan County and was called "Ride Out." Here we are using the version that originally appeared in The Saturday Evening Post, where it was called "Tell Them Good-by." Foote is the author of Tournament, Shiloh, Follow Me Down, Love in a Dry Season and Jordan County. Our use of this story represents the sole attempt to interfere on the part of the Dial Press management. George Joel was the first to publish Shelby, and recommended that we pick up this story. After reading it, we agreed that the interference was not only painless but justified.
—R. G.

The state executioner had set up the portable electric chair in a cell on the lower floor, and now he was testing his circuits. A cable ran from the chair, like a long dusty blacksnake, through the window bars to the generator in the truck parked in the cool October darkness outside the jail. Whenever the switch clicked there was a pulsing hum and an odor of heated copper in the cell. The turnkey, who had helped to install the chair, watched the cable as if he expected it to writhe like a pressure hose with each surge of current, but it lay in loose coils without motion.

Low and wide, with heavy arms and legs, the chair had an unfinished look, as if the workman—a clusmy copyist of pieces from the Louise Seize period—had dropped his tools and walked away. It had been built six months before by a New Orleans electrician who had stipulated that he was to receive no profit from the job. The executioner was more philosophical; he referred to it as "my old shocking chair."

His name was Luke Jeffcoat. Deep lines extended from the wings of his nose to the corners of his mouth. A tall thin man of about forty, he worked now in his undershirt. Tattooed snakes ran down his arms and spread their heads on the backs of his hands. He hummed as he worked, his voice curiously like the hum of the generator, low and on a single note.

Presently three men came into the cell. The first two, the sheriff and myself—I am county physician—were required by law to be there, but the third man, the district attorney, came of his own accord, "to see this thing I'll be sending them to," he said.

The sheriff jerked his thumb toward the window.

"Who are those people out there?" he asked the turnkey.

Under a bug-swirled arc light fifty yards down the alley, a man and a woman sat hunched with long waiting on the seat of a wagon. The two gray mules dozed, and there was a long pine box like a pale shadow in the bed of the wagon.

"It's his mamma," the turnkey said. "She rented a dray and bought a box to take him home in. They been there since about midnight. Just after they got here, I went up and took the horn away from him."

"How is he?"

"I think he went to sleep. Hoskins is up there."

The sheriff took out his watch, a big one with a gold hunting case. He opened it, then snapped it shut.

"Three-thirty," he said morosely. "Where is Doc Benson?"

"He told me he'd be here by three," I said. "But it really doesn't matter, does it?"

"The law says two doctors, and we'll have two doctors." The sheriff shook his head, a big man with wattles like a turkey cock. "Damn these new-fangled inventions, anyhow. The old rope and trap door suited me fine."

We heard the quick, tearing sound of tires on gravel, then an automobile door being slammed. Doctor Benson came in. "Sorry I'm late," he said. "Got held up."

"It's all right," I said. "We aren't ready anyhow."

Jeffcoat threw the switch for the final test, and again there was that pulsing hum and the odor of heated copper. Then he went to the washstand in the corner, soaped his hands, rinsed them under the tap, and dried them carefully, on his undershirt.

"All right, sheriff," he said. "I'm ready if he is."

It may be that I had seen him before, but as far as I know—since, with his shaved head and his slit trousers, he probably did not resemble himself anyway—my first sight of him was when they brought him into the cell a few minutes later. During the past six years I have learned his story, and I intend to set it down in a straightforward manner from beginning to end. I saw only the closing scene, but four people who knew him well have given me the particulars—his mother, who is a cook in this town; Blind Bailey, a pianist in a local Negro dance hall; Pearly Jefferson, the New Orleans jazz musician; and Harry Van, the New England composer. In many cases I have merely transcribed my notes of conversations with these four persons, but to avoid cluttering my narrative with footnotes, I wish to state my obligations at the outset. And now, having done so, I will set it down, as I have said, from birth to death.

He was born in a time of high water, the stormy May of 1913, in a Red Cross tent on the levee at the foot of the main street of Bristol, Mississippi. His mother, whose name was Nora, was fifteen the month before. The birth was not due until six weeks later, but in the excitement of being herded with three hundred other Negroes onto the only high ground within seventy miles—save for the Indian mounds which dotted the Delta, relics of aboriginal times—she became alarmed and the pains came on her. In a steady rain, while water purled up the levee toward where she lay on a strip of salvaged awning, she moaned and bellered through five hours of labor. When the flood reached the level of the river on the other side, and therefore ceased its advance up the levee, the child was born.

From an adjoining camp of white refugee families someone sent her a paper sack of store candy. When the midwife had swaddled the child in clean burlap and placed it beside her, she was quite content, holding her son against her breast and dissolving a lemon drop in her cheek, but she wished the father was there.

His name was Boola Durfee, a tall, flat-chested man from the lower Delta, son of a freedwoman and a half-breed Choctaw blacksmith. Nora was with him only one week, in September of the year before, when the big warm moon of late summer glazed the fields and the tin roofs of the churches and dance halls where he played engagements while she waited outside.

A gaunt, high-cheekboned man, he had no home; he roamed the country, with his guitar and his songs. "I got a itchy heel," he warned her. "Some morning, baby doll, you'll wake up and find me gone."

That was the way it turned out. Four days later she woke with the sun on her face and found herself alone on the pallet bed. For the next ten years she would hear people mention having seen him, sometimes in far places, sometimes near by, still playing for what he called "sukey jumps," but she made it a point never to ask about him. Then she heard that he had been killed in a knife fight in Natchez-under-the-Hill.

She gave the child its father's name, Durfee, for a first name, and attached her family name, Conway, for a surname.

Durfee became Duffy, which was shortened to Duff, and that was how he came to be called Duff Conway.

After the water went down, she got a job as maid in a banker's house, and when the cook left three years later, Nora took her place. She lived alone with her child in a two-room cabin in that section of Bristol known as Lick Skillet. When she had saved twelve dollars she bought a mail-order pistol, a big nickel-plated one, which she kept in a bureau drawer in the front room near her bed, so that she could turn to it in time of trouble, as other women would turn to a man.

Aborted into a flooded world, Duff was undersized and sickly, solemn as a papoose. The red in his skin was like a warning sign to Nora; if the boy could inherit the Choctaw pigment and the high cheekbones, she thought, he might also inherit the guitar-calloused thumb and the itchy heel. So she kept him by her, in her cabin, at church and at the banker's house, where at first she swaddled him in a crib on the back porch and later propped him on a chair in one corner of the kitchen itself. He passed the waking hours of his early childhood amid a clatter of pots and pans and in an atmosphere of spice and frying food. Perched on the tall straight-back chair, his feet suspended with that ungulate and analgesic quality of children's feet, ten inches clear of the floor, then six inches, then two inches, then touching it, and he was seven and Nora enrolled him in school.

Young enough herself to be mistaken for one of the girls in the upper grades, she would take him there every morning and call for him every afternoon. "You going to amount to something," she told him. "Study hard and stay away from riffraff."

On an April afternoon when Duff was in the fifth grade, Nora missed him among the children trooping out of school. She went back to work, and when she came home that night he was in bed asleep. She shook him awake.

"Where you been?" He rubbed his eyes with his fists.

"Let me 'lone."

"Where you been all day?"

"Let me 'lone, mamma. I'm sleepy."

"Sleepy!" She shook him. "Where you been, boy?" Then she whipped him. But he cried himself to sleep without telling her anything, and four days later it happened again.

This time she went looking for him. On Bantam Street, in the red-light district, she saw a crowd of Negroes, mostly silk-shirted sports and their over-dressed women. They were gathered so closely that Nora could not see what they were watching, but she heard strange music. She elbowed her way toward the center and saw four small boys performing on four outlandish instruments—a jug, a banjo made from a cigar box and a length of lath, a jew's harp, and a set of drums invented from a battered suitcase top and a saw horse and three stove lids.

Duff was the drummer. He sat on an upended cracker box, drumming steadily with two chair rungs. He was entering a solo break—his head turned sideways down near one shoulder, his eyes closed tight, his lower lip sucked between his teeth—when Nora caught him by the arm, hauled him off the box and snatched him through the crowd.

"Wait up, mamma!" he wailed, straining back toward the crowd and waving the chair rungs. "I got to get my drums!"

Nora shook him till his teeth rattled. "Wait till I get you home," she said. "I'll drum you."

He was twelve the following month. For nearly two years after the Bantam Street incident it was a contest between mother and son, she trying the only way she knew to keep him from becoming what his father had been, and he revolting against being tied to her apron strings. The four-piece band had been formed at school by the boy who played the cigar-box banjo. At first they would practice during noon recess, but after a while that was not enough. They began to cut school, and then they went professional, playing on street corners for nickles and dimes and an occasional quarter. Late at night, after Nora was asleep, Duff would slip away to Bantam Street.

At the largest of the places, a two-story building known as the Mansion House, there was music every night by a blind pianist famous all over the Delta. His name was Blind Bailey, an enormous old man who had played on showboats until the days when vaudeville and motion pictures drove them off the river. Duff liked him best, but he came to know them all. He would sit under barrel-house windows, listening to ragtime piano and rare three and four man groups, and the next day he would teach the songs to the three other members of his sidewalk band, drumming the rhythm and humming the melody. This way he developed a sizable repertory of the songs which remained his favorites always, the old river-boat and New Orleans classics, "Eagle Rock Rag," "Ostrich Walk" and "Creole Belles"; "Hilarity Rag," "San" and

"Chattanooga Stomp." Just before dawn he would slip back into the cabin and crawl into bed without waking his mother.

The contest between mother and son ended with an event which took him beyond her control. He was indicted by the grand jury for burglary and larceny, arraigned by the district attorney, and tried by the circuit court. On a plea of guilty, while Nora wept into her handkerchief, he was sentenced to be placed in reform school for an indefinite period.

He had been saving his fourth of the coins ever since the day he saw a set of drums in the show window of an uptown music shop. When he had accumulated nearly four dollars in loose change, which he carried in a tobacco sack worn on a string around his neck, he felt qualified to price the drums. He chose a quiet time, when there was no one in the store except the proprietor.

A loose-jointed man with steel-rim spectacles and a receding chin, he sat at a desk in the rear, reading a newspaper. He looked up with a startled expression when Duff said, "How much you ax for them drums in the window?"

"Don't sneak up on me like that, boy." He looked over the newspaper at Duff. His eyes seemed to bulge and recede, goitrous behind heavy lenses. "That's a fine set of drums," he said.

"Yes, sir, sho is."

"You want to buy them, or are you just curious?"

"I want to buy them," Duff said. He unbuttoned his shirt and took out the tobacco sack.

"They're seventy-eight dollars and fifty cents," the proprietor said.

"Thank you, sir," Duff said. He returned the sack and buttoned his shirt carefully. "I be back."

He was short seventy-four dollars and thirty cents. Three nights later he got a chance to do something about it. At the Mansion House—he had graduated from hiding under the window to hear the music; now he came onto the porch to listen—he met a boy about four years older than himself. The boy asked Duff if he wanted to earn some easy money.

"How?" Duff said.

"Take it," the stranger said.

RIDE OUT

"Take it how?"

"Through a window. How you reckon?"

It would be easy, the boy said. All Duff had to do was stand outside the house and whistle if anyone came along. They would split the take. "Fifty-fifty," the stranger said.

"Will it come to seventy-five dollars?"

"Ought to, easy."

"I'm game," Duff said.

But when he turned and saw the policeman coming toward him, his mouth went dry and all he could manage was a faint, low whistle. It was enough, however; the other guy got away. A neighbor had seen them and had telephoned the police.

At the arraignment, the district attorney gave Duff every chance, but all he could do was repeat what he had told the police. He did not know who the stranger was; he could not even give a description of him.

"All right, boy," the district attorney said. "If that's the way you want it." He was a dark man with hard eyes. In circuit court he recommended that Duff be placed in the state reform school until such time as the authorities would declare it safe to return him to society. The judge so ordered.

In custody of a white deputy, Duff and four other Negro boys rode across the flat dark Delta and into the brown loam and loess hills where scrub pine grew and knee-high cotton stalks stood bare in the November rain. It was his first train ride, and he enjoyed it. When they arrived at the reform school that afternoon, it was still raining, a slow steady drizzle which ran down their faces like tears.

The reform school was an all-Negro institution, visited yearly by a group of white politicians on their inspection tour. It was a low gray building of weathered clapboard—a short dog run with a narrow gallery connecting two deep ells, one the prisoners' dormitory, with swinging oil lamps and three-decked bunks along the walls, so that it resembled the crew's quarters in the fo'c'sle of a sailing ship; the other the prisoners' mess and an apartment for the warden and his family—set back from a gray, hard-picked, grassless yard like a surface of zinc, and surrounded by a high wire fence which in the dull light had the flat, deadly glint of gun metal. "Here you are," the deputy said. None of the boys said anything.

They were left in the dormitory on their first day, but the following day they went to the field. Breaking ground for the planting season, Duff learned to run a straight furrow behind the straining cruppers of his mules, to wear the lines looped like a long necklace as he walked, and to reverse the plow with a quick lifting motion as the mules came about at the end of a row. He liked it—the work and the queer, trembling feeling of fatigue which came when he lay on his bunk after lights-out.

Sundays were best. Five of the prisoners had formed an orchestra, and every Sunday afternoon they would play on the gallery from two o'clock till sundown. Duff became friendly with the drummer, a light skinned boy from the piney hills, and was allowed to sit in on an occasional number.

"You pretty good," the drummer said. "But you don't hold the sticks right. Looky here." He rolled a long, pulsing snare passage. "Try it." Duff tried it. "Yair," the drummer said. "That's more like it. But look. Keep your wrists up. Like this."

"Something must be wrong with me," Duff said. "I get it all right, but it don't come out right on the skin. I keep wanting something I can pick up on."

It was six months before he got what he was wanting. Then the cornetist died. There was no one to claim his effects, so the warden divided them among the prisoners.

"I've seen you watching him," he told Duff. "Here. See you can learn to blow it."

Duff took the cornet with both hands. It was heavier than he had expected, dull gray like old silver, nicked and battered along the column and at the bell. He held it against his chest, walking back to the dormitory. This was Sunday, and he sat on the side of his bunk all afternoon, learning to blow it. He found he could control the sound by pushing down on the valves, but it was doubly difficult because they would stick and he had to learn also to pull them up again. He was still there and he was still trying when the others came from supper and began to undress for lights-out. Then he lay quietly in the dark, with his lips pursed, imagining he was practicing.

Two Sundays later he joined the other musicians on the gallery. At first he just blared the horn, backing the other players as if the cornet were a rhythm instrument, but soon he learned to follow the musical line. By the end of the month he was beginning to lead the way, the horn riding rough and loud above the others, and by the end of the year there would be quiet large groups in the reform-school yard, their dark faces lifted toward the musicians on the gallery. They came from miles around, their wagons and dusty automobiles parked hub to hub in a field beyond the road, and sat from a little after two o'clock until well past sundown and into the gathering dusk, when the supper bell would clang, strident and insistent, and the breakup would follow, the boy prisoners going into the low, rambling building, and the visitors dispersing to their wagons and cars across the road.

"That was playing, warn't it now?"

"Sho was. How 'bout that horn?"

"Man! That boy plays that thing!"

"He sho does!"

The warden arranged Saturday-night engagements for them, driving them to Jackson and near-by communities for dances and barbecues. Within a year of the time Duff was committed, the reform-school band was well known in that part of the state. They were offered more invitations than they could fill.

The drummer was nominal leader of the group—they called themselves the Noxubee High Hat Rhythm Kings, in memory of the dead cornetist, who had been sentenced from Noxubee County for manslaughter—but Duff was leader once the music got under way. The others followed his loud, blary horn on every song. They had no other style. They played the things Duff had learned while crouching beneath Bantam Street windows, the old New Orleans river-boat songs which had been great before the boys were born.

"Thump," the drum would beat once, and the others would go right into it. There was no vamping, no announcing of theme, no quiet introduction to set the mood. It came out full and uninhibited, the cornet riding high and wide, the other instruments falling in behind like dry leaves sucked into the rearward vacuum of a speeding truck.

"Man, man," the drummer said once between pieces. "Where you get all that power?"

Duff looked down at the horn in his lap. "I don't know," he said. "In my throat, I reckon."

When he came home in early fall, nearly two years after the train ride with the deputy, there were chocolate bands on houses and trees from the great flood of 1927. In some of the cabins there was soft yellow silt on the beams, left there when the water went down. An abandoned skiff bleached in the yard next to Nora's, derelict, with its painter still tied to the steps. Four children sat in it, their dark faces grave with pretense. Playing steamboat.

It was late afternoon. Waiting for Nora to come home, he sat on the steps holding a paper-wrapped parcel in his lap. When he lay back on the porch floor, the children's voices faded, as if the boat were indeed bearing them away, then passed completely out of hearing. When he opened his eyes, the sun was gone and bull bats were flying and he was looking up into his mother's face.

"Hello, mamma," he said. "I fell asleep waiting on you."

"Get up, boy, before you catch your death of cold." She watched him quietly. "You had your supper?"

"No'm. I ain't eat since I left Moorhead this morning."

He stood up, carrying the parcel. As he limped across the porch toward the door, Nora saw that the fronts were cut out of his shoes. "What's the matter with your feet?"

"Corns," he said. "I got them plowing."

Looking back at Duff as he walked gingerly across the front room, Nora said, "Plowing. Well. Maybe that place done you some good after all."

"Yessum."

"Leastways you won't be breaking in people's homes again real soon, will you?"

"No'm."

Duff sat at the kitchen table, the parcel again in his lap. Nora went to the cupboard and began putting biscuits and cold bacon on a plate. Over her shoulder she said, "What you got in the package?"

"It's my horn," Duff said. "The warden gave it to me."

"Horn? What kind of horn?"

"A horn, mamma, that you blow. It's a cornet, like in a band; to make music with."

Nora halted, the plate in her hand. Then she came forward quietly and put the food on the table before him. "I'll shake up the stove and perc you some coffee," she said.

Duff would be fifteen in May, five feet, nine inches tall and weighing a hundred and thirty pounds, within half an inch and ten pounds of all the height and weight he would ever have, though in later years the wedged shoes and padded suits would raise and broaden him, just as the perfumed grease would straighten the kinky hair which now fitted his head like a thick woolly skull-cap. His eyes were black, with slightly yellowed whites, and his mouth was broad, with even white teeth and bluish lips and gums. His arms and legs were thin and gangling, but his hands and feet were small. His voice was low and he spoke so softly that people often had to ask him to repeat his words.

When he left after supper, he carried the horn with him. At four o'clock in the morning Nora heard a fumbling at the door. She reached for the handle of the bureau drawer where she kept her pistol. Then the door came open, and it was Duff. As he passed her bed on the way to his cot in the kitchen, she saw that he still carried the horn.

"You act like that thing is part of you, boy. Where you been till all hours of the night?"

"I got a job, mamma."

"What doing?"

"Playing this." He held up the cornet. "It's at the Mansion on Bantam Street. I get a dollar a night."

So this time the contest was brief, was over before Nora had time to plan her campaign. He had outgeneraled her so quickly that it ended almost as soon as it began. She lay back and pulled the quilt over her face.

As he stood there waiting, she spoke through the cloth. "Go on to bed," she said.

Now it was Duff who was on the inside, screened by swirling dancers and curtained by stale smoke, making the wild Masion House music while other boys crouched outside the window, as he had done three years before, to hear the musicians they were too young to approach. Blind Bailey was there every night, but the others were transients. Guitar, saxophone, drums or banjo, they never stayed longer than a week. Usually Duff and the enormous old pianist were alone, the two of them a study in contrast. Blind Bailey was gray-haired and wore blue-lensed spectacles and a box-back blue-serge suit. He affected a high celluloid collar and a narrow tie, and he kept a flat whisky pint on the upright. He weighed just under three hundred pounds, with skin so black that it glistened as he sat straight-backed, punching the keyboard with his big hands, the fingers dark and boneless like sausages. Duff was years younger than anyone else in the house. He wore denim trousers, faded sky-blue, and an open-neck shirt. Sitting with his legs crossed and his body hunched over the silver horn, he kept his eyes closed tight against the yellow glare of the light bulb suspended naked on a cord from the ceiling.

When the whisky was good and the music went to suit him, Blind Bailey would sing. They were meaningless songs, without connected thought, and sometimes even without words. He would begin bouncing on the over-sized bench which had been made for his weight, then throw back his head and holler:

"Shake it up, break it up,
Throw it on the wall!"

and then go off into a language all his own, mostly shouts and moans, punctuated with growls and hisses, like an enraged sea lion. Duff learned to conform to these voice improvisations note for note with his cornet, and they were the basis for the spectacular art of his later years.

He played at the Mansion House for two years and a half. A little after two o'clock one cold February morning, a group of young Negroes came laughing and shouting into the dance room. They wore unseasonal white flannel trousers, blue-and-white-striped jackets and two-tone shoes. They were bandsmen from an excursion steamer which had stopped at the Bristol wharf for a moonlight dance. The steamer was lying over till morning because of ice and debris on the river, and the musicians had come ashore to make the rounds of the Bantam Street houses.

They danced with the girls and listened to the music for an hour. Then they went on, taking most of the girls with them. They had been gone half an hour when Blind Bailey began to strum "The Farewell Blues." When it was ended, Duff held the spit valve open and blew out the cornet, and Blind Bailey rapped on the piano lid to waken the boy who slept behind it every night until time to guide the old man home by the coat sleeve.

The moon had risen late. As Duff came down the steps, it shone bright and cold on the flannel trousers and gaudy jacket of one of the steamer bandsmen who stood on the sidewalk, holding out his hand in greeting.

"Howdy do," he said. "I've been waiting to see you. I'd have seen you inside, but I make it a practice never to talk business with regard to hiring a musician while he is actually engaged in playing for someone else. Excuse my glove." Duff felt cold, soft leather against his palm. "My name is Jefferson," the bandsman said. "Pearly Jefferson, they call me." He paused.

"Glad to meet you," Duff said.

"Likewise. Would you like a drink somewhere?"

"I generally get me a cup of coffee at the All Night Café. It's just up the street a piece."

"Fine," Jefferson said. "I'll join you."

Over the coffee, with the same high-flown garrulity he had used in greeting Duff outside the Mansion House, he explained that his orchestra had lost its horn man on Beale Street in Memphis two nights ago.

"I like your tone," he said. "With a little polish, I think you'll fit right in."

There were only two hours before the steamer was to take in her stage plank. When Duff wakened Nora and told her he was leaving, she sat up in bed, clutching the quilt under her chin.

"I can't understand you, boy," she said, shaking her head. "How come you want to run off with strange people?"

Duff kept his eyes on his shoes. "I want to make something out of myself, mamma."

"Humph. You just want to play that scand'lous music; that's all you want. Why'n't you stay home and play it?"

"They going to pay me twenty dollars a week, mamma."

"And what's the good of that," she said. "You'll just spend it on canned peaches and sardines and cigars and suchlike."

"I got to go."

"You ain't got to nothing."

"Yessum, I have. I got to."

She waited a moment, watching him. Then she said quietly, "All right; if you got to, you got to. I ain't holding you."

The stage plank was taken in on schedule. The side wheels thrashed the water, backing the steamer away from the wharf. Then the whistle screamed, steam precipitating onto the deck like rain, and the paddles reversed, driving the boat ahead on the forward slope of a self-made, churning wave. From the rail Duff watched Bristol shrink and fade in the pale light of the winter dawn. When he was a mile downriver, the sun came up big and red, and as the steamboat rounded the bend he looked back and saw the town gleaming blood-red for an instant, buildings and water towers burgeoning in flame. Then, apparitionlike, as the trees along the Arkansas bank swept across it like a green curtain, it was gone.

That night they played Vicksburg, then Natchez, then Baton Rouge, and within a week they were in New Orleans. Duff made two trips on the excursion steamer, to and from St. Louis and fifty river towns along the way. He had the flannel trousers and the coat of many colors now, but he could not wear the two-tone shoes, because the owner of the boat would not allow him to slit them for his corns. Pearly Jefferson taught him to read music and featured him on a share of the songs. In Memphis, Duff bought a new cornet, a golden horn with easy valves and a bright glitter like new money.

After the second trip, Jefferson, who played piano, persuaded Duff to join him on a job in a New Orleans' river-front dance hall near the French Quarter. With four other musicians—drums, trombone, clarinet and bass—they formed a group known as Pearly Jefferson's Basin Six. As a group, the Basin Six probably were not so good as some of the cultists nowadays declare in their volumes on jazz. They were late in the tradition, too late for the "carving contests" held on street corners in the days when rival bands played to attract the public to their respective dance halls and cafés; too late for the days when a band advertised its music by driving around town in a wagon, the musicians hunched in the bed between the pianist, who faced forward against the driver's seat, and the trombone man, who faced rear and moved his slide over the tail gate.

But, late or early, they were in the tradition. They played the same songs for people who had heard them in the old days and they knew musicians who had grown old in the trade, men who had sat on the same rostrum with Buddy Dubray and Cleaver Williams and were willing to talk about it. Duff's four years in New Orleans were not the years of his greatest music, but they did more than other years to develop his final tone and style. Backed by the teachings of Blind Bailey, they were the years which made him what he was when, later, musicians who were supposed to know called him the best horn man of his time.

In March of 1935 he accepted a job with Rex Ingersoll in New York. A tall, handsome Negro with sideburns and a hair-line mustache, Ingersoll was called "the crown prince of jazz" in advertisements for the motion pictures and radio programs which featured him. In New Orleans two weeks before, he had heard Duff play and had talked with him for half an hour. He had been interested in the Basin Six treatment of "Maple Leaf Rag" and had paid Pearly Jefferson a hundred dollars for what he called the "arrangement." From New York he telegraphed Duff an offer of two hundred and fifty dollars a week. Duff packed his bag and took the first train north.

Ingersoll took him to a tailor and had him measured for half a dozen suits. "We'll get that out of the way first," he said. Then he took him to rehearsal. Afterward he said, "Duff, you really blow that thing. It's great. But it's a little different up here. On those passages that belong to you, go right on and ride it out. Like I say, it's great. But other times you have to hold back and melt into the others. See what I mean?"

"Play it soft?"

"Yair, background it."

"All right, Rex."

He tried to do as he was told, and two weeks later Ingersoll spoke to him again about it. "We got to take some of the blare out of it. I think it's great, and if I had my way I'd let you loose all the time. But we got to keep the icks happy."

Duff tried this time too. He kept right on trying, right up to the day when he could not even try any longer. Two years later he explained it this way:

"He told me to hold back on it, and I tried, but sometimes I couldn't. So Rex put a mute in the horn and hung a tin derby over the end of it. That was all right, then. Rex said it was fine. Maybe it was, to listen to. But my wind backed up on me. What was supposed to be coming out the other end got choked back down my throat. I like to bust. Rex liked it, but it got me so wrought up I couldn't sleep. I'd sit up mornings, trying to woodshed it out of me, but that didn't help much. So one night I stayed home.

"When Rex came round next day, I told him how it was. He said I was wrong. He said music wasn't only for the ones that played it. It was for the ones that listened to it, too, he said, and it was up to us to give it to them the way they wanted it. That sounded reasonable. I figured he was right, being top man in the big time and all that. I figured he wasn't clearing three hundred thousand a year without knowing what was right.

"And Lord knows I wanted to stay; all that money and high living, I like it well as the next man. But I couldn't. I would have if I could, but I couldn't."

Next day a drummer he had worked with in New Orleans came to see him. The drummer said, "I heard you left Rex. What you planning to do now?"

"I don't know," Duff said. "Go back home, I reckon."

"Ain't no sense in that, man. You just got here. Look. This friend of mine is opening a place here in Harlem—you know, a gin-mill affair, nothing special. You'd be playing for cakes at first. But come on in with us and we'll make us some music like it ought to be made."

"I don't know, Joe. Seems like my horn don't suit this town. Rex ought to know."

"It'll suit this place. Come on."

There were no tin derbies at the Black Cat, no mutes, no music stands spelling R E X in neon. Opening night, the following Saturday, everything that had been pent up in him for the past six weeks seemed to come out loud and clear. From that first night it got better, and six months later he hit his stride.

"I don't know how it happened," he told Harry Van later, looking back on it. "It seemed like the horn kind of opened up and everything I ever learned came sailing out."

Harry Van had never heard jazz before, not to listen to. It was something he accepted, in the same way a person might accept Joyce or Brancusi, admitting there might be something there and even admitting it was probably sincere, but never caring to study it or give it any real attention. He was twenty-seven then, just beginning to compose the things he had always hoped he would find himself equipped to do—music which was intellectual in concept and execution, with intricate chromatic weavings. He believed he was beginning to find himself. Nothing had interrupted this belief until the night his harmony instructor took him to a Harlem night club.

Over the doorway there was an arched cat with green electric eyes and a bristling tail. The instructor rapped at the door, and a panel opened inward upon a face so black that the eyeballs glistened unbelievably white. The Negro showed an even row of gold teeth when he recognized the harmony instructor. "Evening, professor," he said, and the door swung open, revealing a dingy anteroom and another door. When the second door was opened, they were struck by a violent wave of sound, the ride-out finish of "China Boy," followed by one thump of the drum and an abrupt cessation which left a silence so empty that it, too, seemed to strike them across their faces like an open palm.

On a low dais in an opposite corner there was a five-man group —drums, piano, cornet, clarinet, saxophone—seen dimly through smoke which hung like cotton batting, acrid and motionless, about the small round tables where people sat drinking from heavy cups. Van looked for other instruments, incredulous that all that sound had come from five musicians. As they were being seated, the drum set a new beat, pulsing unvaried; the clarinet began to squeal, trilling arpeggios with frantic hysteria; the saxophone thumped; the cornet gave tentative notes; the piano brought out "One Hour" for eight bars and subsided into the general rhythm of sustained chords. Then it happened.

The cornet man, whose skin had the reddish tint of cocoa, took a chorus alone. Wearing a white polo shirt, high-waisted tan trousers and shoes with the fronts hewn out, he sat with his legs crossed, the snub horn bunched against his face, his eyes closed and his head held down so that, through the early bars, he appeared to be blowing the music into the floor. His playing was restrained; it sounded almost effortless. But seeing him, Van got the impression that the musician was generating a tremendous pressure only to release a small part of it. Toward the close of the chorus, as if the pressure had reached that point toward which he was working, the player lifted his head, the cornet rising above his face, and the leashed energy seemed to turn loose all at once, riding powerfully above what had gone before. It approached that point at which hearing would renege, that farthest boundary of the realm of sound, soaring proud and unvanquishable beyond the restraint of all the music Van had ever known.

The harmony instructor left soon after midnight, but Van was there when dawn paled the hanging smoke. He went home, ate breakfast, walked the quiet morning streets for an hour, and went to class. Looking back on it, that day had the unreal quality of a dream. It was not until two hours after dark, when he passed through the tandem doors of the Black Cat for the second time, that the dreamlike state ended and the actual living world returned.

He was early. The tables were bare and last night's smoke had dispersed. Four of the musicians were there, sitting at a table in a far corner, their instruments on the floor beside their chairs. Soon the crowd began to arrive, and when the room was a little less than half filled, one of the musicians mounted the dais and sat at the piano. Again it was like no music Van had ever heard before; again it was without melody or rhythm, just a vague tinkling in which the black keys seemed to predominate, a strumming such as might have been done by a performing animal, except that there was a certain intelligence in the touch, a tonal sentience beyond Van's comprehension.

The clarinetist arrived. White, about forty years old, with a neat pale tonsure, he resembled a dentist or a haberdasher's clerk. As he crossed the room he took the instrument from the case beneath his arm and began assembling it. He stepped onto the dais without breaking his stride, halted behind the piano, and began to play the shrill, sliding runs of the night before. The three others came forward together, and during the saxophone break Van recognized the melody and realized he had been hearing it all along, even when the piano first stated the theme. It was "I Never Knew," which had been popular at dances in his undergraduate days.

He was there for the closing this second night too. The following day he cut his classes, but he stayed away from the Black Cat that night. Something is happening to me he thought, alone in his room, unable to sleep after the day of idleness. Something is happening that means everything I've done adds up to nothing. I've got to start all over again. He kept remembering the tone of the cornet, recalling whole passages of improvisation by the cocoa-colored Negro. It was incredible that a man could improvise the music he had heard. Maybe he can't even read notes, Van thought. Maybe he came here from a cornfield somewhere, just dropped the hoe and took up the horn and played what his grandfather played in the jungle a hundred years ago.

The next night he found that some of this was wrong. The cornetist could read notes, for one thing. His name was Duff Conway. He had come up from New Orleans two years before, and already he had made a name for himself. Van learned this from an enthusiastic young man who sat at an adjoining table. He had a crew haircut and explained casually, but with an edge of pride, that he was a writer for *Platter*, a trade magazine published by a record manufacturer.

"That's the most horn in the world," he said. "I thought everybody interested in music knew Duff." He spoke a racy jargon which Van could not always follow, and he had a habit of pacing the music by tapping the table with his palm and humming "du-dud du-dud" through his teeth, with a rhythm which Van thought did not always conform to that of the musicians on the dais.

During a break in the music the young man brought the

cornetist to Van's table. "You've been asking about him, so I thought I'd bring him over. Comb them all—Fifty-second Street, and Loop. Twelfth Street in K.C., anywhere you please—you won't find a horn man like this one. Mind what I'm telling you."

"I'm pleased to meet you," Van said.

"Same here," Duff said.

He was twenty-four that month. His manner with strangers was awkward, but soon after meeting Van the uneasiness left him. They became friends and were seen together in such diverse places as Fifty-second Street and Carnegie Hall, the Village and the Metropolitan—one the son of a New England choirmaster and a sea captain's daughter, an advanced student at one of the nation's leading musical institutions, already composing music which even the conservative officials of the school called promising; the other the son of an itinerant guitarist and a Mississippi servant, horn man in a Harlem gin mill, whose name was enough to evoke superlatives from his followers and whose recordings already were collector's items.

For two years the relationship grew, Van being drawn steadily away from the music he had known, into the orbit of the music Duff represented, until he was composing things like those he formerly believed were without melody or harmony or sometimes even rhythm. At first his friends from the institute talked against it, but now he seldom saw them. He was at work on a four-part composition made up of variations of jazz themes and based on Duff's improvisations.

Van had completed more than half of this work when Duff began to feel a weariness in his arms and legs. He had lost weight, and some nights he was so tired he could hardly hold the horn up to his face. He began drinking to fight it, keeping the waiter on the move between the bandstand and the gin bottle at the bar. This took much of the weariness away, but at the end of August, 1939, something happened.

It was near closing time, and Duff was just entering the final chorus of "Body and Soul," one of his best songs. As the horn mounted toward the final note, he felt something rising at the back of his throat, an insistent tickling like a feather against his pharynx. He fell off the note, and there was a moment of flat silence. Someone said, "He fluffed," and it was loud against the sudden quiet.

Duff coughed, and there was a taste of salt at the base of his tongue. He wiped his mouth with the back of his hand. When he saw the darker red against the flesh, he coughed harder, and a bright bubble of blood broke from his mouth, running down his chin and onto the front of his shirt.

Van took him home and sat feeding him cracked ice till morning. At the clinic, when the examination was over and the X ray had been taken, the doctor said, "Come back at five o'clock and we'll see what there is to this thing."

He was a mild, gray-haired man. When Duff and Van returned, the late-afternoon sunlight lay in soft yellow bars across his desk. He held the negative against the light. "Here you are," he said. At first Duff could not see what he meant. Then, as the doctor's finger moved among the smoky branches of the ribs, he discerned a gray smudge about the size of a silver dollar. While he was watching it he became aware that the doctor was speaking. ". . . prescribe in a case like this. What you need is bed rest. I cannot tell you how long it will take to cure you, but I can tell you it will take less than six months to kill you if you stay in that airtight room blowing your lungs out on a trumpet every night. Do you want me to arrange for a sanitarium for you?"

"No, thank you, doctor," Duff said. He stood up, holding his hat. "I'm going home."

Every morning on her way out, Nora would set the big pitcher of milk on the bedside table, and Duff would lie there watching it through the long quiet day. Just before sundown he would tilt an inch of milk into the glass, sloshing it around to stain the glass to the brim. When he had drunk it painfully, sip by sip, he would take the pitcher to the kitchen and, being careful not to spatter any drops she might discover on the sink, pour the remainder down the drain. Then he would compose himself in bed for her return.

Some days a speculative expression would come on his face as he lay there, and soon he would get up and cross the room to the bureau, where the cornet lay in the drawer beside Nora's pistol. He would not touch it. Sometimes he would not even open the drawer, because he could see it quite clearly in his mind, the dull shadowed gleam of gold beside the bright glint of nickel. He had been in the room three months now, hearing strident newsboy voices crying Hitler and the ruin of Poland, while the tree outside the window turned from dusty green to the hectic flare of Indian summer and then stood leafless in the steady rain of late November.

On Christmas Day he took up the horn for the first time since he had put it away four months ago. He carried it back to the bed and played it for an hour, pulling the quilt over the bell to deaden the sound. After that, he began to play it for an hour every afternoon, and by the end of January he was playing it mornings, too, without the quilt. But it was March, the tree budding along its boughs in the abrupt Mississippi springtime, before he left the cabin with the horn. He left quietly, careful not to waken Nora. Except that now he went out by the front door while she slept on the cot in the kitchen, it was like the nights a dozen years before, when he would slip away to hear forbidden music on Bantam Street.

As he went up the Mansion House steps he could hear the piano going strong on "Deed I Do." Looking across the dance room, through the smoke and above the heads of the dancers, he saw Blind Bailey's broad blue back and his gray head bobbing in time to the music. A young man in ragged clothes sat woodenfaced beside him, strumming a guitar. Duff crossed the room and stood behind the piano, watching the heavy black hands moving over the keyboard. He lifted the cornet, waiting for the second chorus, then came in on it, carrying it wide open for eight bars before fading for the piano break, and then they took it together to a ride-out finish.

"Lord, Duff, it's good to hear you," Blind Bailey said, lifting his head. The spectacle lenses were blue disks, flat and opaque as target centers in the glare of the naked light bulb. "How you been so long?"

"Fine as can be," Duff said. "Just you play me some more of that mean piano."

At the cabin four hours later, the lamp was burning and Nora was waiting for him. As was her custom, she had got up in the night to see if there was anything he wanted. Finding the bed empty, she dressed and went to Bantam Street. From the sidewalk outside the Mansion House she heard the cornet. Then she came home, lighted the lamp and waited for him.

When he closed the door, she said, "I ain't going to try and reason with you, because you grown now. But ain't you got no better sense than to be at that place, blowing that horn with them bad lungs that the doctor his own self told you wouldn't last half a year that way?" She waited for him to answer. Then she said again, "Ain't you?"

"No'm," he said.

"All right. Go on to bed."

At first he went to the Mansion House twice a week. By the middle of April he was there every other night, and before the end of May he was going every night. But by this time there was more to attract him than the music. There was a girl. Her name was Julia, a light-brown girl with a wide mouth, big eyes and a boisterous manner. Nineteen, slim, high-bosomed, she had come to Bristol from Vicksburg when her parents opened a café on Bantam Street six months before. With his New York clothes and haircut and his aura of fame, Duff attracted her from the beginning, but the first time he noticed her was when he had just finished a fast chorus of "Wish I Could Shimmy." She was wearing a red dress, and she leaned down and threw her arms about his neck.

"Oh, people, people!" she cried. "Look at my horn-blowing man!"

This sort of thing had happened before, on the river and in New Orleans and Harlem, but this time something was communicated. He looked up and saw her bright eyes and laughing mouth just above him.

"Play it, daddy," she said softly. "Play that thing."

"Back up, gal," he said, "I'll blow one just for you."

He played "Canal Street Blues," and for the rest of the night, whenever he looked toward the dance floor, he saw Julia either watching him or performing for him, switching the red dress or preening like a bird. When the last number was over and the room emptied, she was waiting for him. After late coffee he walked her home, and from her porch swing they watched the dawn accomplish itself. There appeared to be two sources of light, one descending from the sky and one rising from the earth, and when they joined, it was broad open daylight. He had never noticed this before.

In the three weeks that it lasted, Duff experienced something he had never known before. Except for his music and his sickness, he had never been involved in any situation he could not walk away from. At reform school, for instance, he could look forward to a time when he would be free, but there was no such assurance here. Sick as he was, his nervous system upset by coughing fits which were growing more frequent all the time, he was conscious of his inability to hold her. Within a week of the night she threw her arms about him and called him her horn-blowing man, Julia began letting him know his short-comings. Wherever they were, he was always aware that he did not satisfy her wants, either at such places as the All Night Café, where she expected raucous talk to impress people around them with his life in the big time, or in the high back room of the Mansion House, where she would weep with nervous tension and rail at him with all the passion he was unable to relieve.

There were really only two considerations which kept her by him even for the short time that it lasted. One was her wanting to get the full benefit of reflected fame, and the other was a lack of anyone to take his place. Three weeks were enough to exhaust the first. The second consideration also was filled by the end of the third week, but she could not be satisfied with leaving Duff for the other man, even after she had singled him out. She wanted to be won, preferably after a contest which would display her as the object of contention.

The man she chose was likely to furnish whatever violence she wanted. He was Chance Jackson, a gambler well known in the region for his instant willingness to bet on almost anything, as well as for his loud clothes, his pearl-gray derby and the big yellow diamonds he wore. Born and raised in a college town, where his mother was a servant in the home of the president of the university, he had been given his mother's employer's official title, chancellor, as a first name. Faculty members and townspeople thought it a ludicrous name, until he began growing up and it was shortened to Chance, and then they realized how apt it was. While still in knee breeches he became a master at dice, cooncan, pitty pat and all the other Negro gambling games. When he had cleaned his section of the state, he widened his field, and now he went from town to town, staying no longer than the winnings were good.

He was almost forty now, and there were men who had saved between visits for twenty years, waiting for an opportunity to skin him. Once a year he came to Bristol. A section in the rear of the Mansion House dance room was partitioned off by an old theater curtain nailed along its top edge to the ceiling, thus forming an alcove in which two card tables and a blanketed dice board stood under blue cones of down-funneled light. Whenever there was a hush on the dance floor, which was rare, the rattling of dice and the cries of the gamblers came through the curtain. Foot-high letters across its center spelled ASBESTOS and there were faded advertisements of harness shops and restaurants and clothing stores whose dead owners had never guessed the final room their names would grace.

Duff was resting on one of Blind Bailey's special numbers when he saw the gray derby above the red dress. When the piano stopped, Julia came to the rostrum.

"Make him leave me 'lone," she said. "I'm scared of that man."

"What's he been doing?"

"Nothing. But I'm scared."

"Stay 'way from him, then," Duff said.

Half an hour later he saw them together again. He could see that they were talking as they danced. Though he could not hear what they were saying, Julia was telling the gambler that Duff had said he would beat her if she danced with him again.

"He'll do it, too," she said.

"Him?" Chance said, looking at Duff. "He ain't going to beat nobody. Watch here." He danced toward the rostrum. "Hey, horn boy!" he said. "Was you wanting to beat somebody?"

It was between pieces, and Duff sat with his horn in his lap. The gambler's diamonds flashed as he leaned forward with one arm about Julia's waist. "Was you?" Duff did not answer. Chance leaned closer and spoke again, his voice caressing and soft, his face less than six inches away, "I said was you?"

"Move on and let that girl alone," Duff said.

What followed happened so quickly that he was not aware of any sequence of motion until it was ended. Without taking his other arm from around the girl's waist, Chance raised one hand. Not making a fist nor even using the flat of his palm, he touched Duff under the chin with the tips of his fingers, lifted him gently against the back of the chair, and tipped him over backward. There was a loud thump as his head hit the floor, and then he heard the clang as the cornet struck.

"Watch out there!" Blind Bailey said gruffly. "Quit that horseplay round the bandstand!"

Looking up from the floor, Duff saw the pearl-gray derby brim haloing the smiling black face. "Just who was you going to give that beating to?" Chance said.

The cornet, on the floor beside Duff's head, had an ugly dent in the column just behind the bell. He saw it first, and then he saw Julia. The gambler's hand, still clasping her waist, showed dark against the bright red dress, and she was smiling.

Afterward he told himself that it was the smile which caused what followed. His nerves were upset by knowing that she would not stay with him, and his music had been getting worse because he held back on it to stave off coughing fits. When he went over backward, saw the scarred cornet, and then looked up and saw Julia smiling approval, he reached the end of misery, and he knew what he was going to do. As he left the room, carrying the dented horn, he could hear the crowd laughing.

For a moment, the cornet and the pistol lay side by side in the drawer, just as they had done through the early months when he was curing. He turned with the gun in his hand and heard the cot squeak in the kitchen.

"Duff?" Nora said. Closing the cabin door, he heard her again, "Duff!" He left, walking fast, the pistol heavy in his pocket.

Blind Bailey was banging out "Tin Roof Blues" as Duff went up the steps and into the dance room. Chance and Julia were dancing in the far corner. Shouldering his way through the dancers until he was within ten feet of them, Duff took out the pistol and waited. The other couples faded back toward the walls and the room was hushed, except for the loud piano and the cries of the gamblers beyond the curtain, but Chance and Julia were cheek to cheek in a slow turn. The gambler's face revolved toward Duff, until beneath his lowered lids he saw the glint of the pistol. He stopped, still clasping his partner, the gyral movement half completed. He moved Julia slowly aside, never taking his eyes off the pistol.

Chance had time to raise one hand, the palm showing pink in a gesture of protest. "Wait a minute, boy," he said. Then the gun went off, louder than anything Duff had ever heard. The piano stopped like a dropped watch, and there was an abrupt silence. The gambler went backward against the theater curtain and slid down it to the floor. The bullet had passed through his outstretched palm, ranging upward, had entered his forehead just above one eyebrow and had come out high on the back of his head. The gray derby rose, and now it fell, spinning on its crown and showing a new red lining.

There were quick scrabbling sounds as dancers and gamblers went out through doorways and low open windows. Then there was silence again, and Duff and Julia and Blind Bailey were alone in the big room. Forgotten cigarettes raised their plumes among the overturned chairs and half-empty beer bottles. Julia began to back away, her eyes bulged big and her hand against her mouth. "Don't," she said. "Don't." Duff watched her until the end of the curtain lifted and fell, and she was gone.

Alone on the rostrum, under the steady yellow glare, Blind Bailey turned his head, the flat blue disks reflecting no light. "Whoever you are, God bless you," he said. "And please don't shoot a blind old man."

Duff heard steps at the door. Dropping the pistol, he turned and saw a policeman at the far end of the room. A wide tan hat cast a dark parabola down the top half of his face, but beneath the shadow the mouth moved, steady and thin-lipped.

"Don't try anything," the white face said. "Just stand there."

He was in jail three months awaiting trial. It was held during the hottest weather of the year, the first week in September. The judge sat behind a high desk, an old man with clean linen and a black string tie and a habit of clearing his throat with a rattle of phlegm. The jury was out less than half an hour. When the foreman had reported, the judge leaned forward and peered at Duff through thick lenses.

"Do you have anything to say before sentence of the court is passed upon you?"

No one heard Duff say anything, but the judge could see his lips form the words, "No, sir." The judge paused, leaning forward and seeming to gather himself, his forearms flat on the bench. He watched Duff closely, like a psychologist in his laboratory.

"I sentence you to be committed to a felon's cell and there to be safely kept until the tenth day of October, in the year of our Lord, nineteen hundred and forty, at which time you shall suffer death by electrocution, and may God have mercy on your soul."

There was a faint sigh, a collective suspiration, as the spectators rose and filed for the doorway. Two deputies led Duff down the narrow rear stairway, across the rear plot of the courthouse lawn, and back to his cell in the county jail. The door closed behind him, and he sat looking up at the high barred window, the hot bright blue September sky.

Next day, when Nora came to see him she carried a bundle wrapped in clean flour sacking. Even before he unwrapped it he could feel the slick hard shape of the cornet. She had taken it to a gunsmith and had the dent smoothed out. He played the horn whenever the jailer would let him. The notes were less blary now, because his lungs were worse, but the tone was as clear as ever. Every day there would be a group in the yard below the cell window, sitting under trees or leaning against the jail, listening to the cornet.

When Harry Van first heard the horn he was halfway to the county jail. It caught him in mid-stride, as if he had crossed an exact circumference into a circle of sound which had as its center the golden bell of the cornet, and though it grew louder as he neared it, the tone was no clearer beneath the cell window than it had been a block away.

He had taken the midnight train from Memphis—the one natives called the Cannonball, "in indirect ratio to the compliment implied," they added—south through fields showing white as if with incongruous snow in the warm October moonlight. The trip was one hundred and fifty miles, and it lasted eight hours. The coach bucked and rattled, stopping at every hamlet and even backing onto spur tracks to make those off the main line. During the final two hours he could see the countryside clearly, first in the pale sudden dawn and then in sunlight, the corrugated metal gins whining soprano, the slow willow-bordered creeks and bayous with their rackety bridges, the flat ash-gray fields where pickers moved down the rows dragging nine-foot sacks bulged at the lower ends with the fiber which in the moonlight had resembled snow.

In rumpled tweed, with his soft hat and careful collar, his Scotch-grain shoes and foulard tie, juxtaposed among salesmen sleeping upon their sample cases and excursionists returning from their two-day flings in the city, Van was like a visitor from a future generation or even from another planet; the other passengers looked at him once and then let him strictly alone. When at length the conductor passed down the aisle, announcing Bristol, Van took his pigskin bag from the rack and went onto the platform. He stepped onto a gravel quay, deserted now, save for an old Negro who wore a rusty black tail coat. "Pardon," Van said. "Can you direct me to the county jail?" The old man watched him curiously, puzzled by the Eastern syntax. "The county jail," Van said. "Where is it?"

The old man raised one arm. "Yonder way," he said. "Two blocks twill you sees de soldier; dat's de cyotehouse. Hit's in back."

Now it was Van's turn to be puzzled, but he took up the bag and began walking down the sidewalk in the direction the old man had indicated. He paused for an instant when the music reached him, then continued forward, moving in the rich circle of sound, hearing again, after so long a time, the proud, soaring tone known to jazz musicians everywhere. But it did not seem to Van that he was hearing it again; it seemed that he had never stopped hearing it since the night three years ago when his harmony instructor had taken him into Harlem.

When Duff left New York, he said he would be back in a year, but twelve months later one of the waiters at the Black Cat told Van that Duff had been tried for a barrel-house shooting and would be executed in October.

That was late September. Van wrote and waited ten days for an answer. Then he took the train for Memphis. And now, walking along the small-town Southern street, hearing again the horn which had become for him the ultimate expression of all music, he thought: There ought to be two sets of laws, one for us and another for the few like him; because it's not right to expect them to follow something set down and codified in books for men who don't even think the way they do, if they think at all.

He crossed the street toward a wooded lawn where a column gleamed pale among oaks and sycamores. Surmounting the shaft, with one foot advanced, his hands clasping the muzzle of his rifle, the Confederate faced south. His blanket roll was tied neatly across his left shoulder, and the eyes were bland and impervious in the shadow of a wide hatbrim as straight and unyielding as if it had just been lifted from the stamping machine. This was the soldier the old man at the depot had told him to watch for, and the brownstone structure with its new cupola was the courthouse.

Behind this there was a square two-story building of harsh new concrete. There were bars at the windows, and a heavy barred door blocked the entrance. A stout man sat on the stoop. He wore khaki trousers and a faded denim shirt with large half-moons of darker blue beneath his armpits. As Van approached, the man looked up, and Van saw that his eyes were pale green, as if they had been washed with strong soap and the color had not held. There was a lax, mobile expression about his mouth.

Van halted before him, his careful city-cut tweeds more out of place than ever as he stood in the jail yard with his bright pigskin bag against his leg.

"May I see Duff Conway?" he said.

The stout man dropped his glance. He shaved a long curl of pine from the stick he held. Without looking up, he said, "You from up his way?" There was a ring of enormous keys at his belt.

"Yes."

"Figured you were." He looked up. "Sho now. You can see him." He rose and swung the barred door open. "You can put your suitcase there. Won't nobody bother it." His voice was not strong, but it had a staminal quality. "I understand he got sick or something up there and come down here to get well. I don't know if he got well or not, but Luke Jeffcoat is going to give him the big treatment tomorrow, so it probably don't make much never-mind. Were you acquainted with him up there?"

"Yes."

"Lawyer?"

"No, friend."

The turnkey looked at him curiously. "Then maybe you can get it home to him." They were climbing a steep circular stair. The turnkey toiled ahead, his voice continuing with unflagging volubility, "I'm a religious man myself—fact it, I always have been—but I can't talk to him, seems like. I can talk to most of them, but not to this boy. He listens, but it don't get through. So you tell him; tell him to lay that horn aside and get right with his Maker."

Oral personality, Van thought. Does he ever stop?

"Most of them we have to kind of put the damper on, they get so sanctified with all their kinfolks there and two or three jackleg preachers yelling about salvation at the top of their voice, but he can't seem to get it through his head that the time ain't long. Won't see no preacher; won't even pay his mamma no mind; just sits there all day long with that horn, playing them honky-tonk songs. He'd be blowing it all night, too, I reckon, if I'd let him."

They had reached the second story now. The turnkey led Van down a dim corridor flanked with cells. There was a combined odor of creosote and mildew, of rust and something indefinable. The sound of the cornet filled the jail; it was "Rose Room," near the finish.

Garrulous and unwearied, the turnkey continued to talk. "Well, he can blow it tonight if he wants. Most of them ask for a quart of corn and a woman, but I reckon he'll want the horn. The sheriff always gives them whatever they want. If it's possible, that is. Funny thing: last January we had a boy wanted watermelon. Wouldn't nothing else do, he said. And we got it for him, too; out of a freezer at the icehouse. Feller that owned it had been saving it for something special—a wedding or a election or suchlike—but he didn't begrudge it. No, sir; he didn't begrudge it a-tall."

While he told about the watermelon the turnkey stood at the cell door with the key ring in his hand. He selected one of the big brass keys and fitted it into the lock. As he swung the door ajar he said, "Company, son."

Duff did not hear him. Riding out the coda of "Rose Room," he was jack-knifed into the lower section of a double bunk, hunched back against the wall with his knees drawn up and his heels against the iron frame. The cornet was lifted toward the high barred window, its bell catching the light as in a golden bowl. While the final note died away, Duff turned his head and saw Van standing in the doorway. Duff lowered his head and smiled, his teeth showing even and white against his cocoa-colored face.

"Hello, Harry," he said. "You're a long way from home."

"Hello, Duff."

Van had come fifteen hundred miles, but there was little he could say. The three men sat in the cell for an hour, the turnkey doing most of the talking.

As Van got up to leave, Duff looked at him quietly and said, "Don't you feel bad about this business. There wasn't anything anybody could do. It's just that I shouldn't ever have left home. Going away like that, I lost touch with everything I was born to be with. I ought to stayed at home where I belong."

After a moment, Van said, "I'll tell them hello for you."

"Thanks," Duff said. "But you better not make it hello. Make it goodby." He took up the horn.

Halfway down the circular stairway, following again the broad, faded back of the turnkey, Van heard the first note of the cornet. He picked up his bag inside the doorway and stepped outside.

"So long," the turnkey said.

Crossing the lawn, Van could still hear it. The brilliant waves of sound swept over him, surging past the dusty trees and the ugly brownstone courthouse, past the pale Confederate soldier and into the street beyond. There was more than an hour before time for his train to leave, but Van walked fast, wanting to be out of range of the horn.

The sheriff and a deputy brought him into the cell, walking on either side of him, their hands supporting his elbows. His shaved head glistened like mahogany, and his slit trouser legs flapped about his ankles. His eyes glittered, the pupils contracted by the sudden light.

The turnkey followed them into the cell, and Doctor Benson and I and the young district attorney watched from the rear wall. The executioner, who had stood by the chair and watched them come in, stepped forward and took over, beginning the oration, the running commentary he supplied with every job.

"All right," he said. "Here you are for the last ride. Don't be troubled in your mind." He secured the straps and plated cap. "I've had them all kinds," he said. "Some cried and moaned, and some didn't, but they all went. So don't fight back. Hey, there!"

The switch clicked.

For a moment there was the deep, pulsing hum and the odor of burning.

Then Jeffcoat resumed his speech. "Yair! Just one bump on the road to glory, and he never knew what hit him. Yair. Steady now and we'll hit him again; not because he needs it, but because the law says so. Yair!"

There were hurrying footsteps through the cell door, and as I came forward with my stethoscope, we could hear the young district attorney being sick in the hall. I leaned over the chair for a moment, then straightened up and pronounced the prisoner dead.

CHARLES BEAUMONT

Black Country

>   THERE ARE PASSAGES *in this story that seem to have been written while a phonograph played some old Louis Armstrong records. The purists may quibble and wonder what a saxophone is doing in a band like this, but Beaumont's feeling for the music is his license. When I first read "Black Country," I thought there were spots where the writer had worked his way into language situations from which there would be no escape, but he always came out clean. A writer who is not a professional musician takes a great risk when he tries to write from the musician's point of view. Beaumont took the risk and went through standing up. Actually, he does play a little piano—or did, when he was not racing sports cars or turning out science fiction. He is twenty-six.—R. G.*

Spoof Collins blew his brains out, all right—right on out through the top of his head. But I don't mean with a gun. I mean with a horn. Every night: slow and easy, eight to one. And that's how he died. Climbing, with that horn, climbing up high. For what? "Hey, man, Spoof—listen, you picked the tree, now come on down!" But he couldn't come down, he didn't know how. He just kept

climbing, higher and higher. And then he fell. Or jumped. Anyhow, that's the way he died.
 The bullet didn't kill anything. I'm talking about the one that tore up the top of his mouth. It didn't kill anything that wasn't dead already. Spoof just put in an extra note, that's all.
 We planted him out about four miles from town—home is where you drop: residential district, all wood construction. Rain? You know it. Bible type: sky like a month-old bedsheet, wind like a stepped-on cat, cold and dark, those Forty Days, those Forty Nights! But nice and quiet most of the time. Like Spoof: nice and quiet, with a lot underneath that you didn't like to think about.
 We planted him and watched and put what was his down into the ground with him. His horn, battered, dented, nicked—right there in his hands, but not just there; I mean in position, so if he wanted to do some more climbing, all right, he could. And his music. We planted that too, because leaving it out would have been like leaving out Spoof's arms or his heart or his guts.
 Lux started things off with a chord from his guitar, no particular notes, only a feeling, a sound. A Spoof Collins kind of sound. Jimmy Fritch picked it up with his stick and they talked awhile—Lux got a real piano out of that git-box. Then when Jimmy stopped talking and stood there, waiting, Sonny Holmes stepped up and wiped his mouth and took the melody on his shiny new trumpet. It wasn't Spoof, but it came close; and it was still "The Jimjam Man," the way Spoof wrote it back when he used to write things down. Sonny got off with a high-squealing blast, and no eyes came up—we knew, we remembered. The kid always had it collared. He just never talked about it. And listen to him now! He stood there over Spoof's grave, giving it all back to The Ol' Massuh, giving it back right— "Broom off, white child, you got four sides!" "I want to learn from you, Mr. Collins. I want to play jazz and you can teach me." "I got things to do, I can't waste no time on a half-hipped young'un." "Please, Mr. Collins." "You got to stop that, you got stop callin' me 'Mr. Collins' hear?" "Yes sir, yes sir."—He put out real sound, like he didn't remember a thing. Like he wasn't playing for that pile of dark-meat in the ground, not at all; but for the great Spoof Collins, for the man Who Knew and the man Who Did, who gave

jazz spats and dressed up the blues, who did things with a trumpet that a trumpet couldn't do, and more; for the man who could blow down the walls or make a chicken cry, without half trying—for the mighty Spoof, who'd once walked in music like a boy in river mud, loving it, breathing it, living it.

Then Sonny quit. He wiped his mouth again and stepped back and Mr. 'T' took it on his trombone while I beat up the tubs.

Pretty soon we had "The Jimjam Man" rocking the way it used to rock. A little slow, maybe: it needed Bud Meunier on bass and a few trips on the piano. But it moved.

We went through "Take It from Me" and "Night in the Blues" and "Big Gig" and "Only Us Chickens" and "Forty G's"—Sonny's insides came out through the horn on that one, I could tell—and "Slice City Stomp"—you remember: sharp and clean, like sliding down a razor—and "What the Cats Dragged In"—the longs, the shorts, all the great Spoof Collins numbers. We wrapped them up and put them down there with him.

Then it got dark.

And it was time for the last one, the greatest one . . . Rose-Ann shivered and cleared her throat; the rest of us looked around, for the first time, at all those rows of split-wood grave markers, shining in the rain, and the trees and the coffin, dark, wet. Out by the fence, a couple of farmers stood watching. Just watching.

One—Rose-Anne opens her coat, puts hands on hips, wets her lips;

Two—Freddie gets the spit out of his stick, rolls his eyes;

Three—Sonny puts the trumpet to his mouth;

Four—

And we played Spoof's song, his last one, the one he wrote a long way ago, before the music dried out his head, before he turned mean and started climbing: "Black Country." The song that said just a little of what Spoof wanted to say, and couldn't.

You remember. Spider-slow chords crawling down, soft, easy, and then bottom and silence and, suddenly, the cry of the horn, screaming in one note all the hate and sadness and loneliness, all the want and got-to-have; and then the note dying, quick, and Rose-Ann's voice, a whisper, a groan, a sigh. . . .

> "Black Country is somewhere, Lord,
> That I don't want to go.
> Black Country is somewhere
> That I never want to go.
> Rain-water drippin'
> On the bed and on the floor,
> Rain-water drippin'
> From the ground and through the door. . . ."

We all heard the piano, even though it wasn't there. Fingers moving down those minor chords, those black keys, that black country. . . .

> "Well, in that old Black Country
> If you ain't feeling good,
> They let you have an overcoat
> That's carved right out of wood.
> But 'way down there
> It gets so dark
> You never see a friend—
> Black Country may not be the Most,
> But, Lord! it's sure the End. . . ."

Bitter little laughing words, piling up, now mad, now sad; and then, an ugly blast from the horn and Rose-Ann's voice screaming, crying:

> "I never want to go there, Lord!
> I never want to be,
> I never want to lay down
> In that Black Country! . . ."

And quiet, quiet, just the rain, and the wind.
"Let's go, man," Freddie said.
So we turned around and left Spoof there under the ground.
Or, at least, that's what I thought we did.

Sonny took over without saying a word. He didn't have to: just who was about to fuss? He was white, but he didn't play white, not those days; and he learned the hard way—by unlearning. Now he could play gutbucket and he could play blues, stomp and slide, name it, Sonny could play it. Funny as hell to hear, too, because he looked like everything else but a musician. Short and skinny, glasses, nose like a melted candle, head clean as the one-ball, and white? Next to old Hushup, that cafe sunburn glowed like a flashlight.

"Man, who skinned you?"

"Who dropped you in the flour barrel?"

But he got closer to Spoof than any of the rest of us did. He knew what to do, and why. Just like a school teacher all the time: "That's good, Lux, that's awful good—now let's play some music." "Get off it, C.T.—what's Lenox Avenue doing in the middle of Lexington?" "Come on, boys, hang on to the sound, hang on to it!" Always using words like 'flavor' and 'authentic' and 'blood', peering over those glasses, pounding his feet right through the floor: STOMP! STOMP! "That's it, we've got it now—oh, listen! It's true, it's clean!" STOMP! STOMP!

Not the easiest to dig him. Nobody broke all the way through.

"How come, boy? What for?"

And every time the same answer: "I want to play jazz."

Like he'd joined the Church and didn't want to argue about it.

Spoof was still Spoof when Sonny started coming around. Not a lot of people with us then, but a few, enough—the longhairs and critics and connoisseurs—and some real real ears too—enough to fill a club every night, and who needs more? It was COLLINS AND HIS CREW, tight and neat, never a performance, always a session. Lots of music, lots of fun. And a line-up that some won't forget: Jimmy Fritch on clarinet, Honker Reese on alto-sax, Charles di Lusso on tenor, Spoof on trumpet, Henry Walker on piano, Lux Anderson on banjo and myself—Hushup Paige—on drums. New mown hay, all right, I know—I remember, I've heard the records we cut—but, the Road was there.

Sonny used to hang around the old Continental Club on State Street in Chicago, every night, listening. Eight o'clock roll 'round, and there he'd be—a little different: younger, skinnier—listening hard, over in a corner all to himself, eyes closed like he was asleep. Once in a while he put in a request—"Darktown Strutter's Ball" was one he liked, and some of Jelly Roll's numbers—but mostly he just sat there, taking it all in. For real.

And it kept up like this for two or three weeks, regular as 2/4.

Now Spoof was mean in those days—don't think he wasn't—but not blood-mean. Even so, the white boy in the corner bugged Ol' Massuh after a while and he got to making dirty cracks with his horn: *WAAAAA!* Git your ass out of here. *WAAAAA!* You only think you're with it! *WAAAAA!* There's a little white child sittin' in a chair there's a little white child losin' all his hair. . . .

It got to the kid, too, every bit of it. And that made Spoof even madder. But what can you do?

Came Honker's trip to Slice City along about then: our sax-man got a neck all full of the sharpest kind of steel. So we were out one horn. And you could tell: we played a little bit too rough, and the head-arrangements Collins and His Crew grew up to, they needed Honker's grease in the worst way. But we'd been together for five years or more, and a new man just didn't play somehow. We were this one solid thing, like a unit, and somebody had cut off a piece of us and we couldn't grow the piece back so we tried to get along anyway, bleeding every night, bleeding from that wound.

Then one night it bust. We'd gone through some slow walking stuff, some tricky stuff and some loud stuff—still covering up—when this kid, this white boy, got up from his chair and ankled over and tapped Spoof on the shoulder. It was break-time and Spoof was brought down about Honker, about how bad we were sounding, sitting there sweating, those pounds of man, black as coaldust soaked in oil—he was the blackest man!—and those eyes, beady white and small as agates.

"Excuse me, Mr. Collins, I wonder if I might have a word with you?" He wondered if he might have a word with Mr. Collins!

Spoof swiveled in his chair and clapped a look around the kid. "Hnff?"

"I notice that you don't have a sax man any more."

"You don't mean to tell me?"

"Yes sir. I thought—I mean, I was wondering if—"

"Talk up, boy. I can't hear you."

The kid looked scared. Lord, he looked scared—and he was white to begin with.

"Well sir, I was just wondering if—if you needed a saxophone."

"You know somebody plays sax?"

"Yes sir, I do."
"And who might that be?"
"Me."
"You."
"Yes sir."

Spoof smiled a quick one. Then he shrugged. "Broom off, son," he said. "Broom 'way off."

The kid turned red. He all of a sudden didn't look scared any more. Just mad. Mad as hell. But he didn't say anything. He went on back to his table and then it was end of the ten.

We swung into "Basin Street," smooth as Charley's tenor could make it, with Lux Anderson talking it out: Basin Street, man, it is the street, Where the elite, well, they gather 'round to eat a little . . . And we fooled around with the slow stuff for a while. Then Spoof lifted his horn and climbed up two-and-a-half and let out his trademark, that short high screech that sounded like something dying that wasn't too happy about it. And we rocked some, Henry taking it, Jimmy kanoodling the great head-work that only Jimmy knows how to do, me slamming the skins—and it was nowhere. Without Honker to keep us all on the ground, we were just making noise. Good noise, all right, but not music. And Spoof knew it. He broke his mouth blowing—to prove it.

And we cussed the cat that sliced our man.

Then, right away—nobody could remember when it came in—suddenly, we had us an alto-sax. Smooth and sure and snaky, that sound put a knot on each of us and said: Bust loose now, boys, I'll pull you back down. Like sweet-smelling glue, like oil in a machine, like—Honker.

We looked around and there was the kid, still sore, blowing like a madman, and making fine fine music.

Spoof didn't do much. Most of all, he didn't stop the number. He just let that horn play, listening—and when we slid over all the rough spots and found us backed up neat as could be, the Ol' Massah let out a grin and a nod and a "Keep blowin', young'un!" and we knew that we were going to be all right.

After it was over, Spoof walked up to the kid. They looked at each other, sizing it up, taking it in.

Spoof says: "You did good."

And the kid—he was still burned—says: "You mean I did damn good."

And Spoof shakes his head. "No, that ain't what I mean."

And in a second one was laughing while the other one blushed. Spoof had known all along that the kid was faking, that he'd just been lucky enough to know our style on "Basin Street" up-and-down-and-across.

The Ol' Massuh waited for the kid to turn and start to slink off, then he said: "Boy, you want to go to work?" . . .

Sonny learned so fast it scared you. Spoof never held back; he turned it all over, everything it had taken us our whole lives to find out.

And—we had some good years. Charley di Lusso dropped out, we took on Bud Meunier—the greatest bass man of them all—and Lux threw away his banjo for an AC-DC git-box and old C.T. Mr. 'T' Green and his trombone joined the Crew. And we kept growing and getting stronger—no million-copies platter sales or stands at the Paramount—too 'special'—but we never ate too far down on the hog, either.

In a few years Sonny Holmes was making that sax stand on its hind legs and jump through hoops that Honker never dreamed about. Spoof let him strictly alone. When he got mad it wasn't ever because Sonny had white skin—Spoof always was too busy to notice things like that—but only because The Ol' Massuh had to get t'ed off at each one of us every now and then. He figured it kept us on our toes.

In fact, except right at first, there never was any real blood between Spoof and Sonny until Rose-Ann came along.

Spoof didn't want a vocalist with the band. But the coonshouting days were gone alas, except for Satchmo and Calloway—who had style: none of us had style, man, we just hollered—so when push came to shove, we had to put out the net.

And chickens aplenty came to crow and plenty moved on fast and we were about to give up when a dusky doll of 20-ought stepped up and let loose a hunk of "That Man I Love" and that's all, brothers, end of the search.

Rose-Ann McHugh was a little like Sonny: where she came from, she didn't know a ball of cotton from a piece of popcorn.

She'd studied piano for a flock of years with a Pennsylvania longhair, read music whipfast and had been pointed toward the Big Steinway and the O.M.'s, Chopin and Bach and all that jazz. And good!—I mean she could pull some very fancy noise out of those keys. But it wasn't the Road. She'd heard a few records of Muggsy Spanier's, a couple of Jelly Roll's—"New Orleans Bump," "Shreveport Stomp," old "Wolverine Blues"—and she just got took hold of. Like it happens, all the time. She knew.

Spoof hired her after the first song. And we could see things in her eyes for The Ol' Massuh right away, fast. Bad to watch: I mean to say, she was chicken dinner, but what made it ugly was, you could tell she hadn't been in the oven very long.

Anyway, most of us could tell. Sonny, for instance.

But Spoof played tough to begin. He gave her the treatment, all the way. To see if she'd hold up. Because, above everything else, there was the Crew, the Unit, the group. It was right, it had to stay right.

"Gal, forget your hands—that's for the cats out front. Leave 'em alone. And pay attention to the music, hear?"

"You ain't got a 'voice', you got an instrument. And you ain't even started to learn how to play on it. Get some sound, bring it on out."

"Stop that throat stuff—you' singin' with the Crew now. From the belly, gal, from the belly. That's where music comes from, hear?"

And she loved it, like Sonny did. She was with The Ol' Massuh, she knew what he was talking about.

Pretty soon she fit just fine. And when she did, and everybody knew she did, Spoof eased up and waited and watched the old machine click right along, one-two, one-two.

That's when he began to change. Right then, with the Crew growed up and in long pants at last. Like we didn't need him any more to wash our face and comb our hair and switch our behinds for being bad.

Spoof began to change. He beat out time and blew his riffs, but things were different and there wasn't anybody who didn't know that for a fact.

In a hurry, all at once, he wrote down all his great arrangements, quick as he could. One right after the other. And we wondered why—we'd played them a million times.

Then he grabbed up Sonny. "White boy, listen. You want to learn how to play trumpet?"

And the blood started between them. Spoof rode on Sonny's back twenty-four hours, showing him lip, showing him breath. "This ain't a saxophone, boy, it's a trumpet, a music-horn. Get it right—do it again—that's lousy—do it again—that was nowhere—do it again—do it again!" All the time.

Sonny worked hard. Anybody else, they would have told Ol' Massuh where he could put that little old horn. But the kid knew something was being given to him—he didn't know why, nobody did, but for a reason—something that Spoof wouldn't have given anybody else. And he was grateful. So he worked. And he didn't ask any how-comes, either.

Pretty soon he started to handle things right. 'Way down the road from great, but coming along. The sax had given him a hard set of lips and he had plenty of wind; most of all, he had the spirit—the thing that you can beat up your chops about it for two weeks straight and never say what it is, but if it isn't there, buddy-ghee, you may get to be President but you'll never play music.

Lord, Lord, Spoof worked that boy like a two ton jockey on a ten ounce horse. "Do it again—that ain't right—God damn it, do it again! Now one more time!"

When Sonny knew enough to sit in with the horn on a few easy ones, Ol' Massuh would tense up and follow the kid with his eyes—I mean it got real crawly. What for? Why was he pushing it like that?

Then it quit. Spoof didn't say anything. He just grunted and quit all of a sudden, like he'd done with us, and Sonny went back on sax and that was that.

Which is when the real blood started.

The Lord says every man has got to love something, sometime, somewhere. First choice is a chick, but there's other choices. Spoof's was a horn. He was married to a piece of brass, just as married as a man can get. Got up with it in the morning, talked with it all day long, loved it at night like no chick I ever heard of got loved. And

I don't mean one-two-three: I mean the slow-building kind. He'd kiss it and hold it and watch out for it. Once a cat full of tea tried to put the snatch on Spoof's horn, for laughs: when Spoof caught up with him, that cat gave up laughing for life.

Sonny knew this. It's why he never blew his stack at all the riding. Spoof's teaching him to play trumpet—the trumpet—was like as if The Ol' Massuh had said: "You want to take my wife for a few nights? You do? Then here, let me show you how to do it right. She likes it done right."

For Rose-Ann, though, it was the worst. Every day she got that look deeper in, and in a while we turned around and, man! Where is little Rosie? She was gone. That young half-fried chicken had flew the roost. And in her place was a doll that wasn't dead, a big bunch of curves and skin like a brand new penny. Overnight, almost. Sonny noticed. Freddie and Lux and even old Mr. 'T' noticed. I had eyes in my head. But Spoof didn't notice. He was already in love, there wasn't any more room.

Rose-Ann kept snapping the whip, but Ol' Massuh, he wasn't about to make the trip. He'd started climbing, then, and he didn't treat her any different than he treated us.

"Get away, gal, broom on off—can't you see I'm busy? Wiggle it elsewhere, hear? Elsewhere. Shoo!"

And she just loved him more for it. Every time he kicked her, she loved him more. Tried to find him and see him and, sometimes, when he'd stop for breath, she'd try to help, because she knew something had crawled inside Spoof, something that was eating from the inside out, that maybe he couldn't get rid of alone.

Finally, one night, at a two-weeker in Dallas, it tumbled.

We'd gone through "Georgia Brown" for the tourists and things were kind of dull, when Spoof started sweating. His eyes began to roll. And he stood up, like a great big animal—like an ape or a bear, big and powerful and mean-looking—and he gave us the two-finger signal.

"Sky-High." 'Way before it was due, before either the audience or any of us had got wound up.

Freddie frowned. "You think it's time, Top?"

"Listen," Spoof said, "God damn it, who says when it's time— you, or me?"

We went into it, cold, but things warmed up pretty fast. The dancers grumbled and moved off the floor and the place filled up with talk.

I took my solo and beat hell out of the skins. Then Spoof swiped at his mouth and let go with a blast and moved it up into that squeal and stopped and started playing. It was all head-work. All new to us.

New to anybody.

I saw Sonny get a look in his face, and we sat still and listened while Spoof made love to that horn.

Now like a scream, now like a laugh,—now we're swinging in the trees, now the white men are coming, now we're in the boat and chains are hanging from our ankles and we're rowing, rowing— Spoof, what is it?—now we're sawing wood and picking cotton and serving up those cool cool drinks to the Colonel in his chair— Well, blow man!—now we're free, and we're struttin' down Lenox Avenue and State & Madison and Pirate's Alley, laughing, crying— Who said free?—and we want to go back and we don't want to go back—Play it, Spoof! God, God, tell us all about it! Talk to us!— and we're sitting in a cellar with a comb wrapped up in paper, with a skin-barrel and a tinklebox—Don't stop, Spoof! Oh Lord, please don't stop!—and we're making something, something, what is it? Is it jazz? Why yes, Lord, it's jazz. Thank you, sir, and thank you, sir, we finally got it, something that is ours, something great that belongs to us and to us alone, that we made, and that's why it's important, and that's what it's all about and—Spoof! Spoof, you can't stop now—

But it was over, middle of the trip. And there was Spoof standing there facing us and tears streaming out of those eyes and down over that coaldust face, and his body shaking and shaking. It's the first we ever saw that. It's the first we ever heard him cough, too—like a shotgun going off every two seconds, big raking sounds that tore up from the bottom of his belly and spilled out wet and loud.

The way it tumbled was this. Rose-Ann went over to him and tried to get him to sit down. "Spoof, honey, what's wrong? Come on and sit down. Honey, don't just stand there."

Spoof stopped coughing and jerked his head around. He looked at Rose-Ann for a while and whatever there was in his face, it didn't have a name. The whole room was just as quiet as it could be.

Rose-An took his arm. "Come on, honey, Mr. Collins—"

He let out one more cough, then, and drew back his hand—that black-topped, pink-palmed ham of a hand—and laid it, sharp, across the girl's cheek. It sent her staggering. "Get off my back, hear? Damn it, git off! Stay away from me!"

She got up crying. Then, you know what she did? She waltzed on back and took his arm and said: "Please."

Spoof was just a lot of crazy-mad on two legs. He shouted out some words and pulled back his hand again. "Can't you ever learn? What I got to do, god damn little—"

Then—Sonny moved. All-the-time quiet and soft and gentle Sonny. He moved quick across the floor and stood in front of Spoof.

"Keep your black hands off her," he said.

Ol' Massuh pushed Rose-Ann aside and planted his legs, his breath rattling fast and loose, like a bull's. And he towered over the kid, Goliath and David, legs far apart on the boards and fingers curled up, bowing balls at the end of his sleeves.

"You talkin' to me, boy?"

Sonny's face was red, like I hadn't seen it since that first time at the Continental Club, years back. "You've got ears, Collins. Touch her again and I'll kill you."

I don't know exactly what we expected, but I know what we were afraid of. We were afraid Spoof would let go; and if he did . . . well, put another bed in the hospital, men. He stood there, breathing, and Sonny gave it right back—for hours, days and nights, for a month, toe to toe.

Then Spoof relaxed. He pulled back those fat lips, that didn't look like lips anymore, they were so tough and leathery, and showed a mouthful of white and gold, and grunted, and turned, and walked away.

We swung into "Twelfth Street Rag" in such a hurry!

And it got kicked under the sofa.

But we found out something, then, that nobody even suspected. Sonny had it for Rose-Ann. He had it bad.

And that ain't good.

Spoof fell to pieces after that. He played day and night, when we were working, when we weren't working. Climbing. Trying to get it said, all of it.

"Listen, you can't hit Heaven with a slingshot, Daddy-O!"

"What you want to do, man—blow Judgment?"

He never let up. If he ate anything, you tell me when. Sometimes he tied on, straight stuff, quick, medicine type of drinking. But only after he'd been climbing and started to blow flat and ended up in those coughing fits.

And it got worse. Nothing helped, either: foam or booze or tea or even Indoor Sports, and he tried them all. And got worse.

"Get fixed up, Mr. C, you hear? See a bone-man; you in bad shape. . . ."

"Get away from me, get on away!" Hawk! and a big red spot on the handkerchief. "Broom off! Shoo!"

And gradually the old horn went sour, ugly and bitter sounding, like Spoof himself. Hoo Lord, the way he rode Sonny then: "How you like the dark stuff, boy? You like it pretty good? Hey there, don't hold back. Rosie's fine talent—I know. Want me to tell you about it, pave the way, show you how? I taught you everything else, didn't I?" And Sonny always clamming up, his eyes doing the talking: "You were a great musician, Collins, and you still are, but that doesn't mean I've got to like you—you won't let me. And you're damn right I'm in love with Rose-Ann! That's the biggest reason why I'm still here—just to be close to her. Otherwise, you wouldn't see me for the dust. But you're too dumb to realize she's in love with you, too dumb and stupid and mean and wrapped up with that lousy horn!"

What Sonny was too dumb to know was, Rose-Ann had cut Spoof out. She was now Public Domain.

Anyway, Spoof got to be the meanest, dirtiest, craziest, low-talkinest man in the world. And nobody could come in: he had signs out all the time. . . .

The night that he couldn't even get a squeak out of his trumpet and went back to the hotel—alone, always alone—and put the gun in his mouth and pulled the trigger, we found something out.

We found out what it was that had been eating at the Ol' Massuh.

Cancer.

Rose-Ann took it the hardest. She had the dry-weeps for a long time, saying it over and over: "Why didn't he let us know? Why didn't he tell us?"

But, you get over things. Even women do, especially when they've got something to take its place.

We reorganized a little. Sonny cut out the sax—saxes were getting cornball anyway—and took over on trumpet. And we decided against keeping Spoof's name. It was now SONNY HOLMES AND HIS CREW.

And we kept on eating high up. Nobody seemed to miss Spoof—not the cats in front, at least—because Sonny blew as great a horn as anybody could want, smooth and sure, full of excitement and clean as a gnat's behind.

We played across the States and back, and they loved us—thanks to the kid. Called us an 'institution' and the disk jockeys began to pick up our stuff. We were 'real,' they said—the only authentic jazz left, and who am I to push it? Maybe they were right.

Sonny kept things in low. And then, when he was sure—damn that slow way; it had been a cinch since back when—he started to pay attention to Rose-Ann. She played it cool, the way she knew he wanted it; and let it build up right. Of course, who didn't know she would've married him this minute, now, just say the word? But Sonny was a very conscientious cat indeed.

We did a few stands in France about that time—Listen to them holler! and a couple in England and Sweden—getting better, too —and after a breather, we cut out across the States again.

It didn't happen fast, but it happened sure. Something was sounding flat all of a sudden like—wrong, in a way:

During an engagement in El Paso we had "What the Cats Dragged In" lined up. You all know "Cats"—the rhythm section still, with the horns yelling for a hundred bars, then that fast and solid beat, that high trip and trumpet solo? Sonny had the ups on a wild riff and was coming on down, when he stopped. Stood still, with the horn to his lips; and we waited.

"Come on, wrap it up—you want a drum now? What's the story, Sonny?"

Then he started to blow. The notes came out the same almost, but not quite the same. They danced out of the horn strop-razor sharp and sliced up high and blasted low and the cats all fell out. "Do it! Go, man! Oooo, I'm out of the boat, don't pull me back! Sing out, man!"

The solo lasted almost seven minutes. When it was time for us to wind it up, we just about forgot.

The crowd went wild. They stomped and screamed and whistled. But they couldn't get Sonny to play any more. He pulled the horn away from his mouth—I mean that's the way it looked, as if he was yanking it away with all his strength—and for a second he looked surprised, like he'd been goosed. Then his lips pulled back into a smile.

It was the damndest smile!

Freddie went over to him at the break. "Man, that was the craziest. How many tongues you got?"

But Sonny didn't answer him.

Things went along all right for a little. We played a few dances in the cities, some radio stuff, cut a few platters. Easy walking style.

Sonny played Sonny—plenty great enough. And we forgot about what happened in El Paso. So what? So he cuts loose once —can't a man do that if he feels the urge? Every jazz man brings that kind of light at least once.

We worked through the sticks and were finally set for a New York opening when Sonny came in and gave us the news.

It was a gasser. Lux got sore. Mr. 'T' shook his head.

"Why? How come, Top?"

He had us booked for the cornbelt. The old-time route, exactly, even the old places, back when we were playing razzmatazz and feeling our way.

"You trust me?" Sonny asked. "You trust my judgment?"

"Come off it, Top; you know we do. Just tell us how come. Man, New York's what we been working for—"

"That's just it," Sonny said. "We aren't ready."

That brought us down. How did we know—we hadn't even thought about it.

"We need to get back to the real material. When we play in

New York, it's not anything anybody's liable to forget in a hurry. And that's why I think we ought to take a refresher course. About five weeks. All right?"

Well, we fussed some and fumed some, but not much, and in the end we agreed to it. Sonny knew his stuff, that's what we figured.

"Then it's settled."

And we lit out.

Played mostly the old stuff dressed up—"Big Gig," "Only Us Chickens" and the rest—or head-arrangements with a lot of trumpet. Illinois, Indiana, Kentucky. . . .

When we hit Louisiana for a two-nighter at the Tropics, the same thing happened that did back in Texas. Sonny blew wild for an eight minute solo that broke the glasses and cracked the ceiling and cleared the dancefloor like a tornado. Nothing off the stem, either—but like it was practice, sort of, or exercise. A solo out of nothing that didn't even try to hang on to a shred of the melody.

"Man, it's great, but let us know when it's gonna happen, hear!"

About then Sonny turned down the flame on Rose-Ann. He was polite enough and a stranger wouldn't have noticed, but we did, and Rose-Ann did—and it was tough for her to keep it all down under, hidden. All those questions, all those memories and fears.

He stopped going out and took to hanging around his rooms a lot. Once in a while he'd start playing: one time we listened to that horn all night.

Finally—it was still somewhere in Louisiana—when Sonny was reaching with his trumpet so high he didn't get any more sound out of it than a dog-whistle, and the front cats were laughing up a storm, I went over and put it to him flatfooted.

His eyes were big and he looked like he was trying to say something and couldn't. He looked scared.

"Sonny . . . Look, boy, what are you after? Tell a friend, man, don't lock it up."

But he didn't answer me. He couldn't.

He was coughing too hard.

Here's the way we doped it: Sonny had worshipped Spoof,

like a god or something. Now some Spoof was rubbing off, and he didn't know it.
   Freddie was elected. Freddie talks pretty good most of the time. "Get off the train, Jack. Ol' Massuh's gone now, dead and buried. Mean, what he was after ain't to be had. Mean, he wanted it all and then some—and all is all, there isn't any more. You play the greatest, Sonny—go on, ask anybody. Just fine. So get off the train. . . ."
   And Sonny laughed, and agreed, and promised. I mean in words. His eyes played another number, though.
   Sometimes he snapped out of it, it looked like, and he was fine then—tired and hungry, but with it. And we'd think, he's okay. Then it would happen all over again—only worse. Every time, worse.
   And it got so Sonny even talked like Spoof half the time: "Broom off, man, leave me alone, will you? Can't you see I'm busy, got things to do? Get away!" And walked like Spoof—that slow walk-in-your-sleep shuffle. And did little things—like scratching his belly and leaving his shoes unlaced and rehearsing in his undershirt.
   He started to smoke weeds in Alabama.
   In Tennessee he took the first drink anybody ever saw him take.
   And always with that horn—cussing it, yelling at it, getting sore because it wouldn't do what he wanted it to.
   We had to leave him alone, finally. "I'll handle it . . . I—understand, I think . . . Just go away, it'll be all right. . . ."
   Nobody could help him. Nobody at all.
   Especially not Rose-Ann.

End of the corn-belt route, the way Sonny had it booked, was the Copper Club. We hadn't been back there since the night we planted Spoof—and we didn't feel very good about it.
   But a contract isn't anything else.
   So we took rooms at the only hotel there ever was in the town. You make a guess which room Sonny took. And we played some cards and bruised our chops and tried to sleep and couldn't. We tossed around in the beds, listening, waiting for the horn to begin. But it didn't. All night long, it didn't.

We found out why, oh yes. . . .

Next day we all walked around just about everywhere except in the direction of the cemetery. Why kick up misery? Why make it any harder?

Sonny stayed in his room until ten before opening, and we began to worry. But he got in under the wire.

The Copper Club was packed. Yokels and farmers and high school stuff, a jazz 'connoisseur' here and there—to the beams. Freddie had set up the stands with the music notes all in order, and in a few minutes we had our positions.

Sonny came out wired for sound. He looked—powerful; and that's a hard way for a five-foot four-inch bald-headed white man to look. At any time. Rose-Ann threw me a glance and I threw it back and collected it from the rest. Something bad. Something real bad. Soon.

Sonny didn't look any which way. He waited for the applause to die down, then he did a quick One-Two-Three-Four and we swung into "The Jimjam Man," our theme.

I mean to say, that crowd was with us all the way—they smelled something.

Sonny did the thumb-and-little finger signal and we started "Only Us Chickens." Bud Meunier did the intro on his bass, then Henry took over on the piano. He played one hand racing the other. The front cats hollered "Go! Go!" and Henry went. His left hand crawled on down over the keys and scrambled and didn't fuzz once, or slip once and then walked away, cocky and proud, like a mouse full of cheese from an unsprung trap.

"Hooo-boy! Play, Henry, play!"

Sonny watched and smiled. "Bring it on out," he said, gentle, quiet, pleased. "Keep bringin' it out."

Henry did that counterpoint business that you're not supposed to be able to do unless you have two right arms and four extra fingers, and he got that boiler puffing, and he got it shaking, and he screamed his Henry Walker "WooooooOOOOO!" and—he finished. I came in on the tubs and beat them up till I couldn't see for the sweat, hit the cymbal and waited.

Mr. 'T', Lux and Jimmy fiddlefaddled like a coop of capons talking about their operations for a while. Rose-Ann chanted:

"Only us chickens in the hen-house, Daddy, Only us chickens here, Only us chickens in the hen-house, Daddy, Ooo-bab-a-roo, Ooo-bob-a-roo. . . ."

Then it was horn time. Time for the big solo.

Sonny lifted the trumpet—One! Two!—He got it into sight—Three!

We all stopped dead. I mean we stopped.

That wasn't Sonny's horn. This one was dented-in and beat-up and the tip-end was nicked. It didn't shine, not a bit.

Lux leaned over—you could have fit a coffee cup into his mouth. "Jesus God," he said. "Am I seeing right?"

I looked close and said: "Man, I hope not."

But why kid? We'd seen that trumpet a million times.

It was Spoof's.

Rose-Ann was trembling. Just like me, she remembered how we'd buried the horn with Spoof. And she remembered how quiet it had been in Sonny's room last night. . . .

I started to think real hop-head thoughts, like—where did Sonny get hold of a shovel that late? and how could he expect a horn to play that's been under the ground for two years? and—

That blast got into our ears like long knives.

Spoof's own trademark!

Sonny looked caught, like he didn't know what to do at first, like he was hypnotized, scared, almighty scared. But as the sound came out, rolling out, sharp and clean and clear—new trumpet sound—his expression changed. His eyes changed: they danced a little and opened wide.

Then he closed them, and blew that horn. Lord God of the Fishes, how he blew it! How he loved it and caressed it and pushed it up, higher and higher and higher. High C? Bottom of the barrel. He took off, and he walked all over the rules and stamped them flat.

The melody got lost, first off. Everything got lost, then, while that horn flew. It wasn't only jazz; it was the heart of jazz, and the insides, pulled out with the roots and held up for everybody to see; it was blues that told the story of all the lonely cats and all the ugly whores who ever lived, blues that spoke up for the loser lamping sunshine out of iron-gray bars and every hop-head hooked and gone, for the bindlestiffs and the city slicers, for the country boys in Georgia shacks and the High Yellow hipsters in Chicago slums and the bootblacks on the corners and the fruits in New Orleans, a blues that spoke for all the lonely, sad and anxious downers who could never speak themselves . . .

And then, when it had said all this, it stopped and there was a quiet so quiet that Sonny could have shouted:

"It's okay, Spoof. It's all right now. You'll get it said, all of it—I'll help you. God, Spoof, you showed me how, you planned it—I'll do my best!"

And he laid back his head and fastened the horn and pulled in air and blew some more. Not sad, now, not blues—but not anything else you could call by name. Except . . . Jazz. It was jazz.

Hate blew out that horn, then. Hate and fury and mad and fight, like screams and snarls, like little razors shooting at you, millions of them, cutting, cutting deep. . . .

And Sonny only stopping to wipe his lip and whisper in the silent room full of people: "You're saying it, Spoof! You are!"

God Almighty Himself must have heard that trumpet, then; slapping and hitting and hurting with notes that don't exist and never existed. Man! Life took a real beating! Life got groined and sliced and belly-punched and the horn, it didn't stop until everything had all spilled out, every bit of the hate and mad that's built up in a man's heart.

Rose-Ann walked over to me and dug her nails into my hand as she listened to Sonny.

"Come on now, Spoof! Come on! We can do it! Let's play the rest and play it right. You know it's got to be said, you know it does. Come on, you and me together!"

And the horn took off with a big yellow blast and started to laugh. I mean it laughed! Hooted and hollered and jumped around, dancing, singing, strutting through those notes that never were there. Happy music? Joyful music? It was chicken dinner and an empty stomach; it was big-butted women and big white beds; it was country walking and windy days and freshborn crying and—Oh, there just doesn't happen to be any happiness that didn't come out of that horn.

Sonny hit the last high note—the Spoof blast—but so high you could just barely hear it.

Then Sonny dropped the horn. It fell onto the floor and bounced and lay still.

And nobody breathed. For a long long time.

Rose-Ann let go of my hand, at last. She walked across the platform, slowly, and picked up the trumpet and handed it to Sonny.

He knew what she meant.

We all did. It was over now, over and done. . . .

Lux plucked out the intro. Jimmy Fritch picked it up and kept the melody.

Then we all joined in, slow and quiet, quiet as we could. With Sonny—I'm talking about Sonny—putting out the kind of sound he'd always wanted to.

And Rose-Ann sang it, clear as a mountain wind—not just from her heart, but from her belly and her guts and every living part of her.

For The Ol' Massuh, just for him. Spoof's own song:

"Black Country."

CLELLON HOLMES

The Horn

FOR INSCRUTABLE REASONS of his own, Clellon Holmes has become the foremost chronicler of that group of delinquents, aspiring intellectuals, hopheads, advertising men, loafers and merchant seamen who hang out in Greenwich Village bars and call themselves, mainly because Holmes gave them the idea, "the beat generation." Some bop musicians are included in this group. This story is about a musician and a singer. We've put it in because it's the best thing about the modern school of musicians we've found.

Consider that it was four o'clock on a Monday afternoon, and under the dishwater-gray shade (just the sort of shade one sees mostly pulled down over the windows of cheap hotels fronting the sooty elevateds of American cities where the baffled and the derelict loiter and shift their feet), under this one shade, in the window of a building off Fifty-third Street on Eighth Avenue in New York, the wizen September sun stretched its old finger to touch the dark, flutterless lids of Walden Blue, causing him to stir among sheets a week of dawntime lying-down and twilight getting-up had rumpled.

Walden Blue always came awake like a child, without struggle or grimace, relinquishing sleep in accordance with the truce he had long ago worked out with it. He came awake with a sparrow stare, fast dissolving as the world was re-discovered around him, unchanged for his absence. He lay without moving, as a man used to waking beside the bodies of women will most often move either toward them or away, depending on his dream; lay, letting his water-cracked ceiling remind him (as it always did) of the gulleys of shack-roads back home where he would muddy his bare black feet when a child, and where, one shimmering-cicada noon, he had stood and watched a great, lumbering bullock careen toward him, and become a Cadillac-ful of wild zoot-suited city boys, pomaded, goateed, upending labelless pints, singing and shouting crazily at everything: "Dig the pick'ninny! Dig the cotton fiel'! Dig the life here!"; to bump past him, gape-faced there in the ruts, splashing mud over his go-to-meeting britches, and plunging on around the bend of scrub-pines where he once mused over an ant-hill in the misty Arkansas dawns—for all like some gaudy, led-astray caravan of gypsies, creating a wake of rumor and head-shaking through the countryside.

Walden Blue slid long legs off the bed, and for a moment of waking reflection—that first moment which in its limpid, almost idiotic clarity is nearly the closest human beings come to glimpsing the dimensions of their consciousness—he considered the polished keys, and the catsup-colored neck of the tenor saxophone which, two years before, had cost him $150 on Sixth Avenue, becoming his after an hour of careful scales and haggling, and the gradual ease which comes to a man's fingers when they lose their natural suspicion of an instrument or a machine which is not their own, but must be made to respond like some sinewy, indifferent horse, not reluctant to being owned but simply beautiful in its blooded ignorance of ownership. For on this saxophone Walden Blue made music as others might have made love a kind of fugue on any bed; Walden made music as a business, innocent (because love of it was what kept him alive), just what others might mean by "their business," implying as that did some sacrifice of most that was skilled and all that was fine in them. He considered his saxophone, in this first moment of waking, without pleasure or distaste; noting it with the moody, half-fond stare of a man at the tool he has spent much time, sweat and worry to master, but only so that he can use it.

Looking at it, he knew it also to be an emblem of some inner life of his own, something with which he could stand upright, at the flux and tempo of his powers—as others consider a physical feat an indication of manhood, and, still others, a wound; to Walden the saxophone was, at once, his key to the world in which (always like some mild, slouchy stranger) he found himself; and also the way by which that world was rendered impotent to brand him either failure or madman or Negro or saint. But then sometimes, on the smoky stand between solos, he hung it from his swinging shoulder like one bright, golden wing, and waited for his time.

"Hey, there," he said to himself reproachfully, dangling his feet in an imaginary brook, for it was nearing four-fifteen, which meant the afternoon was slipping by; and so he got up, stretching himself with the voluptuous grace some musicians give to any movement, and went about coffee-making. The electric plate was dead in one coil; the pot itself rusty from weeks of four o'clock makings; and, without troubling his head about it, he used yesterday's soggy grounds. Coffee had no taste or savor to him at that hour; it was merely hot and black. He started his day with it, and as though it poured something of its nature into him, by the swirling night-hours, amid smoke and roar, he would be like it: hotter and blacker, if anything. The second scalded cup was as necessary to the beginning of his day as the second shot of bourbon, or the second stick of tea was to its blissful morning end someplace uptown where, for sociability and personal kicks, he would blow one final chorus for himself, with a rhythm section of hardy, sweating souls collected from a scattering of groups around town, and then, packing up, go home empty of it all again. He drank his coffee back on the bed, lean shanks settled down on it, naked as a child; and each gulf re-established him in the world.

His mind was clear; in these first moments, scarcely a man's mind at all, for he had no thoughts, just as he rarely dreamed. One afternoon in L.A.—back four years ago when bop was an odd new sound, and a name for the jazz many of them had been blindly shaping, and something else as well (a miraculous, fecund word because no one then really understood its meaning, only somehow knew)—he sat on a similar bed over his first cup, just like now, and out of the sweet emptiness of his morning-head one thought had come, like cigarette smoke drifting across a shaft of pale sunlight, leaving no visible trace: that he was a saxophone, as bright and shiny and potential as that, and still as well. The night and his life would play upon him. Some afternoons since then, he recalled recalling this thought, and often giggled secretly at its foolish accuracy. But never troubled his head.

Only this afternoon something else was there. That morning—four or five at least, up at Blanton's on 125th Street where, in the back, and after hours, they served coffee and the musicians gathered to listen or play or talk that shop-talk without which any profession in America would be thwarting to Americans—Edgar Pool had been inveigled to sit in with the house-group (nothing more than rhythm upon which visitors could build their fancies), and, as everyone turned to him in the drab, low-ceilinged room, giving him that respectful attention due an aging, original man whom all have idolized in the hot enthusiasm of youth, something had happened. And now Walden remembered.

There are men who stir the imagination deeply and uncomfortably; around whom swirl unplaceable discontents; men self-damned to difference; and Edgar Pool was one of these. Once an obscure tenor in a brace of road-bands, now only memories to those who had heard their crude, uptempo riffs, and managed neither to remember nor forget (their only testament the fading labels of a few records, and these mostly lost, some legendized already, one or two still to be run across in the bins of second-hand jazz record stores along Sixth Avenue), Edgar Pool emerged from an undistinguished and uncertain musical environment by word-of-mouth. He went his own way, and from the beginning (whenever it had been, and something in his face belied the murky facts) he was unaccountable. Middling tall, sometimes even lanky then, the thin mustache of the city Negro accentuating the droop of a mouth at once determined and mournful, he managed to cut an insolently jaunty figure, leaning towards prominent stripes, knit ties, soft shirts and suede shoes. He pushed his horn before him, and, listening to those few records years later when bop was gathering in everyone but had yet to be blown, Walden, striving more with his fingers than his head at that time, first heard the murmur of the sounds they were all attempting. Edgar had been as stubbornly out of place in that era, when everyone tried to ride the drums instead of elude them, as he was stubbornly unchanged when bop became an architecture on the foundation he had laid.

He hung on through fashions, he played his way when no one cared, and made his money as he could, and never argued. One night in 1940, in a railroad bar in Cincinnati, where the gangmen came to drink their pay with their dusky, wordless girls (something in them aching only for dance), he sat under his large-brimmed hat and blew forty choruses of "I Got Rhythm," without pause, or haste, or repetition; staring at a dead wall; then lit up a stick of tea with the piano man, smiled sullenly, packed his horn and caught the train for Chicago and a job in a burlesque pit. Such things are bound to get around, and when Walden met him a year later (on another night at Blanton's) the younger tenors had started to dub him "The Horn," though never (at that time) to his face.

Edgar Pool blew methodically, eyes beady and open, and he held his tenor saxophone almost horizontally extended from his mouth. This unusual posture gave it the look of some metallic albatross, caught insecurely in his two hands, struggling to resume flight. In those early days, he never brought it down to earth, but followed after its isolated passage over all manner of American cities, snaring it nightly, fastening his drooping, stony lips to its cruel beak and tapping the song. It had a singularly human sound— deep, throaty, often brutal with a power skill could not cage, an almost lazy twirl on the phrase-ends; strange, deformed melody. When he swung with moody nonchalance, shuffling his feet instead of beating, even playing down to the crowd with scornful eyes averted, they would hear a wild goose honk beneath his tone— the noise, somehow, of the human body; superbly, naturally vulgar; right for the tempo. And then out of the smearing notes, a sudden shy trill would slip, infinitely wistful and tentative.

But time and much music and going alone through the American night had weakened the bird. Over the years, during which he disappeared and then turned up, blowing here and there; during which, too late, a new and restless generation of young tenors (up from the shoeless deltas and shacklands like Walden, or clawed out of the tangled Harlems and the back-alley gangs) discovered in his music something apt and unnameable—not the sound, but some arrow toward it, some touchstone —over the years which saw him age a little and go to fat, which found him more uncommunicative and unjudging of that steady parade of eager pianists and drummers which filed past behind him, the horn came down. Somehow it did not suggest weariness or compromise; it was more the failure of interest, and that strain of isolated originality which had made him raise it in the beginning out of the sax sections of those road-bands of the past, and step solidly forward, and turn his eyes up into the lights. The tilt of his head, first begun so he could grasp the almost vertical slant of the mouthpiece, remained, the mouthpiece now twisted out of kilter to allow it; and this tilt seemed childishly fey and in strange contrast to his unhurried intent to transform every sugary melody he played, and find somewhere within it the thin sweet song he had first managed to extract, like precious metal from a heap of slag.

Walden felt Edgar Pool threaded through his life like a fine black strand of fate, and something always happened. When he first heard him in the flesh—sometime back in 1942, in the dead-center of war, after learning those few records by heart, after finding his own beginnings in "Brahmin" Lightcap's big band that came in with a smashing engagement in Boston, swamped in publicity and champagne parties (because Lightcap was, after all, the Dean of Jazz, the scallawag from New Orleans cat-houses eventually medaled by the governments of France and Belgium for "good-will spread on a jazz trumpet"), and which went out six months later, a financial bubble, when the trumpet section grumpily enlisted in the Navy and most of the saxes were arrested on narcotic charges; after this, after waiting to hear Edgar, missing him in L.A. by a lost bus connection, getting hung-up in Chicago right after Edgar took up with Geordie Dickson, Walden had come into Blanton's one night, and heard a sound, and there was Edgar, horn at a forty-five-degree angle to his frame, playing behind Geordie as she sang "What Is This Thing Called Love," with a tremble in her voice then that made you wonder. Something settled in Walden that night, and he decided to get out of the big bands, the bus schedules, the dancehalls, the stifling arrangements; off the roads for a while; to stick around New York, which was his adopted pond after all; to give himself his head. It wasn't Edgar actually—just that aura of willful discontent around him; wanting a place, but not any place.

Since then Walden dug Edgar whenever he was around, puzzled and disturbed, but not until this morning in Blanton's had anything come out clear. Edgar had played with weary and indifferent excellence, noting neither Cleo, who played piano with Walden at The Go Hole every night but never got enough and, like so many young musicians (he was only 17) seemed to have no substantial, homely life but jazz, no other hours but night, and so hung around Blanton's till dawn with untiring smiles of expectation, nor the others who wandered in and out, listening to every other bar, gossiping, and showing off their latest women. Edgar stood before them, down among the tables for there was no proper stand, sax resting on one thigh, and Walden studied him for an instant with that emotion of startling objectivity that only comes when a man least expects or desires it. And for that moment he forgot his own placid joy at the night narrowing down to an end and to this hour among his own sort, at the sight of someone so inexplicably isolated from it all, though generally accepted as one pivot on which it turned.

Edgar fingered lazily, ignoring Cleo's solid, respectful chords, one shoulder swinging back and forth slightly, his chin pulled in. His hair was long over his large collar, he padded up and down on exaggerated crepe soles, between solos he chewed an enormous wad of gum soaked in benzedrine. They said he had "gone queer," but there was something soft and sexless about him nonetheless. Then he smeared a few notes over a pretty idea—a crooked smile glimmering behind the mouthpiece, all turned in upon himself, all dark; and Walden alone seemed to catch the sinister strain of self-ridicule behind the phrase, behind the sloppy, affected suit, the fairy hip-swinging; and at that moment the presence of a secret in Edgar reached him like a light.

For if jazz was a kind of growing Old Testament of the Negro race—and of all lost tribes in America, too—a testament being written night after night by unknown, vagrant poets on the spot (and so Walden, reared on a strange Biblical confusion, often thought of it), then Edgar had once been a sort of Genesis, as inevitable and irreducible as the beginnings of things; but now, mincing, chewing, flabby, he sounded the bittersweet note of Ecclesiastes, ironical in his confoundment. Then it happened.

Geordie Dickson flounced in with her cocker spaniel under one arm, and two dark, smirking escorts guiding her, half-tipsy, between them. And the sweaty faces around the room pivoted, and someone hoarsely whispered. For this was the first time in the two years since something unknown and awful had separated them that they had been in the same room. Their lives were fatefully, finally intertwined, for Edgar had found her singing in a back-road gin-mill in Tennessee (no more than sixteen then) and, probably with only a clipped word of command, had taken her away, and brought her north; a sturdy, frightened, bitter girl, one quarter white, raped at fourteen on a country lane by two drunken liquor salesmen, thrown into reform school where she was chained to her iron cot when her child was born out of her dead, finally released to find her family vanished, thrown back for pocket-picking in colored churches, released again in the custody of a probation officer who tried to get her into a whorehouse, and trying to keep off the streets with her voice when Edgar saw her first. He taught her some sense of jazz, got her the initial jobs, backed her up on the records that followed, and took money from her when, all overnight, she became a sensation to that dedicated breed of lonely fanatic which jazz creates. Walden, among the others, had often stood in the vest-pocket clubs on Fifty-second Street during 1943 as the lights faded away and one spot picked her out—mahogany hair oil-bright, the large gardenia over one ear still wet from the florist's, candle-soft eyes, skin the sheen of waxy, smooth wood—and heard the opening chords, on grave piano, of "I Must Have That Man"; and also heard, with the others, the slur, the sugar, the pulse in the voice and known, without deciding or judging, that it was right; and been dazzled too.

People turned wherever she went (although not anticipating a scene as they did at Blanton's that morning), because she had the large, separated breasts of a woman who has spent hours leaning over her knees, working or praying; breasts that would be tipped with wide, copper-colored nipples; breasts that would not be moored; made for the mouths of children, not of men. In all her finery (off-the-shoulders gown, single strand of small pearls, the eternally just-budded gardenia), her flesh and the heavy-boned grace of her body alone had any palpable reality. There was a breath-taking mobility to her—nothing fragile or well-bred—but that extraordinary power of physicality which is occasionally poured into a body. The deep presence of fecundity was about her like an aroma, something mindless and alive; that touch of moist heaviness (suggestive of savagery, even when swathed in lace) which is darkly, enigmatically female. She was a woman who looked most graceful when her legs were slightly parted, who appeared to move blindly, obediently, from some source of voluptuous energy in her pelvis; whose thighs shivered in brute, incomplete expression of the pure urge inside her.

Edgar did not indicate by even the quaver of a note that the excitement and apprehension in the rest of the room had reached him. He played on, as if in another dimension of time, when she took a seat not ten feet from him, the spaniel squatting in her lap, wet nose over the edge of the table, eyes large. Neither did she look, but went about settling herself, nodding to acquaintances, chatting with her companions. She was arrogantly drunk, opulently sensual as only a woman, in the candor of dissipation, can be; and beside her Edgar looked pale, delicate, even curiously effeminate. She had always been strangely respectful of him, even when swarms of white men had fidgeted at her elbow, pleading to fasten her bracelets, even when easy money had turned her life hectic and privileged; she had looked at him, even then, with a tawny, resentful respect, like a commoner with a sickly prince. She had sensed that he could see, and it always, just for an instant, blurred her picture of herself.

Now she was drinking heavily out of a silver-headed, leather-jacketed pocket flask; her eyes grown flashing and wet. The spaniel lay on her thighs, subdued, with the natural humility dogs often have before the antics of humans, and she poked and patted and cooed to him loudly, as if trying to goad him into a bewildered bark.

Edgar finished his chorus and gave it to Cleo on the piano, who never soloed; for whom the dreadful spaces of thirty-four open bars held no terrors, but small interest either; and then he slowly turned his back on her, a dreamy, somehow witless grin weakening his face as he muttered nonsense with the drummer.

His absolute lack of recognition in these first moments was the surest sign to Geordie that he was electrically aware of her movements there in the room, but something in him was indestructible, some merciless pride with which he chose to victimize himself. Only he could smash or break it. Some said, after all, that he had gotten her on the morphine habit she threw only when, at the height of her glittering success, she had been arrested for "possession and addiction"; other rumors went that love between them had been a stunted, hot-house pantomime, always lurching on the shadowy edges of sensations—as queer and deformed as Edgar himself; and certainly he had liberated a gnaw in her that had, ever since, run wild, even amuck, enslaving her to a vision of life he only entertained for himself, an ironical indulgence of whim he had only endorsed, with passion, for a brief season, and then unaccountably drifted away, leaving her stranded in it, gnashing her teeth.

She began to chatter with vicious affectation when he took his reed into his mouth like a thumb and blew a windy yawp—trapped into the chatter as in everything else, because his placid, punishing indifference (not only to her but to all the real world) was yet another symbol of some incalculable superiority. Her mouth, as it snarled and quivered, was (to all the stunned young men like Walden, who, years before, had thirsted after her like an ideal), to them, indescribably, cruelly sensual, as though she were about to faint from some morbid and exhilarating thought. But only her mouth had learned the tricks of contempt, brittleness, and sophistication. Her eyes glowed steadily with something else, and as Walden looked at her, in these first moments that seemed supercharged with tension and thus unendurably long, he saw (as this morning he seemed fated to see everything that had been under his nose for years) the nature of that something else; saw that her long, shapely neck had started to wrinkle; saw she had expensive powder in her armpits where there should have been soft, dark hair; saw some sweet rot in her; and knew there was a flaw now where there had been none before, a flaw developed by a life that had carved a black cross on her forehead; and then sensed the woman in her flesh again, now gone slightly stale, and remembered that some said even the dog had licked it.

Edgar chose this moment to blow sweet, as a final passionless mockery of the auspiciousness or sentiment that others might be feeling in that situation. His sound was disarmingly feeble, in earnest; but meant to prove, by some inmost private irony, that he was, if so he chose, a timeless man. The limpid pathos of his song was somehow a denial of the past, a denial of any power over him but his peculiar self-abusive ability, which he had mastered so totally as to be able to ignore it for years if that was his whim. And at that moment, just as Geordie's eyes drifted across him to something else, the saxophone, hanging limp against one thigh, stirred and came up, and there was (for just that second) a corresponding stir of vigor in his sound; and then he fell back into the vapid, thin tone, his horn descending, as if to say (and Walden heard) that he would be a slave to nothing, not even the genius inside him. His obsession (and all men are dominated by something) was his last secret, the note he carefully never blew.

To Walden (for that moment paralyzed, turned outward, willless), Edgar seemed a mask over a mask; all encrusted in an armored soul. Some said, he knew, that Geordie had once stripped the masks away, one by one, with no intent but desire, and had a hint of the inside, and been driven wanton out of helplessness. The secret must have been (as it most always is) that his need was formless, general; a need which persists only because no satisfaction could ever be fashioned for it; an inconceivable thing in a woman, a thing forever mysterious and infuriating to her; but something peculiarly male, the final emblem of imperfection, impotence, but with a terrifying power to wound or create, the Jeremiah-like power of a fury at powerlessness.

So they were alone in all that room, absolutely locked together and alone, and yet steadfastly refusing to notice each other, and Walden knew that Edgar would blow all night if necessary, burst a lung, dredge himself to obliterate her—and not because he cared, not for her; but because of himself. Already somebody was thinking about how he could possibly describe it to the "cats in his group" the next night. "Man, it was positively the gonest!" would prove far too thin, and by the time word of it reached L.A., K.C., Chicago, it would be a kind of underground history, one of those nights that, passed from mouth to mouth, year upon year, become, in the alchemy of gossip, fabulous and Homeric.

Cleo, alone of everyone, refused to be drawn into the drama of their wills, but looked from Edgar to Geordie, not casually or with suspense as the others were, but with an expression of trembling, clear-eyed sorrow, his little hands automatically making the sad chords on which Edgar was shaping his humiliation of sadness, his lips saying softly over and over again: "Oh, man, what for. Oh, man, why. Oh, man, no!" Edgar only wiped a phrase across the words and wiggled his hips.

Walden, too, was struck dumb, all eyes, somehow horrified, for now Geordie's mouth was capped with straining avidity around the neck of the flask, the spaniel staring up at her with baffled, dark eyes. Even Edgar watched this over his horn with a half-hidden, secretive smirk; and Walden, at that instant, suddenly thought of him as a Black Angel—something out of the scared, rainy nights of his childhood when his mother had tried to remember the Bible her mother had once, long ago in a bayou town, read to her; and gotten it all mixed and filled it in herself in a droning, righteous whisper—till Satan carried a razor and Babylon was a place in midnight Georgia, and the fallen angels were black bucks run wild through the county like the city-boys in the Cadillac, and even Jehovah wore a Kluxer's sheet, and everyone was forever lost. Edgar was a Black Angel, and half the tug Walden had always heard in his music was right there, clear and unavoidable— the dark-half, the damned-half, the sweet-demon-half. Edgar was a Black Angel all right, and Walden suddenly knew; for like many people brought up on the Bible like a severe laxative, he often thought, without whimsy, about angels and suchlike. Not that he believed, that wasn't necessary; but sometimes when he played and stared up into a rose spotlight so as to concentrate, he thought about some possible heaven, some decent kind of life—and groped blindly like any man.

If he had better understood himself and the inconsolable ambiguity of men's aspirations, the unforgiveable thing he did then might not have stunned him so. But he did not understand, and knew little of the concepts upon which men struggle to define their existence (although down in his heart waited a single note of music that he felt would shatter all discord into harmony), and so when he found himself suddenly beside Edgar, his horn clipped to its swing around his neck, and heard himself break into the pedestrian chorus of "Out of Nowhere" that Edgar was blowing, he was filled with the same sense of terror that had swept over him the first time, ten years ago, that he stood up before live, ominous drums and cut out a piece for himself. Only it was worse, because there was a complex protocol to "after-hours"; unwritten, inarticulate, but accepted by even the most beardless tyro with the taped-up, second-hand horn for which he did not even own a case—certain, in his feverish preoccupation with himself, that he had found the idea. There was a protocol and it did not countenance an uninvited intrusion from the watchers, no matter who. Even a man suddenly possessed by an unendurable impulse to blow was expected to wait his time and keep his head. On top of that, Walden (thought of among musicians as a "good, cool tenor," who was reliable, with sweet ideas, and a feel for riffs, but one who had not yet found his way) was presuming upon Edgar Pool, revered from a distance by everyone who came later and blew more; whose eccentricities were accorded the tolerance due to anyone embittered by neglect; and whose lonely eminence as "The Horn" was beyond challenge, a matter of sentimental history. What Walden did, then, was unheard-of.

But he started the next twelve bars nevertheless, keeping a simple tasty line. Edgar, reed still between loose lips, gave him a startled, then slyly amused glance, telling Walden, all in a flash, that for the audacity and stupidity of the move he would do him the honor of "cutting" him to pieces, bar to bar, horn to horn. But the affront had shocked everyone else; the room was frozen, speechless; and Walden knew he was, in effect, saying to them: "I secede from the protocol, the law," and further (and this he did not know, though it was the truth of what he felt): "What I know must be done cannot be done within it." But thereby he was placing himself outside their mercy and their judgment, in a no-man's land where he must go alone. Only Geordie was not transfixed; a slow, quivering smile had curled her lips, and her fingers had left the spaniel's ears.

Edgar leaped back easily, satirizing Walden's last idea, playing it three different ways, getting a laugh, horn hung casually out of one side of his mouth. The drums slammed in perfectly on top of Cleo's remonstrative chord, and Walden started to swing one shoulder, playing sweet when it was his turn, knowing they would take only six bar breaks from then on, to tighten the time, and finally only four, where a man had to make himself clear and be concise; the last gauntlet where a misfingered note could be the end.

Edgar slouched there beside him, as if playing with one hand, yawping, honking, aping him; and only his beady eyes were alive, and they were sharp, black points of irony and rage; not, somehow, at the ill-mannered challenge, but at something else, a memory that made him old in the recalling. And Walden looked into those eyes, and blew a moving phrase that once another Edgar might have blown, and was, at last, victm of the naive core of his heart, the unthoughtout belief that it mustn't be Edgar's way. He looked at Edgar, loving him even in all his savage, smearing mockery, battling not him but the dark side of that black-angel soul; bringing light.

It got hotter, tighter, and Cleo, staring at Walden as at a barefoot man exulting on a street corner, laid down solid, uncritical chords for both of them, that it might be fair and just—all the time his innocent, dewy eyes on the side of sweetness, who ever would speak up for it.

Walden looked at Edgar, sweating now and gloomily intent, and blew four bars of ringing melody, so compelling that Edgar stumbled taking off, unable to remember himself (for "cutting" was, after all, only the Indian-wrestling of lost boyhood summers, and the trick was getting your man off balance). And then Walden came back clear, and suddenly knew (so beyond doubt he almost faltered) that his was the warmer tone, that this was what he had always meant; and so experienced a moment of incredible, hairbreadth joy.

The silence in the room came apart, because music was fair contest. The crowd unwillingly shifted the center of their prejudices, acknowledging that "something was happening," and between phrases Walden could hear Geordie crying sharply: "Blow! Blow!" but, looking to find her rocking back and forth, eyes narrowed now to bright wicks, could not tell at whom she cried, and did not, he realized consider himself her champion; but was only bringing light.

Edgar was shuffling forward and blew four bars of a demented cackle, and, for an instant, they were almost shoulder to shoulder, horn to horn in the terrible equality of art, pouring into each wild break (it felt) the substance of their separated lives—crazy, profound Americans, both! For America, as only they knew it who had wandered like furtive Minnesingers across its billboard wastes to the screaming distances, turned half a man sour, hard-bitten, barren, but awakened a grieving hunger in his heart thereby.

In Edgar's furious, scornful bleat sounded the moronic horn of every merciless Cadillac shrieking down the highway with a wet-mouthed, giggling boy at the wheel, turning the American prairie into a graveyard of rusting chrome junk; the idiot-snarl that filled the jails and madhouses and legislatures; some final dead-wall impact. And in Walden, no sky-assaulter but open-eyed, there was the equally crazy naivete that can create a new, staggering notion of human life and drive some faulty man before it through the cities, to plant an evangelist on every atheist Times Square, a visionary in any godless road-house; the impulse that makes cranks and poets and bargain-drivers; that put up a town at the end of every unlikely road, and then sent someone with foolish curiosity to see what was there. America had laid its hand on both of them.

This time Walden had the last chorus to himself, having earned it. By that same unspoken protocol, it was understood by everyone that he had "cut," and so Edgar stepped back—for though the victor might venture outside the law, the victim, having nothing left, must abide by it. And Edgar accepted. The crowd was on its feet when the drums signified by a final, ecstatic slam that it was over, Geordie standing too, but in all the shouting and heated laughter there, she alone was motionless, grave.

Walden's moment of joy had gone off somewhere, and he felt a chill of apprehension and so swung on Edgar, one hand extended vaguely as if to right himself. But Edgar, unsnapping his horn, half-turned from the room, only glanced at him once—a withering, haunted look, a look he had probably never shown anyone before; and leveled now at Walden, without malice, only as a sort of grisly tribute to his prowess and his belief. It was to be Walden's spoils: that bewildered stare about the eyes of another man, whose effort, even to punish himself out of pride, had been thwarted. It was a look which had a future, from which heavy, fatal consequences must proceed; and with it went a weak, lemonade grin, meant only to cover the wince of nausea; for Walden knew then that Edgar had horrified himself, like a drunk who sees, in the single, focused moment of hangover, the twitching, blotchy ruin of his own face, the shadow across his eyes—knowing all along that the horror will not fight down the thirst, knowing then that he is unalterably damned.

At that, Edgar turned, leaving his horn abandoned there, and limped away, pausing only at Geordie, not to touch her, but only to peer at her for an instant, mutter something almost without moving those stony lips, and disappear into the crowd, making for the exit. Walden's hand still lay, half-spread, on the air, and he felt, for the first waking time, the import of tampering, for whatever the reason, with another man's tussle with fate.

Then Cleo was at his elbow, staring past him after Edgar, eyes moist with alarm, voice choked with shock as he exclaimed in an undertone: "Catch him before he dies! Catch him!" And he, too, ran away through the milling crowd, still on the side of sweetness, knowing where it lay, looking neither to right nor left.

So Walden stood there alone in the light, isolated in his achievement, and by it, breathless and transformed, the way a man feels who has, on an impulse coming up from far down in his soul, totally altered his life all in a moment, and who then looks up, stunned, to discover himself in a new moral position to everything around him. And in that dazzling isolation, only Geordie approached him, coming so close her fragrance swirled thickly through his head, and he saw that she was exhausted, sobered, and somehow resigned. For just a second they were caught in an odd, impersonal affinity, and in that second, she whispered.

"Don't worry. Don't you worry now. You know what he said to me? He only said: 'He sounded good.' Just that. Don't you worry now, honey."

She gave him a last, wan, forgiving half-smile just as her escorts hurried up, one of them snuggling the sleepy spaniel, and Walden knew, for all the smile and for all the words, that she was worried nevertheless. But she turned and glided away then, as though she too was going under; leaving him standing there by himself, while people he had known for years clustered and exclaimed around him as though he were a notorious stranger, and he held his head up manfully under their praises.

Sitting on his bed, it all came back with blinding clarity between gulps of coffee; all of a piece, all in an instant, undamaged by sleep. He got up, shivering with the memory, to pour himself the second cup and realize, with dumb acceptance, that this was to be the first afternoon of his life.

He had brought the light all right, but the conflicts in a man's nature were not to be resolved by light alone. Edgar had fled in disgust and despair at what it had revealed, fled from the light because it was not for him anymore; fled, open-eyed anyway, into the murk that had always stood around him. The light had only shown him an inevitable path. Walden was frozen, even now hours later, by the power one man had over another; it sickened something trusting in him, even though he could not disbelieve the clear impulse which had prodded him to stand up. But the consequences of an action were endless, and he could not see the end of this particular one. He had taken a stand for once, and as he had discovered about his tone, so he had, for once and all, damned himself to going his way.

Then he knew that sometime, perhaps in the cramped, second-sax chair of one of those tireless, all-but-forgotten road-bands of the mythical past, this awful moment of human commitment must have been pushed up to Edgar too, and, without thought or hesitation, he had leapt in, cutting his road alone; and blown, as himself, for the first time, and started down (for that was his unswervable direction) as he went up, started toward that morning and Walden by finally tapping the sources of himself, and letting his sound out. That was the only secret, and Walden wondered, with all the astonishment of a new idea, what his end would be.

From now on, he realized as he stood before the bed, suddenly amazed by his nakedness, there would be dreams through the mornings when he alone slept in the busy world, and, when he awoke, all the irritations and responsibilities of age and work. The armistice with sleep and discord had been forever broken. From now on he had to fight for his life and his vision like every man.

At that, the quiet loneliness of self-knowledge descended over him like a prophetic hint of the shroud toward which all lives irrevocably progress; and, pulling on his shorts, he remembered what Cleo had said just that morning:

"Catch him before he dies!"

And wondered if that was to be part of it too. But, putting the wondering aside for then, he set himself to dressing methodically. This was his first day in a strange, lonesome country, and one part of it, anyway, was knowing that it could not be postponed any longer.

JACK WEEKS

The Funeral of the King

JACK WEEKS WAS a newspaperman for seventeen years in Detroit and Chicago. He specialized in gangsters on duty and in jazz musicians off duty. He later served as executive officer on Yank, with no complaints from the enlisted men. After the war he did a stint as managing editor of The New Republic, then retired for a while to free-lance, turning out a couple of books for teen-agers and a large number of stories for Collier's and other magazines. In 1954 his first novel, I Detest All My Sins, was published. It was brought out by Dell and was not enclosed between boards, and the literary reviews and the daily press ignored it. But it was a fine novel, as this is a fine story.

Blue Tick crawled stiffly out of the boxcar in the Jersey yards. He had never been to New York before but he knew the end of the line when he saw it. It had been a long time, too, since he had beat the trains but never mind that. A man don't forget those things. They put you in jail when you're young and strong and keep you there till you're old and creaky but they don't change you much inside. Blue Tick stood quietly in the shadows, watching the flashlight of a yard bull and the lantern of a brakeman bobbing away

THE FUNERAL OF THE KING 425

together. When it was safe, he left the tracks for the highway and began the last lap of his journey to find Sledge.

Sledge was somewhere in New York, a big man now, the King of the Banjo, they called him. Old Sledge owed him something and Blue Tick had come to collect. It made him laugh to think how Sledge would be surprised to see him after all these years. About forty of them, Blue Tick guessed. Forty weary years. Thirty-five anyhow. He had lost track of them. No sense keeping count because they never gave you credit for good behavior. Eight or ten governors had come and gone before anyone had bothered about a pardon. And then the only reason they turned you loose was it didn't pay to feed you any more, once you got too old to work. Blue Tick was almost too old for anything now but he wasn't worried because Sledge would look after him.

A truck driver took him into Manhattan and told him how to get to Harlem. When he left the subway at 125th Street he asked the first man he met where he could find Sledge.

"Sledge who?" the man said.

"Just Sledge," Blue Tick said. "The King of the Banjo, they call him here."

"The only king I know," the man said, "is King Louis and he plays the trumpet."

"That ain't Sledge," Blue Tick said. "Sledge plays the banjo and sings songs. Old songs and some he makes up. He made up one about me."

"I don't want to hear it," the man said.

Blue Tick looked him in the eye.

"As old as I am," he said, "I could handle you. But I'm too busy."

He walked slowly down the street, stopping other people to ask about Sledge. Nobody seemed to understand him. He began to worry. He was a long way from home and it was cold up here. He was too slow to make out like he used to. Ever since he had got out of Camp Nine and had heard about how Sledge was a big man in the North, singing in the theayters, he'd been counting on Sledge to make it easy for him in his old age. He sniffed the cold air, looked at the light snow drifting past the street lamps and shivered. Then he saw a blind man playing a mouth organ by a newsstand. Blue Tick went up to him and asked the question.

"I don't know him," the blind man said, "but I knew him."

"What do you mean?" Blue Tick said.

He knew but he didn't want to believe it. He didn't want to believe his luck could be that bad.

"I mean Sledge is dead," the blind man said. "He died two days ago."

Blue Tick shut his eyes to get hold of himself.

"You a friend of his?" the blind man asked.

Blue Tick opened his eyes and looked at the blind man's face.

"Yeah," he said, "an old friend. He made up a song about me once, about how I got my name of Blue Tick because I can speak just like a blue tick hound."

The blind man put the mouth organ to his lips and blew a couple of soft notes.

"How does the song go?" he asked.

"I don't remember the tune," Blue Tick said, "but the words go like this:

> "You ought to hear old Blue Tick bay.
> You ought to hear old Blue Tick bay.
> When he makes his sweet music
> The hound dogs just fade away."

The blind man laughed.

"I heard him sing that song once," he said. "Let's see now."

He lifted the mouth organ and began to play.

"That's it," Blue Tick said. "That's the tune."

"Listen," the blind man said when he had finished the song. "If you want to see old Sledge before they put him in the ground you better get goin'. They're burying him tomorrow. Tonight they're holding a service for him up at Grayson's Funeral Home. You just about got time to make it. Three blocks up and three to your right."

There were so many white people at the funeral that Blue Tick couldn't believe he was in the right place. He had never known Sledge to have any friends among white folks. Sledge had got his name from breaking a white man's arm with a ten-pound hammer

THE FUNERAL OF THE KING

and that's how Blue Tick had come to know him the first time in jail in Arkansas. Later on, after their time was up, Sledge had cut a white man in Pass Christian and they had sent him up to Camp Nine for a good long while. They had sent Blue Tick, too, for just standing around when it happened. And now here were all these white people, come to mourn, evidently. If it had been another time and another place Blue Tick would have looked to see which one had the rope.

He began to edge through the people in the lobby of the funeral parlor. He stopped when he heard a man say:

"I think I knew Sledge as well as anybody."

Blue Tick looked at him. The man was fat and bald and had small, plump hands. Blue Tick noticed the hands because the man kept reaching up and smoothing his eyebrows. A tall, round-shouldered girl said:

"I'm sure you did, Van. But don't start a speech about it, darling —please. We've all heard it, anyway."

The bald man looked at her angrily.

"Sweet," he said.

"Don't make a scene, dear,"

"I'm not making a scene. I just wanted to tell you that Sally has asked me to do a piece about him and I thought you might give me your ideas."

He pulled some papers from a pocket and began to read:

"The king is dead. Sledge, who sang of toil and trouble. . . ."

He stopped reading, glanced at Blue Tick and turned back to the tall girl.

"Of course, this is just the first draft," he said. "It's more to give you the feeling. . . ."

"It gives me a terrible feeling," she said. "Let's postpone it for a suitable period of mourning."

Blue Tick moved away and looked into the room where the coffin was. Most of the seats were already filled. A straggling line of people was passing slowly by the coffin. The people were mostly better dressed than any friends of Sledge that Blue Tick could remember, and looking mighty sad. Blue Tick watched a large white woman in a low-cut dress and a hat made out of grapes and black straw stare into the coffin longer than the others and then stagger away, sobbing and blowing her nose. What do you suppose that scoundrel had done to make these people act like this, Blue Tick wondered. Maybe it wasn't the Sledge he knew, after all. Blue Tick thought he better take a look himself to make sure. He got in line, uncomfortable behind a small, thin, blonde girl. The girl seemed to be really sorry. More than ever Blue Tick began to think the blind man had sent him to the wrong undertaker's. His turn came at last and he looked down into the box.

It was Sledge all right, a lot older, but still big and mean looking. The dress suit was confusing but you couldn't mistake the scar that had come from a baling hook in New Orleans. They had been working together on the docks then. Blue Tick couldn't think what that fight had been about but he remembered that they had to run and keep out of town for a while. He went to the back of the chapel and took a seat. He found himself behind the woman in the grape hat. She was talking to a very pale man with heavy-rimmed glasses. Blue Tick leaned forward and listened to them.

"He was the last real minstrel," she said.

"Absolutely authentic," the man said.

"He couldn't be anything else," the woman said. "He knew the life of the people."

He sure did, Blue Tick thought.

A worn-out organ began playing somewhere and the whispering quieted. When the dirge ended five men in lodge uniforms walked in, looking embarrassed. Four sat down in seats that had been reserved for them in the front row. The fifth stood by the coffin with eyes closed for a few moments, then began an oration.

"Friends," he said, "we have come to pay the last respects to this poor clay who was in life Ellsworth Winchester, known in many famous places where he sung his songs as Sledge. He was a lodge brother of ours, joining us when he first come to New York on his journey through the world. We did not see as much of him at the lodge hall and functions as we would have liked to but he was a much beloved brother nevertheless. . . ."

The heat of the funeral hall after the long cold of the freight train made Blue Tick drowsy. He lost track of the lodge brother's words, which made very little sense, anyway. He doubted if the lodge brother had really known Sledge. Blue Tick wondered if any of these people had known much about him at all and what they would think if he got up now and pushed the lodge brother aside and told them the story of Camp Nine and the getaway. He would begin it with the day Sledge found the file.

They had been two years on that chain gang and the time was wearing them down. Later on two years wasn't much but he and Sledge were young then and every day counted. They were working on the road one day when the blacksmith's rig came by and the file fell into the dust. Sledge had it inside his shirt before the guards ever saw him stoop. The first night Sledge filed his leg iron almost through and then smudged over the cut with some charcoal he had got in the mess line. The second night Blue Tick did the same and the third night they got out. They went barefoot through the camp yard, with their shoes stuck in their belts, and the dogs paid them no mind. The minute they got clear Sledge picked up a stone and whenever they stopped to rest he honed the file until he had a fair knife edge.

They made good time through the swamp but they were still a long way from the railroad when they first heard the hounds around daybreak. They stopped and listened and Blue Tick felt his heart grow cold. Sledge leaned back against a cypress tree, panting, honing the file by habit, looking off toward the camp.

"It's too early for them to have found us out," he said. "Somebody must have told. I wish I had him in my hands now."

"You'll have those dogs in your hands soon enough," Blue Tick said.

"That's the truth," Sledge said.

He and Blue Tick looked at the sharpened file and tried to plan about the dogs. The two hounds at Camp Nine were famous all over the state. They were cross-breeds that could trail like a bloodhound and fight like a bear dog. With these dogs there wasn't any need to run them on the leash. The boss just turned them loose and when they caught up with a man they held him till the guards came. And generally chewed him some, too.

"What are we gonna do?" Blue Tick said.

Sledge waved the file back and forth.

"I'll think of something," he said. "If I can't kill a dog I deserve to be in jail."

"Nobody's killed these dogs yet," Blue Tick said.

"Nobody's caught this man yet, either," Sledge said. "Come on. Let's move."

The sun stood above the trees as they started running again and its heat filled the swamp quickly. They were not in good shape for running after the years in chains. The clamor of the hounds behind them was closing in fast.

"We better stop soon," Sledge said, "if we want to be fit to handle them. We got to think what we're going to do. One thing sure, I ain't going back to no road gang."

They came to better ground, rising from the swamp, and a little farther on a gully, cutting through a ridge and leading down into a stream. The stream was waist deep and moved with a steady current. Sledge stopped and grabbed Blue Tick at the mouth of the gully.

"Look here," he said. "We got us an ambush."

"Talk fast," Blue Tick said. "Them hounds is tuggin' at my britches."

"Here's what we do," Sledge said. "We run through that gully right into the stream. Then we turn back and clumb up the bank again and hide on the ridge right at the edge of the gully, see? You take on side. I'll take the other."

"Then what?"

"Then those old hounds are gonna trail right through that gully. When they hit the stream bank they gonna stop and worry a minute. And that's when you and I drop on them and stop them and stop them hollering for good and all."

"What about the boss and them? We ain't gonna drop on them, too? They got guns, man."

"Never mind them," Sledge said. "They're a long way behind the dogs. Come on."

Sledge ran into the gully and threw himself on the ground. He squirmed around for a moment and crawled on into the stream.

"I'm leavin' plenty of Sledge there for them dogs to smell," he said. "I want them to stop and think about me."

Blue Tick did the same and then they climbed up the bank and lay flat in the grass which hung like eaves over the gully.

"You ought to have something to fight with," Sledge said.

"I ain't got time to hunt for it," Blue Tick said. "Can't you hear them dogs?"

"I hear them," Sledge said. "They sound as close as you. If I didn't see your mouth shut I'd think it was you."

At that moment the hounds broke out of the swamp and came to the high ground. Through the screen of grass Blue Tick and Sledge watched them running straight up the hot trail. They came on with no uncertainty, their heads high, mouths wide, giving tongue now in hysterical yelps. They crowded each other into the gully, skidded at the edge of the water, turned back on the heavy scent left for them in the path.

Sledge nudged Blue Tick, slid over the parapet of the creek bank and dropped dead on one of the distracted hounds. Blue Tick saw the honed file flashing up and down. Then he dived himself and tried to take the other dog by the throat. He missed a good grip but got a fistful of hide and held on. The hound reared, snapping and roaring, catching Blue Tick off balance and thrusting him backward into the stream. As he twisted, Blue Tick felt a wrenching pain in his knee. Then the water engulfed him. He held on to the dog, trying to drown it before he drowned himself. Then the dog quit thrashing and Blue Tick stood up. When he wiped the mud out of his eyes he saw that Sledge had killed that dog, too, following him into the stream with Blue Tick and using the file. The other hound lay still in the gully.

"Hurry up, man," Sledge said. "We got no time."

He dragged both dogs into the stream. Then he went back and cleaned away the blood and brushed over the signs of struggle.

"Now we run some more," he said. "Only this time they ain't gonna know for sure which way we went."

"Maybe you're gonna run," Blue Tick said, "but I ain't."

He sat down and wrapped both hands around his knee. He knew from the pain that it was torn inside too bad to fix. In a little while it would be as fat as his thigh and stiff as a fence post. Sledge looked back along the trail, then he looked close into Blue Tick's eyes. He grabbed Blue Tick by the shirt.

"Can't you run at all?" he said.

"I ain't never gonna make the railroad," Blue Tick said.

"You sure?"

"I'm so sure I'm getting ready for that whipping they're gonna give me when they drag me back in."

"Well, then," Sledge said. "You can do something for me. I'll make it good to you. I'll make it up to you some way. I don't know when or how but I'll do it."

"What do you want me to do?" Blue Tick said.

"Listen," Sledge said, shaking him a little by the shirt. "You crawl as far as you can—that way."

He pointed east, away from the tracks.

"And I'll keep on the way we were goin'."

"How's that gonna help us?" Blue Tick said.

"It won't help us," Sledge said, "but it'll help me. Because when you get off a little way you're gonna bay like them hounds. You know how you can do that good enough to fool anybody. You just call those men to you, Blue Tick, because you're finished anyway, you said so yourself. And when they get to you over yonder in the east somewheres I'm gonna be far gone in the west. What do you say?"

Blue Tick looked at him, tried to get up, and couldn't.

"Might as well," he said.

"That's my partner," Sledge said.

He slapped Blue Tick on the back and ran. Blue Tick floundered across the creek and began crawling east. Every so often he rested on all fours and bayed long and sweetly. Then he would grin and think how his voice was traveling back through the trees, beckoning the camp boss down a false trail. It wasn't long before they came up to him but it was long enough to give Sledge his start out of the state.

The lodge brother came to the end of his speech and Blue Tick brought his mind back to the funeral parlor and looked around to see what would happen now. A white man was next on the program. He was pale and scrawny and wore a turtle neck sweater. He carried a big guitar up to a chair by the coffin and sat down and began to do some of Sledge's work songs. He sang them in a tinny voice, nothing like Sledge's bass, but Blue Tick guessed he meant well and it was good to hear them again, even from a man who surely never laid any railroad track.

Then a fat man in a tuxedo got up and said:

"Ladies and gentlemen, this concludes our services except for one little thing."

He looked around and moved his hands nervously. The woman in the grape hat whispered to her friend:

"Get a load of Rudy. The perennial master of ceremonies. He misses the mike."

The fat man cleared his throat.

"You all loved Sledge as I did," he said. "He sang in my club so often that—well, he was like someone in the family. I don't really know what we're going to do without him."

"I'll bet you don't," the grape hat woman whispered. "You'll probably have to close the joint."

"But as popular as Sledge was," the fat man went on, "he never made a great deal of money and he didn't save any. The sad truth is that he came to the end of his life without enough to—uh—"

The fat man put his hand on the coffin.

"—to pay bills like this. Now I think the least we can do is dig down and give him the kind of sendoff a real trouper deserves. I'm going to ask you all to leave something here with Sledge and I mean folding money, too."

The fat man turned toward the doorway and made a little gesture and Grayson, the undertaker, walked in, bearing a deep china bowl. He put it on a small table beside the coffin and backed away.

"I'm starting the ball rolling with . . ." the fat man said, and held up a twenty-dollar bill, turning it slowly, so that everyone could see the value. He held it with both hands over his head for a moment, then dropped it into the bowl. He walked out of the room. The undertaker cleared his throat and shifted his feet. The lodge brothers got up and filed slowly past the coffin, each dropping a dollar in the bowl. The rest of the crowd followed reluctantly.

Blue Tick stood in the back of the chapel watching them and wondering what Sledge had done with all his money. No matter what the fat man said, he must have made some. Then Blue Tick went up to the coffin once more, thinking about his own troubles and wondering how long it took you to starve to death in New York. He stood at the coffin, looking into it and thinking: You old scoundrel, this is the second time you went and left me flat.

When the undertaker tapped him on the shoulder Blue Tick put away all his good resolutions about the law and made up his mind. He reached into his waistband and pulled out the bulldog .38 that he had found in his last landlady's dresser, turned and shoved it against the undertaker's vest.

"Now don't make no noise," he said, "because I need this money bad and besides it belongs to me."

With his left hand he scooped the contributions into his pocket until the bowl was empty. He looked around the chapel.

"Is there any other way out of here?" he said.

The undertaker shook his head.

"There's just the one door," he said.

"You got a key?"

"Yes sir," the undertaker said.

Blue Tick took the key, pushed the undertaker into the chair and backed away.

"Now keep quiet for a while," he said. "If there's any talkin' to be done just let old Sledge do it. He can tell you the whole story."

Blue Tick locked the undertaker in and walked out. He went back to the subway station. The blind man heard him coming. He knew him from his chain gang limp, and called out:

"It's a shame you was too late to see your friend. How was the funeral?"

"Ordinarily I don't care for them," Blue Tick said, "but this one was all right."

ROBERT SYLVESTER

The Lost Chords

BOB SYLVESTER's piece about me and my burglars, which appeared in The Saturday Evening Post, was the first public mention of the barefoot school in a magazine with a mass circulation. Naturally, ever since then, I've held a sentimental regard for Bob and his work. It wasn't sentiment that prompted us to choose this story, however: it was the story itself, a good one, and one that will be appreciated by every musician who had to have a do-it-yourself Who's Who ready for a reporter. Bob manages to work in a lot of the folklore of jazz, which is another reason why this one stands out. In case anybody is wondering where he's met Bob before, he is a columnist on the New York Daily News and the author of a number of successful books.

E. C.

The greatest jazz trombonist of his time, which in his case meant all time, stared bleakly at the cup of black coffee before him while he tore apart the benzedrine inhaler. He got the cardboard shell off, dumped the drug-soaked cotton filler into the coffee, swished it around, and then removed it with the handle of the spoon. He took a tentative sip of the steaming brew and told himself he felt better.

The greatest jazz trombonist of his time was on the wagon. On the wagon for a while, possibly, but surely on the wagon for tonight. Tonight was one of the important nights. He would have to keep his head on his shoulders, tonight. Tonight was important to his career. He looked casually at his wrist watch. Not yet quite time for the boy from the jazz magazine. Five minutes or so to think about other things—things like his career, for instance.

He permitted himself a faint sigh. The night club where he was now working was only a few doors from the combined coffee pot and saloon which now sheltered him. It was no different, the night club, from most of the night clubs in which he had spent forty years of his life. The club was no different and the band he was bossing was no different. Both were typical. Especially the band. Tonight was a typical night in typical surroundings and with typical employees. The cornet player simply hadn't shown, as yet. The clarinetist was working under the handicap of a split lip, the gift of his latest beloved. The guitarist was drunker than usual. The boss of the joint was complaining a little more loudly than usual. The whole thing couldn't jump much longer. Just a few more nights like tonight, and the nights before tonight, and once again he'd be out. Out and looking for one more job just like this one. He could fairly feel it coming. The familiar drag chorus.

The greatest jazz trombonist of his time sighed again, this time a little more deeply, and thought about the boy from the magazine coming to interview him. He waited, staring at the benzedrine-spiked coffee on the enameled table, and told himself he just wasn't up enough to give the boy the same old story all over again. He just didn't have the strength to tell the child how he got to be such a success, the kind of a success who could win the jazz magazine's annual poll year after year. He wondered, idly, if he should tell the boy the truth. Like, for instance, the truth about his current job.

"You play six sets a night," the boss had told him when they signed the contract. "I'm giving you six dollars every time you show up in time for your set and a dollar extra every time you show wearing a clean shirt. You don't like it that way, take me to the union."

No, that wasn't the kind of a story which would do anybody any good. It wasn't even the kind of a story the boy would even want. He looked quickly at his watch and wondered if he had time to go to the corner drug store and get another benzedrine inhaler. He decided he didn't, and cursed himself for his own stupidity in not calling on Dr. Iodine during the afternoon and refreshing his supply of benzedrine pills. Dr. Iodine, whose name was actually Johnson, wasn't much like Dr. Kildare, perhaps, but he was a jazz buff and he could be depended upon for the kind of medication jazz musicians usually believed they needed. He wished Dr. Iodine would come in right now. He would ask Dr. Iodine for a prescription for some benzedrine pills. Or, better yet, he and the doctor would just walk back to the latter's office and have a couple of bennies together. It would help get him through this upcoming interview, at least.

He thought a little more about Dr. Iodine. There was always a Dr. Iodine hanging around any good jazz outfit. Just like there was always The Girl hanging around. And The Expert who hung around, the one who knew all about jazz and had decided that just one man, out of all the jazzmen in the world, was really worth hearing. Those types. They were always there, wherever it was, wherever you played, no matter what. The Doctor and The Girl and The Pusher who handled the junk and marijuana supply. And The Record Collector, who was possibly the biggest drag of all. The same old types. Everywhere. Through the years and across the country. These were the buffs, the only real followers the music had ever had.

He felt, if possible, a little more sorry for himself. The benzedrine inhaler, he decided, must have been pretty well dried out. And, of course, it was his second day on the wagon, always the worst day for him. He let himself sink further into the irritated feeling of persecution. It wasn't fair. The whole thing was wrong. Jazz was an art, the only true American art, and it deserved more from the public than it had ever received. He was comforted slightly by a remark once made by Artie Shaw, the clarinetist.

"The American public," Artie had said with his usual cynical contempt, "for years has been getting music which is far too good for it."

But Artie had been one of the ones who quit, who deserted, who went on to more commercial music. Artie had taken the easy way. But not him. He had started with jazz as a kid and he would stay with it until his lip broke down. It would be time enough then to start thinking of something else. He'd been there at the beginning and he . . . the beginning.

He smiled a little, now, again remembering the beginning. The beginning, for him, had been as a kid on the old Mississippi excursion boat, The Capitol. He closed his eyes and remembered again the music he had helped make on those moonlight sails of the old Capitol. The songs, the songs that so few jazz musicians even remembered, nowadays. But he remembered them. He remembered them all.

He remembered "Skeleton Jangle" and "Good Time Flat Blues" and "Iceberg Stomp." And "Jazz Me" and "Save It Pretty Mama" and "Empty Bed Blues." And "Three Flights Up" and "Rocks in My Bed" and "Didn't He Ramble?" And "Bucket Got a Hole In It" and "Make Believe Rag" and "Funkey Butt Take It Away."

He remembered the dead songs, all right, and he remembered the dead musicians who played them. The names and the faces came back again, came back with the titles of the songs. Long Green and Big Green, Muffle Jaw Chambers and Agile Bacquet. Yellow Nunez and Monk Hazel, Horsecollar Draper and Big Eye Louie. Paul Detroit and John Detroit and Detroit Red, no relation. The old bass player called Slap Drag, the silent oldster known as Dry Bread and the funny one called, for some reason, Shoe Bootie. All dead, he supposed. But he remembered them all, all right. He wished he could turn back the years and be with them for one more river cruise. Those were the best years, the young years. It seemed like nothing could really hurt you when you were in the young years.

He had been a kid when jazz music was still a thing played in Negro funeral parades and he had been still a kid when it suddenly became the popular thing in the Basin Street cathouses. A poor New Orleans kid, luckily a white poor kid, and the first time he had ever handled a horn had been in the waif's home. A big, battered, bent horn—but nonetheless a golden horn with a

THE LOST CHORDS 439

world of fascinating treasure in its simple mechanism. And, also luckily, a horn which had found its way to a charity organization where one adult teacher loved music and was, therefore, willing to spend some extra time and effort on any gutter brat who felt the appeal of music.

The true jazz was still in the bawdy houses, when he first embraced it with the first horn of his own. He got with it on the river, working the river boats, trusting the river, sure the great river would carry its cargo of wondrous music to the great cities of the nation. They were all sure of it, then. All sure they were going somewhere, taking their new musical art with them.

Well, they'd gone places in one sense. They'd gone from the New Orleans cathouses to Chicago dumps and dancehalls and clipjoints. They'd moved from one gutter to other gutters. They'd invaded New York and brought the art as far up—or maybe down —as the speakeasies and sidestreet drops. It hadn't been until the recent years that jazz finally had been discovered as an art. And even this discovery, it was beginning to be obvious, was the wrong kind of discovery.

It was the wrong discovery because jazz had been taken up by a cult. And the cult was as violently prejudiced as the other cults which scoffed at the art. The cult which had discovered the true jazz was convinced that the time for novelty and experiment was over. Jazz might be a product of artistic revolution, but one revolution was enough for it. No new upsets, please. Just play the old songs exactly the old way The same old songs exactly the old way. The same twenty or thirty standards. Play them the way they're supposed to be played, the cult indicated, and we'll sit here and decide whether you play them a little better or a little worse than somebody else plays them the same way. And then once a year our little magazines which are devoted to the true jazz will have a vote by the readers and we'll publish a list of the "greatest" musicians of the year. That was the cult.

His lips twisted bitterly, thinking his private thoughts about the cult. The cult was responsible for that National Jazz Foundation in New Orleans, for instance. Not that there was anything wrong with the Foundation. It meant well enough. But it was discouraging, in a way, that New Orleans had not discovered jazz was a Chamber of Commerce commodity about thirty years sooner.

If New Orleans could have recognized its own creation a little earlier, he told himself, Bessie might still be alive. Bessie Smith, the greatest blues singer of them all. Bessie had died in New Orleans. Died because she was injured in an automobile accident, died because she bled to death on the back stairs of a New Orleans hospital, and bled to death because the New Orleans hospital was a white hospital and Bessie Smith wasn't white.

Now, of course, Bessie was a solid New Orleans jazz legend. It would be funny, he told himself, if only you could laugh about it. But you didn't laugh about it and it wasn't even wise to complain about it. Best just forget it. Maybe the cult could have done something about it if the cult had come along earlier. It seemed nowadays as if the cult was all that the real jazz had left. But the cult just wasn't enough.

Once in a while, of course, some oldtime jazz man would hit it lucky, find some formula which had a wider public appeal. It had happened to him, once or twice, but the results were always the same. The brief flash. The sold out concert and the following confused critical reviews. The hurried recording date which furnished the records which sold only to the cult. The two or three quickly sponsored radio appearances which always went wrong. And then nothing. Nothing except back to a barroom in Chicago or a cellar in San Francisco or another dreary hotspot on Swing Street.

It was harder to laugh off, now. They had been able to laugh it off easier in the old days. He remembered the time Wingy Mannone had built the small band and booked it into a Chinese restaurant near Chicago. They'd taken the stand, that first night, and really set off. They ended the first set by blowing up a real storm with "Tiger Rag." When the set was over Wingy walked over to the pudgy, dead-panned Chinese owner who had been sitting quietly in a corner of the nearly empty restaurant. The Chinaman's name was Mr. Chum, he remembered. Wingy proudly asked Mr. Chum how he liked the band.

"Velly nice band," Mr. Chum told him. "Too much Tigah Lag. Two weeks notice."

How they had laughed, when Wingy came back to the stand and told them about it! They had laughed then and laughed later. It was all a laugh then. It was easy to laugh, when you were young and strong. The old Chicago days, those were the days, those were years for laughing. The days of Hitch's Happy Harmonists and of Roland Potter's Peerless Players. A man could even get a delayed laugh from thinking of those days, days when every jazz band thought it had to have a name like Roland Potter's Peerless Players.

Those were the days, all right, but he knew he could never have them again. Days when you met the rest of the jazz band in some saloon or in front of some stale agent's office, piled six men into a ramshackle touring car or limousine, got the instruments tied on the roof and stuffed under everybody's legs, and were off through the biting cold of late afternoon for some dance palace or hoodlum's hall.

Off for a night of playing music the way it should be played if you were good enough and strong enough to play it. A night which lifted you up, which lifted the customers to a new pitch of excitement, which ended with everybody flying, everybody so keyed up that it was impossible to cool out for a while.

So the cooling out process would take place on the ride back to the city. The bottle would be passed back and forth. And the best stick man would roll the long, thin marijuana cigarette and it would be handed around. Why, in those days a good stick man could roll a marijuana cigarette in an old car going sixty miles an hour over a bumpy road. Roll a stick without losing a speck of the dust.

One night in particular came back to him now, the night he had first met and played with the fabled Bix Beiderbecke. Bix was carrying his cornet in a paper bag, he remembered, and even the he had a pivot tooth which was always loose. Riding back to Chicago over newly fallen snow, Bix had knocked the pivot tooth out of his mouth with the neck of the bottle. The tooth had gone down through the broken floor boards.

They had stopped the car, taken a flashlight and walked back along the tracks in the snow, carefully examining each inch of white surface. Finally somebody saw a tiny hole in the snow.

Bix got down on his knees, felt with his fingers, and came up with the tooth. He put it back in his mouth. It was cold. He took it out of his mouth and put it in his pocket.

"I gotta remember to have that fixed," he told them seriously. "I can't play without it."

That Bix. He'd been a one, all right. He smiled faintly again, remembering the time Bix had been asked to describe the technical difference between a cornet and a trumpet. Bix gave it hard thought.

"You can pack more dirty laundry in a trumpet case," he said at last.

Well, he was too old now to live those days again even if such a chance were offered to him. There were no laughs now. Only the recurrent fears. Things scared him now. Things like what happened to old Bunk Johnson.

Bunk, of course, was a veteran when he had been a kid. Bunk had been one of the teachers of Louis Armstrong. He was the great jazz cornetist of the primitive days and he had come to about the expected end. When they found him, the youngsters who were bonafide members of the cult, Bunk was working as a laborer in the rice fields around New Iberia, Louisiana. He'd lost most of his teeth and long since hocked his horn but Bunk was probably knocking off a week's pay and living in what amounted to peace. But, discovering to their amazement that the legendary Bunk was still alive, the cult couldn't let him be. Oh, no. They had to resurrect him.

So they had outfitted Bunk with a set of store teeth and got him a horn and staked him while he practiced. Then they'd brought him to New York with all sorts of high class hullaballoo and surrounded him with some ancient Dixielanders and set him up in a beer-and-dance hall. Bunk went back so far with jazz that he was a natural for feature stories and exploitation, for a while. But Bunk only had one story and it couldn't last forever.

So two years later Bunk Johnson died. And he died right back in the same rice field where the cult had found him, again doing a day's work without his store teth and without the horn which had tricked him for the second time in his long and empty life. Yes, that was what had happened to Bunk. And what would, in one form or another, happen to him.

He closed his eyes tightly against this recurrent fear. There must be a way to avoid an end like that; there had to be something more for a man who had given a long life to a real musical art. There had to be a way out. Some way out. There had to be, but there wasn't. The only way out was to change over, to go commercial, to be a business man musician.

Well, he had even tried to be commercial, once, and that hadn't worked either. It was bad enough to go through the misery of failure when you believed in what you were doing but it was pure poison to fail when you didn't even believe in what you were doing. The commercial music wasn't for him. Too square for him. Let the cornballs have it.

A man with his reputation in the jazz field could always get some sort of work somewhere. If worst came to worst, there was always the one-nighters. A chill shook him slightly as he thought about the one-nighters and the probability that soon he would have to do them again.

You started out on the one-nighters the way you used to start out of Chicago for a jazz date. You had one or two cars, the men with instruments, and one or two wives as super cargo. You pulled up to the first dance hall, got out, unloaded the instruments, and went to work. The dance hall would be steam-heated and by two a.m. everybody would be perspiring freely. Then you packed the instruments and got back in the car for a ninety mile drive to the next town. Somebody would open the window for a little air. The next day you had the head cold which stayed with you for the whole tour of one-nighters. From the second dance hall to the last one you played trombone with one hand, using the other hand to hold a handkerchief with which you wiped your nose after every few bars. That was what one-night stands meant. And, something told him, he was faced with another jaunt of one-nighters.

The last one was so bad that he had been thoroughly discouraged. So discouraged that he just up and left the damn outfit in Detroit and beat his way back to Chicago, where he went to work in one of those lovely strip-tease saloons. A real haven for real music lovers. The saloon was worse than the one-night tour. He was lower than ever, that period, and he took to smoking more marijuana than usual. So when The Pusher was knocked off and the cops belted him around a little, The Pusher furnished the names of his clients. The cops came and got him and he did 30 days, that time. One more price he had paid for being the wrong kind of a musician.

The unfair part of it was that it was fate which made him the wrong kind. If fate had only had more sense he and the old boys like him would be the right kind of musicians; the other kind would be the wrong ones. The public was more at fault than he was because the public had accepted the wrong music and, by acceptance, made it right. Music in his day was played by musicians and played from the heart. Music today was played by trained mechanics and played from the head. There was no individuality left, no genius, no spark and no lift. No wonder so many old jazzmen were whisky heads or tea hounds or even drug addicts. A guy had to find some release from the emptiness of a lifetime of struggle.

When this kid from the magazine arrived, he probably would ask the same old question about why so many old jazz greats destroyed themselves by dissipation. He would have the stock answer, the answer he always gave. "The hours," he would say, not believing it even as he said it. But there was no use telling a story of failure—not when you had just been voted the greatest trombone player of the year. Again.

He had given the matter considerable thought, himself. He recalled a veteran radio executive who was a real buff and who had tried several times to do something for jazz, each time giving up in despair.

"Dixieland music was born in the whisky bottle," this fellow told him. "Swing came out of marijuana cigarettes and this new be-bop music is a product of cocaine. I'm through with the whole damned nonsense."

Be-bop. The boppers. The new school of jazz. How the old boys hated and feared these kids. They hated them and ridiculed them with an instinctive viciousness. He supposed he ought to hate and fear the boppers himself. Certainly they were a threat to his welfare. They'd taken enough jobs away from him, for sure. Bop was the new kick. It had its own cult, a younger and noisier cult than the old jazz had. These kids confused him and he was convinced they were all the way wrong, but he couldn't hate or fear them. Everytime he tried to hate them he kept putting himself in their places, remembering what a tough struggle it had been with the first revolutionary jazz, the kind he played, the kind which was now a legend.

The bop kids were just trying to find their way. To tell the truth, they had been blocked off from taking up the true jazz. Every good kid who came along was inevitably compared, to the kid's disadvantage, to some oldtimer or dead great. It must surely be dicouraging enough to drive the kids into a new form of jazz. A form that was wrong, of course, but at least was something of their own. Something for which they could devise their own rules and outlook.

It was typical, probably, that the old jazz men had turned so violently against the new school. But the old boys had spent so many wasted years thinking of themselves as daring innovators that any outside innovation was an immediate threat to their lifetime crusade. So they had immediately tried to knock the kids down. And, to their complete amazement, instead of staying down the kids had gotten up and started to knock back. It was developing into a one-sided contest because there were so many more kids and, as kids, they could punch so much faster and harder.

So instead of having two jazz schools working for the good of jazz as a whole, there were now two hostile camps each devoted to the destruction of the other. Nothing suffered except the music itself, of course. It was always that way. It was always taking a worse beating from within than from without.

He just couldn't get mad at the bop kids. Right now they were young and strong but the years would beat them the way they had beaten him. Bop was just another version of jazz and the boppers would one day stumble over all the frustration and defeat which had crippled and beaten the Dixielanders. Maybe, he thought for the first time, there was a curse on jazz itself. After all, the music had been born as marching songs for Negro funerals. Maybe death was somehow linked to it, somehow a part of it, somehow destroying it each and every time the art got started on what should be its upbeat.

There was nothing to be done about it. You spent your life trying for that elusive thing, a spontaneous musical art which came from your imagination and your heart, which every time you came near achieving was so contagious that everybody within earsound was affected by it. You spent your life trying to keep an evasive, tricky art alive. And you wound up nowhere and with the art right back in the slums where you first found it. It was enough to make a man cry real tears.

He sighed and gloomily regarded the empty coffee cup. He looked guiltily at the cuffs of his shirt. It was one of those nylon shirts that you can wash in a handbasin and dry without ironing. He had washed it last night, being on the wagon, and so far it still held its spotless, snowy shine. One more dollar from the boss, anyway. He sighed softly once more.

A man with thick horn-rimmed glasses and a peculiar, disorganized manner came vaguely up to the table and regarded him.

"Sold, pops," the man said.

"Vout," the greatest trombonist of his time answered. Listen, doc, walk me back to your office for a minute, will you? I'm beat down to my socks."

He walked with Dr. Iodine to the latter's grubby office in a crumbling brownstone and allowed the man of medicine to spill four heart-shaped benzedrine pills into his cupped hand. He separated them into pairs, flipped one pair into his mouth, and swallowed a paper cup of water.

"Join me, doctor?" The doctor declined, watching him with childlike admiration. "Then come back to the joint," he suggested, "and I'll blow up a storm for you. I'll really turn it on." The doctor nodded in full agreement. Ah well, he thought, having a buff this way is better than having to pay cash for what you need.

He was feeling better even before he was back on the street and at the door of the night club he was further pleased to find Benny Ferraro, the trumpeter, standing on the sidewalk with his horn. Benny readily agreed to sit in with the band "until and if" the regular horn man showed for work. Inside, the youth from the jazz magazine was waiting for him at the bar. The youth regarded him with open worship.

"Pops," the youth said, wringing his hand, "you're still the mostest."

"Reet," the trombonist told him, feeling almost good enough to laugh. "Don't sit up too close tonight or I'll blow you right out of the joint."

"Solid, father," the youth said worshipfully.

He introduced the youth to Dr. Iodine, referring to the latter as "a medico who really digs jazz," and went happily to the stand. The pills had given him a quick, good lift. His men were in their places, which made him feel even better. He worked the slide of his trombone and sprayed the fine lubricating oil along its length. Tonight he wanted to blow his best. The kid's jazz magazine would surely make a big feature of him. It wasn't a bad magazine; one of the most important, really.

Maybe this would be the night and maybe the kid would write the right article. Maybe this would be the time somebody saw the story, somebody in radio or television, or somebody at the concert hall in midtown. A night like this one could be the turning point. This night, this night which had started out just like all other nights, might be the biggest night of his life. Everything he had worked and fought for might be accomplished now, tonight. He spoke sharply, happily, over his shoulder to his musicians.

" 'Muskrat Ramble'," he told them. "Real bright."

He got the mouthpiece of the trombone against his lips, stomped his foot three times, and the music exploded. Without appearing to watch, he saw the kid from the jazz magazine begin to take notes. He went into the fast second chorus, playing for all he was worth, playing as well as he'd ever played.

This could be it. This could be the night.

GERALD KERSH

The Musicians

THE JAZZ PURISTS *in the audience may insist that the musicians in this story are not, strictly speaking, jazz musicians. Nevertheless, we are inserting it because it is an excellent description of the kind of atmosphere in which jazz thrives, and also because Kersh makes his characters, jazz men or no, come brilliantly and memorably alive. Also, we wanted at least one story with a foreign background. We have no notion of when or why Kersh put down these words; all we know is that it is Dickensian in detail and insight, and full of those metaphoric delights that have won Kersh a world-wide following. Incidentally, more of the above-mentioned atmosphere may be found in two of Kersh's novels,* Night and the City, *and* Prelude to a Certain Midnight.

The Banbury Tavern lies between a pin-table saloon and a black-glass cinema on the east side of a famous square.

If Piccadilly is the heart of night life, the Square is its rumbling, vital gut. The railings round the middle of it enclose benches and a patch of petrol-intoxicated grass: there are people who pass through the Square three hundred times a year without noticing the seats or the greenery. For the frontage of the Square is worth

THE MUSICIANS 449

its weight in banknotes. Here young people are initiated into the joys of life. Boys have committed crimes to get the price of a meal in that Square; girls have sold themselves for a dance, a glass of wine, and a teaspoonful of caviar in one of its cafes. History has been made on every one of its corners. Every brick and stone could sing its little song of money and blood.

The square is the drinking pool for the leopards and the fat cattle of the West End. It has its notorious tributaries and outlets —streets of drinking clubs, billiard halls, gambling dens, and mysterious furnished apartments off dim red-carpeted stairways that lead to the upper parts of all-night coffee shops. A few yards away lies Charing Cross Road, which is the anteroom of Limbo and the waiting place of the pallid damned. Here, day after day, year in and year out, people loiter at the doors of the theatrical agents—midgets, acrobats, tattooed ladies, conjurers; living skeletons, fat men, giants, freaks with rubber faces, dramatic actors in moth-eaten astrakhan collars, cracked tenors, broken wrestlers, legerdemain experts with stiffened joints, equilibrists with no sense of balance. Human encyclopedias whose memories are failing, composers whose vogue is gone and forgotten, comedians who can raise only smiles of pity, beauties whose eyes have wrinkled, soubrettes who nauseate, ventriloquists whose lips tremble, glamour girls as disenchanted as a provincial theatre in gray daylight—all standing in melancholy idleness, with a wan eagerness that is more pitiable than despair, hoping against hope, waiting under the scythe of Time.

Toward Piccadilly, in Archer Street, the musicians segregate themselves. They also stand and wait in little groups. At the snap of a finger you may pick up a swing band, a washboard quartet, a phalanx of xylophonists, a couple of symphony orchestras, a whole encampment of tea-shop *tziganes*, complete with side whiskers, or a hopeful and willing army of men who are ready to croon a Mammy song and play a tuba and double on an electric guitar, or do anything at all for the sake of a job.

People in this locality move in unbreakable circles, like fish in a bowl. Archer Street, Charing Cross Road, and always back to the Square, where the doors of the Banbury Tavern snap like the jaws of an amiable dog.

It was inevitable that theatrical people should take possession of the Banbury. It is a species of Green Room. Everybody knows everybody else. The doorway is always choked with dear friends who have met at the cash desk. There you may see young women of that painted, modish beauty which changes with the seasons and is peculiar to show girls; men from some show across the road, in cyclamen trousers, with their faces still made up; comedians in work; singers in their glory, who make their ten and fifteen pounds a week and eat every day; tap dancers with happy ankles; adagio trios, consisting of two young men as powerful as bullocks and a girl as light as a humming bird. There is also a sprinkling of mixed sportsmen from the old light-heavyweight champion's pub round the corner. Not every Tom, Dick, or Harry may hang about the Banbury Tavern sipping little cups of coffee. This place is for breadwinners; there is a minimum charge. It is, furthermore, something like a club. Everybody is called by a Christian name, and that of an affectionate kind: Maxie, Bunty, Kitty, Jerry, Zena, Peaches, Billy, Hughie, Orchis, Eyelashes, Sweetness, and Toots.

The atmosphere of the tavern is strangely lurid. The light comes from red and green neon tubes, which cast so eerie a radiance that a glowing cigarette end looks yellow and a red cigarette packet becomes orange color. The customers sit in pews, four to a table, and eat American food. They take to sweet corn and waffles as to American accents. So they nourish themselves with hamburgers garnished with carrots, and sandwiches so full of strange vegetables that they resemble little Hanging Gardens of Babylon. The place is never empty. There is a perpetual mutter of conversation, while waiters, swathed in white and scoured like attendants in an operating theatre, dart from table to table with hygienic glass bottles of scientific coffee and surgical trolleys of transatlantic pie.

It was here that I met the musicians.

I had accepted dance music as an ox accepts grass. It was there; I took it in without wonder. There had always been at the back of my mind a vague contempt for the men who played it.

But when I met the three little musicians I was ashamed. They had in the first place a stupendous vitality, these remarkable fellows who drugged themselves with raw rhythm and flogged their nerves with neat noise.

It was not until later that I discovered their profound artistry.

There was nothing about the appearance of the Dougal brothers that distinguished them for other men. Willie, the elder, looked like a youth apprenticed to a serious-minded shopkeeper. He had a timid, preoccupied air, a downtrodden look. There was neat self-effacement in every line of his round, white face, in his primly brushed hair, large round spectacles, and unassuming clothes. He seemed to be brooding over something trivial, say a discrepancy of a farthing in his master's accounts. Jamie, the younger, was thinner, redder in the face, and more vivacious. He also might have been a shop assistant, but in some place where there were boys of his own age and possibilities of a little harmless fun. On second thought I decided that Willie was articled to a lawyer, while Jamie was a medical student.

Anything but musicians, I thought. But the third man, Sid, looked colorful and romantic. He wore his hair long, and creamed so that the comb marks were as clean cut as chisel lines in ebony. He was no bigger than thirteen-year-old boy, and as dark as night; swarthy, sorrowful, handsome, dandified, with profound black eyes and tortured brows that met in a struggling sprout of fine black hair.

And yet they told me they played in a septet. I asked them what they played, and how they played.

"If," said Willie, shyly looking away, "if it wouldna bore you too much, and if you've ten minutes to spare. . . ."

"We've a rehearsal," said Jamie. "Moore's Rehearsal Rooms in Lisle Street."

I followed them. Moore's is soundproofed, yet noise gets through the walls. Passers-by stop dead in their tracks like caracoling horses, shocked to a standstill by shattering blasts from upstairs. There is no end to the fantastic variety of music rehearsed at Moore's. Serious-minded quartets saw out Bach with the assiduity of Newfoundland lumberjacks; Harlem bucks moan songs of mud and cotton.

When I arrived, the septet was arranged on chairs. The musicians had the tense appearance of men condemned to die—

with an underlying cheerfulness, as if they were to die in a good cause. Jamie was moodily poking at one note on a piano. It was the F above the middle C; I remembered it afterward when he told me his story. Willie had a violin in his hands. Sid, with an air of doom, had unclipped a guitar case and was peeping into it as if it contained serpents.

The leader, who clutched a saxaphone, said, "Now," and blew a note. His mouth and hands were full: he conducted with his hips, his nose, and his eyebrows. Two saxophones, a trumpet, a set of drums, Jamie's piano, Willie's violin, and Sid's guitar all exploded at me. I was sitting three feet away from the mouth of the trumpet. With that stunning burst of sound, I expected a high wind. I realized then how a man feels when he is playing in an orchestra, how he becomes part of the music he plays.

The second saxophonist played without moving his body. He was a long, lachrymose man, but as his fingers ran over the keys, complicated as the controls of a submarine, his eyelids drooped, his cheeks fell in, and something like a sleepy smile curved the corners of his mouth, as if he were sucking sweet nourishment out of the reed.

The trumpeter sat still. Only his feet moved, tapping the floor. His eyes were empty. His forefinger fascinated me; it was pure yellow, and this yellow finger rose and fell on a yellow key, letting out clear, cold blasts of rhythmic sound—yellow sound!—while his lips were shut tight. I swear to you that you could not have pushed a knife blade between thoselips. It seemed to me that his instrument was soldered to him; that he must eat and drink through the trumpet; that he was an inexhaustible cistern of noise, and the key was a tap. When he played a sustained note, his forefinger grew rigid; music came out in a hard jet.

The drummer brandished strange weapons. He tickled the parchment with wire and it laughed; rapped it with sticks and it groaned, while the man's face, distorted as if with rage, writhed and grimaced, and a queer fleck of golden light, reflected from one of the cymbals, fluttered around his mouth and forehead.

But Willie seemed to sit above it all. I watched his face, It expressed the mildest kind of astonishment. He held his violin, richly colored like smoked fish, and glanced with a kind of dismay at his left hand, which, leaping out of his cuff, was running wild on the strings. And Jamie clowned. He grimaced, wagged his head like de Pachmann, winked, nodded at me, and pretended to swallow a cigarette, while his hands sprawled and bounded on the keys like spiders on a hot plate.

Sid, fiercely feeling his way over his guitar like a killer after a death grip, picked out pure, profound notes and flicked them into the boiling pot of the music, while the leader, perched on one leg and twisting his entire body, emptied his lungs into his saxophone and screwed up his eyes.

They stopped. "No," said the leader.

Willie blinked mildly, and then, with the power and the subtlety of a master, played half a dozen bars out of Beethoven's "Quartet in C Major."

"Try 'Flat Foot Floogie,'" said the leader.

Later, as he went downstairs, I said to Willie, "Why aren't you billed as a virtuoso? Why aren't you playing in a concert hall?"

"He has done," said Jamie.

When?

"When he was ten years old. You should have seen him, in a little kilt and an Eton collar. Can you imagine? A fiddle, mark you, with an Eton collar. Mother made us wear them. He was an infant prodigy. So was I. Shall I tell him, Willie?"

Willie murmured, "Yes."

We went back to the Banbury Tavern. Sid came too.

The entrance was blocked by another group of musicians. Christian names fell as thick as raindrops. "Look who's there," whispered Jamie, nudging me. A slender, pale man in an exquisite suit of clothes was saying something to a ponderous, pear-shaped drummer. I listened. "The sax sounded like a piece of string!" and the slender man, with an expression of unendurable suffering, turned away and slapped himself in the neck. The drummer shrugged his heavy shoulders, and looked as if his mouth had filled with bile.

"Bert," whispered Willie. "The Bert."

But Bert walked away, still shaking his head, with the black melancholy of ten thousand midnights on his back.

"Maxie," said Sid, jerking a thumb toward the pear-shaped man.

"You wouldn't think it, but he can play the drums like a cannibal," said Jamie. "And look, there's some room at that table—the table there, where the colored fellow is sitting. Hiya, Blue. Do you mind if we sit here? Meet Blue."

Blue, a Jamaican trumpeter with a face that might have been gouged by an Ashantee wizard out of a block of milk chocolate, squeezed my hand in a great dry grip.

"I was telling you about Willie and me," said Jamie.

A wild-eyed man came and whispered in his ear.

"I can manage half, if that's any use to you," said Jamie, producing coins.

"Thanks, Jamie, thanks a lot, Jamie. Thanks a whole lot."

"Money," said Jamie, with some bitterness, when the stranger was gone. "That, in a way, has been the ruin of Willie and me."

Though we are musicians (he said), we come of a respectable family, from Aberdeen. Father and Mother are simple, ordinary people. Willie and I are crazy. Music—I don't know how it is, but music just broke out among us like an epidemic. Our sister has it, too. She plays the cello.

I don't know exactly how Willie took to it. It began with his having a fiddle—a little sawed-off, half-sized thing—when he was six years old. They took him to a teacher. Willie was so shy he didn't dare to ask where the bathroom was and had an accident. But as soon as he was told what to do with this queer little violin of his, well, he simply played. It came natural to him. You ought to have seen him, weeping with embarrassment but playing away for dear life. I can't explain it. He had a natural talent. Willie played that violin just as a duckling swims. It must have come from somewhere. God knows where. Have you ever bothered to look at his hands? Look, and you'll see: he has muscles that nobody else has.

Well, Willie was learning to play the fiddle. So I, of course, had to learn the piano. I was sent to some old lady who gave lessons. She was a worried soul. You know the kind of thing—letting a few rooms, cooking meals, minding babies, and teaching piano, all at the same time, for about sixpence an hour or something equally absurd. She had a very depressing little house a few streets away from where we lived—och, a horrible little house! But the pride of her life was her piano.

THE MUSICIANS

It was a great Bechstein grand, a black one. She must have spent two hours a day polishing it. You could see your face in any part of it. The first thing she said to me was, "Jamie, this piano cost a hundred and fifty pounds." I was terrified of it. I hardly dared to hit the keys. A hundred and fifty pounds, I thought.

Well, I, also, had a little talent. Nothing quite like Willie, mind you, but not bad at all. I was shaping very well, as a matter of fact; that in spite of the fact I was only about seven years old and considering who was teaching. And I liked having those lessons two or three times a week.

Pass me the sugar. One afternoon—it was a Saturday, and I remember it well: it was pouring with rain and I had to wrap myself up in a big coat and wear my little rubber Wellington boots—I say, one afternoon, when I went for my lesson, this poor old lady was in a devil of a state. She was cooking a dinner, or something, and scrubbing the stairs at the same time. I know she had an apron on. I took my coat off and watched my reflection in the piano lid—it was like one of those funny mirrors in a side show, you know—and waited for my lesson. I didn't dare to lift that sacred lid without permission.

The teacher came in and opened the piano and said, Jamie, my boy, do you mind running over some scales for ten minutes or so until I'm ready for you?"

"Why, yes," I said, and sat down. It was a pleasure, you understand. She went out, shutting the door. I went over some scales. And then I heard something rattle.

I looked down at the keys, and I swear that my heart simply stopped beating. It did. Because something awful had happened. The little oblong of ivory on the F above the middle C had come off. And there, on this marvelous white keyboard, there was a dreadful brown patch. I picked up the bit of ivory, looked at the brown patch. It had some traces of glue on it. I spat on the glue, and tried to stick the ivory back, pressed it down with all my force, touched it, and it came off again.

Then I went into a panic. A hundred and fifty pounds' worth of piano ruined, I thought, and sweat just poured off me. I put the ivory in my pocket, then thought, "No doubt she'll fetch the police and I'll be searched." So I took it out again and dropped it into my right boot. My heart was going like a little steam hammer when she came back. "Sorry to have kept you waiting, Jamie," she said. "Now—" And then she stopped and there was a silence you could have cut with a knife. My eyes felt like fifty-six-pound weights. "Jamie," she said. I said, "Yes?"

"What have you done?"

Silence.

"Jamie, what have you done to my piano?"

"Nothing," I said.

"You have."

"I haven't."

"You have. That note there.

"What note?"

She pointed to the brown patch. "Why," I said, "it was like that when I came in."

"No," she said. "I looked at that piano just before you came in and it was not like that."

"It was," I said, and burst into tears. "Perhaps it fell through a crack between two of the notes."

We looked over all the notes. No bit of ivory. We looked under the carpet. No ivory. And all the time I had a dread—a real, awful dread—of being searched. And at last the moment came. "Jamie," she said, "turn your pockets out." I did so, one by one. Out came marbles, lumps of toffee, spinning tops, bits of elastic, yards of string, a knife, a water pistol, half a broken watch, seven pencil stumps, a black mask—everything in the world but the missing bit of ivory.

I looked up at her. Saved, I thought. She sighed, and seemed about to burst into tears. "Jamie," she said, "if you've got that key, tell me, just tell me. Tell me the truth, Jamie," she said, "for God's sake"—that scared me, that "God's sake"—"for God's sake, Jamie, tell me."

"I haven't got it, I swear," I said, weeping like a tap.

"Ah," she said, and paused. I knew what was coming. "Jamie, it might have fallen into one of your Wellington boots."

"No!" I yelled, in absolute horror. "No! No!"

"Take them off."

"I won't! No!"

THE MUSICIANS

She caught hold of me, got my left boot, pulled it off in one jerk and shook it. Nothing fell out. The ivory was in my right boot. "Now the other one," she said. But you would have had to saw my leg off to get that boot. I clung to it, kicking and screaming, and at last she had to let me go. Sobbing and sniffling and palpitating, and feeling that my last hour had come, I ran home. I never dared to breathe a word about that bit of ivory. It haunted my dreams for months afterward. When I went back for my next lesson, she looked at me so bitterly that I couldn't play. And it was the same afterward. By the time I came under a decent teacher, it was just the slightest shade too late. I could become a good pianist, an excellent one, but not quite a master pianist. For that incident—I was a sensitive little soul, like Willie—that bit of ivory, and all that horrible business connected with it, had worked itself into my nervous system. And to this very day, I have a kind of flash of distaste whenever I have to play the F above the middle C. That is odd, eh? But there it is.

All the same, I got along. But Willie was a born artist. You have to be, to take to a fiddle as he did. A violin is very different from a piano. Willie, here, was born with something that it takes years to learn. At the age of seven he could play a Mozart concerto, a Bach concerto, and even the Brahms violin concerto. At nine he was an accomplished performer. At ten—

Listen. There is a thing called the Sir James Caird Scholarship, open to all Scotland. Willie entered for it. It was ridiculous. One had to produce an original composition, and the devil knows what besides. And there was Willie, a weeping infant in the kilt I told you about and an Eton collar. It's practically a physical impossibility even to play a violin while you are wearing an Eton collar, anyway. You just imagine—wee Willie surrounded by strapping great men of thirty or so; serious students with lifelong experience, with their pockets full of quartets and I don't know what else, and all the grim-faced examiners. There wasn't a chance.

He had brought nothing but his silly little sawed-off fiddle. Nobody noticed him. He trembled in a corner. Men got up and played. They sounded like Kreisler—you know what I mean: men with all the tricks. They bowed and they agonized and they went about their business like finished performers.

And at last came Willie. "What have you got?" He was tongue-tied, and stood there wondering where the bathroom was and clutching his toy fiddle. Finally he played. And when young Willie played, his heart and soul went out at his finger tips and came up through the strings. He played one simple tune of Schubert's. At first the examiners—you could see it in their faces—were determined not to take much notice. They certainly weren't going to be impressed by Willie's timidity and youth—that pasty-faced little moon-calf!

But they melted. It was like steam over icicles. The sheer purity and simplicity of the music he got out of that kipper-boxwood fiddle won them over. No master could have played better. It was exactly perfect, and full of feeling, understanding, and soul. They were unanimous in their praise, I tell you, and awarded him the scholarship without argument. He was to go abroad and study. The newspapers gave him headlines. Menuhin? Bah! Discovery of Child Prodigy!

But the very idea of going so far away from home simply broke young Willie down. He couldn't do it. And back he came.

But that wouldn't have made so very much difference, or at least it might not have. I don't know. I really think that it was what happened afterward that did the real damage to Willie as a master violinist. Because he was as good as Kreisler had been at that age—an infant prodigy, neither more nor less.

You see, we used to give little performances at concerts. We, as the little prodigies, were in great demand. Well, one day there came a man with a rattling voice who ran a variety show in Greenock. I don't know what Greenock is. We didn't then, I shall never forget the offer he made us. I, as the sharp younger brother, took charge of the business side.

"Give you twelve," he said. I was incredulous. Twelve shillings for a week's playing! Six shilling each! It was a fortune. He saw me hesitate, saw the joyous surprise, in my eyes, and said, "All right, I'll make it thirteen." "Done," I said. When I saw in the contract that he had meant pounds instead of shillings, I fainted.

We went to the hall in Greenock. It was the toughest place in the town. The scum of the yards used to go there for the pleasure of razzing the performers. The more cat-calls one got, the better.

They had to have wire netting over the stage, to protect the performers from bottles and vegetables thrown from the auditorium. All that was part of the fun.

We went on through a perfect uproar of razzberries and boos and whistles. We were going to run away. "You are doing fine," the manager said, and pushed us back. So there we stood while a fusilade of apple cores and orange peel bounced off the wire netting, and a houseful of roaring men and screeching women shouted us down—playing Strauss, Schubert, and the stickier classics.

So we were shouted off every night for a week. The manager was pleased. He gave us our thirteen pounds and sent a chucker-out to see us safely on the train. And that was the end of the matter. We had appeared in public—Willie, delicate as a new-born butterfly, and me, with my nervous kink about the F above middle C. I got over it all right. But it did something to Willie. Willie, genuinely a prodigy, really a budding master.

He can still play as well as anybody but the very finest fiddlers. But something has got into him that stops him. One day, maybe, you'll hear him play the stuff he likes to play. But now—ha, he itches and jumps. Fiddler in a dance band—a good one, a perfect one, but a fish out of water. You should hear him when he doesn't know you're listening.

So there it is. They drove the music back into him. I don't express myself as clearly as I could wish. The kettle was boiling and they riveted the lid down—there's all the force, all the heat, imprisoned. For myself I don't mind much. But Willie? That's bad. Ah well, if he'd been born in Budapest—excuse me, you've a smut on the side of your nose—he'd be Dear Master. But a pennorth of ivory, a dock rat with an apple core—it's astonishing what damage they can do.

Oh, by the way, Blue. Have you heard Ted White's latest number? "Blackout," he calls it. I've heard worse.

To hell with music.

It was dark now. We walked southward.

"I started to write a ballet once," said Sid suddenly.

"What kind of a ballet?" I asked.

"Oh, a ballet. Once I did a descriptive piece." He lit a cigarette. In the light of the match, which blazed like a beacon in the blackout, I saw his eye, moody and dark, full of something strangely formidable. "One night," he said, "I was on tour, staying in an apartment house. Did you ever listen to a boarding house about midnight? A sort of—undertone of nervous headache. Bongg—bongggg—the house relaxes—and other things join in: outside a tram, the last tram, and a cat, and a bicycle bell. Then in the room upstairs somebody trying to get comfortable on bedsprings. Next door some voices, a man's and a woman's, and a tap running and two boots falling. A gas fire. A kettle. Then . . . well, it ends Ahh-hhaa, boom-ba-haaa boom-bahaa—you know, your heart beating, and the rise and fall of breathing. One day. . . ."

"Yes?"

"Nothing. You'll see."

"Charing Cross," said Jamie. "We go down here."

I saw them go down. A train shouted, a lift gate clashed. The whole town then seemed to whistle and hoot, killing with one universal catcall a million unsung songs and broken symphonies.

OSBORN DUKE

Oh Jazz, Oh Jazz

ORIGINALLY WE HAD *planned to include "Struttin' With Some Barbecue," Osborn Duke's first jazz story—but it already had been reprinted and also had been made into a television play. Then a friend told us about this one, which appears here for the first time. It is strictly a musician's story; few others have ever managed to capture, as this one does, the spirit and single-mindedness of musicians united stubbornly in a band that is a success only in the eyes of its members. Duke is the author of a recently published novel about jazz,* Sideman.

I banged the keys and got up from the piano, hungry. I opened my trumpet case, thinking maybe there'd be a candy bar. There wasn't so I banged it shut.

"Come on. Let's eat," I said to Durf.

"You don't have to wait on me," he said.

Durf and I were alone. Everyone else had gone out to eat. We usually went to eat together after the job, but tonight Durf just sat there after we played the good-night medley. He didn't even get up and stretch. It was his last night with the band and he just wanted to sit there by the music he'd played night after night for five years. He held his trumpet on one knee and a fifth of Walker's on the other.

The ballroom was dark except for the bandstand. It was an island of light. It could have been a lighted fight ring in a dark stadium with Durf a retiring champion taking a last look around.

Outside the red neon sign saying Mattie's Casino was off. There was no more car noise from the parking lot. Only the band bus and Mattie's Cadillac remained. The marquee was bare. *Bly Washburn And Band With New Trumpet Sensation Durf Green* lay in a pile like paste-board alphabet soup beneath it.

Joe Cater came in and made his way through the rows of chairs and white-clothed tables still askew in after-the-ball-is-over fashion. He kicked an empty whiskey bottle and sent it bowling across the waxed dance floor. Joe was eating a hamburger.

"Ain't you eat?" Joe asked as I broke off a piece for myself.

"I'm waiting on him," I said. We both looked up at Durf. The band was still set up. The music stands were small and square and had BW painted in white on them. They looked like fifteen red tombstones. Durf was sitting on the highest tier, perched there like a big owl. His hair was mussed and he still had on his uniform, the brown cardigan and yellow tie.

"What you think you is?" Joe asked, laughing. "A one-man band?"

Durf just sat there owl-like.

"What you waiting on, anyhow?" Joe asked. "Why don't you just go on if you're going?"

Durf still didn't answer. Joe stooped down and started folding up a sax stand. He had no set way of tearing down and setting up a band. He would always start in on the part nearest to where he happened to be standing. Joe had been bandboy for Bly Washburn even before the war when Bly's band was polling among the top ten in America. He came back after the war when Bly reorganized, when Durf and I came on the band. Joe was a trumpet player himself in the old days, before jazz became a nice word. He went crazy over Durf Green.

"That boy Durf," he'd say, "he plays the way I wanted to. But my old lip went hard on me." And he'd rub the dime spot of white on his upper lip thoughtfully, the spot where twenty or thirty (or forty) years ago a trumpet mouthpiece had fit.

I started playing "Clair de Lune" to pass time. But I'm a pretty bad piano player, doing good to get past the da-da-da (dum) dadada part.

"D-flat in the bass," Durf said softly.

"Yeah?" I asked. "B-flat?"

"D. D as in damn," he said. "Want another nip?" He held out the fifth.

"Not now. I want something to eat."

"Not till I finish this," he said.

"Bring it with you."

"You mean Soldier?" he asked, holding up the fifth. "Remember, suh. This here's de South!"

"All right. Soldier," I said. "But let's eat."

"Not till I finish Soldier."

"That's how you get ulcers," Joe Cater said, "drinking it like that."

"Hell, Jess," Durf said, "go eat. Don't wait on me. Joe's here with me. Aren't you, Joe?" He was egging Joe on. They had been fighting each other ever since Durf decided to leave the band. Joe was against Durf leaving. Durf got a smirk on his face like a school boy who knows he's being mean and the teacher can't do anything about it. "Ain't you, Joe Cater?" he shouted.

Joe let a music case fall plop on the floor. "I ain't saying no more. If you want to go, go! Don't be bothering me. I got work to do." Joe stood spraddle-legged, the back of his wrists on his hips and his hands hanging like flappers, his arms making a triangle on each side of his fat stomach. It was a stance his mammy must have had as she leaned over to scold her children. "All I got to say is, a man what plays horn like you ain't gonna be happy doing nothing else. Don't care how much he make or how easy he living!"

Durf shut up and became an owl again. Joe went back to work and I started playing "Clair" again, putting a d-flat in the bass. Then Mattie yelled something from the office.

"What's that?" I shouted.

"Green. Telephone." Mattie must have counted her money and found we didn't make any for her. She sounded mad.

"That must be Eliza," Durf said quietly.
"Who's calling?" I shouted. No answer.
"Take it for me, Jess," Durf asked.
"What'll I say?" I asked.
"Say I'll be there."
"The airport?"
"Yeah."
"Three-thirty?"
"Yeah," he said soberly. "Tell her just to send my things on out. I'll meet her there."

Mattie had her back to me when I came in to get the phone. She was putting a rubber around some hundreds.

"Eliza?" I asked. "This is Jess." Then I gave her the message.

"Thanks," Eliza said and hung up. Not even goodbye. And she said it in a way that meant she wasn't sorry we were no longer friends.

"Green's leaving, huh?" Mattie asked without turning around.

"I guess so," I said.

"Can't Bly pay enough to hold him?" Mattie asked.

"Maybe not."

"Listen," she said, turning to look at me, "why don't you guys get wise? Start playing something folks can dance to."

"I thought that's what we were doing."

"Either that or quit calling yourself a dance band," she said. "Any band that can't make money on Saturday night in Charleston ain't *no* band! No wonder Green can't support his wife. And kid."

"You've been talking to Eliza," I said.

"It wouldn't kill you guys to play something with the old one-two, one-two." Mattie stood up and danced several steps with a make-believe partner.

"We're musicians, not boxers," I said.

"Don't get smart, son. You know what I mean. The business man's bounce."

"Talk to the leader. I just play third trumpet myself."

"There's bands come here don't work half as hard as you birds."

"Play the old one-two, huh?"

"You bet they do. Take Lucky Barry."

"You take him," I said.

"Green ought to be with a band like that."

"He'd go crazy playing that hogwash."
"At least he could support what's-her-name. His wife."
"Eliza," I said.
"And he wouldn't be on the road like a damn gypsy all the time."
"He likes it with Bly."
"Ain't there some other band good enough for him?"
"Maybe. But he don't want to work with them."
"My God! What's he going to do? Starve?"
"He's going to work in papa's bank."
"Whose?"
"Her's."
"Oh," Mattie said. "So that's it." Mattie looked out of the box-office window at Durf. "What's he doing anyway? Just sitting up there drinking?"

Durf was seated as I left him. He hadn't moved. Joe Cater was slowly busy around him, packing up. It looked like Durf was a king watching his kingdom being torn down beneath him.

I started to walk out of the office. Mattie caught my arm. "How much will he make at that bank?" Mattie asked.

"It's not that," I said. "He wants to settle down and live a little."
"But how much actual money? Ten thousand?"
"Maybe."
"He'd make that with Lucky," Mattie said. "He wouldn't have to travel so much. Lucky stays a month every time he comes here."
"It's no use," I said.
"I'm a good mind to call Lucky. He's a personal friend of mine."
"I know Durf. He'd rather hang up for good than play that crud."
"What's so bad about Lucky's band?" Mattie asked. She was suddenly angry. "They may not play as loud and high and fast as you birds! They may not do all that screeching! What does that mean, anyway? Tell me that!"
"They play the old one-two."
"You birds play the fast too fast and the slow too slow."
"We play music!"
"Music my eye!" Mattie said. "People don't come here to hear music. They want something they can dance to. They go downtown when they want a concert."
"How much did you lose tonight?" I asked.

"What!" Mattie was startled.

"You heard me."

"Listen, son," Mattie said, shaking her finger at me pistol-like and backing me out the door, "I may just break even. But I never lose. Not me!"

There was a light on in the popcorn stand. I walked over to see if there were any leavings. I wondered what I would do if Mattie offered to get me on with Lucky Barry. For a bill and a half I could stand a lot of the old one-two. And it wouldn't be apostasy if I took it. I'd just be quitting. No one's calling me the White Hope or the New Trumpet Sensation. Not that I'm running myself down. I play good section horn and I've got connections, the kind that only want to know one thing: "How does he play?" Stammer and say, "Well, he's an awful nice guy!" "Yes, but damn it *how does he play!*" I'm not Durf Green but I'm a long way from the At Liberty columns: A-1 trumpeter; good habits, reads, ad libs; owns tux; will travel.

"Mr. Green didn't hurt hisself, did he?" the colored girl asked. She was cleaning the popcorn machine.

"Not that I know of," I said, putting a handful of cold unfluffy corn in my mouth.

"How come he just sits there that way?"

"Maybe he's tired."

"Oou-ee!" she said. "I'd be tired too. He sho makes that trumpet talk!"

"How'd the band sound?" I asked.

"Well," she said, "kinda loud. You know I hears all kind of bands working for Miss Mattie. The one I likes is that Lucky Barry. He smooth!"

"My God," I thought, "when even colored folks don't like what we're playing there must be something wrong!"

"What was that last se-lection you-all played?"

" 'Home Sweet Home'," I said. "Wasn't that smooth?"

"I never heard nothing like that before," she said. "No wonder Mr. Green all tired out."

"Home Sweet Home" was our way of saying good-night, a brass chorale voiced six ways, voiced close and then opening up on the no-o-place-like-home part and sounding like dawn coming up like thunder. Durf usually ended it with a high G. Tonight he went up to a big double-C.

Molinari came in, wearing his overcoat with the collar turned up and wrapped tight around him. He got sweaty playing drums and had to be careful about catching cold.

"Didn't you eat," Molinari asked.

"I'm waiting on Durf," I said. I offered him some corn. He took a few grains, then spit it out.

"My God!" he said. "That's worse than the hamburger."

"Is that all you had?"

"That's all was open in the whole town," he said. He paused a moment. I watched his head going up and down. It was a nervous habit he had. His head went up and down all the time like he was watching a vertical tennis game. "The Crow was there," he said.

"Looking for Durf?" I asked.

"She didn't speak to anybody," Molinari said. "She just walked in and looked all around."

I didn't want to hear anymore about Eliza. "You haven't taken your drums down," I said as we walked over to the bandstand. He was finicky about his drums. He wouldn't let Joe Cater touch them.

"I was thinking Durf might want to blow some," he said. I thought I could hear his head moving up and down even when I couldn't see it.

Joe Cater had torn down all the music stands but Durf's. It looked like a lone tombstone. Durf still sat behind it with Soldier and his horn, looking quietly drunk and desperate.

"Was that Eliza?" Durf asked.

"What?" I asked.

"Was that Eliza?" he asked again.

"Yeah," I said.

"What's she say?" Durf asked. He was thick tongued and sitting unsteadily in his chair.

"She said 'Thanks'." I said. "I told her you'd be there. You got about an hour yet."

"Maybe I will and maybe I won't," Durf said. "Say, did you ever get the feeling that you wanted to go? And then you got the feeling that you wanted to stay?" He thought he was being cute. He laughed and almost fell out of his chair.

"You just as well go on, boy," Joe Cater said. "Bly done already got Jake Harrison."

"Jake Harrison!" Durf sneered. "Jake Harrison!"

"You got no right making fun of Jake," Joe said.

"Jake Harrison will be in Norfolk," Durf said rapidly. "He won't have to be in Norfolk till midnight, 'cause you can't dance in Norfolk on Sunday so the job doesn't start till midnight!"

"Is you going crazy, Durf?" Joe put in.

"And you can stay in that new hotel in Portsmouth and catch the ferry across. And coming back the milk man will be on the ferry and you can drink a quart of milk right off the wagon just as the sun is coming up."

"Boy, you better give me that bottle," Joe said. He went over and tried to get Soldier away from Durf. But Durf pushed him away.

"God!" Durf said seriously. "Don't you get tired of seeing that sun come up every morning just as you're going to bed?"

"I wish you'd come down to Norfolk and talk the book over with Jake," I said.

"Me tell Jake Harrison how to play?" Durf pretended to be astonished.

"There's so much left-handed stuff in it," I said.

"Jake can do all right," Joe said. "Jake reads like an adding machine."

"You hear that, Jess?" Durf asked. "Jake Harrison reads like a damn adding machine!" Durf was quiet a moment. Then he pointed his finger like an accusing judge at Joe. "But tell me this, Joe Cater. How's his jazz?"

Joe was evasive. "Jake's a hell of a nice fellow. Get along with anybody. Me and Jake worked for Bly back before you ever came along."

"I think Jake plays might pretty myself," I said.

"But how does he play jazz, Joe Cater?" Durf asked, saying each word separately and still pointing his finger at Joe.

"What's the matter with you, Durf!" Joe stopped zipping the cover over the giant hat-box music case. He stood up and took his mammy-washwoman stance. "You want me to say it? All right, I say it. It don't bother me none to say it." His eyes bore down on Durf, and Durf became suddenly ashamed and bowed his head.

"Jess here, he say Jake plays pretty. Sure he do. Plays smart horn too. Learned to play in college." He paused a moment, looking around to me and Molinari. "But there ain't nobody I knows of plays like this boy here." He stared at Durf again. "And you ain't through yet. You just starting!"

"Yeah," Durf said soberly, "just a growing boy of thirty-one."

"That ain't old," Joe said.

"Aw, let him alone, Joe," I said.

"Jake's already on his way," Molinari put in, his head moving fast like the tennis game had speeded up.

"Bly could pay him off. He'd do it too," Joe said. "Just let Durf say the word."

"But wait'll you hear that Jake Harrison," Durf said, wild again. "Wait'll you hear those high notes, Joe Cater." Durf shouted. "F, G, A, double-B-flats. I hear he got up to P one night and couldn't find the pot!"

"Boy, is you jealous!" Joe said, laughing, jolly as a Negro Santa Claus.

"Aw, shut up." Durf had a way of fighting with Joe, even cussing him, that was man to man, not white man to black. It was something Joe was proud of.

"Yes, sir," Joe laughed. "You sho is jealous."

"I said shut up!"

Cyclops came up on the bandstand. He was a young sax man and arranger who wore black glasses that sat like picture frames on his pale little head. He was carrying manuscript paper and a thick book. Cyclops was ambitious. He was always reading, either philosophy or sex, or working on a new arrangement.

"The guys in the bus have a message for you, Joe Cater," Cyclops said, sitting down at the piano.

"I got a message for them too," Joe grunted. "Ain't nobody going to get to Norfolk in time to sleep in no bed."

Cyclops read from a note, pretending he was a page reading a king's proclamation. " 'To the Black Prince of Whales: Your highness: We've slept in the bus three nights in a row. Hurry up'."

"When I gets done, I'm done," Joe said. "Ain't nothing going to get lost or busted either. Let 'em get some young punk if they don't like the way Joe do it."

Joe Cater was as much a part of the band as the rhythm section and he knew it. Griping at him to hurry was a nightly ritual, for he took hours to do what a younger bandboy could do in minutes. He was slow but careful. I'd trust my own horn with him.

"Hey, Jess," Durf said suddenly. "What'd she say?"

"What did who say?" I asked.

"Eliza."

"I told you. Everything's O.K. Just relax," I said firmly. Durf had let his head hang to one side like the whiskey had broken his neck.

"Jeez, Durf," Cyclops said, "it's not going to seem right without you blowing back there."

"Have a drink, kid," Durf said.

"No-o. . . ."

"Come on," Durf said. "Where I'm going I won't tell." Cyclops was only seventeen and we'd promised his mother we'd see he got no bad habits. Cyclops took a nip and Durf took a big drink. "What you writing?" Durf asked.

Cyclops waited for the whiskey to stop burning. " 'My Old Flame'," he said.

"Good tune," Durf said undrunkenly. "Got good chords." He blinked his eyes several times, trying to focus them on the manuscript.

"Say, it goes up to an F-sharp here," Cyclops said, pointing to the part and singing in a do-dee-dum monotone that only he could have understood. "Can Jake Harrison play that all right?"

I waited for Durf to scream. He didn't. He just sort of wiggled around and fell backwards chair and all off the tier. When we got around to pick him up he was lying like a bug on its back, holding his horn and Soldier in his hands an arm's length above him.

Durf wanted to get back behind his music stand again, but Joe said he had to pack it because the boys out in the bus were in a hurry to get to Norfolk. So Durf sat down on the piano bench besides Cyclops.

While we were listening to Cyclops try over "My Old Flame" on the piano Birkeland came on the stand. I could tell he was disgusted and had something to say, but he didn't say a word till Cyclops finished, the way you don't go in and sit down in church until the praying stops.

"Did you guys eat?" Birkeland asked.

"I did," Molinari said.

"Where, for God's sake?" Birkeland asked. "I walked all over town looking for a decent place. Dear, dear old Southland!" he said bitterly, pounding his forehead with the palm of his hand.

"I got a hamburger down by the square," Molinari said, his head bobbing rhythmically.

"That's where I wound up," Birkeland said. "The hamburger was rotten. And that waitress! What a stupe! 'You all is from the Nawth, ain't you,' she says. Acts like she don't want to wait on me 'cause I don't say you all!" Birkeland was a big talker when he was disgusted and he was disgusted most of the time. "Man, what I'd give to be in New York again," he went on. "At least where a man can get a meal after nine-o'clock at night! God, what I'd give for an offer like yours, Durf. What a break!" He looked at Durf, but Durf just blinked his eyes disinterestedly and said nothing. "Me, I haven't even seen my wife and kid for three months. If that kid of mine ever so much as looks like he wants to be a musician I'll pinch his goddamn head off!"

"Quit if you don't like it," Durf said softly. He was still beside Cyclops at the piano, picking out a melody with one finger on the high keys.

"What else could I do?" Birkeland asked, trying to interest Durf. "What else could I make a living at? It wouldn't be so bad if we got some decent booking. You know we've got two weeks coming up on the tobacco-warehouse circuit?"

"Quit if you don't like it," Durf said angrily. "Go back to playing the hotel bands."

"Damn it, I would quit," Birkeland said, angry too, "but I can't even get enough money ahead to hold me while I'm getting another job. You know it's been six months since we had more than three days in one spot. Six months and I've saved sixty mother-grabbing dollars!"

"We've had it rough lately all right," I said.

"Maybe if Bly would play something people could dance to for a change," Birkeland began.

"Don't you say nothing about how Bly runs this band!" Durf shouted.

"I'm not, I'm not," Birkeland said. "Sure he's a nice guy. The nicest any of us will ever work for. What I mean is we ought to play something just for the dancers once in awhile. A business man's bounce or a rhumba."

"Oh, give up, sad!" Durf said, and began picking out the one-finger melody again.

"I know we got a good band," Birkeland said. "But it's a musicians' band. Ordinary people just don't get what we're trying to do. And Bly gets us guys that bow down when you say the word jazz." He made a swami like a Hindu and said, "Oh, jazz Oh, jazz! We're glad to play for kicks. Oh, he lets us have our own way. Sure. Play the way we want to play. A guy can do anything he's big enough to do on Bly's band! Swell. Fine. O.K. But what about us poor guys who love to play for kicks but have to make a living too? What about us?"

Durf stood straight up, suddenly sobered by anger. "Is that all this band means to you, Birkeland?"

"Listen to who's talking, will you!" Birkeland said.

"Take it easy, Durf," Joe Cater said. "Birkeland's got a right to red-shirt if he wants to."

"He's always red-shirting," Durf said, staring at Birkeland but speaking to Joe. "I'd like to see him quit so he'd be happy once."

"Who does he think he is anyway?" Birkeland said, staring back at Durf but saying it to Joe. "He's always thought he could get by with anything just because he's Durf Green. The Great Trumpet Sensation!"

"You son-of-a-bitch!" Durf said.

They started for each other. Joe and I caught hold of Durf. Molinari and Cyclops went over to Birkeland.

"Don't you start advising me, Mr. Trumpet Sensation," Birkeland said, just wanting to talk and not wanting to fight. "Oh, you can talk big. You got it made, boy. Easy street! You got that blonde sugar-tit. . . ."

Durf broke loose from us.

"Don't hit his lip!" Joe yelled.

Birkeland didn't expect a fight. He wouldn't even put up his hands. Durf hit him hard and knocked him down. Then he sat back down at the piano and let his head slump down in his arms on the keyboard. Birkeland just lay there. Joe was over him, seeing where he was hit.

"Your lip's all right," Joe said, giving Birkeland a handkerchief to hold on the bleeding spot. "It's just your chin."

The blow must have been a shock treatment for Birkeland, like shaking a hysterical woman. "I'm sorry, Durf," he said, raising up on his elbow, "I didn't go to say all that."

"Forget it, man," Durf said without lifting his head.

"It's just that I get so goddamn fed up sometimes," Birkeland said.

"We all do, Birke," Molinari said.

"You'd be the first guy to complain if Bly turned commercial," Joe said to Birkeland.

"I know it, Joe. I'd just as soon not play if I couldn't work for Bly."

"You can't help wondering sometime what's going to happen when you get too old to travel," Molinari said, his head yea-saying very fast.

"Which you are at thirty-five," Birkeland said.

"And jazz styles change so fast it's all a young man can do to keep up," Molinari said. "Some kid comes along. Lots of talent and push. Blows the new way. Looks young and fresh and crew-cut on the stand."

"That's the trouble with music business," I said. "A guy with talent can always make it hard for the rest of us."

"The tension wires are always up," Birkeland said. "The minute you relax you might as well hang up."

"We're going to discourage young Cyclops," Molinari said.

Cyclops had been jotting ideas down on the manuscript paper. "Not as long as Bly keeps playing my arrangements," he said.

"You know what's beginning to get me?" Birkeland asked, getting up off the floor. His chin had stopped bleeding. "Those damn kids in front of the band sweating you every night. All ears. Just hoping you'll screw-up. Then they wink at each other." He looked at Cyclops. "You watch, kid. They'll bother you some day, too. 'Ha!' they say. 'The old boy's slipping. Getting old. Played a major seventh out of tune. Missed an entrance'."

Joe Cater went over and put his hand on Durf's shoulder. "You hearing that, boy. See how lucky you is to be getting out?"

"Give up, Joe!" Durf said. He gave Joe a shove that almost floored the old man. Then he stood up, very drunk. "Sure I'm lucky. I'm not going to be carried off the stand some night like Jimmy Sands was. Have hell in my kidneys. Have some doctor say, 'Sorry. Can't do a thing for him.' I was with him when he died. Don't you think I know what he went through! Laying there swelled up like a balloon. Singing to himself." Durf was trying hard not to fall. He held to the piano for support. His lower jaw hung loose and he was slobbering. "And I'm not going to end up like you guys," he pointed his finger at us, "playing for beer and kicks when you're fifty years old. Playing's for young men. Dear Mom. It's a wonderful band. Having wonderful time. Please send me five dollars so I can eat!"

"You better go sit down, boy," Joe said. "You're sick."

"I'm going to be living. Really living! Sleeping in the same bed every night. Money in the bank. No more seeing that damn sun come up either, Joe Cater, no sir. It's going to be fat living! Fat!" He pounded on the piano. "Like Jimmy Sands used to say. 'Man, it's fat living!'"

Durf gulped a drink that came within about five shots of finishing Soldier. Then he gagged.

"God, Joe. I'm sick," he said.

Joe put his arms around Durf to steady him and led him off to the toilet. "Let's throw it up, boy. You'll feel better," Joe said.

Cyclops got up from the piano and picked up his book. He sat down on the edge of the bandstand with his feet dangling and began to read. I got at the piano again and Molinari started dismantling his sock-cymbal. Birkeland said he was beat and was going out to the bus and go to sleep.

"Can't you just picture Durf behind a desk," Molinari said to me, his head bobbing to the tennis game slowly now, "saying 'Let me tell you about our *Special* Checking account, Mr. Lipshitz!'"

"About ten in the morning," I said, "when he's usually just turning over."

"Or just getting up to go to the can," Cyclops put in.

We were quiet again. The only sound was Molinari's head.

"Durf sure played tonight," Cyclops said.

"What a beat he got!" Molinari said.

"He played five choruses on 'Flying Home'," I said. "I counted them. And he never played the same idea twice."

"He must think with notes instead of words," Cyclops said.

"Yeah," Molinari said. "He must think with notes."

"I've been thinking of him and Jimmy Sands," I said.

"I bet if Jimmy hadn't died Durf wouldn't be leaving," Molinari said.

"Remember the time we got so dragged playing that hotel job for six weeks?" I asked.

"Oh, man! That was the lowest," Molinari said. "I was ready to quit."

"That was before my time," Cyclops said.

"Durf and Jimmy would do anything for laughs," I said. "So they came to the job wearing crazy suits."

"And eating celery off a stalk!" Molinari said.

"Orange coats and purple pants ballooned at the knee and so small at the ankle they had to take their shoes off to get out of them."

"What characters!" Molinari said. "And Bly made them wear the suits right on the stand."

"Intermissions they'd walk around eating this celery," I said. "Nobody could play. It was too funny. We just broke-up. Then when we did start playing we played better than we had in weeks."

"That Bly!" Cyclops said. "He knows musicians!"

"Durf's not like the same guy," Molinari said. "That Blonde Crow fixed him."

I didn't say anything.

"Like I said," Molinari repeated. "If Jimmy Sands hadn't died Durf wouldn't be quitting."

"I hate to see him go," Cyclops said.

II

I began a progression of chords on the piano, piecing chord into chord, trying to go as far as I could without resolving them.

It reminded me of cutting pastel strips of art paper and pasting them together to make a chain, way back in kindergarten. I was thinking of Durf and Eliza and Jimmy Sands.

I hated to see Durf quit, too. I'd known him longer than anybody in the band, back when the war clouds that were over Europe in 1939 had finally let a little rain fall in both our lives, via Pearl Harbor. We were in the same army band. We had a game we played lying on our bunks at night after lights out: I wonder how such and such would have played trumpet.

"Henry Ford?" I asked.

"Yeah," Durf said, "yeah, he could. But we'd never heard of him if he did."

"Lincoln?"

"Him we'd heard of." Durf pulled out a five and struck a match to look at Lincoln's lips. "Man, what chops," he said. "You know who he'd sound like? Like Louis Armstrong. Like Louis was playing back in the 'thirties. A tone as big as all hell!"

Durf was nobody then. Just another kid that made Sergeant fast because he played good. You'd never have thought the magazines would be calling him New Trumpet Sensation. They might not have either if he hadn't met Jimmy Sands. Jimmy was big-time before the war. A real fine trombone man. I don't think Durf ever thought of playing as being anything more than a good way to make a living till Jimmy came along. We used to say Jimmy was Durf's John the Baptist.

"Stick to your horn," Jimmy used to say. "There's nothing like playing." And it wasn't long till Durf was just like Jimmy. He wouldn't talk to a guy who wasn't a musician.

"The guy's not a musician," Durf would say, "so what are you going to talk about?"

Durf learned everything he could from Jimmy Sands, not only how to play good jazz but how to think and act the way a musician ought to think and act. And how to drink. Jimmy said to keep working and he'd get both Durf and me on Bly Washburn's band after the war.

"Bly's is a band you can grow on," Jimmy said. "I think I'd hang up and sell apples or something if I couldn't work for Bly."

He meant it too. Right before he died he turned down a two bill a week job in the Chicago studios to stay with Bly.

And play! Too bad Jimmy's records don't do him justice. He didn't play a sensational style like Durf. Just easy and gentle, not that circus-band tone most jazz trombone men have. He sort of fondled each note, like a baby playing with its mother's breast. But Jimmy had power too. He could shake the windows when he wanted to. Durf used to kid Jimmy about the unorthodox way he stood. He wouldn't hold his horn with the slide straight out like you're supposed to. He'd just aim it at the floor and blow.

"Hey, man," Durf would ask, "how come you stand like that?"

"I learnt to play in a telephone booth," Jimmy would say.

They could have been martyrs if they hadn't been such clowns, for they had the Cause and the Call. Jazz was gospel to them and playing was preaching their gospel, not just making a living. But they were too funny to be martyrs. They believed in the gospel of a good laugh too. Let the band get brought-down and they'd come up with something just for kicks like the wild suits and the celery.

It was lucky they got with Bly Washburn. Most leaders would have fired them the first time they cut-up or popped-off on the bandstand. Not Bly. He knew what a good laugh could do for morale just as he knew they weren't ordinary musicians. And they were lucky to be with Bly because his book had good jazz arrangements, the kind you could still hear something new and interesting in long after you'd played it enough to know your own part by heart. Even the 4th sax or the 3rd trumpet, like me, could play things like his "Laura" night after night and still look forward to playing it again. Not that it was an easy book. Even when you knew the arrangements by heart you still had to work to play them right. And you couldn't play them without improving yourself. It was a musician's band all right, especially for those like Jimmy Sands who would say, "Everything's expendable but playing, man. Stick to your horn."

Durf and Jimmy boozed a lot but seldom got really drunk. They were pint a day men. Then one night in Scranton it hit Jimmy right in the middle of his solo on "Laura." We had to carry him off the stand and three days later he was dead. Kidney poison. The doctors couldn't do a thing. He swelled up like a balloon and

Durf said he was singing riffs to himself right to the last. He'd sing and say, "Man, that knocks me out. Where's my horn? Get me my horn." Out of his head all the time.

We had to get a coffin as big as the telephone booth he said he learned to play in, he was so swollen up. Durf took what was left of the pint Jimmy was drinking when it hit him out of Jimmy's old beat-up trombone case. He stuck it away in his own trumpet case. Jimmy's was long and square at the ends, big enough to hold his dirty underwear and socks and shirts as well as his pint and trombone. When we put it in the box car beside the telephone booth coffin it looked like a miniature coffin. There was something ridiculous about it, like a gag Jimmy might have thought up himself.

Durf was a wild man after Jimmy died, drinking only to get drunk and a pint a day was only a starter. That's why it seemed like a blessing when he met Eliza. Even guys like Molinari, who call her the Blonde Crow now, thought it was a blessing. Durf passed out on the stand three nights in a row.

"Boy, you going to have the kidney poison too," Joe Cater said, helping him off.

Durf spent all his time getting drunk and playing. His horn would hardly get cold from the time he woke up in the hotel to the time he either passed out or went to sleep in his chair, jamming after the job. And he was hell on the band, shouting any time anyone made a mistake.

"Come on! Play or go home!" he'd shout.

One night he was jamming while we were waiting on Joe Cater to pack up. Molinari was at the drums and Cyclops was at the piano. He stopped playing suddenly and started fooling around with a blues melody. Cyclops couldn't find the right chords for it.

"That's not it!" Durf screamed. They tried it again and Cyclops still couldn't get it. Durf was furious.

"Listen, damn it!" he said. He stuck the bell of his horn right in Cyclops' face and blew it again as loud as he could. It scared Cyclops so he cried. But he got it at last. Then we all got out our horns and began fooling with Durf's melody. It was a wistful thing that made me think of a rainy day that kept me from going out to play when I was a kid. We each fooled around with it until we had a complete head-arrangement. We didn't even need to write down our parts. Durf said to call it "Lament for Jimmy." There was a quiet spot of twenty-four bars. Just the rhythm played there. It was where Jimmy's chorus would have been.

We quit thinking about Jimmy except when Bly would call up the "Lament," and I guess we thought more often what a character he was than how he played. But Durf didn't forget. He kept the pint Jimmy was drinking the night it hit him under his stand every night. By the time he met Eliza he'd quit being a wild man, drinking and shouting and staying on his horn all the time. He started being say-nothing and sad.

"Ain't no use you moan-groaning around here," Joe Cater would say. "Just go on and live your own life."

I heard about Eliza before I met her. They said she was a tall blonde, sort of a Billy Rose type, and that she was rich. Her father was connected with Standard Oil. And I remember Joe Cater standing in his washwoman way saying, "That one ain't going to be nothing but trouble!" They said she knew all about jazz. She could tell you how many times Bix Beiderbecke blew spit out of his horn in 1930 and who played 3rd sax with Benny Goodman in 1939. I thought that was good. She would be somebody Durf could talk to, even if she wasn't a musician.

Durf was happier after he met her. He was still quiet and sad but he started playing better. His playing had got to be lousy. He was missing things like high F's that were usually child's play for him.

"What's she like?" I asked Durf one night at intermission.

"Real fine," he said. "Wonderful legs. They look *new* somehow. Like something out of a modern design. I don't think she even has to shave them."

I met Eliza with Durf at the Three Deuces on Fifty-second Street when it was known as The Street by musicians, back in the pre-bebop days when some of the finest small-band jazz that has ever been played was being played there. I gathered Eliza was busy putting second things first in her life, concentrating on the things money can't buy, one of which was the fine art of Jazz.

"After all," I remember her saying, "jazz and skyscraper architecture are America's only original contribution to culture."

Eliza was never my idea of the Queen of the Universe, but I was glad Durf married her. She seemed right for him, and Durf couldn't have been happier. He stopped putting Jimmy's pint under his stand every night but he still carried it in his case. It was after he married that the magazine stopped calling him the White Hope and started the New Trumpet Sensation.

Eliza didn't like the road. She told me that herself. But she stayed on even when things were rough.

"When a man and woman get married," Eliza said, "they ought to be together. That's the only rule I know."

She tried to be a musician's dream wife. She'd come out to the job every night and sit there like a bobby-soxer. When we played good she told us so. When we didn't she'd just sort of raise her eyebrow and say nothing when we asked, "How'd the band sound?" She even learned to copy parts in her spare time, although it was sometimes funny the way she'd get the sharps and flats on the wrong line before she got the knack of transposing from a score.

I liked it when Eliza would ask me in to supper. She was a good cook and it griped her not to have her own kitchen. But she could do wonders even in a hotel room. And it was fun to be with her and Durf. They always had a lot of private jokes that I wasn't in on, but I liked it just the same. After supper she'd have a cigar in a metal tube for Durf and me. I didn't smoke cigars but with her and the food it all seemed good and wholesome and I liked it.

"Papa always smoked after dinner at home," Eliza said. "I like that about a man."

"He's with Standard Oil, isn't he?" I asked.

"Oh, no," she said. "I guess he might have some Standard stock. But he's a bank executive."

It was a shame when Eliza started having the leg pains, for she sure had fine legs, and in those heavy elastic stockings they might as well have been made of wood. She quit coming to the jobs on the nights they hurt the worst. One night after supper they got me drunk. I tried to put my hands on Eliza's legs while Durf was in the bathroom.

"I was just trying to see what varicose veins look like," I said. They thought it was awful funny. That's how close they were.

She didn't get mad and he didn't get jealous. They just thought it was funny.

Eliza stayed on with Durf when the other wives were sent home, when Bly couldn't get a location job for more than a week-end and a jump from Omaha to Salt Lake City or Chicago to Galveston for one-niters was routine. In the golden days of the post-war boom we'd played the way we wanted to play and laughed at the Mattie's all over the country that pleaded for the old one-two. We could play musical music and still get all the work we wanted. And we made good money too. The reckoning came in '47.

It was supposed to be things getting back to normal after the post-war boom, but was in reality a depression that put bands like ours out of the business and left only the commercial guys like Lucky Barry working. But we were die-hards. Some of the guys quit when the salaries went down. Three out of fifteen quit. But we knew Bly was only getting eight hundred or a thousand a night where six months before he was getting three times that.

The road wasn't easy. We were usually getting in fifteen bus hours a day between jobs, and often sleeping only in the bus for days at a time.

Eliza and Durf bought a little Ford and trailed along after the bus, splitting the driving when her legs weren't hurting. Once when Molinari was complaining about the callouses on his behind Eliza said something to him that made his head stop bobbing for a moment.

"What do you want to bet," she said, "that my fanny can't match yours callous for callous!" Molinari told that in the bus afterward. She was some gal. We liked her then all right.

I knew when something was wrong. I could tell by the way Durf was acting in the section. He was having fits again when someone played a wrong note, just like after Jimmy died. I figured it was her legs. She hadn't been to the job for several weeks. It came to a head one night in Dallas. Eliza had to go to New York for an operation and she wanted him to go with her. I heard it all through the thin walls of the Camel Hotel.

"You can take off," Eliza said. "We wouldn't be gone a month." She was crying.

I couldn't hear what Durf said.

"I'm not asking you to quit," she said. "Just take off."
"Who'd play my book?" Durf asked.
"There must be somebody," she said. "You're not *that* good!"
"Shut up," he said.
"It'd be different if we were making anything," she said. "We haven't even broken even for two months."
I couldn't hear.
"When people get married they ought to stick together," she said.
"You won't be gone long, honey," he said.
"It's the least you can do," she said. "Haven't I gone through hell to be with you!"
"Oh, my God!"
"I *have* gone through hell!"
"You ought to thought of that before you married me!"
"*I* married you!" she screamed. "You married me as much as I married you!"
"You knew how I live," Durf said.
"Like a damn nomad!" she screamed. "What if we had a baby!"
"You're hysterical, Eliza!"
"I'd name it little Nomad Green!"
"Please shut up."
"Or you think I'll sit around somewhere while you're bouncing around the country with Mr. Bly Washburn!"
"You're shouting!"
"What if I am!" she screamed. "You say I married you. All right, I married you. Not this goddamn band business!"
I heard the door slam when Durf walked out. Eliza took the plane for New York the next morning. Alone.
It was a month before Durf saw Eliza again.
"I don't care if she's gone to hell," he said. But I didn't believe him. I knew him before he fell in love and afterwards. I could see the difference and I figured that if she'd gone to hell he'd soon be going after her. I was right. When Bly got sick and we had to take a lay-off Durf aimed his Ford for New York and drove night and day getting there.
The lay-off lasted six weeks. When we went into rehearsal again several of the old guys were missing. Durf Green was one of them.

We put off rehearsal three days more while Bly and Joe Cater and I got after Durf to come back.

I knew how Durf felt. Sleeping in the same bed under the same roof and eating regular home-cooked meals was hard to give up. I thought more than once about not coming back myself. But after all I didn't belong anywhere else.

Durf came back but without Eliza.

"Is everything all right?" I asked.

"Fine," he said, and laughed. "She's pregnant."

"My God!" I thought.

"Henry, that's her Papa, offered me a job," Durf said.

"Does he have a band too?"

"A bank job. Executive, I guess," Durf said. "I told him I'd think it over."

"You mean quit playing?"

"If I do quit Bly I'll hang up," Durf said. "There's nobody else I'd want to play for. Eliza thinks I ought to take it. She figures we wouldn't be making enough to keep the baby with us on the road."

"What do you think?" I asked.

"Too bad playing horn isn't just a business," he said. "Hell, I can make more in one year at the bank than I could in five playing. And we wouldn't have to travel either."

Things were looking good for us after the lay-off. We got a new agency and they got us good bookings, locations for a change. We made a movie short and some records that caught on. "How High the Moon," featuring Durf, was collecting juke-box nickles all over the country.

We had a month at the Casino Gardens on the West Coast. Eliza came out to be with Durf, but she stayed clear of the band. They had me in to supper once. It was supposed to be like old times. But it was strained and unfriendly. I tried to leave early.

"Where you going?" Eliza asked.

"Oh, couple of things I want to do before the job," I lied.

"Here," she said, throwing a cigar in a metal tube at me. "Take this with you!"

"Eliza!" Durf said. He got up and left the room.

"You sure have changed, Eliza," I said. I picked up the cigar but didn't smoke it.

"You can tell that by looking at me," she said with a hard laugh. She was three months gone. "You're going to see me change a lot more."

"You mean!"

"Why not?"

"I didn't think you're supposed to ride in a car."

"I want to be with my husband," she said. "I guess that's very inconsiderate of me!"

"You sure have changed," I said.

"One of us had to!" She was angry, breathing so hard her whole body moved with each breath. "I don't ask him to quit playing. He could get in the studios."

"Why not a hotel band!"

"He didn't pledge allegiance when he came on Bly Washburn's band."

"Bly's band made Durf," I said, getting angry too.

"Made him what?"

"A damn fine trumpet man! And he'll be even better. He's not through yet."

"Sure, 'Bly's is a band you can grow on,' " she said, mocking what we believed. " 'It's collective. None of us are as good individually as we are playing together!' "

"Eliza, for God's sake!"

" 'Something happens when we play together that happens with few White bands. Something important!' "

"By God, it's the truth and you know it!" I said and walked out, leaving the cigar in the metal tube on the table.

It was no surprise when Durf told me he was giving notice. It was one night after the job when we were eating together.

"She won't go home unless I go with her," he said. "She's sick all the time now."

"I've got to hand it to her," I said.

"Jess, you know that pint of Jimmy's? The one I got in my case?"

I said yes.

"Put it in your case when I leave, will you?"

I said I would.

III

I was still at the piano piecing chords together in a way that made me think of a kid making a chain out of pastel art paper. Cyclops sat reading. Molinari had dismantled everything but his snare drum. He was still hoping Durf would want to play some. Then I heard the scrubwomen squawking out in the dark.

"Where you going there!" Then, "Oh, I'm sorry, Mr. Washburn." Bly must have said something funny to them for I could hear them laughing. He came walking across the wet floor not bothering to tip-toe.

"Where's Durf?" Bly asked. He didn't come up on the bandstand. He stood on the dance floor looking up.

"Back in the can," I said. "Drank himself sick."

"Joe with him?"

I nodded.

"I called the hotel and Eliza said he was still here," Bly said. "He's not going to miss his plane, is he? It's the last one out till Monday."

"He can still make it," I said. I got Durf's horn and put it in his case. There was Jimmy's pint. I didn't feel like taking it.

Bly was kidding Cyclops.

"What is it this time?" he asked. "Sex?"

"John Dewey," Cyclops said, holding up the bible-thick book.

"What's he say?" Bly asked.

"He says a sailor is intellectually at home on the sea," Cyclops said. He liked to show off in front of the leader. He took off his picture-frame glasses. "This is what Durf ought to tell his wife," Cyclops said. He made a prissy face and said in a falsetto voice, "I can't come work in Papa's bank. You see, I'm intellectually at home on the trumpet!"

We were laughing at Cyclops when Durf came back. He was walking alone now, Joe Cater following him.

"What's so funny?" Durf asked.

"Feel better, man?" Bly asked.

"Much better." He didn't look good. His eyes were blood red. His face was like white bread and his lips like bread crusts. "Going to finish Soldier now," he said.

"You crazy!" Joe said. He got the bottle away from Durf.

"Durf," Bly began.

"Got a speech for me, Bly? A testimonial?" Durf asked, smiling.

"No," Bly said, smiling too. "Just goodbye." He shook Durf's hand. "Joe, what did I tell Jimmy Sands the first time I heard Durf blow?"

"You said, 'There's a chair on my band for that boy any time he wants it,'" Joe said.

"That still goes, Durf," Bly said, not smiling. "And I figure my arteries are good for another ten years." Bly turned and walked away rapidly. "See you guys in Norfolk," he called. "At midnight."

Durf sat down at a table at the foot of the bandstand and let his head fall into his folded arms. Joe Cater put his last load on the dolly to take it out to the bus.

"You better come on with them drums," Joe said to Molinari. "We about ready to go."

"Durf might want to play some," Molinari said.

"Don't see how he going to play any more tonight!" Joe said.

Durf seemed to be asleep at the table when Eliza came in. She was walking stiff-legged the way she walked when they hurt her. They were spread apart like a person galled in the groin. She came right over to where Durf was, moving carefully on the waxed dance floor. She didn't even look up on the stand. Molinari and Cyclops both got up and went to the toilet. I wished afterward I'd gone with them.

Durf wasn't asleep. "What's the matter? 'Fraid I wasn't coming?" He asked. He didn't raise his head off the table.

"Are you coming or not?" Eliza asked.

"It's too late."

"No it isn't," she said. "The plane's behind time. We've got till 4:00."

"Wait till Monday."

"No," she said. "We're going tonight. Now come on!" She was trying hard not to yank him up, not to hit him. She breathed hard. Her belly was big and fractious looking as if she had a huge egg under her dress. "I'm going to be on that plane. You better too. Or it'll be the last you'll ever see of me. Or the baby!"

She gave Durf's horn case a kick that glided it across the dance floor and into a post. Then she turned and walked out as cautiously as she had walked in.

I went over and picked up Durf's case. There was a puddle of whiskey beneath it. "She broke Jimmy's pint," I thought. "The Blonde Crow!"

"Let's play something," Durf said, getting up from the table. "Cyclops! Molinari! Where are you!" He found Soldier where Joe Cater had put it down and finished what was left. "Let's play something!" he roared.

Cyclops and Molinari came back from the toilet, and Joe Cater came in too. Molinari got behind his snare and started a rhythm. Cyclops got at the piano.

"What do you want to blow?" Cyclops asked.

"Anything! Something wild!" Durf said. "Who's got my horn?" I took the horn out and gave it to him. I didn't want him to see the broken pint.

"Let's play . . ." Durf began, and fell over. Joe rushed over to him.

"Well, look here," Joe said. "Looks like my boy Durf done passed plumb out!"

We took our time getting away from the Casino. It was long past plane time when we stopped the bus in front of the hotel and went in to see if Eliza had left any of Durf's things. Durf was still out, sleeping in the back of the bus. Joe Cater and I went in together. We were feeling so good we were singing. I asked the night clerk for the key to Green's room.

"It's already out," he said.

Joe and I exchanged silent glances that carried one message: defeat. We went back out to the bus and got Durf and took him up the elevator and down the hall to 307. He was still out. I knocked.

"Come in."

Eliza was sitting in a comfortable chair, knitting. The only light was by her chair. She had her legs propped up on an ottoman. They were bare, without the thick elastic hose. The way the light hit them made me wonder again what varicose veins look like.

"Put him on the bed," Eliza said, still knitting. Joe and I exchanged looks again and obeyed. Then we put down his horn and overcoat and went out, careful not to slam the door as if we were leaving a sick room.

That was the last time I saw Durf. We got a card when the baby was born. They named him Jimmy Green. On the back was a note saying he hadn't even got the dent out of his horn that got in it the night he passed out.

DATE DUE		
SON 15 '84 F		